Japanese Industrialisation

How did Japan not only escape imperialism but emerge to challenge the West?

What are the social and cultural factors in Japan's industrial success?

> This is a highly readable text that adopts an imaginative approach to the description and analysis of Japan's economic development since 1603. Unlike many works on Japan's modern economy, it takes a wide-ranging conceptual approach, and also seeks to locate the Japanese experience in a broader geographical context, comparing it with other economies and assessing its impact on Asian development during the period since the Second World War.
>
> Janet E. Hunter, London School of Economics

This book presents the major aspects of industrialisation in Japan from the beginnings of the Tokugawa period in 1603, to the present day. It interprets Japan's surprising industrial success in social, cultural, institutional and technological terms. Inkster combines historical research with a broad analysis which considers issues such as:

- The role of the state
- The process of cultural selection and engineering
- The crucial importance of technological change
- The character of Japan's private-sector institutions

Japanese Industrialisation features detailed treatments of East Asia, China, the US and 'the West' as essential parts of the global context of Japanese historical experience. It considers many of the unusual institutional features of Japan's corporate enterprise and political regime and controversially interprets them as deliberate expressions of industrialisation under conditions of late development and escape from Western colonialism. It also identifies many of the constraints on future growth as geopolitical rather than cultural or environmental. This book is an essential resource for students and academics in areas including Asian Studies, Japanese History and Industrial Development.

Ian Inkster is Research Professor in the Department of International Studies, the Nottingham Trent University. He has published widely on the history of science and technology, focusing on the causes, character and consequences of industrialisation. His previous publications include *Science and Technology in History* (1991) and *Technology and Industrialisation* (1998).

Routledge Studies in the Modern History of Asia

1 **The Police in Occupation Japan**
Control, corruption and resistance to reform
Christopher Aldous

2 **Chinese Workers**
A new history
Jackie Sheehan

3 **The Aftermath of Partition in South Asia**
Tai Yong Tan and Gyanesh Kudaisya

4 **The Australia–Japan Political Alignment**
1952 to the present
Alan Rix

5 **Japan and Singapore in the World Economy**
Japan's economic advance into Singapore, 1870–1965
Shimizu Hiroshi and Hirakawa Hitoshi

6 **The Triads as Business**
Yiu Kong Chu

7 **Contemporary Taiwanese Cultural Nationalism**
A-chin Hsiau

8 **Religion and Nationalism in India**
The case of the Punjab
Harnik Deol

9 **Japanese Industrialisation**
Historical and cultural perspectives
Ian Inkster

Japanese Industrialisation

Historical and cultural perspectives

Ian Inkster

London and New York

In memory of my wife
Lorraine Inkster
(née: Anne Rich)
1949–92

First published 2001
by Routledge
11 New Fetter Lane, London EC4P 4EE

Simultaneously published in the USA and Canada
by Routledge
29 West 35th Street, New York, NY 10001

Routledge is an imprint of the Taylor & Francis Group

Typeset in Baskerville by Florence Production Ltd,
Stoodleigh, Devon
Printed and bound in Great Britain by University Press,
Cambridge

British Library Cataloguing in Publication Data
A catalogue record for this book is available
from the British Library

Library of Congress Cataloging in Publication Data
Inkster, Ian.
Japanese industrialisation: historical and cultural
perspectives/Ian Inkster.
p. cm.
Includes bibliographical references and index.
1. Industrialization—Japan. 2. Japan—Economic conditions.
I. Title.
HC462.I577 2001
338.952–dc21 00–062796

ISBN 0–415–24444–7

Contents

PART III
Modern Japan 159

Illustrations

Tables

Figures

Preface and acknowledgements

The approach of this book goes against the grain of many of the conventional treatments of Japanese industrialisation. A muscular economics may seem attractive to some, but sadly inadequate to others. By taking the long period from around 1603 to the year 2000, and by placing Japan in a frequently rehearsed international context, I hope to have attracted an audience beyond that of specialist students and academics. Of course, the danger which follows is that I lose an expert audience in favour of courting something more popular or accessible. But life is never that simple, and, barring a few great authors, texts are always more complicated than they intend to be. So this book does include most of what you might need to know about Japan in order to write essays on its industrial or economic history or to make informed comparisons of Japan with other systems or nations, and it does embrace more detail about social structures, technologies and institutions than might normally be found in a general treatment. The book hopes to be an interesting analytic statement in the guise of a textbook.

Prologues to each of the three parts of the book give brief overviews and outline chapters – especially Chapters 2, 3, 6 and 9 – provide basic data and chronology for the whole span of time. In each of such chapters, major themes, problems and possible syntheses for the period are displayed prior to the more detailed chapters which follow. I have attempted to weave interpretive elements together in the narrative and towards the end of all chapters. There is much detailed cross-referencing in the text, and the index makes a special attempt to allow threads and themes to be identified and pursued in differing contexts. Given the extensive range of the book, I have not managed complete coverage of all possible topics (e.g. agriculture or public finance), but have instead opted to focus on selected interpretive elements (culture, institutions, technologies and foreign interactions in particular) and on periods of great importance, such as the Meiji years of industrialisation (1868–1912) or the fast growth of the 1960s and 1970s.

I have also chosen to abandon an enormous paraphernalia of research footnoting and referencing. Except for a few instances where notes add to an argument, references are at the end of each chapter. Highly select lists of 'Further reading' provide precisely that and are listed alphabetically. The 'References' sections refer to all the sources named and quoted in the text and are listed in the order in which the associated themes or arguments appear. Such bibliographical resources have been kept to an absolute minimum, although they tend to rise in number as we approach the more contentious recent past and as statistical sources become of greater significance. References are mostly in English, but at some points this could not be kept to, and I would like to thank Naotake Ito and Makato Kuwabara of Tokyo for help with nineteenth-century Japanese newspapers, records and published texts, and Jerry Liu of Nottingham Trent University for help with Chinese sources in Chapter 11. In order to clarify the bibliography and index, Japanese personal names are arranged in Western style.

The book is based on my teaching of undergraduate and graduate students of Japanese and Asian economic history since 1973, as well as upon my own more narrow research interests in the history of Japanese industry and technology. I have been very fortunate in having enthusiastic classes on Japanese development in which around one-half of the students were either East Asian or of East Asian origins, the majority coming from Chinese-speaking backgrounds. This has over the years produced a different sort of response or feedback than would have arisen from an entirely anglophone or European student audience.

I can not thank all those in Japan and elsewhere who have helped me pursue my Japan interests. From the late 1970s the Institute of Developing Economies, Hitotsubashi University and the United Nations University, all in Tokyo, were generous with time, understanding and hospitality. Naotake Ito and Makato Kuwabara of the Diet Library were tremendously helpful in securing research material and with translations. More recently, the International Institute for Advanced Studies, Kyoto has rekindled some earlier interpretive thoughts, many of which were initially developed for meetings in Sydney (May 1978), Tokyo (June 1980), Hobart (May 1983), Oxford (October 1983), Brisbane (August 1987), New Delhi (May 1988), Suva (December 1988), Windsor Castle (December 1988), Saragossa (August 1993) and Nice (1995). I would like to thank all the discussants and antagonists who encouraged me to think again, as well as my then research students Bill Purcell, Michael Johnson and Rhonda Roberts. Between 1973 and 1996 my closest colleagues and friends in Sydney and in Australia more generally suffered much Japan talk, and I would especially like to thank John Perkins, Steve Nicholas, Barrie Dyster, S. Ambirajan, Imran Ali, Mike Pearson (and the 1980s MA in Asian History team at the University of New South Wales), John Merson from the ABC and Science and Technology Studies, Sidney Crawcour at ANU, Ross Mouer, Gavan McCormack and Yoshio Sugimoto in Melbourne, as well as the late Gordon Rimmer for not only listening but allowing my interests to be properly reflected in my teaching. The Australian government financed research trips to Japan during 1991–3 in order that I might continue work on the largely problematic Multifunctional Polis, for which see Chapter 10 'Pacific partnership'. The Japanese academic friendships and research programmes have kept me going throughout, and I owe much to the International House of Japan Inc. (Tokyo) during 1979, to the then President of the IDE in Tokyo, Noboru Kanokogi, to the members of the UNU Project Team on Technology Transformation, Takeshi Hayashi and Shigemochi Hirashima, and to Kenjiro Matsutani, Hiromitsu Umehara, Masao Kosaka, Ryoshin Minami and Kenkichiro Koizumi, as well as to the advice of foreigners in Japan who were far more learned than I, especially James Goode, Sudhin Mukhopadhyay, Adnan Fawaz, and the late and great John Thavaraj, whose singing shall always be remembered. Most recently, the Global History Seminar of the Institute of Historical Research, Senate House, London, has been a constant reminder of the widest of contexts, and once more I would like to thank Patrick O'Brien, Alan Macfarlane and Gerry Martin for the display of intellectual challenges well beyond the concerns of a Eurocentric world. Since 1996 my history colleagues at The Nottingham Trent University have helped nourish my growing interest in cultural engineering, whilst my postgraduate students and colleagues at Nanhua University, Dalin, Taiwan have continued to stimulate my comparative reflexes.

My children have, as usual, acted as a challenging element, but were prevented from actually stopping me by my wife Lesley. The book is, however, dedicated to the memory of my wife Lorraine, who died in May 1992. One of my abiding memories is of Lorraine tramping alongside me into the Diet Library in Tokyo during 1980, heavily pregnant with our son Toby, helping me with my research into technological change. Lorraine was trained as an historian and I have written the book in her memory. She was a true support and remains a great inspiration to my family and friends.

1 Prologue 1878

Anxious visions in Meiji Japan

> One day when I was passing the Shimbashi bridge, I observed on a pillar of the bridge, an inscription 'Constructed in the 100th Year of Meiji'. Wondering at this, I looked at the bridge and found that it was not like that in the olden time, having glittering pillars of copper, and railings of iron: the houses in the surrounding streets were splendidly built and some of them three, and others five stories high; flags from every merchant's house were waving in the air; all kinds of precious articles were displayed in the shops and carriages and horses were incessantly passing to and fro. Indeed, a most flourishing state of trade was actually before my eyes.

So began a *Dream of the Future* – of the year 1967 – accounted thus in Japan during late 1878 by the editor of the *Hochi Shimbun* newspaper, Mitsuomi Tachibana. This was a most traumatic time, one of extreme cultural, political and institutional disarray, in the midst of years of doubt and uncertainty, of prolonged equivocations felt by those many tens of thousands of Japanese whose lives were lived well beyond those of the modernising elite. Just months before this the famous Satsuma Rebellion had failed to disturb the government from its determined trajectory towards a national Restoration based on its own strange admixture of tradition, cultural engineering and modern technologies.

But our editor continues his story of Japan in 1967 as dreamt in 1878:

> Greatly puzzled at this, I went into a shop and found that the master of the shop was a White man with blue eyes and red hair, wearing handsome clean clothes and sitting in an easy position by a desk; and that those wearing scanty and torn apparel and in the employment of the master of the house, were none but the yellow-coloured and high-cheek-boned brethren of ours. The noise of a carriage was then heard and on turning my face towards it, I saw a party driving in a carriage ornamented with glittering gold and silver. On inquiring of the bystanders as to who it was, they told me that the gentleman was a Mr John Tale the proprietor of the Silk Filature manufactory in

> Joshiu. At this, my wonder increased and on asking as I passed on, the names of the proprietors of certain stores and which I presumed to belong to large merchants, I was informed that this was the dry goods store of Henry Siebold, that was the tailor-shop of William Zekenon, and so on – all the large houses in the main streets being occupied by the Whites. Where a large flag was waving in the air and a high building towering to the sky, was a bank established by an English firm, Manrin and Co. Where several three-storied stone buildings are seen, covering several Cho of ground and employing many hundreds of labourers who work without intermission, is the tea firing place of an American, Mr Balcon.

Here, then, is limited imagination – the industries are tea and silk and clothing, the riches in the form of gold, and apparel, carriages and houses. The Westerners named are British, American and Germanic, involving no known contemporaries but containing allusions enough – thus to Philipp Franz von Siebold, student, traveller and prisoner in Japan some forty years earlier, who returned as an unsuccessful diplomat just prior to the Restoration of 1868. The imagination belongs to the global political economy and to the cultural insight rather than to the niceties of subsequent industrial development *per se*.

Tachibana continues:

> Seeing all this, I was surprised to find that our country was so prosperous, but at the same time, I wondered why the masters of such prosperous places were only of the Western people. I then passed into the bye-streets and on looking at the state of the houses, I saw none but immense numbers of my countrymen flocking together like sheep or pigs, in a few poorly-built houses, using straw for flooring, their scanty dress leaving portions of their body uncovered, without being able to afford sufficient vegetables to fill their stomachs, their wives were weeping from the cold, and the children crying with hunger, the husbands being employed by the Western people, and were earning scarcely sufficient wages to fill the mouths of their families. Indeed, those who were born of rich families and who used to wear handsome dresses and partake of rich food, and who possessed large plots of ground in the main streets and were noted for their wealth, have now come to reside in the bye-streets and to live a life of hard work and poverty.

Note, then, this description of destitution is not Dickensian. The blame here for hard times lies not with the Bounderbys and Gradgrinds of the world nor with the failed moral economy of urban living. The rich have suffered too, if not in terms of the luxuries of a romantic backlash, then through a simple, direct and more powerful loss of riches. The world is global and dualistic. Japanese are not hurting each other day by day, Japanese *have* hurt each other over a period of almost one hundred years by adopting a policy of coexistence with foreign capital and intellect, a juxtaposition that must surely be eventually to their loss. Foreign interaction spells sovereignty at bay and the antagonism between the main streets and the byways, the occasions of a drop from the one to the other, captures well those global underdevelopments and biases of the twentieth century analysed so well in Michael Lipton's *Why Poor People Stay Poor* in the 1970s (a book on urban bias) or, in a different way, by Gunder Frank's *ReOrient* in the 1990s (a book on historical bias).

With Tachibana (who describes things much better!) we go on.

> The scenes were as if one were actually looking at the pictures of Hades and Paradise. Those who were enjoying the happiness of Paradise with luxurious food and warm clothing, being all Western people, whilst those who had sunk to the bottom of Hades, and were working hard, were all Japanese. I, seeing this could hardly keep from weeping and was sorely puzzled why my countrymen should have fallen to such misery, whilst the western people were so prosperous. When I reached the Kiyobashi bridge, I saw a respectable looking gray-haired old man standing on the bridge in a sorrowful state, as if he were waiting for somebody. I approached him and after bowing to him, I asked 'Is this country Japan? Is this the capital, Tokei? How is it that the Western people alone are enjoying such great wealth, whilst the Japanese are in such a miserable state? Although there are some remains of the old state in the streets, our countrymen are all being employed by and working for, the Western people, in fact, it seems as if they are all masters, and we, their servants. Is it a fact that, this is not our country, but a place where the poor people of our country have emigrated to, and are being employed by the Western people and that the streets have been, by their orders, built in imitation of our capital of Tokei?

The wonderful dualisms of modernity are here in this dream: Paradise and Hades out of masters and servants, main streets and byways, the West and the East. And it is these which prepare the ground for a new dualism and the meaning of the Dream.

> The old man then replied. – 'How strange your questions are! Do you not know the cause of our country's having fallen to this state? I will explain to you briefly. Since our government, eighty years ago, allowed the Western people to live in the interior, and abrogated the law forbidding them to possess immovable property and thus allowed them to use their capital freely in the interior, on account of the great difference between their business capabilities and ours, affairs have

> gradually come to the present state – and although, of course, their *capital and intellect* having been employed in the interior, there are some among our countrymen who have gained some profit, they are only the go-betweens, those who gained their wealth by running about between the western people and ourselves and giving assistance to both sides. Generally however, the people were outdone by the superior strength of *capital and intellect*; and now, although the country is Japan and the capital, Tokei, those who have control over the wealth of Japan and are employing the Japanese labourers are none but the Western people. Is it not very sad? Eighty years ago, if there had been some courageous statesmen who opposed the opinion of the public and had not allowed the wealth of the Western people to penetrate into the interior, we would not have had to see the sad state of the present day. This is indeed what I am constantly regretting.' On saying this he disappeared. At this, I was very sad and deeply affected, and I was on the point of bursting into tears, when I suddenly awoke and found that it was all a dream. My whole body was covered with perspiration and I found myself beside a table in an upper room, and it was yet in the eleventh year of Meiji.

And the offices of the *Hochi Shimbun* were on the main street. Note here the way that the distinction between *capital and intellect* is made to work. Capital from other nations does not bring its intellect with it in some neutral, osmotic-learning sense. John Stuart Mill is wrong. Rather, those who bring their capital also wield their intellect. And in this Dream they do so in such a manner as to capture Japan. In particular, Tachibana with his reference to Japanese go-betweens, identifies exactly the many twentieth-century expressions of *economic brokerage*, defined by Norman Long as 'those individuals and social categories who play a major part in connecting local production systems with the wider socio-economic framework and who control the crucial sets of relationships involved'. In most of the twentieth-century underdeveloping regions of Asia, Africa or Latin America, such brokerage was linked intimately with expatriate capital, tended to emerge as a new disruptive elite and to transfer profits from indigenous development further towards the global agents of modernity. And in the twentieth century all of this unfolded within and between all the other elsewheres in the world.

This may not be great prophecy, nor canonic literature. *Japan's* future turned out well enough. As early as the 1930s the London working class were eating Japanese canned salmon, North American living rooms were illuminated by Japanese electric light bulbs, South American children played with Japanese toys and the urban employed of the Philippines rode to work on Japanese bicycles. By the 1960s of our Anxious Vision the Japanese economy was growing at a rate which doubled its size every seven years. But Tachibana's *Dream of the Future* is worthy of our consideration. To the extent that there can ever *be* such a thing, it was intended as a counterfactual prediction, a vision of that future which *would* unfold if Japan truly opened its doors to the West. Importantly, it reminds historians that the *trajectory of the modern* was not inevitable or foreseen, even in a culture such as that of Japan, too commonly and dismissively visualised as an exception which proves a set of very doubtful rules and precepts. The enlightenment of Japan into the pale of industrial modernity was stuffed full of such anxieties.

It is also surely of importance to be sometimes reminded of how a progressive and effective *modern stance* could be forged out of just such uncertainty. Let me be explicit enough. The Dream predicted that if the choices before emerging Japan were to be badly taken, then the white men with blue eyes, foreign capital and confident intellect, would forge a future so disastrous as to demand a vivid description as a solemn warning. In 1878 our editor might be forgiven his dream of a future tense, filled up with the failure to cope with that Westernism which so speedily encroached upon an unsuspecting population of some 35 million souls. There is absolutely every historical reason to believe that the wholesale introduction of Western capital into early industrialising Japan would have been entirely disastrous. On this matter more generally, both John Stuart Mill (as Gradgrind if you like) and Karl Marx (but here there is no literary equivalent) were equally wrong headed. Mill, whose writings were much appreciated amongst the intellectuals and policy makers of Meiji Japan, believed in the great transcending power of capital as it moved between nations, and his seeming assumptions about the unproblematic diffusion of technology to areas beyond its original creation laid the foundations of a major historiography. Similarly, Marx believed in the naturally transforming power of capital and technique in combination as they moved out beyond their points of origin. Thus in one of his famous *New York Daily Tribune* essays he was forthright in his claim that 'when you have once introduced machinery into the locomotion of a country, which possesses iron and coals, you are unable to withhold it from its fabrication'. More universally, but with an eye on China and the East, Marx argued that trade, capital and technique combined to produce just that civil unrest which in turn would bring in a brave new world of modernisation to replace the unmoving 'fossil form of social life'. Our editor, and many like him, rejected the whole range of Western ideology on capital, from market liberalism *à la* Gradgrind through to Marxian critical analysis. The Japanese mode was to modernise using foreign technique *without* social revolution, and the logic of our editor's dream resulted in his wholesale rejection of foreign capital. The transfer of Western technique in the absence of Western capital and capitalists demanded a multitude of statist interventions and the initiation of just that policy of industrial targeting which has become the hallmark of developing Japan from Meiji to the present and is today associated with the so-called *Confucian Renaissance* which has occurred throughout industrialising Asia since *c.* 1970.

In the forthcoming pages I attempt to present the essential industrial history of Japan alongside a more broadly-based interpretation of success. Although he held it in common with many other Japanese, the editor of the *Hochi Shimbun* was wrong in his prediction because he was in no good position to forecast accurately the nature of the technological and institutional changes which were to set the nation on a dynamic economic trajectory. In the very year in which our editor penned his vision, Japan was busily resisting foreign capital, imbibing Western knowledge and devising its own institutional innovations. We shall insist throughout our text that the essential dynamics of Japanese economic history may not be uncovered within the features of its conventionally-defined 'economy' alone. All economies, whether markets or commands or merely confused, are bounded by institutions and attitudes. But these latter are subject to change as well as stasis, and it is in the historical relations between economy, technology and institutions that the key to an interpretation of Japanese industrialisation may be found.

Part I
The beginnings

Introduction

In a dispatch to Earl John Russell of 19 November 1864, Sir Rutherford Alcock, a representative of British interests in Japan who understood the international arena far better than he understood Japan, warned how 'all Treaties made with Japan have been forced upon it; and until great changes have taken place in the character, institutions and government of the people, it is vain to expect that Treaties so entered into can be maintained by a religious abstinence from the use of force as a means.' During 1867 and 1868 force broke out in all directions, although on a relatively small scale. Without doubt, the Meiji Restoration of 1868 was some function of Western intervention, or, as Russell judged, arose 'almost exclusively from the relations that have of late years been established between Japan and foreign nations.' The 'great social revolution' was perhaps best marked in the memorial of Chōshū, Satsuma, Hizen and Toza which was addressed to the Emperor in the autumn of 1868 and which defined the Tokugawa regime as illegitimate, as a culmination of a six-hundred year baronial rampage reflected in the 'boundless despotism of the Shogunate'. Traditional structures of authority had been improperly usurped and abused. Now a class was to extinguish itself; by the edict of spring 1871, 'The clans are abolished, and prefectures are established in their place.'

The Meiji Restoration of 1868 can, therefore, be viewed as a political and economic watershed formed of both Western interventions and internal dissolutions. Distress and the related movements for social change which occurred in the 1830s were clearly strengthened by the fears surrounding the arrival of the Westerners in 1853. The subsequent Tokugawa compromises meant a great weakening in the legitimacy of the State itself, and this provided an opportunity seized by the dissenting *han* and the political intellectuals and progressive bureaucrats. In such a view the industrial modernisation of Japan was born of a complex mixture of social, political and military forces.

This section considers industrialisation in the Meiji years in some detail, stipulating a broad approach to the interpretation of success. Chapter 2 details the dynamic elements within the Tokugawa economy (1603–1868), from which Meiji industrialisation emerged. Chapter 3 measures the economic success of the Meiji years and suggests the significance of appropriate government policies, the relevance of an institutional approach and the complex character of the 'Western impact'. Chapters 4 and 5 serve as interpretive extensions of the analytical narrative and together show how Statist intervention was crucial in explaining the central features of Japanese economic dynamics, but particularly with regard to the exploitation of Western knowledge and technique.

2 The dynamics of the Tokugawa economy (1603–1868)

Pax Tokugawa – the 250 years peace

> These people are the delight of my heart.
>
> (St Francis Xavier *c.*1550)

Despite a great deal of recent scholarship, Tokugawa Japan (1603–1868) remains something of an enigma. With a population of around 30 million, Japan was demographically larger than any European nation, and physically larger than any nation in Europe other than Sweden, France and Spain. On the other hand, with 75 per cent of the area composed of mountain, the density of lowlands settlement meant that a very large population was mainly organised within a series of interacting communities. Across most of the area most of the time, Japan's climate was temperate, but Tokugawa Japan's domestic economy lay on the edge of the monsoon area, periodically exposed to typhoons, floods and famine. The tremendous cultural hegemony of China in East Asia embraced Japan throughout the years to 1868, yet that influence was much modified. The phonetic alphabet emerged as a partial replacement and extension of Chinese characters, Japan's Confucianism was not a replication of the Chinese model. As with Britain, Japan lay somewhat outside the mainstream of continental life, and external influences were forever being amalgamated in a distinctive culture.

After the battle of Sekigahara in 1600, which effectively closed the phase of Warring Barons, Ieyasu Tokugawa, (1542–1616) began to erect the system of social control and national seclusion which was to last until the 1850s, and upon which the hereditary military dictatorship, or *shōgunate*, was to depend for its political and financial hegemony. Pax Tokugawa was forged from war and tempered in peace. The rights of the Emperor, which had been delegated during the civil wars, were transferred as the rights of the new lay government in peace. Will Adams could write of the Japanese in 1611 that 'there is not a land better governed in the world by civil police'. On the other hand, the developing notions of control demanded the exclusion of foreigners from the interior, and this entailed the ruthless suppression of Christians and Christianity after the peasant uprising of 1638. The number of Christians who died as martyrs or from extended ill-treatment was enormous.

Yet – and still enigmatically – this was not a religious persecution of the European type, nor was closure of the nation inspired, as has been argued for Ming China, by fear of foreign ideology or world views. From Ieyasu onwards, the Shōguns of Japan were moved by fear of domestic uprisings. The exclusion re-enactment of 1637 was triggered not by intellectual debate but by the Eastern movements of the Spanish empire. Exclusion, expulsion and censorship were all aspects of the same phenomenon, the fear of loss of inner cohesion and control.

With the Emperor and his court relegated to the obscurity of Kyoto and the Shōgun's government (*Bakufu*) established in the new capital of Edo (Tokyo), the system of controls was further extended during the years 1634 to 1643. Forced alternate residence (*sankin kōtai*), whereby the lords (*daimyō*) of each domain (*han*) sent familial hostages regularly to the capital, was a key element of both martial and fiscal control, for the cost of dual residence was designed to render the coffers of the lords empty. Fear of the truly powerful *han* such as Satsuma or Chōshū, was demonstrated in legislation which created an internal passport system, which monitored the marriage alliances of the *daimyō*, which forbade contact with the Kyoto court, which limited permission for castle-building, which forced large, debilitating projects upon individual *daimyō* and which, in 1643, prohibited the alienation of land as a check on *han* power and as an affirmation of faith in the moral economy arising from the small peasant producer.

Amidst such sanctions emerged rewards. The Tokugawa were themselves vast landowners. In addition, in the earlier years, the revenue the government derived from the rice tribute approximated 30 per cent of the total yield. Whilst the *tozama* (outsiders, those who had fought against the Tokugawa until the battle of 1600) *daimyō* were principally sanctioned through *sankin kōtai* and other restrictions, the *fudai* (inner, allied) *daimyō* were also rewarded with positions in the increasingly complex *bakufu* bureaucracy. Both loyalty and meritocracy were rewarded with civil and military offices and the stipends or land grants which such service brought. A system of obligations, developed from the warrior-peasant distinctions that had emerged after the Ōnin War of 1467, raised the self-image of even those lesser nobles and vassals (*samurai*) whose talents or position did not bring increased, more tangible rewards of money or power. But notions of what was 'tangible' in the Edo era should not be conditioned by modern materialist or Eurocentric assumptions. The service or *gun yaku* obligations of the *samurai* estate embraced the policing and warrior functions. At the same time, the higher peasants (see pp. 17–18) owed *buyaku* or labour service, borne by the individual or the family in the form of village duties, manpower for castle construction, irrigation projects and so on. Whilst *yaku* formally captured the flow of obligations in the hierarchical social system, peasant *yaku* transformed as including all service and tax obligations, just as the *chōnin* (commoner townsmen) secured business rights in the cities in return for labour and service obligations. Thus, and perhaps especially after the 1720s, the *yaku* flow of obligations became more socially pervasive and was increasingly definable as a status reward as much as an economic burden or opportunity cost.

But – as we shall be showing – all of this is a little bland and not properly applicable to the whole period, to all regions and groupings. Despite their efforts, the Tokugawa never exerted much more than a loose hegemony over the motley collection of 250 or more *daimyō*, nor did they prevent the rise of the *chōnin* and merchant estate. At the centre of the social control system, the huge expenses of *sankin kōtai* involved closer and repeated financial linkage between the *daimyō* and the merchants, as the former increasingly depended upon a flow of specie which they had little right to coin. At the same time, the continued power and more sophisticated organisation of individual *han* and the later shift of production and merchandising to the progressive rural areas, associated with an increased capacity to generate incomes outside of the rice economy, led to a movement of financial payments in opposition to the flow of service obligations as well as a weakening of the financial position of the government itself, whose tax share of total yield reduced to around 25 per cent by the end of the period.

Most certainly, our real concern in the rest of this chapter is not with the ill-conceived question of whether Tokugawa Japan would have eventually and inevitably passed through an industrial revolution in the later years of the nineteenth century in the absence of the several interventions of the West which occurred from the 1830s and accelerated during the 1850s. As will be demonstrated, the answer to such a question is perfectly obvious. There is no reason to believe that a wholly isolated Japan, deprived of trade with the Atlantic or the European empire in Asia, of Western technology and of European ideologies, would have experienced an industrial revolution even approximately equivalent to those of the Atlantic economies prior to 1914 or even 1937, the year of the formal outbreak of the Japan–Chinese War. Our purpose here is to briefly uncover the primary dynamics of the Tokugawa economy and explore those features of the nation which were especially conducive to a reception and settlement of Western knowledge and technologies once the nation did, under extreme pressure, find itself 'opened' to Western expansionism in the mid-nineteenth century.

Economy and population

Notions derived from a knowledge of European economic history must be driven from the mind. At the base of the Tokugawa economy lay intensive rice cultivation. Rice culture of a sort reached Honshū around the third century AD. Long prior to 1603, the peasant farmers of Japan had delivered rice as tax and themselves consumed the products of dry land agriculture e.g. wheat or barley. Technological improvements after 1603 allowed the peasantry to grow irrigated rice for themselves and for the market, and the increase in rice varieties in these years was quite tremendous. The provision of good government and improved roadways (both of which related to the establishment of *sankin kōtai*) had an all but immediate impact on efficiency and knowledge diffusion. It is possible to sketch a picture of Tokugawa which outlines adequate housing, clothing and a nutritious cuisine as well as an increase in male literacy to around the 40 per cent to 50 per cent mark. It has been suggested that it was indeed the growing *gap* between socio-political efficiency (rising) and economic backwardness (remaining) which made the prospect of modern economic growth all the more promising by the nineteenth century.

The principal technical improvements of the Tokugawa years embraced commercial fertilisers, irrigation, new threshing machinery (*semba-koki*), multiple cropping and crop diversification.[1] That is, most improvement represented a *diffusion* of existing technique, required little in the way of fixed capital, and was land- rather than labour-saving. In progressive rural areas, often proximate to large cities or good transport systems, a combination of these biological advances (as distinct from mechanisation) allowed a better spread of labour employment throughout the year, that is, a reduction of the seasonal underemployment of familial labour.

Whilst much in the way of irrigation, drainage and flood control technologies was constructed from human labour at the village level or under order from the lords, multiple cropping, seed selection, fertiliser usage and the utilisation of improved hoes, water pumps and ploughs, as well as the introduction of draught animals, remained with the peasant family. Primarily, it was the family farm of one hectare or less which also provided the skilled labour for the by-employments of textiles production, tea and oil pressing, grain milling, pottery and rice wine, paper and ink manufacture. Fertiliser (from night soil and sewer mud to purchased oil cake and dried sardines) might involve the expenditure of up to 50 per cent of an eighteenth-century peasant's total annual cash income. But the improvements which such fertilisers permitted, including multiple cropping or crop diversification, did not in themselves require further cash expenditure. With the possible exception of the thresher, there was no obvious tendency towards labour-saving technology. This suggests that the fuller employment and better organisation of small-plot family labour lay at the very heart of technological change in the Tokugawa rural economy. Thus the use of fertilisers undoubtedly reduced the labour time previously devoted to tramping of leaves, grasses or ash into the fields. But, combined with better irrigation, the productive utilisation of fertilisers demanded new tasks of labour; seed treatment and selection, row planting, intensive weeding, the application of insecticides (oil), attention to frost protection and so on. Together with the conversion of dry field to paddy and a move to high yielding rice varieties and double cropping, it seems evident that acreage, yields and labour intensity all increased significantly during the Tokugawa period. Between 1600 and 1720 alone the acreage under cultivation doubled, at which time the cultivation of rice probably reached something of a plateau. But production in the rural economy did not stultify.

Wet rice agriculture lends itself beautifully to productive combinations. Mulberry trees (for silk) may be grown on high land along the banks of rice fields, silkworm droppings are fertiliser for rice, fish live in irrigation channels. Especially in the south, a major impetus to drain uncultured (*shitsuden*) fields might have been that they could yield wheat and barley. Thus, if we continue with our deduction about improved annual employment of family labour, the intensification of wet rice paddying was complementary to the growth of cash crops (silk and cotton, rapeseed, indigo, tobacco, tea and sugar) and to handicraft production in rural areas. In many regions handicrafts were organised by merchants, using both familial and wage labour, and the rise of rural wages in such industries as silk and brewing is an indication of labour shortage, especially after the mid-eighteenth century. Merchants supplied spinning frames, reeling machinery and looms to farmers and paid them for their work by piece. Such a putting-out system dominated the specialised regions of handicraft production, such as the Kinai cotton region or the silk production of Fukushima, the sugar of Satsuma. The imperatives of the factory were absent from Tokugawa Japan, and the very rare utilisation of water power was mostly for grinding and crushing of rice, wheat and some minerals. In summary, the expansion of production in both agriculture and manufactures was associated with an increase in the number of more productive producers, not an increase in the size of the productive unit.

The question of the 'commercialisation' of the rural sector is a vexed one, for it waits on both evidence and a working definition. Undoubtedly, the seventeenth century saw the increased use of cash, a buoyancy of rural markets and more evident regional specialisation. The seventeenth-century development of the city as a vast consumption centre (see fully pp. 16, 20–3) and the increased urbanisation of both merchants and *samurai* almost certainly led to rural diversification and the emergence of pockets of high prosperity, dynamism and cash advances. Within the peasant estate, differentiation into rentier, tenant and family groupings occurred as reclaimed land was purchased by the more prosperous, or as land was mortgaged from poorer peasants. Village authority – responsible for tax payments – increasingly passed into the hands of the *gōnō* or upper peasantry on a hereditary basis, a reward for service. The merchant entrepreneurs of the seventeenth century, especially the *tonya* or wholesale merchants of Ōsaka, the centre of rice exchange (for cash) and for the trades in cotton, silk, paper and oil, certainly became the focus of a more monetarised economy.

Many merchants expanded out of debt-financing of the upper estate into the purchase of reclaimed land and land mortgaging. But holdings did not increase in size, and indeed the competitive position of larger holdings probably decreased with time. The precise nature of traditional skills, the need for constant monitoring of cultivation and the close alliance between agriculture and handicrafts in most regions, meant that very few producing units captured positive returns to scale in such a way that they could establish market hegemony over other producers. Nor, with the exception of rice, was there a national market in the sense of a unified, competitive price system. Most regions remained self-sufficient. Tenancy may have reached 30 per cent of the farm population in the most advanced regions, with cash replacing rent in kind, but was below 10 per cent in many others. Because of the commanding roles of irrigation and tax collection, the organisation of the village became more central to social life, not less. The Tokugawa rural economy had certainly progressed during the seventeenth century, but in most part it would have been immediately recognised and understood by a Chinese farmer. This is not to imply that efficiency had not increased substantially within the basic agrarian-handicrafts structure, and there is good evidence of increased attention being given to thrift, quality control and technical proficiency. In the terms of Susan Hanley, Japan became a more 'resource-efficient culture' in farming and handicrafts as population pressure rendered basic resources scarce.

The early eighteenth century appears to have been a turning point in the history of the Tokugawa domestic economy on several counts. First, a significant growth in population between 1600 and 1720 seems to have come to a halt. It is reasonable to assume that population growth in the seventeenth century stimulated the adoption of labour-using technology, while the years after that were more dominated by the continuous reduction of seasonal underemployment through a further spread of agricultural and handicraft techniques. It is possible that periods of population growth were associated with periods of land reclamation. The fact that technique became increasingly standardised from around the 1750s suggests that there was little pressure to move towards labour-saving methods. At the same time, this unusual halt of population at around the 30–33 million mark prompts the historian to reflect on the degree of change in the rural sector. *Mabiki* (infanticide) is not readily explained in terms of a general rise of prosperity, indeed it is possible that Malthusian checks to further population growth were emerging in many areas. The fact that most of the new cities were located in already prosperous rural areas suggests that strong neighbourhood effects induced standardisation of superior techniques in those areas, but that many regions lay outside the stream of economic advancement, particularly in the north east. Second, the focus of dynamism appears to have moved away from the cities and towards the advanced rural areas. At least in these regions, labour became a marketable commodity and rural entrepreneurial peasants emerged as a lower strata of landlord. Third, it is from approximately this point that larger constructions, requiring investment funds, became more common in the rural areas. Thirty-kilometre canals or the bay head reclamations which involved 50-kilometre embankments and a significant organisation of effort, were associated with the transfer of merchant capital and interests from the city to the village. Lords and merchants (especially those of the Kinai plain) were involved in the largest post-1720 projects in agriculture, from the conversion of marshes to the paddying of volcanic flanks and tablelands. Fourth, and closely related to the above point, the urban innovations of the seventeenth-century merchants were gradually replaced by their many rural commitments. The urban, innovating merchant was transformed into a more conservative rural landholder and producer. Last, from the early eighteenth century the major input into further output was almost certainly the reduction of underemployment in the rural areas, until in advanced regions a point was reached where the price of hired labour began to rise.

Moral economy – aspects of social structure

> Technical changes in production are never socially innocuous.
>
> (T. C. Smith, 1966)

In a classic study, T.C. Smith has shown how the small plot, family unit became the 'ultimate integer of peasant society'. After the 1720s, population stability accelerated the trend to small-holdings as the labour of any one farm worker became more diverse and intricate. The handicraft character of rural labour was strengthened. The larger holdings of the village were increasingly displaced by the combination of small family holdings and tenant farms. At the same time, an earlier cooperative production of fertilisers, firewood or clothing was replaced by family-based purchase of such inputs.

But alongside this stress on the family plot came transfers of money from the commercial sector, as merchants and peasant money lenders became tenant-using landowners through reclamation of waste land under contract. For many poor peasants, the severe combination of intermittent *corvée* labour, rent, land and purchase taxes, debt payments and localised extortion, meant that between 50 per cent and 70 per cent of income was extracted from the household. The differential impact of economic advance within and between regions is what explains periodic flights to the city, peasant rebellions and the localised undermining of the financial position of many lower *samurai*. Interlocked grievances were evident in the Western provinces rebellions of 1783–7, when peasants rose against merchants *as* landowners. In 1823 peasants in one of the Tokugawa domains rebelled against the combined interests of rice merchants and corrupt local officials. The penetration of merchants into the village, especially after the 1720s, undoubtedly led to a range of relatively new social tensions. Some of the *tonya* silk or cotton merchants controlled forty or more spinners and weavers.

In contrast, the city was affected by the emerging *culture* of merchants and artisans. Owing an array of commercial obligations as well as sporadic forced loans to the *daimyō* or government (*goyōkin*), a partial compensation for the merchants developed in the larger urban settings as artists, authors, actors and master craftsmen created an urban culture which, at points, allied the *chōnin* as a collective with the *samurai* groups within the city. Whilst in many rural areas the *samurai* were becoming an absent 'lumpenaristocracy', in the cities the culture of the middling *samurai* was more characterised by realism and robustness. Although the importance of such micro-cultures within the city should not be exaggerated, the eighteenth century witnessed the growth of a more activist *samurai* group and some merging of the immediate interests of *chōnin* and urban aristocrats.

Compared to most European nations, the Japanese upper estate was very numerous indeed, comprising perhaps 6 per cent or some 2 million of the total population. Nor was this an Asiatic average. The highest estate of Japan was three or four times more numerous as a proportion of population than was the scholar gentry estate of contemporary China. We might distinguish three principal groupings of the *samurai* estate. At its apex was the *karō* or the upper *samurai* of the *daimyō*'s court. The middling *samurai*, or *hirazamurai* were increasingly settled within complex bureaucratic functions, mostly located in urban areas. Below these two were the lower *samurai*, including the *goshi* or rustic *samurai*, providing military and local functions. With the overall decline of the military role and the rise of bureaucratic peasants in the village, many of whom gained such special privileges as the wearing of swords, the position of the last and most numerous grouping of *samurai* was constantly under threat. The difference in real income between even middling and lower *samurai* might be in the order of 50- to 100-fold. *Daimyō* reformers, ambitious to recover their status by increasing yields, at times forced a range of new, low-status tasks upon the rural *samurai*. Thus Harunori Uesugi (1751–1822) of the Yonezawa domain, faced with declining income and rising expenditure, attempted to turn the *samurai* into a productive labour force in agriculture, crêpe and indigo-dyeing ventures and in an improved educational system. The logic of capitalism had entered the *han* and had challenged the traditional obligation and status systems. For many of both *samurai* and peasants the moral economy based on a Confucian ethos of community and hierarchy was weakened as individualism, law and contract, and the exigencies of survival cemented a new system of social relationships. A reaffirmation of the code of the *bushidō* was but one aspect of a conscious attempt to posit ties of loyalty and obligation against the newer flows of work, service and income.

Figure 2.1 depicts in stylised form the social relations of the moral economy.

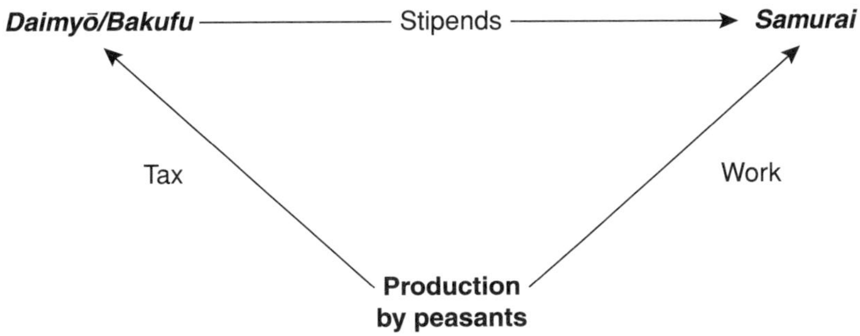

Figure 2.1 Income and work flows of the moral economy.

Here, the net flows of work and payments accorded with the flow of obligations. Thus the stipends paid by *daimyō* to *samurai* were balanced by service obligations flowing in the opposite direction. The fief incomes (*chigyō*) which some *samurai* received directly from the work of the peasantry were balanced by the traditional protection that the warriors or administrators owed to their domain peasants within the moral economy. The taxes in kind of the peasantry, based on surveyed yields and reaching 50 per cent of output, satisfied their need for domain protection and the requirement that the traditional service of the *samurai* should be paid for. In this system the hierarchy of four estates (*Shi-no-ko-shō*: *samurai*, peasants, artisans, merchants) made both moral and financial sense. *Kikoku-senku* (revere grain: despise money) was a phrase which captured the high esteem in which agricultural labour was placed.

Admitting that most but not all of the real upward social mobility of Tokugawa Japan took place *within* the estates, as successful peasants rented out portions of land or controlled the mortgages of others, or as literate and well-placed *samurai* took on bureaucratic functions, Figure 2.2 captures the essence of social change. It must be remembered that the picture drawn is composed from the social landscapes around such prosperous areas as Ōsaka and the Kinai plain, but is not a portrait of the many areas all but untouched by the new financial relationships.

Figure 2.2 illustrates the social structures bounded by *net* flows of work and income, and does not therefore preclude some lesser flows of income in the opposite direction. The moral economy is reflected in the two arrows marked 'Z'. The upper peasantry paid and organised the taxes upon which the finances of the regime and the *han* were based, and generated the original income for the highly esteemed flows to the *samurai* through stipends, grants and salaries. Such flows balanced the reverse flows of moral obligations required of the upper estate. However, it should be noted that the traditional stipendiary payments were reduced as the period progressed. Just as their expenditures rose, the military and local functions of many *samurai*

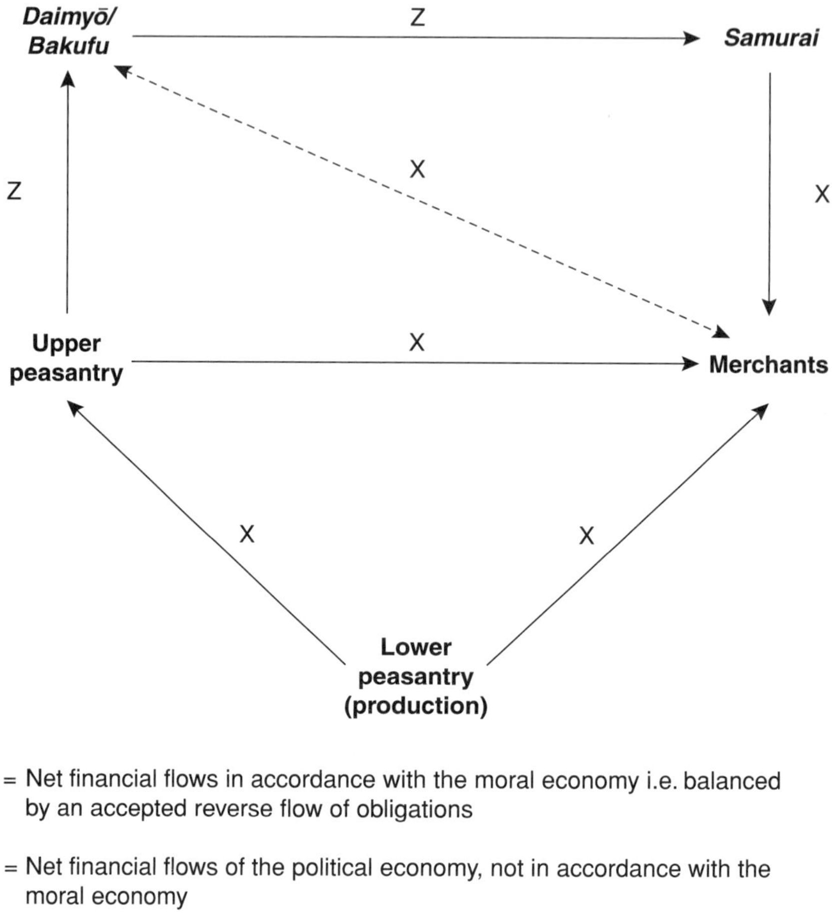

Figure 2.2 Political economy: income flows and social change in Tokugawa Japan.

declined. At the same time, the proportion of flows flowing from the peasantry to the government and *daimyō* fell as their non-rice income grew or as lower peasants became more indebted to merchants and money lenders.

The back of the moral economy was broken on the flows marked 'X'. The fractionalisation of the peasantry and the integration of the merchants is clearly indicated. Indebted peasants were now borrowing from richer peasants and from merchants and this resulted in a continual flow of funds which was not legitimated in the existing moral order. Merchants also received a net flow of income from the handicraft work of the putting-out system, from rents and their commercial transactions with the lower and middling *samurai*. Again, such flows of income were not balanced by an established reverse flow of obligations. The financial links between the merchants and the *daimyō* and government were the most problematic of all, and whatever their net direction they could entail little in the way of acceptable moral relationships.

In the development of *Shingaku* and other philosophies[2] the merchants could claim that their activities represented a series of moral obligations, to the *han* or State. But there was little justification for any recognition by the daimyo of the social importance of the merchant class. Yet the two-way flow of finances between *daimyō* and merchants was ever strengthening. Obviously, the upper estate was increasingly indebted to merchant financiers and agents, but the net balance of payments is difficult to judge overall. Merchants paid commercial taxes and forced loans (*goyōkin*) to the *bakufu* and *han*, which by the early nineteenth century may have represented some 50 per cent of total revenue in the *bakufu* domains. Because such commercial dependencies had no status in the moral economy, debts were often simply repudiated. Also, and especially in the shōgunal or *fudai* domains, merchants paid guild fees and for commercial licences and monopolies.

It is clear that the bonds of finance were beginning to blur the earlier firm distinctions between the estates. Especially in advanced rural areas, the passing of both land and bureaucratic power to the richer peasants altered the *samurai*–peasant relationship. The merchants' increased control over land in turn challenged the hierarchical assumptions governing peasant–merchant relationships. The debt of the *samurai* and the need for financial services threatened the *samurai*–merchant relationship. Yet for the merchant, the financial rewards of the moral economy were increasing dramatically. When it emerged in the 1850s, the demand for political change came not from the merchants or the peasantry as a whole, but from the *han* governments, the rural entrepreneurs and the middling *samurai*, whose expectations were rising.

Sparked by regional distress, the period of the Tempō reforms (1830–43) combined provincial effort at self-strengthening with the conservative reaction to such pressures instigated at the centre of government. Regional famines and risings occurred throughout the early nineteenth century, but were perhaps best symbolised in the Ōshio riots in Ōsaka and those led by Yorozu Ikuta in Niigata. Heihachirō Ōshio (1792–1837) was an officer of civil police who advised the governor of Ōsaka to open the city's reserve stocks of rice to relieve rice famine distress. Refusal led to a popular rebellion against Ōsaka castle and to looting of the merchant quarters. Although the rebellion was quelled, it is of note that Ōshio was a follower of the Ō-Yōmei school of Confucianism that emphasises *action* rather than contemplation. From such a combination of new exigencies and novel thought emerged the provincial *shishi* or 'men of good will'. Both distress and the reform movement were particularly strong in the tozama domains of western Japan, especially Chōshū and Satsuma, whose large *han* revenues were now dependent upon loans or commercial dealings with the merchant estate. In the case of Satsuma, the interest due on loans in Ōsaka and Edo was greater than the annual cost of administration, and debts were often abrogated. We can not write of a national anti-*bakufu* movement in the early nineteenth century, but key, powerful centres were in turmoil and confusion and sought a greater degree of commercial autonomy. The central government's reaction to distress and to *han* reforms was primarily conservative and ineffectual. This was the immediate political and economic background to the acceleration in knowledge and technology transfers from the West. The impetus then, was not that of political revolution or intellectual conviction, but rather a search for new tools of *han*-based self-strengthening. By the time of the American navy's arrival and Commodore Matthew Perry's note requesting foreign commerce (June 1853), which was dispatched to all *han* during the next month, several regions were prepared to accept Western trade as a means of obtaining both improved physical armaments and general prosperity.

Limited change

We have yet to describe more formally the underlying characteristics and limitations of change in the economy. Which combination of forces disturbed the earlier balance in the moral economy? What was it that induced the spread of better techniques in the rural sector? To uncover the dynamics of the Tokugawa economy requires something more than a description of change. The absence of key statistics (even the population figures may be debated) and the impossibility of recovering the micro-history of each regional economy, prompts a search for an approach which is reasonably sturdy in terms of its own inner logic and which admits contemporaneous changes in agriculture, urbanism, industry and social relations. Such an approach should also take cognisance of the seeming deceleration of population and urban economic growth after *c.* 1720.

Figure 2.3 takes the analysis back to the *jōkamachi* of the seventeenth century. With the decline of older centres and the rise of new administrative regions in the initial years of Tokugawa, the castle towns boomed. Hall has argued that for the years 1580–1610, which saw the tremendous growth of Ōsaka, Edo, Hiroshima, Okayama, Sendai and Nagoya, it would be 'hard to find a parallel period of urban construction in world history'. This represents a clear and unusual starting point for an analysis of change. The castle towns of the new *daimyō* domains controlled the plains and the main lines of communication. The edict of 1615 demanded the destruction of all but one castle town in each province. Domain-level *sankin kōtai* drew the vassals into the cities. Of some 150 such castle towns, forty or so gained populations of over 10,000 or represented 10 per cent of their domain populations, whilst Edo grew to over 1 million, and Ōsaka and Kyoto to over 300,000 each. Around the year 1700 the *jōkamachi* reached their maximum growth.

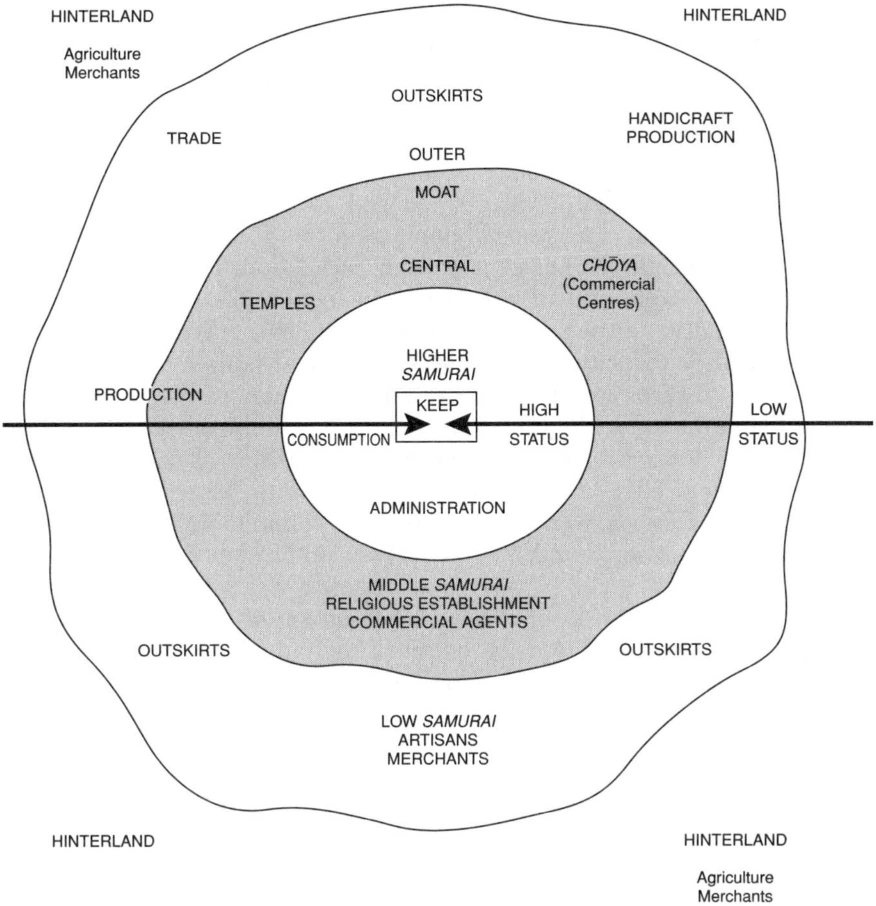

Figure 2.3 Socio-economic structure of *Jōkamachi* (highly stylised).

In and around the central keep was located the conspicuous consumption of the *daimyō*, their retinues and the upper *samurai* bureaucrats. Beyond this but within the inner moat were found the middling *samurai* and the regular administrators of the city. Between the inner moat and outer moat or barricades congregated a mix of *samurai*, merchants (crowded into the *chōya*, commercial centres) and temple populations. Within this band 50 per cent of the townspeople lived on perhaps 15 per cent or 20 per cent of the land area. In contrast, 70 per cent of a city's area might be devoted to *samurai* residence. Here, a strict social hierarchy of location broke down, although *samurai* tended to be located inwards, merchants outwards. These urban sites were the places where formalities broke down and new mobilities and ambitions emerged, where according to the late seventeenth-century writer Saikaku Ihara, 'it is training rather than birth which counts'. Beyond the outer moats were the city outskirts in which the lower merchants, artisans and lower *samurai* were settled. The place and extent of an individual *samurai* residence was basically determined by size of stipend. In and beyond the outskirts of the city lay the hinterland of *production*, dominated by commercial agriculture and handicrafts. Thus the city itself was a centre of consumption, services and exchange, with its hinterland and nearby villages devoted to increasingly varied production. Given that the *samurai* population of a city might at times reach 40 per cent to 70 per cent of total population, it is relatively easy to explain the expansion of production as determined by the city but located beyond its borders. Social mores pushed the merchants and artisans away from the city, just as the pressures of commercial exchange pulled them towards it. The continued indebtedness of the upper estate together with the expansion of merchant interests in the outskirts and rural hinterlands is what best explains the increase in the relative position of rural production after about 1700 or 1720. It must be recalled that the sites of most *jōkamachi* were well chosen, as commanding fertile plains, river crossings, harbours and the most advanced production of rural areas generally.

The rising conservatism or social internalisation of the merchant estate is also understandable. From the outset of the era Ieyasu Tokugawa had requested Kinai merchants to set up their businesses in the city to provide financial services for hostages and retainers and to import rice, silk, oil and other necessities. The merchants developed into two broad categories. These were the merchants who brought in products from the hinterlands or outskirts, and those who utilised the exchange centre of Ōsaka to link the domain with the wider economy. The most centrally located merchants, the *goyō shōnin* or chartered merchants could gain tax exemption, some autonomy and something of social advantage from their increased commercial communion with the inner, upper circles of the city. It was within such a 'mass milling' process that a fusion of merchant and *samurai* interests at times took place, a process which worked at some spatial distance from the resentments felt by lower *samurai* at their loss of status on the urban outskirts. At least in the larger cities, the spread of information followed this spatial and social location of the estates. On both sides of the outer moats were the *chōnin* areas which acted as the primary recipients of the ideas and practices circulated from the centre to the periphery. At the same time, seclusion and an absence of any large foreign trade removed from merchant culture the stimulus of foreign contacts and competition. Usury was, then, a source of possible financial and social advantage, as well as a sink for surplus profits originally generated at the outskirts. But its extent was also a measure of the limits to change. At its extreme, *sankin kōtai* cost up to 70 per cent or even more of a *han*'s cash outlays, and usury increasingly filled the gap between such forced but habit-forming conspicuous consumption and the tax-paying capacity of the peasantry.

Within the city, the financial pressures on the *samurai* also produced important social results. Many of those who could not shift to a bureaucratic function entered commerce or agriculture or converted their debts to the *chōnin* into marriage alliances or adoption contracts. The educated middling *samurai* also chose a role as educators of the administrative class, this further strengthening a rise of the *jinzai* (men of talent) and the notion of an urban meritocracy (*jinzaishugi*).

It was this mixture of spatial and social forces that limited the power of new information or technologies to transform the nation's economy. The great size of the *samurai* estate led to a massive withdrawal from the flow of income for competitive, wasteful consumption purposes. Isolation limited the opportunities for alternative investments. Information dispersed between and within small areas of the cities, but rarely across them. Communication across social estates remained limited through diverse but pervasive regulations, tolls and surveillance systems. Clearly, a *chōnin* culture developed which stressed the virtues of thrift and diligence. Writing in 1727 Sorai Ōgyū (1666–1728) typified city life as like 'living in an inn'. But most urbanites were in fact untouched by commercialisation and the merchants themselves sought justification in terms of loyalty, rather than efficiency. Social and financial tensions mounted in the city, but traditional moral obligations were still adhered to. After the seventeenth century, the agricultural productivity of the villages continued to increase on the basis of the diffusion of superior known rather than new techniques, and the slim thread of Western learning (see Chapter 4) had no impact on construction and engineering technique.

Most importantly, it is very doubtful whether socio-legal restrictions in Tokugawa Japan were at all conducive to the spread of the factors of production and superior techniques from advanced areas (composed mainly of cities and well-placed hinterlands) to areas of relative deprivation. The decade of the 1830s witnessed earthquakes, flood, famines, fire, peasant revolts and rice riots, most of which went unrelieved. By the mid-nineteenth century the income per head of Japan was firmly below that of the income per head of European nations at the time of their transition to industrial revolution. A far greater proportion of the national wealth was locked into the traditional system of social relations than was the case in Europe and America, or even other areas of Asia. Not only did advanced regions accumulate derived advantages of skills, finance and information, the backwash effects of taxation and indebtedness almost certainly created a net flow of resources into such regions over a long period. There is little evidence of any 'leading sectors' operating in such a fashion as to induce growth in new sectors or regions after *c.* 1720.

Japan in context – Tokugawa dynamics and the 'Western model'

> Japan with its purely feudal organisation of landed property and its developed petite culture, gives a much truer picture of the European Middle Ages than our own history books, dictated as these are, for the most part, by bourgeois prejudices.
>
> (Karl Marx)

There exists no single 'European' or 'Atlantic' model of industrialisation against which the character of Tokugawa economic development may be compared. A dominant, if narrow, view of such a 'Western model' of industrial dynamism might begin with the traditional forces of land, labour and capital. Agricultural and commercial revolutions are a prerequisite to industrial transformation for they provide the labour and the funds which entrepreneurs bring to new pursuits embodying new ideas and techniques. The new industrial techniques were, in this model, principally forged in applications of knowledge indigenous to this successful group of nations. Similarly, the diffusion of better techniques was induced under the pressure of rising market forces, principally the search for profits generated by rising demand. Thus eighteenth- and early nineteenth-century European history becomes a story of national conflicts, social transformations and military compromises as a small group of early-start industrialisers begin to depart from the traditional pattern of sporadic economic growth. The conflicts of the French Revolution and the Napoleonic Wars are hallmarks of change; the Crimean War and the American Civil War, demonstrations of the new power of industry.

A broader perspective on Atlantic development might begin (rather than end) with a model of socio-institutional change and an interpretation of the movement of technique and ideas between nation states. After all, not all of Europe developed at once. In many nations of Europe, where a regime of rigid social orders prevailed, strong systems of obligation were common. These involved patterns of social behaviour which may well have retarded the emergence of individualistic profit seeking and income-dominated consumption. In the France of Louis XIV (1638–1715) the idea of fealty between client and protector, between *fidèles* (men) and *maître* (lord) served social stasis in a way that seems at least loosely equivalent to the obligations of the moral economy in Tokugawa Japan. Indeed, fealty between subject and lord in Europe could be so strong as to perhaps explain and justify revolution against central authority, a political potential not dissimilar to the actual conflicts which took place between the *han* and the government in nineteenth-century Japan.

Within the West the early industrialisers were those nations whose traditions were fractured by earlier religious or social conflicts, or weakened by outside influence, or forged in a world made new (the American colonies). So, it has been argued that French industrialisation in the nineteenth century was held back, not by absence of capital or technique as such but by significant social and institutional barriers to innovation, imagination and the taking of risk. More generally, Karl Polanyi had argued passionately that 'social not technical invention was the intellectual mainspring of the Industrial Revolution'.

The new ideas of individualism, competition and profit-seeking were not necessarily natural, organic growths of economic change, but more often raised from the hot-bed of the competing, nationalistic state. For Polanyi, the great transformation to the 'Western model' occurred only when the traditional configuration whereby the economic order was subsumed in the social order was upset. The sustained accumulation of capital and the diffusion of new techniques and needs demanded 'nothing less than the institutional separation of society into an economic and political sphere . . . a singular departure'. Herein emerged the new 'scientism', whereby the ideologies of capitalism were understood not merely as the creation of Adam Smith or David Ricardo, but as extensions of nature and of nature's laws, as in Ricardo's assertion of an iron law of wages or Thomas Malthus' population doctrines. Although many of the institutions of economic liberalism in fact arrived somewhat later on the scene than this simple scheme suggests (for instance, the British cotton industry developed under protectionism, not free trade) and although a few great thinkers within the system did resist the onslaught, J. S. Mill and Karl Marx being perhaps the greatest of them, the general point is well enough made. Western industrialisation waited upon social and institutional change, the separation of moral economy from political economy and the church from the state, constant interactions between 'winner' nations despite periodic warfare and, in the terms of Max Weber, the growth and spread of 'a rationalistic economic ethic'. Clearly, a central aspect of the market system and the 'capitalist spirit' is the greater impersonality of relations between individuals and groups, cutting across and eventually overriding earlier systems of community, locality, hierarchy and obligation, and allowing for such common behaviour as overpricing, money lending, bargaining and a more aggressive, competitive and conspicuous consumerism. Furthermore, it now seems that such a socio-institutional transformation was not necessarily a very slow and laborious process but could at times be brought about quite deliberately by the social engineering of states or empowered groupings who saw advantage in industrial dynamism.

This chapter has suggested that in terms of the more conventional perspectives on the transformation to industrial modernity, Tokugawa Japan had much in common with the West. Land was much improved and greatly extended. Labour was highly skilled, variably underemployed, literate to European standards. Capital does not appear to have been in short supply. Infrastructure, particularly roadways, waterways and ports was invested in to a disproportionate degree. In addition, Tokugawa Japan represented a clearly legitimate nation state, more so than many of those in Europe. The nation was very large indeed, the level of urbanisation significantly high, the degree of social and political control from the centre greater than could be found in any nation of that population size in Asia and as great as could ever have been expected in a nation of that population size in the West at that time. On the other hand, again in fairly conventional terms, population growth had all but ceased in the early eighteenth century in contrast to the demographic transition in Europe, the Japanese nation was isolated from the outside world and savings were almost certainly directed from productive pursuits towards aristocratic consumption more efficiently than was the case in most nations of Europe. These latter factors combined gave rise to a situation of large pockets of conservative commerce, of money-making content with the status quo. Japanese merchants were not challenged by the new innovations of foreign commerce, they were not revolutionaries. Other than in exceptional cases, Japan's intellectuals were not stimulated by ideas and ideologies from abroad. Japanese production techniques was not forever modified and stimulated by streams of incremental improvement from outside. Japanese values were not fundamentally disturbed.

However, the process of limited economic change which we have outlined above did depend upon and involve social and institutional change and a challenge to the earlier Tokugawa moral economy. The seeming deceleration of economic dynamism during the eighteenth century (noted in more detail on pp. 14–15) may have been a reflection of the slowness and regionalism of change in the moral economy. The years of the eighteenth and early nineteenth centuries might, then, have represented a shifting of barriers and constraints lying in the areas of social structure, values and behavioural patterns, rather than a period of economic downturn caused by the more conventional factors of labour and skill shortage, lack of demand, internal political strife and heightened risk. Dynamism in the Tokugawa economy, in this interpretation, took the form of significant structural and production changes, followed by tortuous socio-institutional accommodations. It might well be that the process of accommodation would have gone on for even longer without any regime change in the continued absence of outside interference. The conflicts of the Tempō reform period were fading by the 1840s and 1850s. It is true that certain *han* were becoming dangerously well-equipped and frustrated. By the early nineteenth century, Satsuma controlled 28,000 armed *samurai*, Chōsū perhaps some 11,000, well-beyond the legal allowance. The expenses of the *bakufu* were high and the tax base possibly diminishing. The crop failures of the 1830s compounded the problems of the authorities. There was no obvious political solution in sight. But we should not be confounded by our present inability to find the obvious. The central authority of Tokugawa Japan had withstood challenge for many years. The difference that unfolded in the mid-nineteenth century was that internal conflicts were being waged at the same time as a very strong and independent outside threat was mounted. The regime change of the Meiji Restoration and the subsequent move to a centrally inspired industrial drive in the 1870s and 1880s were determined by outside influence, which provided to a relatively hitherto closed system new weapons, knowledge and expectations. However, and this is a vital rider, the *success* of Japan's 'response' to the Western model was compounded of both the activities and new dynamism of the years 1868–1912 as well as the institutional, industrial and other resources provided by the Tokugawa era itself. Japan leaned on the West, but it did not fall over.

Notes

1 The best introduction to agricultural change is T. C. Smith, *The Agrarian Origins of Modern Japan*, reprinted Atheneum, New York, 1966. The wooden framed thresher appeared first around Osaka prior to 1703 and replaced the *kōki-hashi* (large-size chopsticks) in drawing the rice stalks. Smith makes the point (p. 102) that, even here, labour saved at harvest was used to plant a winter crop immediately after the late harvest.

2 A merchant philosophy founded by Baigan Ishida (1685–1744), Sekimon Shingaku argued, amongst other things, that frugality is a virtue and that profit is just. Thus Baigan: 'My "stipend" is the profits I earn through transactions. I receive them from my customers, if they tell me to come, I will come, just as a samurai will hasten to fulfil his duty'. Shingaku, then, is an epitome of the attempt to collapse the moral economy with the new political economy of the eighteenth century.

References

Hanley, Susan (1997) *Everyday Things in Premodern Japan: The Hidden Legacy of Material Culture*, Berkeley, CA: University of California Press, p. 58.

Hall, John W. (1955–6) 'The castle town and Japan's modern urbanisation', *Far Eastern Quarterly*, 15: 37–56.

Ihara, S. (1959) *The Japanese Family Storehouse* (1959 edition translated by G. W. Sargent), Cambridge: Cambridge University Press, p. 24.

Polanyi, K. (1957 [1944]) *The Great Transformation: The Political and Economic Origins of Our Time* (new edition) Boston, MA: Beacon Paperback, pp. 71, 119.

Weber, Max (1961) *General Economic History*, New York: Collier Books, p. 260.

Further reading

Bito, M. (1981) 'Society and social thought in the Tokugawa period', *Japan Foundation Newsletter*, IX, June: 1–9.

Bray, F. (1986) *The Rice Economies*, Oxford: Blackwell.

Dore, R. (1958) *City Life in Japan*, Berkeley, CA: University of California Press.

Francks, P. (1983) *Technology and Agricultural Development in Pre-War Japan*, New Haven, CT: Yale University Press.

Furushima, T. (1963) *Kinsei Nihon nōgyō no tenkai*, Tokyo: University of Tokyo Press.
Hane, M. (1991) *Premodern Japan: A Historical Survey*, Boulder, CO: Westview.
Hanley, S. B. and Yamamura, K. (1977) *Economic and Demographic Change in Preindustrial Japan, 1600–1868*, Princeton, NJ: Princeton University Press.
Hirschmeier, J. and Yui, T. (1975) *The Development of Japanese Business 1600–1973*, London: Allen and Unwin.
Korhauser, D. (1976) *Urban Japan*, London: Longmans.
Lehmann, J.-P. (1982) *The Roots of Modern Japan*, London: Macmillan.
Minami, R. (1982) 'Water wheels in the pre-industrial economy of Japan', *Hitotsubshi Journal of Economics*, 22: 1–15.
Minami, R. (1987) *Power Revolution in the Industrialisation of Japan*, Tokyo: Kinokuniya.
Moore, R. A. (1970) 'Adoption and samurai mobility in Tokugawa Japan', *Journal of Asian Studies*, 29–3: 617–32.
Morris-Suzuki, T. (1994) *The Technological Transformation of Japan*, Cambridge: Cambridge University Press.
Norman, E. H. (1940) *Origins of the Modern Japanese State*, Institute of Pacific Relations. Reprinted with other relevant material in J. W. Dower (ed) (1975) *Origins of the Modern Japanese State, Selected Writings of E. H. Norman*, New York: Pantheon Books.
North, D. C. (1955) 'Location theory and regional economic growth', *Journal of Political Economy*, 63: 243–58.
Sheldon, C. P. (1958) *The Rise of the Merchant Class in Tokugawa Japan 1600–1868*, New York: Russell.
Shinmi, K. (1965) *Kakyu shizoku no kenkyu*, Tokyo: Maruzen.
Smith, H. D. (1978) 'Tokyo as an idea', *Journal of Japanese Studies*, 4: 45–73.
Smith, R. J. (1960) 'Pre-industrial urbanism in Japan', *Economic Development and Cultural Change*, 9: 241–57.
Smith, T. C. (*c.* 1966) *The Agrarian Origins of Modern Japan*, reprinted New York: Atheneum.
Smith, T. C. (1977) *Nakahara, Family Farming and Population in a Japanese Village 1717–1830*, Stanford, CA: Stanford University Press.
Smith, T. C. (1997) *Native Sources of Japanese Industrialisation, 1750–1920*, Berkeley, CA: University of California Press.
Takeo, Y. (1968) *Social Change and the City in Japan*, Tokyo: Japan Publications Inc.
Tsukahira, T. G. (1970) *Feudal Control in Tokugawa Japan: The Sankin-Kōtai System*, Cambridge MA: Harvard University Press.
Yamamoto, S. (1983) 'The capitalist logic of the samurai', *Entrepreneurship*, (Tokyo), no.7, December, 1–11.

3 An outline of Meiji industrialisation (1868–1912)

Economic performance

> Since intercourse with the foreigners has been opened, the Western arts have been gradually introduced and are flourishing daily and monthly, so that our old manners and customs are totally changed.
>
> (*Hochi Shimbun* 1878)

> Clearing the stage; scattering the past about, comes the new age.
>
> (Matthew Arnold)

Japan's drive to industrialisation from 1868 started from a population base of 34 million and a labour force of some 24 million, more than 70 per cent of whom were employed in the agricultural sector. At around 100 persons per square kilometre the density of population was significantly higher than that of the industrialising European nations and North America. A relatively gentle population growth rate of less than 1 per cent allowed for an increase in income per head of about 2.5–3 per cent per annum average, accelerating from a lower figure until the turn of the century. Although light manufacturing and transport infrastructure headed the growth of the economy, technological and institutional innovations in the agricultural sector yielded surplus income and food flows towards industry, much of which was itself located in small-scale, rural enterprises.

The growth rate of agricultural production is disputed because earlier estimates of up to 4 per cent per annum were based on tax returns (see pp. 34–5, 80–1), the collection of which increased in efficiency as the years went by. However, any examination of the official notifications of 1873 or 1884 indicates that the authorities were well aware of the problems of land conversion, reclamation, pledging, revaluation, improvement and concealment, all used as tactics in the attempt to escape the tax on land value, set at 3 per cent. A reasonable guess would be that the sector grew at the rate of around 1.5 per cent per annum, or significantly above the rate of population growth. Improved performance was based on increases in labour productivity, the dissemination of the best known techniques, including novel rice varieties which responded well to a new range of commercial, chemical fertilisers. A major contribution of the industrial sector to the agricultural was in the provision of low cost chemical fertilisers. The government instigated the *rōnō* or veteran farmer system (1880–95), which focused on the interaction between new methods and established skills and undoubtedly helped in the diffusion of double cropping, dry paddy cultivation, animal husbandry, the introduction of hybrids in sericulture and better methods of rice selection, irrigation and mechanical pumping. Such biological improvements (i.e. efficient water and chemical usage, as against new machinery) tended to be labour absorbing, employing more people and spreading the use of workers more evenly throughout the year. The strong regionalisation of agricultural progress in the Tokugawa years (see Chapter 2) suggests that Meiji agricultural growth was distinguished by a greater diffusion of productive practice, encouraged by better transport infrastructure, which reduced costs as it uncovered new pockets of demand which innovating producers could exploit.

Whatever the actual growth rate in agriculture, the sector clearly served to produce food and labour at a rate sufficient to keep down the wages of workers in industry, whether urban or rural based. Although it is true that between 1894 and 1903 net food imports mounted to 25 per cent of all imports, this reflected a change towards non-food production within the sector as well as the availability of cheap food from Japan's new colonial acquisitions following the war with China (1894–5). By far the most obvious mechanism whereby agriculture was forced to contribute to industry was the land tax reform, which began in 1872–3. At that time some 50 per cent of total rice production was extracted by the state and by upper feudal estates; by the 1890s between 80 per cent and 90 per cent of production was retained by the agricultural producers themselves. A key to this turnabout was the abolition of feudal payments and of the tenure of the lords as well as the introduction of free sales of land and distribution of the product of the land, including its export abroad. Peasant and other proprietors paid tax in money, whilst their rents were paid in kind by tenants, the proportion of whom in total agricultural labour rose from around 20 per cent in the beginning to around 45 per cent at the end of the Meiji era. In the early years, in the absence especially of significant revenue from customs because of the unequal treaties which permitted a tariff of only 4 per cent or so, or of revenue from tax on industrial production (e.g. purchase taxes, stamp duties, permits), returns from the land tax were of tremendous importance to the government's programme of industrial and commercial advance; in 1875 it provided 85 per cent of total national revenue. In systematic terms, the land tax represented a distribution of income away from conspicuous consumers (the old upper estates) towards industry and commerce via the investment and other behaviour of government. In addition the surplus products of the agricultural sector, in particular silk and tea, earned vital foreign exchange when exported abroad.

It was in the peasant households that the silk industry had always been embedded, from the growing of mulberry bushes and the rearing of the silkworm to reeling and weaving on hand looms. In the 1870s silk production became a replacement income for many peasant households threatened by tenancy, taxation and imports of cotton. Government demonstration projects in the early 1870s hastened the diffusion of mechanical powered reeling. Between 1868 and 1883 the output of raw silk doubled, its export expanded at an even higher rate. In time the export of eggs gave way to that of reeled and woven silks. By the 1890s large enterprises, encouraged and monitored by government, had entered reeling, but weaving continued to thrive in small-scale units. Cotton textile production first suffered from foreign imports and this sector depended for its early growth on the import substitution policy of government (see pp. 33–4). The great expansion of this branch awaited the later 1880s and resulted from a combination of previous government assistance, technological innovation and adaptation and the exploitation of cheap, powerless female labour, as well as, on the demand side, a greater accessibility to Asian markets as Japan vastly improved its transport, military and political influence in the region. A measure of structural change in the Japanese industrial economy was that imports of raw cotton from the US were added to imports from China and India during the 1890s. Again, the technical and institutional development of weaving lagged somewhat, and this is some explanation for the great export surge in cotton spun threads until 1900. Power looms were introduced from the 1880s and by 1907 some 9,000 were in operation, providing woven cloth for export to Korea, Manchuria and China. In total, the textile sector was the most important of manufactures; in 1912, 60 per cent of workers employed in 'factories' (five or more persons) were producing textile goods. Yet due to abundant cheap rural labour, technical simplicity and the predominance of traditional skills, most production was still domestic and often did little to disturb the physical and social landscape of Japan. Such modernised but rural and small-scale production was central to the generation of a manufacturing growth rate of around 4 per cent per annum.

Infrastructure development took place at an even faster pace, especially from the 1880s and was closely associated with government encouragement. Transport (roads, rail and river improvement, but including docks, harbours, lighthouses and telegraph systems and, later, shipbuilding) alone grew at a rate of perhaps 10 per cent per annum and improvements here indisputably reduced the cost of the movement of goods, raw materials and machinery for manufacturing firms, and opened up the domestic and export markets. Despite the fact that railroads in particular absorbed large lumps of capital at once but only generated profit somewhat later and in a very diffused manner, there is little evidence of a lack of capital in the financing of large projects. Thus the railway bonds issued by government for the construction of the *Nakasendō* line in 1884 were subscribed to very rapidly by not only banks but also thousands of individual investors to the tune of some 20 million yen. Together with the military and colonial imperatives of the nation (conscription was established in 1884), infrastructure development determined the character of growth in the heavy industries (iron and steel, engineering and shipbuilding) and mining (especially coal, iron and copper). The dual strategic role of railways, as a series of projects encouraging the development of mining and engineering as well as a component of increased military potential, meant that government activity was very important, both in original investment and technological innovation and in providing orders. In 1907 the government established the Yawata Steel Works, the demonstration effect of which led to the emergence of a number of private enterprises. By 1912 domestic pig iron production fed nearly 50 per cent of total Japanese consumption, while domestic production of steel supplied some 34 per cent of the nation's requirements.

Government was also active in mining and engineering. The authorities were quick to bring foreign technology into mining (see Chapter 4). Although by the end of the period some 100 mining companies employed 172,000 workers in coal production alone, partnerships between larger firms and the government were common. This is true too of other aspects of mining, engineering, shipbuilding and metal production generally. The reasons for this are understandable – many such undertakings originated in *han*-based projects prior to 1868, the character of capital investment was generally lumpy and substantial and banks tended to favour larger producers. Sustained forward investment in large projects depended on government contracts almost entirely until the private sector began to exert effective demand for ships, machinery and larger quantities of more standardised raw materials. Perhaps of even greater importance in explaining the rise of a government–large firm link is the simple point that only the relatively large-scale businessmen or business groups could effectively take advantage of the sales of state enterprise in the 1880s, which tended to concentrate around projects of either strategic or technological urgency (see Chapter 5).

It is of great importance to note that industrial dynamism did not mean the falling away of established or traditional industries and enterprises. Cement, sugar, glass, pottery, brewing, sake, paper, chemical and fertiliser production still owed a great deal to small-scale production methods. Such enterprises were often rejuvenated by new power units (steam or later electricity) and better transport and commercial services. Although the emerging *zaibatsu* (financial clique) firms entered these arenas too (e.g. Mitsui in paper manufacture and the *zaibatsu* involvement in Formosan sugar production and trade), most of the output in such manufacturing arose from small, often rural based enterprises. The commercial buoyancy of this middle sector of the economy, lying somewhere between agriculture and the government-activated, large-scale manufacturing economy, was essential to labour absorption, general technical diffusion and the maintenance of nearly full employment at slowly rising incomes, as well as to the protection of existing skills. The prosperity of such enterprise also testifies to a continuity of consumption patterns across the divide of the 1860s.

The ratio of the value of total foreign trade to national income probably varied during the Meiji years within the range 10–20 per cent, by no means a large figure compared to such industrialising nations of Europe as Italy, Germany or Sweden, or to areas of recent settlement such as Australia, where trade ratios reached up to 40 per cent. Low but rising incomes combined with sheer large size to minimise the trade ratio and it seems clear that Japanese industrialisation was primarily satisfying an inflating *home* demand for goods, services, raw materials and capital in both the private and public sectors, rather than significant expansion of autonomous export demand. Exports rose because internal costs were falling, rather than vice versa. But to then argue that, because of this, foreign trade did not act as any 'engine of growth' (a term used by Alfred Marshall and others to explore trade's potential) is to emphasise the demand side to the exclusion of historical supply dynamics. Quite simply, *foreign imports revolutionised domestic technique throughout Meiji.* The ability to produce chemical fertilisers or to build efficient dockyards cannot otherwise be understood. Increased exports from Japan reflected not so much foreign demand but rather the increased efficiency of production within Japan, itself fed by imported techniques. The context of technology transfer is explored in far greater detail in Chapter 4. The mechanisms of technology transfer were many, but a principal medium of transformation and increased internal capability was trade. Already in the 1870s equipment, chemicals and raw materials for industry represented over 25 per cent or more of all imports; by the 1890s these items accounted for well over 30 per cent of a rising total. Industrial machinery was imported at the rate of about 300,000 yen per annum to the mid-1880s, but for the rest of the period the annual import bill for such technology averaged at around 12 million yen. If anything, the Japanese trading and industrialising economy was increasingly dependent on foreign techniques as Meiji progressed, a dependency which by no means stopped with the First World War. At the same time, the expansion of transport and commercial facilities involved in the importing of technique and materials and the exporting of textiles and tea, produced cost-reducing services which stimulated increased production in small new enterprises whose exports may not be otherwise easily explained i.e. firms whose exports were not clearly a result of cost reductions within such enterprises themselves.

Of even greater significance, perhaps, was the dynamic political import of foreign trade. The years immediately prior to 1868 had been dominated by aggressive Western penetration, marked first by the forced entry of Perry and then the signing of the so-called Treaties of Amity and Commerce in 1858, which allowed the US, Holland, Russia, Britain and France extraterritoriality and fixed a minimum tariff protection for Japan at around 4–5 per cent at a time when Western tariffs were commonly 10 per cent or 15 per cent. In fact, Japan's export trade prior to 1868 grew very rapidly at a rate of 15 per cent per annum because of the nature and quality of Japanese goods (especially silk and tea), but this did not spell any gains of foreign currency or bullion. Shipments were in the hands of foreign merchants whose facilities and services (e.g. insurance) had to be paid for. Also, Western traders tended to pay for Japanese goods in depreciating silver just as they demanded gold from the Japanese for foreign imports.[1] It was this failure to gain from trade which determined the new Meiji government on its path of industrial development and, particularly, import substitution. The lack of effective protection added to the great demand in Japan for iron, machinery and equipment and cottons, led to a tremendous deficit from 1868 to 1881: the gold and silver stock diminished by 60 per cent in the transition years 1869–72 alone. Trade was being financed from feudal accumulations. Import substitution policy was one of survival. Government investment and loans for cotton spinning and silk reeling in turn encouraged the technical development of traditional semi-manufacturers. A silk worm disease in Europe[2] and the opening of the Suez Canal in 1869 furthered the expansion of exports. Between 1881 and 1896, years which incorporated the great deflation of Masayoshi Matsukata, ennobled for his services in 1884, exports moved into surplus over imports. Although successful deflation has been pointed to as the sufficient cause of the trade turnabout the evidence is not convincing. Exports continued to surge through time because of the cost-reducing impact of technological change, a policy set in course by government long prior to 1885 and facilitated by an import of foreign technique which continued with some interruptions for another century. Between 1897 and 1912 import substitution clearly gave way to overt industrial export promotion. Japan's successes in transport and in war, more than the art of persuasion, secured revision of the treaties with the Western powers in a series of agreements from 1899, whilst the build up of shipping meant that some 80 per cent of trade was in Japanese holds by 1919.

On the whole the growth rate of capital formation was greater than that of national income. If reparations gained from China (1894–5) and Russia (1904–5) are excluded, Japan financed its own industrialisation.[3] The Meiji government was probably the most industrially active in the world at that time, but it was never a big spender and did not intrude on the internal capital market so as to crowd out potential private opportunities, despite much debate which took place to the contrary during the 1880s. The solid tax base centred on the land tax, steadily falling as a percentage of the total, as indirect taxes rose on sake, tobacco and sugar, and was added to by income tax and customs duties at the turn of the century. Tax never amounted to more than 10 per cent of national income. Revenue was added to by printing money in the early years and by the release of government bonds, including special bonds for infrastructure projects. It must be emphasised that in the first decade or so government was forced to pay huge financial outlays as compensation to the ex-*samurai* (*shizoku*) and for the quelling of the Satsuma (1877) and other rebellions. As late as 1884 the national debt stood at 260 million yen, 176 million yen of which was due to pension bonds. Such income transfers in the budget fell from the mid-1880s and there was consequently more room for government encouragement of industry through infrastructure construction, military investments, technological diffusion activity and direct subsidies. In all, although the savings rate was generally high it does not seem to have been extraordinary in comparison to other nations at that time and the apparent abundance of funds for development was almost certainly a consequence of the pattern or trajectory of economic dynamism. The economy was constantly moving towards a more efficient usage of labour in productive enterprises which were either directly or indirectly influenced by techniques and institutions whose prototypes originated in Europe and the US. For most of Meiji the principal carrier of technique and instigator of institutional innovation was the government itself, a point returned to in Chapter 5.

As might already be seen, the years from 1868 to 1884 were ones of tremendous institutional and technological change, dominated by the government's determination to combat the West with the tools of the West. Henceforth we shall refer to these years as those of the *industrial drive*. In this phase of dynamism there was no realistic (i.e. historical) alternative to government activity other than failure and consequent political retributions. The physical, institutional and financial infrastructure laid down by government in this phase, at whatever social cost, was apprehended as the environmental input into the output of private enterprise after 1884. Within the industrial drive industry grew faster than the economy at large, labour moved in large numbers from agricultural employment to some form of manufacture or service employment, new techniques diffused, including the Japanese-developed throstle spinning (*gara-bō*) in cotton which could be harnessed to water wheels. This was the period of model factories in cotton and silk and spectacular mining and transport projects, not only embodying but publicly applauding the techniques and agencies of the West. The rise of private enterprise was on the back of government infrastructural and service investment and technological diffusion policies, training and educational schemes and a social engineering which successfully kept opposition at bay.

This lagged impact of the public sector on private enterprise, measures the transition to *industrial revolution* from 1885 and a more cost-efficient period of economic dynamism replacing the crucial institutional and attitudinal breakthroughs of the industrial drive. For instance, railway construction, hitherto pursued at a cost of about 30–50 per cent above that of corresponding American projects, now became more efficient and was increasingly the concern of private enterprise. The transition was not smooth or unambiguous. The 81-mile Tokyo–Mayebashi line was constructed in 1883–4 at a rate of $23,000 per mile 'independent of foreign assistance', although indeed $686,000 had been spent in Europe on foreign equipment. The Miike coal mine at the extreme South West of Japan had in earlier years been worked at an output of around 300 tons per day by Mitsui acting as a sole agent for government. When Mitsui bought the mine for £750,000 and the government had invested some £200,000 in machinery and improved transport, a programme of further technical updating was instigated, including locomotive traction and vastly improved harbour and canal facilities. Output rose from 302,000 tons in 1887 to 600,000 tons in 1891, 50 per cent of which was exported. It might be that the transition from industrial drive to industrial revolution can be epitomised as a movement towards greater efficiency of *technique* and *organisation* increasingly instigated by private entrepreneurship which utilised a range of institutional and physical resources created by government prior to 1885. The result was a higher rate of overall economic and industrial growth and an increase in the range of modernising industries.

Japan in context

Japan began its industrial drive at an income level well below that of European nations at the time of their early industrial modernisation. Not only does this point to the importance of non-income measures (such as levels of technique, skills or social cohesion) in determining success, it explains the difficulty Japan faced in altering its industrial ranking amongst the world's developing economies. Around 1870, Japan possessed an income per head about 25 per cent that of Britain and 50 per cent that of Italy, whilst the proportion of the population engaged in agriculture was far higher than that of other industrialising nations with the exception of Russia. If Japan's agricultural and industrial output is ranked against that of ten European nations and the United States, its position lies at twelve in 1860, but remains at twelve in 1880 or in 1910 i.e. at the end of Meiji industrialisation. Because the Atlantic economy was itself fast expanding, even the tremendous changes of the Meiji years failed to move Japan from its position of relative economic backwardness. Other late developers, notably Germany, Sweden and Switzerland, were also industrialising, using the tools of earlier industrialisers such as Britain or Belgium or France to finance and construct new industries in new regions. From the US to Italy and Germany, all late industrialisers had reaped benefits of external financing and technology transfer.

Japan's specific achievement lay in industrialising outside of the Atlantic at a pace with European late developers. Just as a series of nations, from Egypt and Turkey to India and China, succumbed to Atlantic-based industrialisation, Japan resisted the onslaught of the West. Meiji industrialisation should not, therefore, be judged primarily in terms of economic growth rates but in terms of politico-cultural escape. This is so simply because the escape was not a result of luck, magic or one individual or theory, but rather involved the gathering of very real resources in order to employ Western techniques and agencies, yet trade freely and resist foreign capital and, by the early nineteenth century, encroach upon Western ambitions and vested interests in Asia itself. The historical relationship between the Atlantic and the Pacific is a subject to which we return in Chapters 12 and 13.

Interpretations

> A caterpillar has to contract its body and draw up its many legs before it takes a step forward.
>
> (*Jiyū Shimbun* March 1884)

It is increasingly accepted that Japan's early industrial dynamism is not well explained in terms of conventional factors, particularly those of capital and land. The major conventional factor of production which was more fully employed in Meiji Japan was labour. Hence, the historical backdrop of skills, literacy and social cohesion of the Tokugawa era may be harnessed in explaining the Meiji breakthrough into industrial modernity. But any of the possible combinations of conventional factors, including that implied in a surplus-labour model, takes place within some sort of institutional setting, and for most of Meiji this 'setting' was itself dynamic and the predominant agencies for change were not those normally associated with the liberal market economy. As we shall see further in Chapters 4 and 5, government infrastructural, investment, and institutional interventions were crucially important in mobilising the 'response' of the Japanese economic system to the new external and internal political systems. Furthermore, the Meiji economy did not simply slip into a predestined place within the global economy of nations, nor did technology pass osmotically from the Atlantic to the Pacific without human agency, institutional innovation and cultural conflict. Internally, the political transition from the *Bakumatsu* regime to the Meiji restoration programme was fraught with conflict, debate and physical unrest, for the cultural requisites of the moral economy were by no means sufficient to ensure social continuity or political quietism. The replacement of 2 million nobles with 100,000 bureaucrats was never a sleight of hand but represented a social class shift in the power-structure as the ex-*samurai* or *shizoku*, in the words of the *Hōchi Shimbun* 'were compelled to resort to trade and commercial pursuits in order to earn their daily bread'. But in this lies the rub. What determined the direction of social adjustment at such points? A simple mechanistic account of economic transition would fail to note that these powerful groups should have resisted such a 'compulsion' and by their reaction added such enormous social and financial costs to the system that it would have failed by the early 1870s.

It must also be said that most 'cultural' arguments fail to systematically attach convincing cultural *explanans* to major economic *explanandums*.

It appears to be sensible to begin an interpretation of Meiji industrialisation with some version of the late-starter hypothesis. Economic development under conditions of relative economic backwardness allows for the possibility of financial borrowing and technology transfer as well as the exploitation of vast export markets for raw materials, foodstuffs and semi-manufactures. However, as Marion J. Levy once so aptly put it, 'the gaps that latecomers must jump guarantee a considerable impact of strangeness'. Not many nations captured the advantages of their backwardness and this was because a tremendous array of cultural, social and economic resources had to be fairly rapidly mobilised in order to exploit the fleeting potential; fleeting because such possibilities were soon greatly curtailed by protectionism, colonialism and war. Furthermore, Japan did not have vast raw materials for export, capital import was minimised and the external sector of the economy remained relatively small compared to the domestic economy. Several features of the industrialisation of Meiji Japan clearly do, however, illustrate the workings of a late development effect, in particular the predominance of government activity and the strategic significance of technology transfers. In addition, the concurrent growth of agriculture (and its technical upgrading) with industrialisation, as well as the political pressures arising from social dislocation do fit the picture of late development. Too often the activity of government and the capacity for technology transfer (both dealt with in more detail in Chapters 4 and 5) are seen as peculiar to Japan, as highlights of behaviour which originated in the persistence of the family nation, or of extreme nationalism, or of a structured obedience to hierarchy, and so on. The late development perspective might at least serve as something of an antidote to such extreme cultural determinism, as well as to conventional Western perspectives which see Meiji development as the mere continuation of a trajectory first established in the 'prerequisite' era of Tokugawa.

Synthesis

For a synthetic interpretation of Meiji industrialisation we must return to the phraseology of the first section of this chapter. We will show in Chapters 4 and 5 that it is not sufficient to concur with Ryoshin Minami in his statement that the period 1868–84 'was a transition period leading up to, not the beginning of modern economic growth'. If political, institutional and technological change in the industrial drive (prior to 1885) at least partially and perhaps mostly determined the character of industrial advancement after 1885, then the conception of such a 'beginning' to modern economic growth in 1885 becomes either trivial or a mere acknowledgement that 'modern economic growth' is being defined only in terms of its fairly narrow conventional measurement rather than in a manner which allows for its interpretation. This yet permits an account of the success of Meiji industrialisation which involves the contribution of the Tokugawa era, as outlined in Chapter 2. Furthermore, much of the innovative response of the industrial drive was not only in fear of the West but in apprenticeship to the West. The presentation here does somewhat weaken the idea of 'a transition' from feudalist Tokugawa Japan to politically and socially rejuvenated industrial Japan, and tends to emphasise the deliberate character and crucial role of the years 1868–84, for it was within this short period that the successful social engineering of the Japanese elite created the institutions, social overhead capital and strategies which were to form the industrial trajectory of the economy thereafter. We may not divorce the telegraphs, railroads, roadways, ports and harbours, nor the schools, colleges, prisons and legal systems of the industrial drive from the private entrepreneurship of the industrial revolution. Minami admits that such earlier institutional reform 'hastened the formation of nation-wide commodity markets . . . and facilitated population mobility and contributed to the formation of labour markets'. At the same time, the present interpretive framework does not require the Japanese entrepreneur of the industrial revolution to either arise majestically from an institutional wasteland or to be a natural, inevitable outcome of social changes which had occurred many years before in Tokugawa Japan or even earlier. Rather than focus on the entrepreneur as a type, the distinction between industrial drive and industrial revolution draws attention to the conditions under which entrepreneurial acts are most likely to occur.

Innovative business activity does not occur in revolutions nor when a system is under physical threat from the outside world, as was the case in Japan during the 1850s, and as could well have been the case thereafter if the new government had not instigated its own institutional innovations. Entrepreneurship is similarly unlikely in the absence of knowledge and of capital, is difficult if faced with negative social sanctions, and in most cases requires a supply of labour which is appropriately skilled and either amenable to persuasion or entirely powerless. No individualist profit-seeking ethos will in itself generate the conditions within which business innovation might occur. But Meiji Japan may demonstrate that the provision of such conditions can strongly influence the character and extent of private sector involvement in new ventures. If, as in Joseph Schumpeter's famous dictum, 'capital is nothing but that with which the entrepreneur subjects to his control those concrete goods which he needs', then it follows that capital formation may have been of far less importance in dictating the economic dynamics of Meiji Japan than was institutional innovation, a process led by government and influenced from afar.

Themes

A major theme in any account of early industrialisation in Japan must surely be that of the mechanism or process of socio-political control. In so many nations of the nineteenth and twentieth centuries, state-led, rapid industrialisation ended in political and moral disaster, often on a vast scale. In understanding the retention of control in Meiji Japan there are at least three possibilities, none exclusive of the other: (a) Tokugawa Japan contained within it the socio-cultural seeds of continuity; (b) the process of industrialisation in Meiji Japan was not so disruptive of existing institutions and patterns of rural life as was the case elsewhere; and (c) *within* the Meiji industrial drive efficient methods of socio-political control were instituted at minimum cost.

Social control may relate to a second main theme, that of labour absorption. High levels of unemployment of peasants, urban workers and the intelligentsia might well lead to loss of inner political control. Perhaps 75 per cent of the increase in the non-primary labour force in Japan was due to the movement of workers from one sector to the other. A simple late development model would postulate a capital-intensive, technically sophisticated manufacturing sector at the spearhead of economic dynamics set against the backdrop of a labour absorbing agricultural sector. Surplus labour would ensure low wages in the modern sector, whose growth rate would be primarily determined by the growth rate of capital accumulation. Clearly, this model generates growth only if there is a significantly high rate of growth of capital in the modern sector as well as an effective labour surplus, i.e. appropriately skilled or experienced workers must be released from agriculture at a low constant wage rate, set slightly higher than that in agriculture.[4] In Japan, labour absorption on a grand scale, and thus to a great extent social control also, was generated not only in agricultural but in small-scale traditional and new enterprises operating over a range of industries (see pp. 30–3). The tripartite (as against the dual) economy allowed an import of the best from the West in the modern sector, a rejuvenation of agriculture through relatively inexpensive and labour-using *biological* improvements (involving a huge increase in fertilisers imported from industry), and labour absorption in both a transforming and growing agricultural sector and a multifarious small enterprise sector which rewarded traditional skills and, hence, contributed to social control. The starkness of the division between modernised industry and backward agriculture found in a case such as Tsarist Russia during the 1890s was never evident in Japan. At the same time, the accoutrement of state-based modernity – the universities and colleges, hospitals, legal services and general bureaucracy – provided gainful employment for Japanese intellectuals, precisely those who were most aware of the alternative political possibilities inherent within a phase of rapid social and economic transformation. It seems that Meiji dynamics evidenced important historical links between technology transfer, sectoral change and political control.

These themes are considered further in Chapters 4 and 5. The foreign influence on Japanese industrialisation was not confined to the import of machinery or the lodging of patents. A newly 'opened' national system received not only Western technologies but also disruptive Western ideologies. On several levels, a continuing foreign presence in Japan exerted an impact on the character of economic change.

It is fashionable to minimise the function of government in successful economic transformation. In particular it is frequently argued that manifold illustrations of government economic activity are no measures of the contribution of the public sector to growth, for such activity is costly and inefficient. Government intervention might well, then, actively retard economic growth by, for instance, extracting scarce capital from the private sector where it would be far better employed. Chapter 5 suggests that such an argument is inapplicable to Meiji Japan. The sustenance of economic development across the industrial drive in the face of foreign aggression required measures of socio-political control and cultural suasion. Analysts who dismiss such action as exogenous to the world of economic dynamics fail to interpret Meiji economic achievement. Historians who focus on costs at the expense of institutions and the long-term impact of infrastructure and demonstration seem to imply an alternative scenario of nicely operating markets for land, capital, labour and information in a world where conflict is only at the margin and dischargeable through the satisfaction of existing wants within a panoply of efficiently operating private enterprises. Such perspectives also appear to ignore the simple fact that, at any one time, an economic system is lying in some sort of trajectory, and that this is made up of real time and real institutions, technologies and expectations. The odds that any approach involving so many omissions might in fact come up with a sturdy interpretation of the historical dynamics of the Japanese or any other economy seem very small.

Notes

1 The Japanese government nominated gold coinage as the standard but also minted silver coins for transactions among merchants involved in foreign trade. Within Japan gold and silver coinage was set at a fixed ratio for exchange yet new discoveries and exchange variations lowered the international price of silver from the mid-1870s. Foreign merchants therefore brought silver into Japan to exchange for gold, gold flowed out and the government was caught in the situation of having to mint more silver coinage to replace gold coinage.

2 The outbreak of silkworm disease began in Europe and spread through trade. Europeans, particularly the French, attempted to recover by buying in healthy eggs from elsewhere, particularly Japan. It was foreign merchants operating in Japan who advocated quality control of Japanese silk, including better technical instruction for both dealers and growers, limiting of production to most suitable provinces, confinement of reeling to only full size silk and the stoppage of the export of silkworm eggs.

3 The Chinese indemnity was approximately $146 million (360 million yen or about 25 per cent of national income). Henceforth Japan received far greater amounts of capital as a result of its heavy industry and military programme and the high estimation held of the nation by foreigners after the defeat of China and then Russia: war and capital were intimately linked through the decisions of international

investors. Perhaps 30 per cent of net capital formation came from abroad in the years 1896–1913, much of this from bond issues rather than as direct investment.

4 The empirical problems of the classic Lewis model of surplus labour relate to the 'real' availability of labour, i.e. throughout the year, of appropriate skill and work ethos etc., as well as to the production assumptions of the different sectors. But, primarily, there is no intermediate or informal or alternative sector in the Lewis model, and this is too great an abstraction for Japanese history to bear. If labour has a productivity of zero or below its income, it may be drawn from one sector to another at little cost and with no loss of production. It might be noted that the proletarianisation of many of the ex-*samurai* added to the numbers of potential workers in a perhaps significant manner. See J. C. Fei and G. Ranis, *Development of the Labor Surplus Economy*, Homewood, Illinois: Richard D. Irvin, 1964; Ian Inkster, *Japan as a Development Model?*, Bochum: Brockmeyer, 1980.

References

Levy, M. J. Jnr. (1972) *Modernisation: Latecomers and Survivors*, New York: Basic Books, pp. 12–13.

Minami, Ryoshin (1986) *The Economic Development of Japan, A Quantitative Study*, London: Macmillan, pp. 10, 24.

Further reading

Inkster, I. (1979) 'Meiji economic development in perspective: revisionist comments upon the industrial revolution in Japan', *The Developing Economies*, 17: 45–68.

Kinmouth, E. (1981) *The Self-Made Man in Meiji Japanese Thought*, Berkeley, CA: University of California Press.

Lockwood, W. W. (1968) *The Economic Development of Japan, Growth and Structural Change* (expanded edition), Princeton, NJ: Princeton University Press.

Macpherson, W. J. (ed.) (1994) *The Industrialisation of Japan*, Oxford: OUP.

Mass, W. and Robertson, A. (1996) 'From textiles to automobiles: mechanical and organizational innovation in the Toyoda enterprises 1895–1933', *Business and Economic History*, 25(2): 8–19.

Nakagawa, K. (ed.) (1977) *'Labor and Management', Proceedings of the 4th International Conference on Business History*, Tokyo: University of Tokyo Press.

Nakamura, J. I. (1966) *Agricultural Production and the Economic Development of Japan 1873–1922*, Princeton, NJ: Princeton University Press.

Ohkawa, K. and Shinohara, M. (eds) (1979) *Patterns of Japanese Economic Development: A Quantitative Appraisal*, New Haven and London: Yale University Press.

Ohkawa, K., Shinohara, M. and Umemura, M. (eds) (1965–) *Chōki Keizai Tōkei: Suikei to Bunseki (Estimates of Long-Term Economic Statistics of Japan since 1868)* vols 1–14, Tokyo: Toyokeizai Shinposha.

Ranis, G. (1955) 'The community-centred entrepreneur in Japanese development', *Explorations in Entrepreneurial History*, 8(2): 80–98.

Smith, T. C. (1955) *Political Change and Industrial Development in Japan: Government Enterprise 1868–80*, Stanford, CA: Stanford University Press.

Taira, K. (1970) 'Factory legislation and management modernisation during Japan's industrialization 1886–1916', *Business History Review*, 44: 84–109.

Tsunoda, R. *et al.* (1964) *Sources of Japanese Tradition* vols 1 and 2, New York: Columbia University Press.

Tsurumi, E. P. (1990) *Factory Girls. Women in the Thread Mills of Meiji Japan*, Princeton, NJ: Princeton University Press.

4 The foreign influence

Introduction

Following several of the points made in Chapters 1 and 2, we may now suggest that a principal reason for the industrial success of Meiji Japan lay in the precise nature of the country's interaction with the Western economies after 1868. This interaction was conditioned by at least three elements: the *timing* of the Western interventions, the *attitude* of the West towards Japan, and the *character* of the political economy of Japan. Having sketched out a process of limited change during the Tokugawa era, we will now indicate the major forces which dictated the first two elements.

In the course of administering the European interest in Java during the Napoleonic Wars, Stamford Raffles was reportedly deeply 'impressed with the importance of opening a commercial intercourse with the Japanese', and he went on to comment on the energy and intellect of the leaders of the nation. But in 1819 the influential British intellectual journal, the *Quarterly Review* believed that 'the wants of this people are few and their superfluous produce neither great nor valuable' and that, therefore, any lost opportunities were merely diplomatic and marginal. So, the first half of the nineteenth century was in fact characterised by significant degrees of freedom in the relationships between Japan and the advanced Western economies. An aesthetic rather than a commercial interest dominated, and the 'queer and quaint' image of Gilbert and Sullivan's *Mikado* (1885) represented a fairly standard perception. In 1870 the *Japan Weekly Mail* commented that the Japanese 'are inclined to be satisfied with a ready-made knowledge', and as late as 1881 the *Japan Herald* proclaimed that 'the Japanese are a happy race, and being content with little, are not likely to achieve much'. Until at least the Sino-Japanese war of 1895 and probably the Russo-Japanese war of 1904–5, Japan did not posit a large threat, nor did it represent a commercial or strategic challenge of very great moment. Japan appeared as a minor victim of global expansion.

Japan possessed a natural geographical protection. Between them, the vast steppes of Siberia and the Crimean War (1854–6) prevented Russia from effectively pursuing its plans for Far Eastern colonisation. On the other side of the Northern hemisphere, the Manifest Destiny of the Americans first focused on forays against the Amerindians and Mexico (1846), and only the whalers saw Japan as of any consequence. The important investments of Europe were in India, China and Indonesia, and Dutch trade had effected commercial links between Japan and China rather than between Japan and the West. The very early failure of British trade under the East India Company had prompted the idea that Japan could not become 'an Object of Attention for the Manufactures and Produce of Great Britain'. It was the securing of Hong Kong by the British in 1842 which stimulated the ambitions of America in the Far East. Perry's visit and the consequent treaty of Kanagawa (1854) opened the ports of Shimoda and Hakodate, and from then American diplomats urged that a peaceful Japanese–American treaty would keep at bay the British and the French, already at war in China. The 1858 Treaty of Ansei opened Kanagawa, Nagasaki, Niigata and Hyōgo and from thence Japan was stripped of trade protection against the West. It was this which encouraged the anti-*bakufu* element amongst the *han*. Indeed, the relative *absence* of any effective foreign interventionism during 1860–5 may well have been crucial in promoting a degree of freedom in which to prepare for positive response. Economic distress and frequent rebellion characterised the internal politics of Japan just as Britain was heavily engaged in the end-games of the Taiping Rebellion in China, as the Americans fought their civil war and as France intervened in the affairs of Mexico. Such diversions, and in particular the real importance of China, combined with the Franco-Prussian War (1870) to permit an internally determined restoration of sovereignty during 1867–70. From thence, a new national economic response to the West could begin.

The long prelude

Even in seclusion, Japan was not entirely deprived of the influence of other nations. Figure 4.1 summarises the major phases within which a knowledge of Western science and technology was transferred.

The early phase of *Nanbangaku* was dominated by Jesuit influence and saw the introduction of the Western calendar, surgery, navigation, firearms (the musket), the printing press and globes. This period was probably of greater importance than has previously been realised. The Portuguese Jesuit, Christovao Ferreira, who arrived in Japan during 1610, translated and provided commentaries for a synopsis of Western knowledge, eventually published in four volumes in the 1640s as the *Kenkon bensetsu* (*Heaven and Earth, Commentaries*). This introduced the Aristotelian and Ptolemaic systems but was further modified by the Confucian commentaries of Mukai Genshō (1609–77), whose frequent interpolations explained the empirical content of Western knowledge in terms of Neo-Confucianism. That is, he stressed the loose analogies between the four elements of Aristotle and the

Years	*Phase*	*Characteristics*
1543–1639	**Nanbangaku** (Period of Southern Barbarian Learning)	Awakening, southern European influence, translations Little impact on technique
1639–1720	**Sakoku** (Seclusion)	Absorption, renaissance Little impact on technique
1720–1830s	**Rangaku** (Dutch Learning)	Pragmatic rejuvenation Dominated by physicians Official monitoring
1830s–1868	**Tempō-Bakumatsu** (Decline, Reaction and Renewal)	Acceleration in transfers of both knowledge and technique Wider representation of European nations Knowledge as power Decentralisation of transfer activities and mechanisms Military imperatives The exploitation of degrees of freedom
Post-1868	**Yōgaku** (Western Science and Learning)	Pragmatic acceptance Far greater variety of transfer mechanisms Renewal of importance of centralised transfers Diffusion

Figure 4.1 Phases in the transfer and absorption of Western science and technology.

five of Confucianism, the transformation of elements, and an identity between Aristotle's 'ether' and the Confucian notion of *ki* (continuous energy). Ferreira went on to compose other Japanese versions of Western science, including works on surgery and astronomy which were to influence the court physicians of the seventeenth and eighteenth centuries.

The subsequent work of Joken Nishikawa sketched a breakdown of the Confucian unity of natural and moral laws and inserted the Western distinction between *physis* and *nomos,* the 'is' of the laws of nature as against the 'ought' of moral laws. The proclaiming of such distinctions may be seen as an important prelude to *Rangaku.*

The years of seclusion or *Sakoku* allowed some absorption of a very limited corpus of Western knowledge. They were more characterised by a renaissance of ancient learning, the establishment of a school of Chinese classical medicine and some innovations in mathematics and calendar reform. But in this period there is very little evidence of any link between agricultural practice and the spread of Western knowledge. Indeed, the new treatises on agricultural technique and methods, especially the *Nōgyō Zenchō* and *Nōgu Benri Ron* of the years after 1697 owed everything to developments in Chinese agriculture. Interaction with the West was limited to

Spain and Portugal. Artefacts such as muskets, globes, navigation figures and printing presses were introduced on a limited scale. In mining there is some evidence of Western influence, with galleries replacing open-cut operations and the adoption of cupellation in refining during the second half of the sixteenth century. It is also known that the introduction of the matchlock gun by the Portuguese set off a process of technology replication throughout Osaka and Shiga and elsewhere, based on the precise skills of indigenous swordmasters. In 1641 the Dutch took over the previously Portuguese factory at Deshima at the head of Nagasaki bay. Strong censorship and limits on internal passage confined the transfers of knowledge to the small group of *rōjū*, or government inner counsellors, who were the recipients of Japanese translations of official reports on Western developments (*fūsetsugaki*) delivered to the Shogun during compulsory annual visits to Edo.

There is little doubt that it was during the years 1720 to the 1830s, the period of *Rangaku* (Dutch learning), that effective Western tutelage began.[1] In an attempt to solve administrative problems, the Tokugawa regime relaxed the exclusion rules and allowed an inflow of knowledge of Western medicine, science (Newtonian dynamics) and technologies. With an increased emphasis on *Jitsugaku* (the study of real things) a flow of discrete information took place not only through Dutch settlement but through European publications directly imported from China. In 1796 the first Dutch–Japanese dictionary was published, and this was followed by a series of academy and school foundations in which Western learning was included. An important element of *Rangaku* which developed from then was *Bussangaku* or 'knowledge of production', which emphasised practical rather than abstract themes in Western culture. The formal text was by no means the only artefact of *Rangaku*. From the 1720s Dutch ships brought into Japan almanacs, dictionaries, lexicons, foreign flora and fauna, globes, maps, paintings, telescopes, magnets, microscopes, sextants, scientific and medical instruments, magnifying glasses, electrical equipment, thermometers and barometers, and clocks, as well as fire engines, lathes, air pumps and cannon. Together with books introducing the work of Newton and Linneaus and Western techniques of copper mining and mine drainage, many such symbols of the West were formally requested of the Dutch by not only the shogunal court, but by the College of Interpreters in Nagasaki, local officials, commissioners and governors.

The avenues of information dispersal were certainly widened after the early eighteenth century. At times the libraries of Deshima surgeons and officials were ceded or auctioned to the College of Interpreters or to the physicians of the Edo court. The Japanese translation of the work on anatomy by J. A. Kulmus, produced as *Kaitai Shinsko* in five volumes in 1773 probably owed its origin to the availability of such literature. By the time of the residency of K. P. Thunberg (1743–1822) in the 1770s some fifty interpreters were associated with the Deshima outpost, several of whom acted as go-betweens for Japanese scholars of astronomy and medicine. Undoubtedly, this thin thread of *Rangaku* spread to Edo and through the urban cultural system more generally. In 1788 Gentaku Ōtsuki (1759–1827) published his *Rangaku Kaitei* (*Ladder to Dutch Learning*) and established an academy in Edo. By the late eighteenth century *Rangaku* academies and *han* schools ranged from science and the fine arts to medicine and military technology. From the middle of the eighteenth century *Ranpeki* or 'Dutch mania' embraced an increasing number of scholars, whose educational institutions were to spawn many of the intellectuals, administrators and military leaders of the Meiji period. Thus, the 'new men' of the cities had available to them at least some avenues for the absorption of Western knowledge and technique. It was they who provided something of an audience to P. F. Von Siebold's (1796–1866) lectures on Western medicine and surgery in Edo during the 1820s, by which time Western medicine had been introduced to an educated elite by Genpaku Sugita (1733–1811), Copernican astronomy by Yoshinaga Matoki (1735–94) and Newtonian dynamics by Tadao Shizuki (1761–1807).

But until the 1820s and 1830s there were definite limits to the diffusion of any authoritative knowledge of Western science and technique. Western chemistry and mathematics were all but absent from the *Rangaku* scene. The translations of Keill's or Lalande's astronomy texts omitted Western mathematical technique. The small coteries of intellectuals, physicians and officials who imbibed Western ideas were not supported by a network of societies or journals for information reportage and synopsis. The starkly epiphenomenal nature of Western science was indicated by the continuous coexistence of Japanese, Chinese and Western traditions, especially evident in astronomy, medicine and mathematics. The notion of *kyūri* (the purpose of things) may have captured the discernment of a very few Japanese scholars that behind the new Western practices and results lay a wider and diffused ethos of experimental investigation and intellectual challenge. But the limitations of language inhibited the passage of a more incisive Western intellectual influence. Thus Tadao Shizuki's *Rekishō Shinsho*, which was designed to introduce elements of the Newtonian system wrestled with an absence of clear meanings for such terms as 'particle' or 'mechanics'.

Whilst problems of language and meaning remained, the years after 1837, from which time the regime was thrown into crisis through a combination of internal and external challenges, provide evidence of a real quickening of Western scientific and technological transfers prior to the Meiji Restoration of 1868. In this period of decline and search for renewal, labelled in Figure 4.1 as *Tempō-Bakumatsu*, the diffusion of Western knowledge took place at more socially inclusive and provincial levels and through an expanding range of mechanisms and imperatives.

With the publication of *Kikai Kanran* (*A Study of Nature*) and other works during the 1820s, chemistry and pharmacology were introduced into Japan for the first time. The spread of a knowledge of Lavoisier's nomenclature and Dalton's atomic theory was associated with fief-level developments in armaments at Kagoshima and elsewhere. In 1837 Yōan Udagawa published his influential *Principles of Chemistry* which incorporated many recent Western advances through reference to more than thirty Dutch books on chemistry, including a Dutch edition of Lavoisier. Of perhaps even more significance, the *Bakumatsu* years saw a closer integration of Japanese natural science and mathematics (*wasan*). Gokan Uchida (1805–82) developed the notion of *Zappakū Sūri* ('mixed mathematics') as a Japanese version of applied mathematics.

The effect of earlier *Rangaku* learning was to make Japanese elites aware of their relative economic backwardness. The effect of later developments was to introduce specific technologies. There was a speeding up of transferences. P. van der Burg's *Erste Grondbeginselen der Naturkunde,* a survey of new industrial technologies, was first published in 1844 and translated in Japan in 1854. The military needs of the clans dominated the immediate pre-Meiji years. The Saga fief established the *Nirayama Banshō Honyaku kata* (Nirayama Dutch book translation office), designed to bring together scholars of Western learning and workmen engaged in the casting of cannon. Although the dominant focus of such a broadening of interest and activity was the *han* military interests, at points the government also responded to the new sense of crisis. In 1845 Chomel's *Encyclopaedia* was translated as *Kōsei Shimpan* along with other books by the shogun's Office of Translation. During 1854–6 the *bakufu* established the *Banshō Torishirabesho* (Office for the Study of Barbarian Writings).

Induction into Western knowledge was somewhat strengthened by improvements in education. Basic literacy was raised by a renewed growth in the traditional *terakoya* (parish schools for commoners) run by priests and *samurai.* The annual opening rate of new *terakoya* increased from 13.8 in 1789–1800 to 56.3 in 1818–29, to 306 in 1854–67. Although most of such schools concentrated on literacy and moral conduct, there was a trend towards specialised instruction and some introduction of Western languages, medicine and military technique. By 1868 12,000 *terakoya* enrolled 830,000 pupils. In addition, *Shijuku* (private schools for all estates) showed a much accelerated opening rate between the 1800s and 1830s. In several *han,* private schools began to act as loci for Western learning. Schools of the Dutch type, which had initially been established in the late eighteenth century, boasted large increases in enrolments in the early nineteenth century. Kōan Ogata's *Tekijuku* academy for medicine, military science and chemistry took in 600 students after 1844. The fief schools of Kagoshima and Saga established elementary laboratory-workshops for photography, cotton spinning, sugar refining, metal plating, acid manufacture and for the construction of models of reverberatory furnaces and steamships. Saga, responsible for the defence of Nagasaki, introduced knowledge of Western engineering at its *Seirenkata* (technical laboratory) and established a naval school which employed models of steamships and locomotives.

The military *applications* of Western learning became more evident from the 1830s. Ulrich Huguenin's (1755–1834) work of 1826 on iron metallurgy and the construction of reverberatory furnaces was multiply translated and published in several provinces for use in *han* construction of furnaces at Kagoshima, Kamaishi and Hakodate. The Dutch tradition remained important to the military ambitions of Saga, Satsuma, Higo and Nanbu clans, for the construction of boring machinery, mortars, dry docks and steamships. In 1854 Sadayoshi Baba produced the first Japanese text on metallurgy based on Western translations and was associated with the erection of Western charcoal blast furnaces at Kagoshima. At the same time, another scholar of Western science and technology, Tan-an Egawa constructed a reverberatory furnace at Nirayama on the Izu Peninsula. Huguenin's work was used as a guidebook for furnaces using pig iron produced by the indigenous *tatara* methods. In 1857 this led to an adaptation of the Western blast furnace by Takatō Ōshima at Kamaishi, designed to make use of the iron sands of Japan.

Again, the *Bakumatsu* years provided increased personal interaction between Western agents of technical change and Japanese officials and intellectuals. Over 200 foreign technicians and educators were employed by government and *han* during the *Bakumatsu* years. The increased purchase of Western machinery and armaments in the 1850s and 1860s demanded the use of foreign skills and stimulated Japanese missions abroad. From 1854 the naval training school at Nagasaki was run by a Dutch team. The Japanese graduates of this school became lecturers in Edo.

For the Dutch government, as with other European powers, technological tutelage was visualised as part of a wider diplomatic and commercial mission in Japan. After the 1858 trade treaty, British commerce represented some 75 per cent of total foreign trade and British merchants were pervasively involved in much of the destabilisation of the 1860s, with arms sales to the *daimyō*, the smuggling of students abroad and dubious alliances with disaffected *han*. In 1858 an English school was established in Nagasaki, British technicians from Platt Bros of Oldham were important to the erection of the Kagoshima spinning plant, and British entrepreneurial interests were involved in the employment by the Bakufu of the mining engineer G. H. M. Gower in Hokkaidō coal mining. Prior to 1868 perhaps $2 million had been spent by the Japanese government on the French-dominated naval training, dockyard and arsenal complexes at Yokohama and Yokosuka. Over a four year period something in the order of 2,000 Japanese students had received some training in naval engineering and tactics.

Similar influences encouraged Japanese missions abroad. The trading and spinning firm of Glover and Co. of Nagasaki forged strong commercial links with Satsuma and Chōshū and smuggled clansmen out to England in 1863 and 1865–6. These joined the trickle of travelling students which had been started in 1860 by the shogunate. A mission of 1860 to the US was followed by an 1862 mission to Holland and one of 1863 to Britain. In 1863 a student of Chōshū apologised for the cost of such travel, and on behalf of the student group asked the government of the clan 'to pardon them for costing it so much money on their account as they are sure to become good living machines'.

It seems that the last years of the Tokugawa period witnessed a real strengthening of the mechanisms of knowledge and technique transfer and a greater diffusion of Western knowledge amongst those Japanese who were outside the favoured circles of court physicians or translators. It is probably true that Western natural science was grafted on to an essentially unchanged Confucian vision of the natural and moral universe. Although this limited the probability of any meaningful intellectual transformation, the *Bakumatsu* years did serve as a most valuable interregnum between the slim line of *Rangaku* and the more wholesale tutelage of the post-1868 *Yōgaku* era.

Screening the world

> The American people are simple and honest like Japanese born in the mountains or on the farm. The Russians are like the Americans. The English are jealous and have a very bad disposition. Occasionally they cheat others and are impolite.
>
> (Japanese Mission to the USA, 1860)

The borrowings of the Japanese were never indiscriminate. Rutherford Alcock, the British envoy in Japan, noted how in the late 1850s the governor of Nagasaki refused to allow foreigners into the coal mines 'even for the purpose of offering the assistance of scientific and practical men to insure them more profitable working', and in a letter of August 1859 complained how 'to be hustled and pelted with stones is a daily occurrence'. Arson against the property of British and American residents at Nagasaki cost some 250,000 US dollars in one fire in late 1859. Referring to the state of affairs in January 1860 Alcock concluded that 'the ruling classes are unmistakably inimical to all foreign relations'. In fact, the ruling classes were already, prior to the Restoration, screening the world for the techniques and technicians of Atlantic industrialism.

As already hinted, the Japanese investigations of the 1860s were astonishingly thorough and precise, eschewing the diverting romance of Paris, London or Boston for the industrial rationalism of Lyon, Pittsburgh and Clapham. The Satsuma search party of 1865 which visited the Britannia Ironworks at Bedford, England did so in the company of scientific and engineering academics from Glasgow, London and elsewhere, and were reportedly 'astonishingly quick in comprehending the various details'. The

1872 Japanese official visitation of Britain spent little time in London but a considerable time in Liverpool, Manchester, Sheffield, Birmingham, Hull, Glasgow, Newcastle, Bradford, Leeds, Halifax, Coventry, Reading, Brighton, Portsmouth and the mines of Cornwall, in each place visiting the principal manufacturers and engineering workshops across the entire range of nineteenth-century manufacture, transport and communications. Between 1868 and 1895, 2,500 students and officials were sent by government to Europe and North America for study and investigation of best techniques. Between 1868 and 1910 Japanese participated in at least thirty-eight major international exhibitions. At the 1867 Paris exhibition a party of sixty-six from Japan attended and produced a ninety-five-volume report on the economic, institutional and technical advances displayed there. To the 1873 Vienna Exposition were sent seventy Japanese delegates, including twenty-four technical workers from the private sector whose task was to search and buy appropriate techniques. From Austria the group brought back the latest textile looms, which were then tested and leased to various provincial entrepreneurs after regional public display. Japanese internal industrial exhibitions began in 1877 and by the 1890s they were attracting over a million visitors. More spectacularly, the Meiji government established its own model factories and utilities not only to demonstrate but to test alternative Western modes of production. The government's Akabane Engineering Office (1874) was designed to construct selected and tested machinery for purchase by private enterprise, a function also performed by the government printing office.

Official screening of Western technique and practice was never limited to general inspection, nor did the process become any less important as the years went by. In partnership with private enterprise, the Japanese government utilised the detailed catalogues of British, American or German machine makers to derive exact specifications, and all purchases were on the competitive tender principle. By the mid-1890s British firms were beginning to lose out to American and then German machine suppliers as the Japanese tracked the best choices by way of the foreign merchants of the treaty ports. Japanese government inspectors were everywhere and reputedly worked under the motto, 'if in doubt, reject'. As one British machine supplier complained of imported equipment, 'It is no unusual thing for them to be pulled apart entirely and for the whole of the paint to be scraped off the surface of the castings and other covered parts'. At the same time, well trained if yet inexperienced Japanese advisers based in London regularly sent out designs and specifications of best technique to almost all the major Japanese merchant houses, especially in the fields of heavy equipment designed for government armaments and transport systems. The frequent trade commissions sent to Japan from Europe and America obtained only limited results unless they went through the merchant and bureaucratic screening nexus. Successful foreign merchants were at times given some freedom in arranging contracts with Western machine makers. One such American merchant in 1902 placed over £50,000 worth of contracts from the Japanese government to such firms as Morris Machine Co., GEC, and the Bickford Machine Tool Co. In other, fairly exceptional, cases particular suppliers secured a monopoly. A sole agency agreement with Mitsui Bussan meant that the British machine builders Platt Bros of Oldham supplied some 90 per cent of the nearly 2 million cotton spindles in Japan to 1909. But it is also true that the Platt connection with Japan preceded the 1868 restoration and operated on several levels.[2]

Screening included men as well as machines. The appointment of Henry Dyer as Principal of the Engineering College in Tokyo was made as a result of the extended enquiries of Japanese ambassadors in Britain, who sought advice from British academics as well as H. M. Matheson of the Public Works Department in Japan itself. W. E. Griffis was only invited to Fukui (200 miles west of Tokyo) after he had shown expertise in teaching physics to Japanese students in America. Indeed, most of the senior foreign employees of the Japanese government (the *Ōyatoi*) appear to have been carefully vetted prior to any firm offer of employment being made. Further screening took place as foreigners moved from level to level within government or transferred from the public sector into private enterprise at a later date. The Japanese did not take the West on trust.

The moving frontier: layers of influence

The notion of a 'Western impact' is a misnomer, for there was no immovable interface and the influence of the Western powers was constantly changing, pervasive as much as explicit, part and parcel of the process of development as much as an initial given stimulant. In contrast to the cases of India and China, that influence was fragmented and partial. Threat and encroachment were real enough, but Japan lay at the limits of imperial ambition, which was fully occupied with regions nearer home and of at least potentially greater political and economic importance. It is also very clear that an arrangement of the 'leading figures' of Meiji Japan across several fields of endeavour would result in a disproportionately large degree of Western education or educational influence in the biographies of the sample. In addition, the Western influence upon the strategic elite was extended in the proximate, living presence in Tokyo, Yokohama, Ōsaka, Niigata, Kōbe and, often illegally, in the hinterlands of large urban areas, of vocal and culturally aggressive foreigners.

The authorities absorbed foreign influence through the period in a variety of ways, from the advice specifically required of hired employees to that gratuitously offered by foreign newspapermen, diplomats and local politicians. Nor was this simply shouting in a vacuum, for there is evidence of official response and reaction. The highly influential *Meirokusha* group of intellectuals and bureaucrats, which included Yukichi Fukuzawa (1835–1901) and Arinori Mori (1847–89) amongst its leading activists, was responding to foreign comment in the treaty ports as early as 1875. At one point some of its members – Fukuzawa, Mori and Katō – complained to the editor of the *Japan Weekly Mail* over its publication of debates in their private meetings on such sensitive issues as representative government.[3] In early 1877 the *Weekly Mail* began its 'educative' series, 'A primer of political economy' in the knowledge that it would be read by leading figures in the Japanese administration after translation and widespread distribution in the more political of the nation's newspapers: 'the Japanese Government and the Japanese trade should be guided in the right way'. The editor proceeded to instruct the bureaucracy in such vital issues as the unequal treaties, mineral exploitation, the introduction of foreign machinery and personnel, the economic impact of the advocated replacement of the Mexican trading dollar by the silver yen, and so on. By that time, Japanese bureaucrats were themselves addressing the foreign community on matters of policy, e.g. the series of letters by Hiyakasho Teraki concerning the improvement of roads, communications and taxation.

The foreign employees have too frequently been dismissed as servants of the government, implementing given requests from above. In fact, at many levels they influenced individuals and policies. The Imperial University, so often argued as the training ground for both bureaucrats and intellectuals, was dominated by the foreign element in both technology and political economy, and the former was seldom completely divorced from the latter. Such early directors of the University as Katakayama Yoshinami were intellectual cosmopolitans as a result of early training, in his case education at New Brunswick, an initial appointment at the Department of Public Works and as one of the earliest Japanese members of the Japan Asiatic Society which met at Tokyo and Yokohama. Science professors such as Perry and Ayrton at the Imperial College of Engineering, involved their students in research programmes which went beyond pure science into what, today, would be called science policy work – on mineral exploitation, surveying, medical and sanitary reform, investment in national seismological research, mechanical engineering, architecture and so on. When the engineer R. H. Brunton attacked the teaching at the Engineering College the reaction of the authorities exposed their sensitivity to foreign opinion. A government notification of early September 1875 had clearly forbidden government officers (i.e. all employees) to communicate the activities of their departments to newspapers, although all 'scientific commentary' was excluded. When, later in that month, Brunton suggested inadequacies in engineering education in Tokyo a new notification was issued by the *Kōbushō* (Public Works Department): 'No officer of the Cobusho shall publish or communicate or show to any person or persons . . . unconnected with the office or department to which he belongs any official document [or publish] anything upon the subject of or in connection with the business or activities of his office'.

The influence of the foreigners was not to be contained within the ambits of their official positions. Foreign advisers at the Colonisation

Department (designed to expand industry and settlement in Hokkaidō), such as Antisell, Warfield and Capron, stretched the bounds of duty in suggesting the best modes to adopt in planning for regional development. Capron *et al.*'s *Report and Official Letters to the Kaitakushi* of 1875 were full of such advice and included arguments for a far greater formative role for the hired foreigners. Thus, in his official dispatch of 1873 Capron complained that: 'One of the first and perhaps greatest obstacles to success, is the want of candour on the part of the officials of this Department, . . . the ways and means have been a sealed book, and I have compelled to grope my way in the dark . . . no man can do himself or the Government that employs him, justice under such conditions'.

The real value of such examples is the measure of bureaucratic sensitivity which they provide. Several cases might be given of a positive welcoming of foreign advice even when it involved re-specification of policy or adoption of new policy implements. The application of new engineering and other techniques to real projects often involved a more or less implicit political economy, and this impinged upon the nature of the instruments of government. Carl Netto's incisively detailed analysis of Japanese mining techniques and potentials, first offered before members of the Tokyo *Deutsche Gesellschaft fur Natur und Voelkerkunde Ostasiens*, were translated into English and published by the Japanese government on ad hoc initiative as an aid to the stimulation of industrial innovation. Similarly, the Englishman Hodgkinson, officially employed in the Education Department, discovered new coal deposits during his travels in the interior and prepared plans for exploitation which were immediately taken up by the central authorities. E. Piquet, a non-government silk inspector of the firm of Weber, Hall and Co. was highly influential in determining government action in controlling the quality and volume of export of silk cards and raw silk, and publicised his findings through such associations as the Silk Committee of the Yokohama Chamber of Commerce. Experts emerged to meet needs and in turn transformed general demands into more formal procedures. The public lectures of the Dutchman Sieber, who was employed by the government in the translation bureau of the finance Department were officially encouraged and held in the meeting rooms of the Home Department. An audience of high- and medium-ranking officials from Finance listened to his plans for a revision of the land tax. Dr P. Mayet, although employed at the Education Department, so impressed the bureaucrats with his lengthy scheme for insurance in Japan – as originally formulated at the Asiatic Society which met at Yokohama and Tokyo – that he was appointed to the Home Department in order to further investigate possible insurance reform. From this new base Mayet went on to propose change in Japan's financial policy, gave detailed arguments in favour of the level of internal debt, and was rewarded through promotion to the position of adviser to the Financial Section of the newly-established Council of State. Quite as appropriately, obviously self-interested gratuitous advice was ignored – the private memorandum sent to the Privy Council by the commercial firm of Simon, Evers and Co. of Yokohama in October 1880, which supported such newspapers as the *Sei Dan* in their agitation for a foreign loan, was studiously disregarded.

One of the major Japanese commercial journals, the *Chūgai Bukka Shimpō* (*Home and Foreign Commercial Progress*) offered a clear agenda for foreign business and technological interaction. Any direct capital importing should be eschewed in favour of joint enterprises where foreigners provided the equipment and know how, 'for all other things except this, the native material and labour may be employed, the money expended therefore would all remain in Japan, and thus, what foreigners would actively gain would only be the net profit, after having deducted all [Japan based] expenses i.e. original value'. If successful, foreigners should be encouraged to invest their profits and knowledge into further, new Japanese enterprises, but at most on a joint basis. The *Chūgai Bukka Shimpō* severely castigated 'those foreigners who, notwithstanding the present prohibition, are purchasing, in the names of Japanese, Government bonds or holding immovable property, or under various pretexts are, in reality, assisting in mining works etc. Such cases are indeed beyond calculation'. The ideal 'system of intercourse' was that which extended the range of transfer agents but curtailed the foreign ownership of or influence over Japanese assets.

Technology transfer: mechanisms

> The country is burning with eagerness to acquire the knowledge of the West, it behoves the government to supply this knowledge through pure channels and to superintend its absorption into the Body Politic in the manner best suited to be a valuable reproducing agent.
>
> (*Japan Weekly Mail*, September 1870)

The first and most explicit mechanism of technology transfer was international trade itself. As William Lockwood put it, 'a few steam engines served to unlock for Japan the secret of great concentrations of mechanical power independent of climate and terrain'. Indeed, as early as 1886 over 300 steam engines were located in the principal silk factories (182), rice hulling (44), coal mining (43), shipbuilding (16) and cotton spinning (13). Machinery imports rose from 14 per cent of total manufactured imports in that year to 30 per cent in 1890 and 50 per cent in 1895, at which time they were valued at 7 million yen. By the end of Meiji, annual average imports of machinery, parts and instruments had reached nearly 40 million yen.

As we have suggested (pp. 52–3), most machinery imports were arranged or handled by foreign merchants, many operating from the open ports of Japan. Table 4.1 gives some idea of the relatively small number of firms concerned in the early years. Among foreign firms handling machinery

Table 4.1 Foreign firms in the five open ports of Japan, 1874–83

	British	*American*	*German*	*French*	*All other Western*	*Chinese*	*Total*
1874	155	–	–	–	215	95	465
1875	109	–	–	–	148	84	341
1876	80	–	–	–	141	72	293
1877	83	–	–	–	149	53	285
1878	92	–	–	–	155	40	287
1879	90	–	–	–	141	89	320
1880	108	–	–	–	150	102	360
1881	109	49	36	42	32	78	346
1882	98	39	37	17	17	252	460
1883	91	94	34	16	24	346	545

and equipment, Britain remained at the forefront until the turn of the century, when German and American firms increasingly out-competed them in the battle for Japanese contracts.

Such firms commonly represented information systems, available at a price to Japanese agents in both the public and private sectors. Independent commercial enterprises often emerged on the basis of expert knowledge of Japan gained under official auspices. A good example is the machinery and equipment importing firm founded by J. Favre Brandt, who had been first attaché to the Swiss mission in Japan from 1862. On the return of the Swiss envoy in 1864 Brandt remained in Japan to generate a firm supplying arms, munitions, machinery and scientific instruments to the government. From the early 1870s the firm not only supplied machinery to Japanese private enterprise but also engaged formally in instructing buyers in usage and best practice. Other firms, such as Frazar and Co. had carried on business in Asia for generations. The company introduced the first electric light plant in 1887 (made by Thomas Edison and installed in the Imperial Palace), Tokyo's first tramway system and gained the Japanese agency for both Baldwin locomotives and the Ford Motor Company (1909). Ahrens and Co., who operated in Japan from 1870, maintained an important link between German and Japanese officialdom, as its principals remained attached to the German consular service throughout. Fluent in spoken and written Japanese the principals organised the sale of German machinery to the government arsenal in Mito, the silk throwing mill in Shinmachi, the gun-foundary in Ōsaka, the Megoro gunpowder mill, and the mines of Aomori and Inai. Once competitive tendering was formalised, the foreign firms in Japan were forced into competitive bidding and marketing. In most contracts, local foreign agents were held responsible, as guarantors, for the delivery and quality of machine products, which was also regulated by frequent government inspection. In one example involving the import of 16,000 tons of cast iron piping and equipment for the Tokyo Waterworks, a British supplier won the major

Table 4.2 Patents, designs and trade marks in Japan, 1885–1905

Year	*Patents*		*Designs*		*Trade marks*	
	Total applications	*Granted applications (%)*	*Total applications*	*Granted applications (%)*	*Total applications*	*Granted applica-tions (%)*
1885	425	23	–	–	1,296	73
1886	1,384	15	–	–	624	81
1887	906	12	–	–	757	48
1888	778	23	–	–	568	77
1889	1,064	20	176	13	1,029	65
1890	1,180	20	498	16	819	71
1891	1,283	28	290	40	898	62
1892	1,344	28	262	18	1,146	51
1893	1,337	24	250	23	1,243	52
1894	1,250	26	336	19	1,350	65
1895	1,122	20	310	30	1,373	67
1896	1,213	14	300	32	1,578	54
1897	1,542	12	320	28	3,228	72
1898	1,789	16	265	20	2,232	71
1899	1,915	31	342	41	2,837	68
1900	2,007	29	397	33	2,776	64
1901	2,397	25	514	27	2,608	62
1902	3,095	28	930	27	3,529	57
1903	3,253	31	1,180	31	3,743	60
1904	2,618	48	1,378	41	3,105	62
1905	2,897	57	1,562	49	3,810	65
Total	34,808	28.5	9,319	33	41,432	62

contract against Belgian and British rivals, not on the basis of price or quality but because the risk was guaranteed by two known, locally based merchant houses, one British and the other Japanese. Local foreign merchants frequently collaborated with Japanese agents in getting a particular machinery supplier on to the select list of manufacturers used by both government and business. Japanese machine specifications often requested by name both makers and merchants.

Prior to the turn of the century, foreign patentees had little prospect of gaining any control over technical innovation in Japan through the patent system. Table 4.2 shows that, particularly with regard to patents, the Japanese government exerted strict control over the amount of licensed manufacturing production within the country. From the table several points are noteworthy. The industrial thrust of the 1890s is reflected in patent and related activity. There is some evidence of bureaucratic preference for innovative marketing rather than innovative manufacturing, with trade marks being twice as likely to be secured than designs, and nearly three times as likely to be secured than patents. Such characteristics reflect the foreign economic relations of Japan at that time. Until 1896 foreign

Table 4.3 Foreign applications and registrations in Japan, November 1896–December 1904

	Patents		*Designs*		*Trade marks*	
	Total applications	*Granted applications (%)*	*Total applications*	*Granted applications (%)*	*Total applications*	*Granted applications (%)*
Total (all Japan)	18,616	29	5,327	32	24,058	64
All foreign	1,938	65	25	50	4,018	76
UK	442	64	12	75	1,731	74
US	973	71	1	100	532	77
Germany	289	47	7	14	1,332	78
Total foreign (%)	10	220	0.004	156	17	118
Total US (%)	5	245	0.0002	312	2	118

patentees found it almost impossible to gain any protection within Japan or to enter manufacturing directly. Foreign residents in Japan were, with exceptions, similarly restricted to trade and commerce, and could not engage in direct manufacture. But we have seen that this in no way prohibited the Japanese from *importing* machine tools, chemical, construction and other processes etc. as capital imports, many of which had previously been patented abroad. At the same time, the Japanese could reproduce foreign technique with impunity and market such products under trade marks identical to those of their foreign rivals. As the Board of Trade Journal put it in 1896: 'No foreign inventor by applying through a Japanese citizen can obtain a patent except by fraud . . . It is precisely the same with trade marks and designs – there is no registration and no protection. As might be expected, the result is that every other ware of British produce and manufacture of which the label is worth copying can be bought all over Japan of Japanese manufacture, and at a quarter to a fractional part of the cost of the original and genuine article.'

However, in that year some elementary protection was granted to foreign endeavour under a Ministry of Agriculture and Commerce Ordinance. By the new law a foreigner resident abroad could apply for a patent or trade mark in Japanese through a deputy resident in Japan, often a foreign merchant. The immediate results are shown in Table 4.3. It seems that under the new regulations foreigners were most concerned with their trading status (foreigners representing 17 per cent of all trade marks applied for in the period) and somewhat less involved with patents, (with a figure of 10 per cent of the total applications). This was due to the slightness of direct production opportunities in Japan combined with the continued restrictive nature of Japanese patent law. Although foreigners appear to have secured over twice the chance of nationals in having their patent applications granted, the incentive to so apply was relatively low. Interestingly, the Americans were well ahead with their patent effort, although the British and Germans jointly led the assault on internal trading.

The foreign communities of Japan represented much more than mere merchandising. They were the entrepôt of Western attitudes, knowledge and technique. Of the Westerners in Japan, Patt Barr has written that 'soon their foreign settlement areas became living examples, exhibitions almost, to the provincial Japanese of the Western way of life'. The leaders of the communities were themselves convinced that it was the day-to-day 'contact with Europeans' which had forced the Japanese to recognise the 'powerless, stationary and ineffective' condition of their nation. The most obvious exemplars were the technologies themselves, artefacts of the varied interests of the Westerners in mining operations, medicine, road and rail building, military provisioning, silk marketing and so on. Furthermore, it was at this level, within the treaty ports, that the effective carriers of Western technique repeatedly and informally met the leaders of Japan's industrialisation programme. Merchants, educators and hired technical experts from the West mingled with foremost members of Japan's political and intellectual elite. Here was a mechanism of technology transfer which breathed life and fire into trade and capital.

When, in May 1881, the Japanese Seismological Society launched its first major public celebration, including demonstrations of equipment and lectures by foreign experts, the attendance of over two thousand included Japanese nobility and intellectuals as well as key figures of the industrial drive, such as the head of Mitsui Bussan Kaisha (established for direct trade to Europe), the Chief Secretary of the Home Department, and the Vice-Minister of Agriculture and Commerce. The Great National Industrial Exhibition of the same year began and ended with speeches from the Emperor. The distribution of awards for technical or commercial excellence and the major award speech to the 31,000 exhibitors were made by the Emperor, surrounded underfoot by princes and nobility, officers of state and Western diplomats and consuls. A little further afield were the Western residents and Japanese spectators, mixed in with a splash of Korean guests, the bright robes of the latter forming 'an agreeable oasis in a desert of black and neutral tints'. With daily visitors of some 10,000 to 20,000 the exhibition acted as an enormous international industrial mart, illustrating in the words of Prince Kita Shirakawa 'how sensible an impetus exhibitions impart to manufacturing diligence'. The emperor's main theme was the need to 'develop a spirit of industry and perseverance'. Prize-winners included ex-nobles and ex-*samurai*, modern factories and filatures as well as individual craftsmen in ivory, enamelling and metal working.

At the other extreme, and more surprisingly, were the varied, small forums which actively combined Western intellectuals and experts with important figures in Japan's political life. At a time when leading Japanese intellectuals were pursuing the notion of 'barbarian expelling', as in Kanichi Kubota's essays in the *Nichi Nichi Shimbun*, the little known Free Speech Society of Tokyo drew together influential *ōyatoi* (government foreign employees) and Japanese intellectuals. Here Westerners addressed the Japanese on political matters in the vernacular, and meetings were widely reported in the political press, such as the *Akebono Shimbun*. This society appears to have gone underground under pressure from the repressive laws on public meetings but it re-emerged in 1879 as the Society for Public Lectures which met fortnightly in Tokyo. Contemporaneously, a political society, the *Kyōson Dōshin* began to hold its meetings in the English language in order that Japanese members who 'have visited England and America' might exercise their skills. Western intellectuals addressed the meetings of the *Kenyusha* (Political Lecturing Society) and the chemist R. W. Atkinson gained an audience of some 700 at his lecture before the members of the *Risshisha* (Self-Help Society).[4] Although it must remain difficult to accurately estimate the influence of such forums, their very existence indicates that the agents of change in both the West and in Japan met other than in official settings, and that the transfer of knowledge and technique was taking place within a very complex setting. It seems reasonably clear that such complexity and variety of interaction was as much a key to technology transfer as was the availability of funds or the willingness of technicians.

Technology transfer: case studies

The introduction and diffusion of Western technology in silk reeling well demonstrated the variety of available transfer mechanisms. The city of Maebashi was the location for the first private reeling mill of 1870. This used Western technicians. But the series of private enterprise mills which flourished in the early 1870s drew primarily upon the model of the Tomioka Mill, a government project constructed by French constructors in 1872. It was this demonstration plant which introduced water power winding and steam boiling and established Italian and French systems of filatures. The researches of the French sericulturalists Charles Garnier and Paul Brunet led to a recommendation of provincial government filatures of 200 to 300 basins. Brunet returned to Europe to provide the necessary machinery and was the principal supervisor at Tomioka. Here all the key staff initially were Europeans, who operated the steam powered system and maintained low costs by employing over 400 female operators. The technical details of the mill were speedily diffused in the vernacular by such newly created organs as the *Shimbun Zasshi*, which was predominantly filled with reports of European methods of silk egg weaving and animal husbandry. By 1875 or so the Tomioka mill passed entirely into the technical control of the Japanese, and key Western personnel then transferred to the developing private mills. By 1892 Tomioka had trained over 1,000 reelers in modern techniques. A second government mill was built in Tokyo in 1873 and this utilised both French and Italian technology and was leased to private enterprise in 1879. European blueprint technology was not entirely appropriate to Japanese cocoon quality so the government initiated a series of adaptations: iron was replaced by wood in construction, scale was reduced, steam engines were replaced by water power or manpower. Japanese officers were sent to France and Italy to import latest improvements and knowledge diffusion was further stimulated by official screening and searching activity in foreign markets, centred on Japanese consulates abroad. This was soon followed by the activity of direct foreign trading companies such as Mitsui Bussan and Hara Gōmei, enterprises which gained and diffused expert marketing and technical information. As early as 1881 over 100 silk mills were steam or water powered in the private sector and machine reeled silk composed 30 per cent of total production. During the 1880s machine filatures overtook hand reeling, and from that time Japanese copies replaced the imported reelers for domestic use at a fraction of the cost.

At the other extreme of the transfer process the overt military demands of the Japanese state engendered a process of technological borrowing which involved larger capital in the production of final and intermediary goods which were not only sophisticated but for which there was, initially, little *private* demand. Kōzō Yamamura has argued that it was demand arising from the military operations of government which was responsible for assuring the survival and 'growth of often financially and technologically struggling *private* firms in the shipbuilding, machinery and machine tools industries'. Of course, military demand also had a tremendous impact on the government-based iron and steel industry more generally (see pp. 65–6). But Yamamura is particularly pertinent to our approach here in emphasising the public sector–private sector linkage; 'the most significant effects of the Russo-Japanese war were the rapid dissemination of modern technology to a large number of private firms and a suddenly accelerated growth in the fledgling and often struggling private machine and machine tool makers who received increased and timely military demand and technical assistance'. The arsenals and shipyards provide good evidence of the formative influence of Western technology from the very earliest years of Meiji until its end. Within the emerging military–industrial complex new technologies transferred especially quickly; the water-jacket blast furnace developed at Detroit in 1882 was being used at Ashio in 1890; the first successful application of the Bessemer steel process to copper refining was in America in 1884, was uncovered by Japanese in America in 1890 and was operating on a large scale in Japan in 1893; electrolytic refining processes developed in America in the late 1880s were installed in Japan by the mid-1890s, even though their use required a support structure of hydroelectric power plants, electrical generators and water pumps. Prior to the First World War, the government-operated Yawata Steel Works reached a level of technical sophistication comparable with that of its German tutors.

The Yokosuka arsenal of the 1870s was a microcosm of the technology transfer and internal diffusion nexus. The change from wooden to iron ships was no simple affair of purchase – it involved steam hammers, docks, riveting machines, blast furnaces, cranes, ores and cokes, and skilled workers, all imported, adapted and brought together on a significant scale of production. The Yokosuka arsenal was originally administered by F. L. Verny, a French naval engineer and former student at the École Polytechnique. An initial outlay of $2,400,000 provided docks, ships, workshops, and the machinery required to construct steam engines of 400 hp. Established prior to the Restoration, by 1865 the arsenal already had a staff of engineers, accountants, foremen, and skilled workers, whose salaries ranged from $50 weekly to $400 monthly. Verny himself drew a salary of $10,000. From the very beginning, Japanese contractors were used for all large civil engineering tasks, such as levelling and dry dock excavation (1867–8), and this continued through the Meiji years, with the new government providing a monthly maintenance grant of $25,000. By December 1875, 177 Japanese and 128 foreign ships had been repaired there. By that date the Japanese employed within the arsenal included 74 engineering officers, 121 foremen, 27 accountants, 30 watchmen, 1,342 workmen and 250 or so 'employed by the public contractors'. This technological project exerted dynamic system effects both within and without. In 1865 the village of Yokosuka had comprised 1,263 inhabitants; by 1875, 3,673 villagers were mostly employed in the manufacture/fabrication of arsenal supplies. For instance, the village manufacture of bricks and hydraulic mortar, having been taken from the arsenal, made rapid progress, the initial purchase price falling from $12 to $4–6 per 1,000 bricks by 1875. More formally, the arsenal's École de Maistrance (School for Petty Officers) provided elementary and technical instruction in Japanese, the students being 'chosen from amongst the workmen and foremen, who for the most part belong to the families of artisans . . . Some however, are *samurai* who seek service in the arsenal with the desire of bettering their condition.' There were also higher classes taught by French instructors and the arsenal was regarded as the 'practical school' for students of Tokyo Naval College. The basic instruction in the latter included navigation and navigational astronomy, algebra and trigonometry, with examination weekly. Of the special engineering department students enrolled during mid-1895, half had previously been trained at Yokosuka arsenal. The facilities of the college included a model factory with 12 hp engines, pattern shops, a foundry, and fitting and erecting shops, 'furnished with all the necessary appliances for constructing small engines'. Finally, the college had an extension facility which in 1876 provided European engineering instruction to 600 Japanese students in outlying *ken*, and included a preparatory school and a higher mathematical course through a separate Marine Artillery College.

During the late 1870s, the reach of the arsenal extended firmly into the private domestic sector. The Home Department's ironworks at Yokohama were placed under Yokosuka supervision, and provided materials to private manufacturers. Material and bridges for the Shimbashi–Yokohama railway were also made at the arsenal and later assembled, as were the iron rails of the Tokyo tramways. Speaking at Tokyo University in 1877, the engineering professor R. H. Smith emphasised that the military projects were both the forum of transfer and the conduits for internal diffusion. Furthermore, although Western technique arrived at all points, the most modern technologies filtered into the private sector through the arsenals; 'the only places where you can meet with labour-saving machinery is inside the new government workshops, and even there the most of it is destined to the manufacture of war materials'.

Such insidious technological system effects were multiplied throughout Japan during the 1870s and 1880s. By the early 1880s, the arsenals were directly employing 10,000 workers in comparison with the 3,000 in the private machinery establishments. Diffusion from the nodal projects to the private sector was common. Six of the ten textile firms operating during the 1880s used spindles from such suppliers as Platt Bros in conjunction with steam engines made at Yokosuka. The Ōsaka arsenal produced machinery used by several private firms, including a large-scale cotton textile company from 1882.

The transfer-diffusion effects accelerated after the demonstrated success of the war economy in 1894–5. Henceforth, Japan was to receive foreign capital at will, just as China was to become the victim of not only transfers of Western technology and influence, but also indirect transfers of Western power via Japanese imperialism. Table 4.4 provides a clear survey

Table 4.4 Government versus private factories in the machinery industry in Japan, 1902

	Factories		*Horsepower*		*Workers*	
	No.	*(%)*	*No.*	*(%)*	*No.*	*(%)*
Army arsenals	10	3	6,099	33	10,492	15
Navy arsenals	9	2.5	9,022	48	24,461	35
Other government	5	1.5	365	2	3,831	6
Total government	24	7	15,486	83	38,784	56
Private factories	326	93	3,135	17	30,964	44
Total	350	100	18,621	100	69,748	100

of the technological importance of the military–colonial establishment at the turn of the century.

Although they represented only 5.5 per cent of all factories in the machine industries in 1902, arsenals held 81 per cent of horsepower capacity and employed 50 per cent of all workers in the sector. Even such dominance does not entirely capture the relationship between the military–colonial technologies and the private sector technological projects. Thus the revival of Kamaishi Iron and Steel Mill after 1882 resulted almost solely from the demand for pig iron for Japanese ammunition factories. This in turn permitted Kamaishi to exploit the use of charcoal in the furnaces, that is, it induced technological progress. This resulted in the establishment of the famous Yawata Steel Mill which drew from the skilled workers of Kamaishi and the engineering knowledge of new German employees. War/colonial ambitions encouraged the growth of private firms such as Sumitomo Iron Works (1901), Kōbe Steel Works (1905) and the Japan Steel and Iron Works (1907), the last incorporating a joint technology venture between Mitsui and Armstrong, UK. All of these manufacturing ventures or technological projects relied on military demand, colonial expansion and skilled workers and engineers from the arsenals or Yawata Steel. Again, the navy shipyards provided technologies for the infant Japanese electrical and machinery industries.

As shown, the iron and steel industry was clearly associated with the government's military programme. Huge imports of steel, reaching 200,000 tons annually by the late 1890s, were evidence of the dependency of the entire system on foreign trade and provided the principal motive for direct intervention by government. The history of the sector suggests a natural history of technology transfer. Prior to the construction of the state-owned Kamaishi Iron Works in 1874, technology transfer into the iron industry had already taken several forms. In the 1850s the blueprint Western technology of the *han* was derived from an 1826 text by Ulrich Huguenin (1755–1834), a major general in the Dutch army who headed the Liege iron cannon foundry. Translated independently into Japanese in several *han*, Huguenin's book became a basic manual for the construction of reverberatory furnaces to cast cannon in Saga, Kagoshima, Hagi, Nirayama and Moto. At this stage, small high status information networks were vital to progress. At Nirayama was established the *Banshō Honyaku-kata* (Dutch Book Translation Office) designed to combine scholars of Western learning with technicians engaged in the casting of cannon. A key figure in the movement from reverberating to blast furnaces was Takatō Ōshima (1826–81) a *samurai* of Nambu and a scholar of Dutch learning. In 1857 he established a Western style small-scale blast furnace at Kamaishi against the background of increasing *han* technical competency. It was Ōshima, working with the foreign expert Louis Bianchie who was selected by the new government to modernise Kamaishi technology in 1873. However, the government's later adherence to the Western blueprint technique and rejection of Ōshima's plans for smaller-scale furnaces utilising more Japanese expertise led to technical failures. Following investigations by a British employee of the *Kōbushō* (Ministry of Industry), the engineer G. H. Godfrey, millions of yen were spent on railroads and furnaces. British equipment and engineers dominated the project during 1880–2, machinery including two 25-ton blast furnaces. In 1883 the Ministry of Industry closed down the Kamaishi works. The event points to a failure of decisions rather than mechanisms. The technological gap between Japanese charcoal making and Western technique was debilitating, the physical location of the furnaces was inappropriate, the operation of the furnaces by the British disregarded the exact qualities of Japanese iron ore and coal. When the entrepreneur Chobei Tanaka (1834–1901) established the Tanaka Iron Works after taking over the Kamaishi works in 1887, he began production using Ōshima-style smaller charcoal blast furnaces. It was a Japanese scientist and innovator Kageyoshi Noro who then succeeded during the late 1880s in developing new methods of producing coke from coal which permitted the establishment of Japan's first coke blast furnaces at Kamaishi in 1894.[5] By then total blast furnace pig iron production at Kamaishi was greater than production from all traditional *tatara* furnaces.[6]

In effect, the government's Yawata Steel Works of 1901 emerged from the several streams of Kamaishi technique, steel manufacturing technologies developed in the arsenals and dockyards and expertise gained by key Japanese engineers. Thus, Kamaishi technicians moved over to Yawata under German supervision. Again, the German metallurgist who assisted in the establishment of Yawata in 1897 had influenced Kageyoshi Noro during the latter's trip to Europe in the early 1880s.

Again, technical failures occurred in the early stages. Much was at stake. The plant was modelled on the Krupp works at Essen and utilised a Siemen's open hearth furnace, a Bessemer converter and rolling mills at a total capital cost of around 10 million yen. As a government adviser, Noro identified structural defects in the furnace, a faulty blending of the charge and repeated blast stoppages, all due to an unhealthy acceptance of the techniques of 'aliens' and an inappropriate use of raw materials. Subsequent modification and adaptation of the imported technique took place under Japanese auspices and the two dozen German technicians in the plant were dismissed during 1902 and 1904. By 1912 some 80 per cent of Japan's pig iron production came from Yawata and the project acted as a training centre from which many skilled personnel moved to private enterprise.

It is clear that the final, Japanese-controlled production of iron and steel in the 1900s rested on a chain of transfer agencies and processes stretching across both time and other industrial pursuits. A central feature of the history of modernising industries was the periodic conjunction of foreign technique and domestic expertise, public sector demonstration and private enterprise development. Furthermore, Japanese industrial dynamics during the Meiji years seem to illustrate the crucial importance of tacit knowledge and the space for learning, experiment and adjustment gained in such special microcosms of modernity as arsenals, dockyards, training centres and demonstration projects.

Hakurai to *hakugaku*: an interpretation of success

> In considering the real nature of Japanese civilisation, it will be seen that its material factors have largely come from foreign countries, while its spiritual and mental features have been derived chiefly from purely native sources.
>
> (Niichiro Matsunami 1933)

Commenting on the Japanese, Western contemporaries frequently referred to their 'extraordinary aptitude for imitation'. Japan was a *tabula rasa* upon which foreign cultural traits had hitherto represented *hakurai*, mere importations. Under an astute programme of state-led industrialisation, Japan might progress rapidly, indeed faster than the West, for 'they have no past, no religious difficulties, no political hatreds, no foreign complications, hardly any prejudices in their way. They have the accumulated experiences of the West to guide them.' Moreover, the perpetual discussions, compromises and confabulations of liberal democracy would not impose any halt to the transfer process because 'they are under a despotic government . . . any beneficial change can be introduced (with certain limitations) almost as soon as it is recognised as such by a sufficiently strong party in the government'. By such determination the status of Western technology within Japan would move from that of *hakurai* towards *hakugaku*, or erudition. Foreign technology would be internalised. And although it must be noted that most of Western science and culture remained epiphenomenal to Japanese society in these years, Western technology did appear to enter into Japan much more deeply.

Yet technology transfer, especially from industrialised to non-industrialised nations, nearly always fails. This is so because success in the borrowing of entire technological systems involves processes working at and between at least four levels, each of these of great complexity in themselves. It should already be reasonably clear that an interpretation of Japan's success in technology transfer requires some acknowledgement of: (a) the international context of the movement of manuals, men and machines, and in particular, the condition of the international economy; (b) the physical nature of the technologies, which had implications for the cognitive processes of understanding, learning, translating, modifying and adapting; (c) transfer conditions, that is, structural aspects of the receiver environment, such as transport or training facilities and the provision of funds, as well as the level of indigenous technological capabilities; and (d) transfer mechanisms, of the sort discussed more fully on pp. 56–61. It might be seen that the character of the last of these four categories of factors was highly dependent upon the nature of the other categories. For instance, a colonial relationship between source and recipient of technology (see (a) above) would be unlikely to give rise to the variety and informality of transfer mechanisms depicted in this chapter.

Technology transfer in Japan occurred at a time of expanding international economic relations and a tremendous surge of novel Atlantic-based technologies in manufacturing, transport and communications. Once the major task of the Meiji oligarchs was defined as that of dealing with the West, then the Atlantic economy itself offered the tools of emulation and survival. The goals of import substitution and technological sovereignty could not be fulfilled, in the case of Japan, by resorting to protectionism. The only other direction available was that of innovative borrowing led by the direct interventions of the state itself. Competition amongst Western suppliers and experts spelt the real existence of a technological shelf from which Japan could select. In some important cases, such as railways, or electrical technology, entire packages of Western expertise were imported through the normal channels of the international economy.

Second, the physical nature of technology was mainly either machinofacture or inorganic chemicals and was represented in actual, purchasable commodities. The improved lathes and milling machines of the metal using industries demanded skills which, once learned, were transferable from industry to industry. Kranzberg has emphasised that 'the transfer of technology involves a disruption of previous work habits and thought patterns', but the *extent* of such disruption is not standard and varies with the size of the gap between what is already known and accepted and what is required to be known. As the case studies and illustrations above have shown, much of the technology transfer into Meiji Japan either required only modest new skills or was embedded in projects which themselves supplied a learning and training process. Again, much of the technology introduced into agriculture and textiles required only very modest outlays of capital: agricultural practice was revolutionised by the introduction of commercial fertilisers.

Third, the conditions for transfer were decidedly improved through the complex activity of government during the industrial drive, 1868–85. Because the ultimate goals of the principal agent of transfer went well beyond commercial profits and into the defence of the nation, the transfer process was continued despite high costs and technical failures in the early years. In such a situation the 'market' choice would have been to confine transfers to the importing of cost reducing devices and to the final products of Western technologies rather than extend to the process-technology required for import substitution.

Contemporary experience suggests that technology transfer is more likely given a wide range of transfer mechanisms. Turnkey projects unloaded with insufficient preparation may leave political scars and an enclave of modernity within, but detached from, the indigenous economic system. In Meiji Japan, the predominant modes of transfer owed little to foreign capital and ownership. Sustained personal interactions between Japanese and Western agents took place within and between the public and private sectors, and at times involved the most notable of Japanese businessmen, bureaucrats and statesmen. Much has been made of the shedding of foreign experts from government employment during the 1880s, but in fact this often represented a redeployment of Westerners from the public to the private sector. Furthermore, the replacement of key Western personnel by Japanese in major projects did not decrease the dependency of such projects on foreign equipment, patents and licences.

Finally, much of the material above testifies to the significance of the retention of social control within the nation at a time of enormous challenge. Late industrialisation is often associated with vast programmes of technological modernisation that are broken on the back of cognitive, cultural and political dissonance. It is simply not good enough to try to explain Meiji industrialisation in terms of the wisdom, foresight and actions of the strategic elite. It was the *ability* of the Meiji elite to act, to limit the power of the West in Japan while exploiting the artefacts and ideas of the West, and to do so without a revolution from within, which differentiated Japan from any other non-Western nation of the late nineteenth century.

Notes

1 Some historians of Japan might disagree about the ending of Rangaku in the 1820s or 1830s or with the idea of a qualitatively distinct period of Westernisation from then to 1868. The division here is primarily based upon a judgement concerning the widening of the Western science imbibed, including chemistry and mathematics, a deepening of the social groups involved, an increase in the number of transfer mechanisms involved, and the more emphatic emphasis on the applications of knowledge to machinery improvement and civil constructions.

2 As early as the 1840s Platts of Oldham exported some 50 per cent of their cotton machinery. Satsuma's plan for a cotton mill (in 1862) was probably the first significant attempt at modernised technology transfer divorced from armaments. In March 1865 Satsuma sent nineteen men to England and they purchased twenty-eight spinning mills by Platt Bros and 100 weaving machines by Beresford Boiler Co. of Stockport. The mission also reported that Platts should draw up a plan for a cotton mill at Kagoshima. Engineers from Platt arrived in Japan in November 1866, and the mill began successful production soon after.

3 The *Meirokusha* have been described as the most articulate political elite of the time, most members espousing democratic radicalism at some point in their careers, leading members being born in the 1830s and in full intellectual maturity in the early years of Meiji. Yukichi Fukuzawa, intellectual and educator, was perhaps the most influential and the most lucid and attractive in style. Arinori Mori became Minister of Education in 1865 and was assassinated on the day of the proclamation of the constitution (11 February 1889). Hiroyuki Katō became

senator, director of the academy for European studies at Hitotsubashi, the Kaisei-gakkō, and from 1886 was rector of the University of Tokyo.

4 The *Risshi-sha* was founded in 1874 and joined other groups in the general opposition to government on human rights and democracy – see Chapter 5. The society was strongly identified with *shizoku* who had been confined under Meiji government commercial and social policies.

5 Kageyoshi Noro (1854–1923) was then a professor at the Engineering College of the Imperial University, and was an expert on Western ferro-metallurgy. After graduating at Tokyo in 1882 he studied in Europe.

6 The *tatara* process of making iron from iron sand: the *tatara-ro* were bellows-blown furnaces, and yielded steel of very high quality during the eighteenth century.

References

Lockwood, W. W. (1954) *The Economic Development of Japan*, (expanded edition 1968) Princeton, NJ: Princeton University Press, p. 324.

Barr, Pat (1968) *The Deer Cry Pavilion*, New York, Harcourt, Brace and World Inc., p. 33.

Yamamura, K. (1977) 'Success illgotten?: the role of Meiji militarism in Japan's technological progress', *Journal of Economic History* 37, pp. 113–35, 123.

Nihin Sangyo Kikai Kogyo-kai, *Sangyo Kikai kogyo hatten Katei* (Development Process of Industrial Machinery Industry) (Tokyo, NSKK, 1965). Source of Table 4.4.

Kranzberg, Melvin (1960) 'What constitutes an industrial revolution?', *Foreign Policy Bulletin* 39, p. 96.

Further reading

Ames, E. and Rosenberg, N. (1963) 'Changing technological leadership and industrial growth', *Economic Journal*, March: 13–31.

Bartholomew, J. R. (1989) *The Formation of Science in Japan*, New Haven, CT: Yale University Press.

Boxer, C. R. (1951) *The Christian Century in Japan 1549–1650*, Berkeley, CA: University of California Press.

Boxer, C. R. (1986) *Portuguese Merchants and Missionaries in Feudal Japan*, London: Macmillan.

Developing Economies, The (1979), 17 (Special issue), Technology transfer and adaptation – the case of Japan.

Goodman, G. K. (1986) *Japan: The Dutch Experience*, London: Macmillan.

Honja, E. (1967) 'The views of various hans on the opening of the country', *Kyoto University Economic Review*, 9(12): 154–72.

Hughes, H. J. (1974) 'Bakumatsu foreign employees', *Monumenta Nipponica*, 29: 305–27.

Inkster, I. (1991) 'Catching up and hanging on: the formation of science in modern Japan', *Annals of Science*, 48: 393–406.

Inkster, I. (1991) *Science and Technology in History, An Approach to Industrial Development*, London: Macmillan.

Inkster, I. (1998) *Technology and Industrialisation. Historical Case Studies and International Perspectives*, London: Ashgate.

Inkster, I. and Satofuka, F. (eds) (2000) *Culture and Technology in Modern Japan*, London: I. B. Tauris.

Jansen, M. B. (1971) *Sakamoto Ryoma and the Meiji Restoration*, Stanford, CA: Stanford University Press.

Jones, H. J. (1980) *Live Machines: Hired Foreigners and Meiji Japan*: Vancouver, University of Columbia Press.

Kawajiri, N. (1976) 'The missed influence of the French encyclopedists on Wasan', *Japanese Studies in the History of Science*, 15: 79–95.

Maclean, J. (1974) 'The introduction of books and scientific instruments into Japan 1712–1854', *Japanese Studies in the History of Science*, 13: 9–68.

Merhav, M. (1969) *Technological Dependence, Monopoly and Growth*, Oxford.

Mikami, Y. (1931) *Mathematics in China and Japan*, New York: Chelsea Publishing.

Mikami, Y. and Smith, D. E. (1914) *A History of Japanese Mathematics*, Chicago: Open Court Publishing.

Mitsutoshi, N. (1992) *Edo bunka hyobanki: Gazoku yuwa no sekai*, (*Directory of Edo Culture: A World of Harmony between the Refined and the Popular*), Tokyo: Chuo Koronsha.

Nakayama, S. (1968) *A History of Japanese Astronomy*, Cambridge, MA: Harvard University Press.

Nakayama, S. (1984) *Academic and Scientific Traditions in China, Japan and the West*, Tokyo: University of Tokyo Press.

Nakayama, S., Swain, D. and Yagi, S. (eds) (1974) *Science and Society in Modern Japan*, Tokyo: University of Tokyo Press.

Paske Smith, M. (1930) *Western Barbarians in Japan and Formosa in Tokugawa Days*, Kobe: Paragon.

Pittau, J. (1967) *Political Thought in Early Meiji Japan 1868–89*, Cambridge, MA: Harvard University Press.

Ranis, G. (ed.) (1972) *The Gap between the Rich and the Poor Countries*, New York.

Sansom, G. B. (1949, 1973) *The Western World and Japan*, New York: Knopf.

Saxonhouse, G. R. (1974) 'A tale of Japanese technological diffusion in the Meiji period', *Journal of Economic History*, 34: 149–65.

Scheiner, I. and Najita, T. (1978) *Essays in Tokugawa Intellectual History*, Chicago.

Seki, K. (1956) *The Cotton Industry of Japan*, Tokyo.

Shand, R. F. (ed.) (1973) *Technical Change in Asian Agriculture*, Canberra: Australian National University.

Takahashi, H. K. (1965) 'Quelques remarques historique sur la répartition sociale de la propriété funcier au Japan depuis le XVI siècle', *International Conference of Economic History*, 3rd Section, Munich, pp. 421–34.

Tanaka, M. (1971) 'Development of chemistry in modern Japan', *XII Congress Internationale D'Histoire des Sciences*, 6, Blanchard: Librairie Scientifique et Technique.

Yuasa, M. (1965) 'The scientific revolution and the age of technology', *Journal of World History*, 9(2), and other essays in this special issue.

5 The state and economic development

Introduction: the contested state

> The economics of development is not very complicated; the secret of successful planning lies more in sensible politics and good public administration.
>
> (W. Arthur Lewis, *Development Planning*, 1966)

Chapters 3 and 4 have demonstrated, time and again, the importance of government action in mobilising the economy of Japan after 1868. Furthermore, we have also suggested in Chapters 2 and 3 (pp. 24–7, 36–41) that a foremost economic position for the state might be expected in any case of industrialisation under conditions of relative economic backwardness. For instance, R. H. Green has generalised that 'it is an historical fact that, with quite minor exceptions, the later a political-economic unit has embarked on a serious development effort and the greater the disparities between its own levels of institutional and productive forces and those of highly developed political-economic units, the greater has been the role of the State . . . the first element in development is increasing national self-reliance'.

Much hinges around the term 'role', for questions do arise as to the efficiency (i.e. the real function) of government economic activity. All late developers exhibit active state intervention, but this does not in itself provide proof of the economic efficiency of such interventions. Other players may have been in a position to perform a proximate economic role to greater effect.

As we shall see further, government intervention in the economy did not go unchallenged by leading contemporaries, and debate over the optimum extent or best mechanisms of intervention raged in the public arena for decades. The classic position, held in the minds of many students of Japan to this day, was well-expressed by 'A Samurai', writing in an English-language Japanese newspaper of the mid-1880s:

> The Government, ever since the Restoration, vigorously set itself to many difficult works which involved the total change of the national foundation – a task which cannot be achieved by weak governments.

> The people too, recognised the permanent influence of the Occidental civilisation and flung themselves headlong into the race with other nations, in spite of the numerous sacrifices, expecting nothing but a fair treatment at their hands.

The images here are very clear: Consistent and efficient action, legitimised by the ready concurrence of the nation, urged on by the exigencies of the international economy. At centre stage, the government was the bearer of the hopes and aspirations of a new Japan. At around the same time, a leading article in the *Jiji Shimpo* pleaded for 'A rest on the way'. Because 'the progress of a nation in civilisation far outstrips the intellectual development of the individual', it seemed that government's instigation of civilisation in the form of railways and telegraphs must be slowed in order that not too much social dislocation might occur. Indeed, contemporaries saw the Matsukata deflation of the early 1880s in just such terms. Some months earlier the *Chūgai Bukka Shimpo* had characterised the government interventions of the 1870s as both inefficient and insufficient for the needs of the nation. All such commentary evidenced close attention to foreign affairs and to Western economic doctrine.

Unequivocal modern judgements about the economic impact of the Meiji government are hard to find. The relatively low rate of government investment and the 'selling up' of government enterprise to private interests in the early 1880s have often been taken as signs of failure. Clearly, they may be as readily viewed as signs of success – minimal expenditures yielded significant results and selling-up was part and parcel of the strategy of technology diffusion (see Chapter 4). Furthermore, most of those historians who now minimise the role of government in Meiji industrialisation restrict their analyses to rates of savings and capital accumulation and assume that the alternative to government action was a working market system. Such analyses seem to be predicated on the belief that the government *intruded* on an already established system for the production and distribution of goods, information and services, using modernised or Westernised technologies and organisations. The same historians ignore the social underpinnings of economic development and the economic impact of state action in the areas of education, training, information dispersal, property rights, risk reduction and social control.

The costs of continuity

> United and peaceable, taught to give due worship to the gods, due obedience to the laws, due submission to their superiors, due love and regard to their neighbours.
>
> (Engelbert Kaempfer 1692)

> The public should remember that there is a certain limit to the exercise of benevolent intentions which if carried too far becomes a kind of tyranny.
>
> (*Nichi Nichi Shimbun*, April 1878)

Two hundred peasant uprisings occurred between 1868 and 1878, a rate of recorded rebellion far greater than ever took place even in the most distressed years of late Tokugawa, such as the famine decade of the 1780s or the anti-merchant disturbances of the 1820s. In the opinion of T. C. Smith 'never in modern times has Japan been so close to social revolution'. Reasons for popular unrest were manifold – high rents, tenancy disputes, usury and new forms of taxation provided a basis for peasant revolt led by discontented and independently armed *shizoku*. By the early 1880s there is evidence of coherent political opposition arising in silk and textile regions, particularly in the face of competition from imported cottons. At the same time, violent political opposition became somewhat less populist and reactionary and increasingly wedded to coherent political programmes, most of which embraced alternative strategies for industrial and commercial development. Thus, the famous Satsuma Rebellion of 1877 may well have represented, in the words of Barrington Moore Jnr, 'the last bloody convulsion of the old order', but violent activity continued well into the 1880s as an integral component of a more politicised or ideological opposition to Meiji government policies.

For Japan, knowledge of and from the West brought the best of times and the worst of times. The tremendous industrial impetus provided by foreign technologies was matched by the disruptive impacts of Atlantic ideologies. Meiji economic development took place within a global context of massive Western incursions into India, China, Africa, Central Asia, the Middle East and Indochina. The notion of 'civilisation' which confronted the statesmen and intellectuals of Meiji Japan reflected a Western statist ideology compounded of such commanding ideas as the balance of power, the self-regulating market, the liberal industrial state. Together such elements symbolised a political 'enlightenment' more or less forced upon an *ancien régime* overwhelmingly dominated by the privilege, hegemony and corruption of the traditional landed classes. Nor was such external influence a matter merely of books and representations generated from afar.[1] As we have seen, the influence of the foreigner was everywhere within Japan itself. This is especially true in the case of such liberal democratic societies as the Tosa-based *Risshisha* (Society of Free Thinkers) or the similarly minded intellectuals of the *Meirokusha* (Meiji Six Society i.e. founded in the Sixth year of Meiji), which included foremost Japanese intellectuals and statesmen like Yukichi Fukuzawa and Arinori Mori. In 1878 the American scientist R. W. Atkinson was invited to the capital of Tosa, a centre of rebellion, to lecture before 700 members of the *Risshisha*, amongst them Taisuke Itagaki, the leading radical democrat of his day.[2] Within the Free Speech Society of Tokyo during the 1870s, influential Westerners addressed and debated with Japanese intellectuals in the Japanese language. Contemporaneously the political society *Kyōson Dōshin* (Coexistence Circle) began to hold its meetings in the English language in order that its Japanese members 'who have visited England and America' might utilise their new skills. An editor of the influential newspaper, the *Mainichi Shimbun* was imprisoned for publishing material from the *Japan Gazette* 'of such a character as to excite the people and which might incite them to rebellious acts'. From the ideas of J. J. Rousseau and Emile Zola to those of J. S. Mill, Western ideology and activists furthered the cause of political opposition during the 1870s and 1880s.

The major aim of political opposition prior to 1885 was the securing of a national assembly. But all calls for constitutional democracy included programmes for economic reform. Political liberty and economic individualism were seen as two sides of a civilisation coin, and they could only be attained by further shifts in the class and power structure. When over 500 *shizoku* democrats met in the provincial capital of Fukuoka their object was 'not only to discuss individual rights and liberties, but also to bring forward measures for the development of husbandry, industrial works and trade generally, in fact all questions for the benefit of the people and the enrichment of the country'. According to the *Chōya Shimbun*, a newspaper which had been temporarily suspended by government in early 1880, the 'selfish and usurped interests' of the merchant classes yet dominated government thinking. There should be a shift towards the support of 'independent and respectable men who take as much interest in the affairs of the nation as they do in their own private matters'. The culture of business was preferable to that of 'unnecessary officials and expenses'. In 1880, the *Mainichi Shimbun*, in commenting on the possible impact of new repressive laws on public meetings, summarised the changing character of political agitation:

> If we compare the present movement with that at the close of the Tokugawa domination, which had for its object the restoration of the imperial authority to its original position, we find that it is ten times greater both in power and intensity. Then the Samurai and upper classes in the Western provinces alone took part in the restoration; while the traders and farmers knew little and cared apparently less, about what was going on. But now the whole population of the country is actuated with one burning desire for representative institutions, and the movement has become as powerful and uncontrollable as a vast conflagration or the current of a mighty river. Under these circumstances, if the government has promulgated the new regulations with a view to stifle the political aspirations of the people, we greatly fear, that instead of tranquillity and peace, the enforcement of these laws will result in fearful disturbances, with all their long train of abundant evils.

There was without question a significant political and social element in the famous Satsuma Rebellion of 1877, and we may claim something of the sort for the less well-known civil uprisings and conspiracies of

Kumamoto, Tosa, Takebashi and Kagoshima, as well as the several disturbances which followed the influential memorial of January 1874 on representative government. Rebel activists were by no means limited to major urban centres. Of the 1,137 Southern rebels who were sentenced by the Kyūshū Special Court from May to December 1877 some 60 per cent or more were divided fairly evenly amongst a dozen provincial *ken*, each of these areas providing between 4 per cent and 7 per cent of the total. Disaffection was dispersed. Much of the physical unrest was political and gave rise to longer-term local political traditions in crucial areas of the country. Tosa witnessed physical unrest in 1877 and 1878 but by 1879 appears to have become a centre of sustained political debate. The *shizoku* gathered in large numbers as members of the political societies and were foremost in discussion of political rights, freedom of the individuals and representative government.

Yet by 1885 it was all over. In the words of E. H. Norman 'By 1885 the government offensive had triumphed everywhere. The first and most serious challenge to autocracy was beaten back'. Government involved itself massively in social control measures during the late 1870s and 1880s. The most obvious expression of this was in the defeat of physical risings. For all its investment in industry and education during the industrial drive, by far the greatest proportion of government expenditure went into social control. The costs of continuity were huge. At a time when the total yield from the land tax was around 40 million yen (approximately £8 million), the expenses of the Satsuma rebellion alone totalled 42 million yen. Such costs were met by inflationary financing, borrowing and reserve funding. Ōkuma's budget figures of that year estimated an accumulated internal national debt of some 219 million yen, made up mostly of financial liabilities to the *samurai* and *han*, which 'is the extinguishment of the pensions awarded to them in consequence of the events of 1868–71'. Policing and military operations also added to the expense of control. Together the cost of continuity completely overshadowed the direct costs of industrial advancement; in the three years to 1878 government had expended in total some 6.2 million yen on the *Kaitakushi* (Colonisation Department of Hokkaidō), 2.5 million yen on direct loans to industry and 4.5 million yen through the *Mombushō*, or Department of Education.

The Western adviser Dr Paul Mayet viewed all expenditure on social control as ultimately productive in his very detailed analysis of the 1879 budget: 'we see that the most important domestic reforms are those of an economical nature; efforts to lighten the burdens which for ages have ground down the farmer; advancement of the formerly despised artisan and merchant classes; attempts to absorb the hitherto only consuming class of *samurai* into the producing mass of the population'. Mayet went on to show that the government's accumulated debt on account of its 'historical past'; amounted to some 272 million yen, made up primarily of pension redemption, but including the Meiji state's assumption of debts contracted by individual *daimyō* with Japanese subjects 'during the last 50 years before the Restoration'. The expenses of civil war, including Satsuma, added another 53 million yen.

Soft control was far less expensive. From 1873 to 1877 some 4,500 major directive notifications were issued by government departments. The very weight of administrative formality circumscribed political behaviour. In addition, the wide ranging agitation of the mid-1870s gave way during the 1880s to a channelling of energies into the demand for a popular assembly. Provincial discontents were met by bending to the wind. As early as May 1878 at least nominal representation in local matters was increased through the introduction of a general assembly of provincial governors. When in early 1880 the power of the local assemblies was increased, many of the popular societies who continued to press for institutional reform were placed in an increasingly marginal position. The legal closure of the means of diffusion and sustenance of radicalism (the media, public meetings, study groups) shattered the remaining opposition groups. In addition, the character of Meiji bureaucracy appears to have permitted the absorption of many *shizoku* dissidents and intellectuals. state-financed universities and colleges employed Western-educated intellectuals. According to an estimate of 1880, over 90 per cent of senior government officials were of *samurai* origin. Upward mobility through the bureaucracy absorbed outsiders and produced inner cohesion and a progressive, Western orientation among a strategically placed group of decision-makers. The high status given to Western technique and its relative simplicity meant that bureaucrats returned from the West could comprehend and control innovations quite readily. The labour-absorbing character of much small-scale technique (see Chapter 3) was such as to minimise its 'displacement' effects on employment, skills and regional balance. Regional planning in Hokkaidō was viewed as a means of relieving unemployment and political problems by removing *shizoku* away from the centre to technological projects far removed. Decreasing pressure on land tax revenue meant that at least one of the major basic causes of rural unrest was greatly reduced during the 1880s. Finally, the fact that both agriculture and many by-employments thrived under the new regime meant a continuity of organisation in older sectors and established regions and a retention of non-urban social institutions.

We may conclude, then, that mechanisms of control were deliberately forged during the Meiji industrial drive as part and parcel of an overall strategy of industrial modernisation. It may be that the effectiveness of such social engineering in some way depended on a set of social values and norms unusual to Japan. We shall return to this theme in more detail in Chapters 12 and 13. At present we may suggest that political continuity was necessary to the success of Meiji industrialisation and owed much to the considered and costly interventions of the state.

Strategy: the debate over foreign capital

Japan's crisis year was 1878. The expense of Satsuma and the conversion of *samurai* pensions to bonds combined with a drop in tax revenue to stifle the budget. In a letter to the Prime Minister in late 1877, the Japanese Minister of Finance Shigenobu Ōkuma pleaded for strict economy. The state had issued 27 million yen worth of paper currency and borrowed 15 million yen from the banking system. Hardly surprisingly, it was in this year that the debate over the need for foreign capital surfaced within the bureaucracy and the media. According to the *Chūgai Bukka Shimpo* the development of Japan's natural resources, requiring 'labour, its intellectual direction, and capital' would halt in the absence of new finance from abroad. Policy should alter to 'let foreigners subscribe the capital for Japan's public works', for joint-stock companies would also bring in technical knowledge and force the Western powers to review the regulations enforced upon Japan regarding tariffs and extraterritoriality. The presence of foreign capital and the operation of sophisticated Western enterprises would help to concentrate dispersed Japanese capital in the form of bonds and small savings, small monies 'would again assemble and become productive capital'. As to the exploitation of Japan by the Westerners, 'Even supposing that they did take away the profit to their homes, if our countrymen should become thereby incited to commence public works for themselves, the advantage thus gained would be out of all comparison to the loss of foreigners taking away a portion of the net profits'. Ironically to modern minds, proponents of foreign capital cited India, China, Turkey and Egypt as examples of the efficacious adoption of foreign investment. The writers in the *Chūgai Bukka Shimpo* also judged that the success of late developers in Europe itself had been predicated on the combination of advanced capital and intellect derived from earlier developers. Success in relatively backward economies had been attained 'through their having well foreseen the future and obtained capital and intellectual labour widely from both home and abroad'.

Foreign capital would spread modernised industry from the urban points of contact to the hinterlands, 'the people in the interior would be excited and take works in hand one after another'. A host of commentators joined in defence of foreign capital during the late 1870s. The link between capital and diplomacy was never doubted. Foreigners committed to Japanese mines or businesses, in the opinion of the *Chōya Shimbun*, 'would have quitted the stronghold of extraterritoriality to come within the sphere of our laws'. Westerners quickly saw the opportunity to influence policy. In countering claims that foreign capital could lead to commercial exploitation, Western advocates provided examples which we may now view with a certain circumspection: 'Has this happened in Spain, Portugal or in any of the southern countries of America where foreign capital has opened up the resources of these places?' By the early 1880s the proponents of foreign capital were emphasising the argument of J. S. Mill to the effect that the legislators of poor nations should not 'encroach' upon domestic capital but should favour domestic accumulation and foreign borrowings. The seeming abundance of domestic capital for large public projects only represented a movement of financial resources from the private enterprise sector to the public sector. Such public investments merely absorbed scarce domestic capital 'with the certainty of abstracting it directly from the wages fund, thus curtailing the subsistence of the people and the employment of labour'.

Yet, as the Prologue to this book suggests, the proponents of foreign capital failed to convince the government or the people. If for J. S. Mill foreign capital simply represented 'the overflowings of the general accumulation of the world', for Japan it posited a risk not worth the taking. The *Jiyū Shimbun* was adamant that the limits of Japanese economic growth were not set by capital but by 'the sagacity, experience and skill' of capitalists and bureaucrats. It may be argued that the decision on foreign capital helped determine an overall trajectory for the economy throughout the Meiji period. Advocates of foreign capital proposed a freeing up of the economy, less government interference, the 'abolition of political oppression' in order to attract innovative foreign enterprise. Opponents urged the opposite. Government must continue to raise and concentrate capital into industrial enterprises and must set itself to instil a spirit of entrepreneurship in the absence of the Western model. Thus the *Hōchi Shimbun'*, judgement that 'if the spirit of enterprise would develop itself in our countrymen, and if they still continue assiduously to study the arts and sciences, although our country may not be able to at once become as civilised as the Western nations, it is certain that we could, without incurring the risk of much loss, establish profitable enterprises and secure the foundation for an increasing production in the interior, and thus advance to an equal rank with foreigners'. Similarly, the Matsukata deflation of the early 1880s should be seen as the conservative alternative to foreign borrowings. Not only did the deflation incorporate an artificial cheapening of government assets (see p. 86) in private hands, but the general recession dampened the demand for new capital in the private sector yet permitted continued investment in the public sector. Again, the government position on capital furthered the emphasis on social change and income redistribution towards more ready investors and away from unproductive usage. Japanese merchants 'keep seventy yen idle for every thirty yen they employ profitably'.

The most difficult argument to face was that concerning the learning impact of foreign enterprise in Japan: 'Even *bantōs* [bathmen] and petty clerks in foreign employ have succeeded in amassing great wealth after years of steady perseverance'. The ultimate answer was to eschew foreign capital but to employ foreign expertise in the creation of an efficient Japanese learning system.

Financing industrial change

> Given the level of administrative inexperience which must have prevailed, one wonders how the government managed to survive.
>
> (Henry Rosovsky 1966)

Public expenditure as a percentage of national income was around 10–12 per cent in the mid-1880s, rising to 17 per cent in 1900 to over 20 per cent by 1910. Compared to other nations, these proportions were not especially high. Of course, war brought on considerable extraordinary expenditure: the Russo-Japanese war of 1904–5 led to 75 per cent of government expenditure being devoted to military purposes. Ordinary revenue was derived mainly from the land tax in early years (providing 90 per cent of all tax revenue) but was later greatly augmented by purchase taxes, income tax (from 1887), customs revenue, profit from government enterprises and stamp duties. Issue of government bonds were especially important in times of emergency such as the Satsuma rebellion (pp. 74–5), the Sino-Japanese war (52 per cent of costs met by issue of securities) and the Russo-Japanese war (80 per cent of costs met by issues of government securities).

As might now be expected, a massive portion of government expenditure was devoted to compensating the *shizoku*. In the terms of Kōichi Emi, the costs of 'liquidating the old system' were around 50 per cent of total government expenditure during 1868–75, and these were primarily financed by issues of paper money, and domestic and foreign borrowings. As late as 1890 some 20 per cent of government expenditure took the form of income transfers and represented a greater spending than did total government capital formation.

According to the famous estimate of Henry Rosovsky, the government's share of gross domestic capital formation never averaged less than 40 per cent, a figure which included the large durable weapons of war such as ships and ordnance. Most non-military government investment was in construction and infrastructure rather than in manufacturing as such, while military capital formation was mostly in the area of large durable equipment. Most government direct subsidies went to shipping (first to Mitsubishi) and railroads. As late as 1900 government invested five times as much in transport and communication than it did in manufacturing and mining. At the same time the government's current expenditure on goods and services in the field of education reached four times that in manufacturing. It would appear that the multifarious linkage effects of government activity described in Chapters 3 and 4 were secured at low cost, especially in comparison to the financial outlays involved in statist social engineering, military expansion and basic infrastructure provision. The general expenditure pattern clearly suggests that the major economic function of government lay in reducing commercial risk through controlling social conflict and diffusing commercial and technical information, the one an expensive pursuit, the other relatively inexpensive but demanding care and precision. To such environmental investment should be added the tremendous cost-reducing impacts in the private sector of improved infrastructure and manufacturing technologies instigated in the public sector.

More indirectly, the government boosted industrial financing through bank policy. New regulations of 1872 permitted the growth of so-called National Banks, of which there were some 150 by 1880. Pockets of merchant and agrarian capital were organised into smaller private banks which in total were of equal importance in financing businesses as were the nationals. During the 1890s major companies such as Mitsubishi began to convert their own financial departments into banks in order to raise long-term, company specific capital. Several government banks provided particular functions. The Bank of Japan began the issue of convertible notes in 1885, the Yokohama Specie Bank from 1880 financed and encouraged the export sector and the Japan Industrial Promotion Bank of the 1890s provided long-term loans across all productive sectors. The paid in capital of all banks rose from around 52 million yen in 1880 to around 450 million yen in 1910.

Education, training and technology

Japan represents one of the few historical cases where a large and successful import of knowledge and technique occurred alongside the development of an indigenous technological capability. Transfers did not swamp or retard internal development. Our interpretation of this complementarity revolves around the nature of the transfer mechanisms (Chapter 4) and, closely associated with these, the character and extent of government involvement in education, training and information collection and dispersal. The nature of the underlying dynamics of the industrialising system is best revealed at this level. Here government activity was clear, unchallenged (the private sector was incapable of fulfilling this role), expensive, pervasive and *necessary* to an overall strategy for development which forbade the learning process normally associated with the introduction of foreign enterprise on one hand, yet required the emergence of a strong and innovative private sector on the other.

Meiji education strategy depended upon a thoroughgoing exploitation of the assets inherited from the Tokugawa period. A variety of schools, from the small Buddhist temple schools for commoners and *samurai*, the *terakoya*, to *han* schools for *bushi* and private schools for higher learning, accommodated a total of some one million students at the end of the Tokugawa period, a figure about equal to total school attendance in the first year of the modern school system (1873). Up to 50 per cent of male children and perhaps 15–20 per cent of females received some form of instruction, and most historians agree that the Meiji rulers inherited a high literacy level. After the primary school ordinance of 1872 much of the physical and human capital of the *terakoya* and other schools was harnessed to the new elementary and normal school system. By 1890 some 3 million students were in attendance, by 1910 some 7 million.

Although the *terakoya* tradition rested on basic literacy and social learning, the quite dramatic expansion of fief schools for *samurai* (*hanko*) the private schools for *samurai* and commoners from the late 1780s and the *kyō-u-sho* or centres of instruction for adult commoners was associated with a widening curriculum, including elements of Western science – medicine, military technique, languages. At Kagoshima and Saga during the nineteenth century the fief authorities established laboratories attached to *hanko* for the exploration of photography, cotton-spinning, sugar refining, glass manufacture, as well as mechanical construction of furnaces and telegraphs. In contrast to fief schools, the private academies (*Shijuku*) enjoyed relative autonomy and their provisions included subjects banned from the *hanko* and *terakoya*. In these, students were free to learn unconventional Confucian theories, medicine, navigation, mathematics and military science as well as Western languages and philosophy. We may estimate, then, that early Meiji education rested on the twin pillars of traditional elementary instruction encompassing literacy, docility and national culture, and a more recent (post-1780s) trend towards innovative scholarship and a more Westernised curriculum. Although this division followed social class lines this was not invariably so. Many commoners were exposed to the winds of change during the early nineteenth century.

The Meiji government accomplished a massive task in extending this system relatively rapidly. Mass education was a function of local government and involved expenditures far in excess of central government support for higher learning and training. The total cost to local government of mass education during the Meiji era accumulated to around 1,000 million yen, about 30 per cent of all local government expenditure and equivalent to the suppression of over twenty Satsuma rebellions! By 1908 six years of schooling was made free and compulsory, raising the attendance rate to around 95 per cent.

Mass education included technical and vocational training as well as the normal schools, designed to fit between lower and higher education. The latter were considered by Arinori Mori, Minister of Education in the 1880s, as the focal point for training in physical fitness and citizenship. None the less, the rate of social and economic change in the early Meiji years ensured that character construction gave way to learning. The traveller Isabella Bird described a normal school situated in Kobota (Akita) in the extreme north of Honshū, 200 miles from the nearest open port of Niigata. Twenty-five teachers taught 700 pupils ranging from 6 to 20 years of age: 'they teach reading, writing, arithmetic, geography, history, political economy after John Stuart Mill, chemistry, botany, a course of natural science, geometry and mensuration'. American influence ensured that the normal schools became a vital link between the practicalities of elementary instruction and apprenticeship and the abstractions of higher learning. They also harboured a tremendous amount of upward social mobility, training a large number of teachers as well as later governors, local officials and military officers. It was here and in more explicit vocational education that the Meiji government effected a weakening of older distinctions between highly valued mental work and despised hand work, a vital component of technological diffusion and skill accumulation.

The main development of explicit technical education came in the 1890s with the 1893 Regulations on Supplementary Technical Schools and the 1894 Regulations on Apprentice Schools. The new schools under the 1893 regulations were strictly vocational and admitted graduates of elementary level schools. According to one estimate, in 1896 some 66 per cent of total hours in such schools were devoted to metal working or mechanics courses, 14 per cent were devoted to design and technical drawing, some 5 per cent to Japanese, the rest to a mix of mathematics and science. At many vocational schools classes were held on Sundays, in the evening and during off-harvest seasons. Apprentice schools were principally designed to counter the problem of declining quality in traditional industries such as silk, woodworking and varied handicrafts. Pioneers in scholastic apprenticeship training included the Aizu Lacquerwork Apprentice School, the Seto Ceramics School, and Minami Tsuru Weaving and Dyeing School. Many schools were entirely concerned with quality improvement in strictly local products.

Around 2–3 per cent of central government expenditure went to higher education and training, an arena of spending which was quickly contracted in times of emergency or recession but was expanded around the time of the promulgation of the constitution (1889–90). The symbolic centrepiece of this was the University of Tokyo from 1877, and the initial backbone of this was the College of Engineering which consisted of faculties of civil, mechanical and electrical engineering, naval and general architecture, arms and explosives, applied chemistry and mining and metallurgy. Agricultural education was influenced by American experts and advisers, this being especially true of the Sapporo Agricultural School from 1876. The 1883 Regulations on Agricultural Schools divided instruction into fairly distinct layers, a lower grade meant for practical farmers and an intermediate level intended for students who would go on to higher technical education. A similar distinction was made in the 1884 Regulations on Commercial Schools.

Bridging the gap between the vocational and technical schools and the universities and colleges were a series of special technical institutes and mechanics schools, established from the 1880s. By 1884, 103 such schools had been established with some 9,000 students, thirty-two specialising in medicine, twenty in mathematics, nine in agriculture.[3] The Tokyo Higher

Technical School emerged as the principal industrial school, supplying courses in dyeing and weaving, ceramics, applied chemistry, mechanical technology, electrical engineering and industrial design. In such special schools the entire curriculum was devoted to practical training and included very specific, apprentice-like training units – weaving practice, refining of mordents, texture dissection, chemistry of colouring.

Attention to technical education in Meiji Japan was greater than could be found in most other industrialising nations, but shared the general tendency to relegate its most vocational and applied aspects to an ancillary or remedial position. More distinctly, however, technical education was a receptacle of Western influence and knowledge transfer. Many foreigners found employment in the various levels of the technical education system; in the years 1871 to 1899 the College of Engineering in Tokyo alone hired twenty foreigners from England, the US, France and Germany.

By the beginning of the twentieth century some 1,600 institutions provided specialised technical instruction of some type, this including over 1,000 agricultural technology courses attached to lower and normal schools as well as special agricultural colleges. Around 100,000 students were in attendance. The higher institutes of technology all taught European languages, basic science including chemistry and mathematics, some elements of political economy. The emphasis on the development of technical education was a sustained one: between 1880 and 1940 there was a forty-fold increase in the number of students enrolled in higher scientific and technical education and an eighty-fold increase in the number of students in further technical and commercial education. This not only expanded training in modernised technique but provided an additional avenue of social mobility in a rapidly changing society.

Between 1868 and 1885 the Ministry of Industry paid out some 5.6 million yen in the form of salaries to foreign engineers, mostly employed in government railways, (2 million yen in salaries) mining, lighthouses and mechanised manufacture. On average, payment to foreign employees (*ōyatoi*) accounted for over 40 per cent of the total expenditure of the Ministry, a figure peaking at 67 per cent in 1877. This excludes payments to large numbers of foreign employees in the ministries of education, finance and home affairs. Total government expenditure on foreign experts between 1868 and 1892 cost something in the region of 20 million yen. Most foreigners were employed in infrastructure construction rather than directly in manufacturing. To even these expenses must be added the cost to government of sending officials and students to America, Europe and Asia, which adds another 6 to 10 million yen to the expenses of government. Most Japanese went to America in the early years and then increasingly to Britain and Europe.

The effect of such training and information dispersal activity was boosted by other government action, of a more regulatory than financial nature, the importance of which is difficult to estimate accurately. The standardisation movement of 1875–91 cost little in the way of financial resources, but metrication, standardisation in medicines and pharmaceuticals and clearer specifications in government contracts for supply of raw materials hastened the process of knowledge diffusion. The establishment of hundreds of trade associations under official auspices from 1884 were designed to control product quality but eventually emerged as regional technical extension centres.

The state and the entrepreneur

> The common people, no less than the civil and military officials, shall each be allowed to pursue his own calling so that there may be no discontent.
> (Article 3 of Meiji Charter Oath, 6 April 1868)

Chapter 3 (pp. 38–9) began to sketch out an argument relating activity in the public sector to the emergence of a viable entrepreneurial culture in the private sector. The more conventional approach to Meiji business has been to consider the long-term conditions behind the emergence of entrepreneurial groups. Thus, a now standard argument runs that the slow erosion of the status of the *samurai* during the Tokugawa years and the acceleration of this in the early years of Meiji created a group of Japanese with both the need and the wherewithal to attempt something very new. Whereas the merchants of the large towns preferred to invest in trade and consumer loans and could only rise socially by ingratiating themselves with central feudal elements to obtain quasi-social benefit (e.g. the right to carry swords, to assume family names and so on), the *samurai* could become the essential dynamic force turning Japan away from the Tokugawa status quo and towards industrial modernisation. This was especially so given the destruction of the merchant class under the new Meiji conditions of freedom of commerce and open ports, guild abolition and the widespread social and geographical movement of new middlemen and traders. *Ryōgaeya* (money changing) business, which had depended on the use of silver money, was ruined by the currency reforms of 1871.

In Everett Hagen's version of the argument, the *motivations* of *samurai* groups are crucial, as is the withdrawal of status respect from such groups during the Tokugawa era:

> The nature of the humiliation made it clear that technological progress was the only possible road to the restoration of national dignity, just as the internal situation made it clear that economic prowess offered the greatest opportunity for the subordinated groups. Because they offered strength, and because they were an honoured indigenous group, the nation followed them. With circumstance favourable, Japan entered upon continuing technological progress.

We depart from this sort of very generalised approach when we turn away from the entrepreneur towards *entrepreneurship* and the conditions of the creative or progressive commercial act. As Robert Bellah once very nicely expressed it, however important 'motivational factors may be they have proved time and again to be highly sensitive to shifts in institutional arrangements . . . it would be advisable to consider motivation in close connection with institutional structure and its historical development'. Indeed, even those who do concentrate on the entrepreneur as a type, long in the creation, do not omit all reference to context. Johannes Hirschmeier is clear enough: 'Entrepreneurship must be viewed as a result both of individual personality and of the favourable economic and social conditions provided by the group and the cultural milieu. If there is too wide a distance between the new goal and the established standards of the group, even strong and talented persons will achieve the goal only with great difficulty'. The fault here lies in the restricted conception of context, for in early Meiji Japan the major contextual features emanated from the varied activities of the public sector. So it may now be strongly suggested that the conditions for entrepreneurship were closely bounded by at least *six* activities of government during the years of the industrial drive, 1868–85;

1. Social control activity which reduced risk.
2. Model factory and project construction which induced imitation.
3. Stipend commutation which clarified social position (p. 76) and produced financial resources.
4. The 'selling up' process of 1880–5 which diffused technologies and augmented capital at low cost.
5. Infrastructural, especially transport, developments which reduced private sector costs and extended markets.
6. Labour force education and training which reduced costs (docility plus skills) and induced further organisational innovations.

Most of these public sector activities have been related in the previous chapters. Perhaps the best focal point for interpretation is that of the Matsukata deflation and the associated policy of 'selling up' of government enterprises.

Money printing and the expenses of the Satsuma rebellion generated a very serious inflation during 1878–81.[4] Influenced greatly by Western economic doctrine, the new Finance Minister, Masayoshi Matsukata (1835–1924) brought in a general policy of deflation which included a drastic reduction of public sector direct support to manufacturing. The deflation period to 1885 has been seen as that of a generalised transition to *laissez-faire* on the part of the Japanese government. For instance, citing as his authorities Chalmers Johnson and William Lockwood, Ryōshin Minami claims that the 'basic attitude of the government after this period was "*laissez-faire*"'.[5] Yet the evidence is far from clear. The material of this chapter and Chapter 4 shows that government accelerated its economic interventions in the fields of infrastructure and construction, education and training, technology applications and information dispersal, military contracting for industry and raw material supplies, as well as its indirect support for manufacturing through increased regulations relating to finance, quality control and the encouragement of manufactured exports. None of this reads like *laissez-faire* in any acceptable sense. The continuity of projects (e.g. the Hokkaidō development project and railway and ship construction) across the Matsukata divide and the low valuation of government assets during 'selling up', suggest that the movement away from direct investment in manufacturing was part and parcel of an overall strategy of multifold interventions, the timing of which was certainly influenced by the need to cut expenditure whenever possible and reduce inflation. Of course, economic individualism mixed with Social Darwinist sentiments could be found aplenty. Thus Heigorō Shōda of Mitsubishi: 'I say that if we expect enterprises to progress they must be left alone – left to natural selection and the survival of the fittest – without artificial intervention'. Yet Mitsubishi was and had been the recipient of tremendous government support. Most Japanese businessmen also believed that it was the task of government to regulate and restrict commercial competition. Most Japanese, including the bureaucracy, concurred with the *Chūgai Bukka Shimpo* that free competition was a good idea but not at a time when Japanese capitalists possessed finance but little else: 'Now, if without questioning what intellect the capitalists possess, but simply seeing that they are possessed of capital, we should persuade them to commence business in which they are not experienced, they would at once become a prey to cunning and experienced merchants, and although one or two out of 1,000 or 100 may fortunately succeed, they would mostly naturally all come to ruin'. Japan could not wait for the organic development of an entrepreneurial culture and technical expertise, for then 'foreign countries will advance before us and we shall finally have to lose our natural wealth'.

E. H. Norman's emphasis on the changing tactics of government intervention during the early 1880s appears more relevant and sturdy. Government turned towards more indirect forms of encouraging industry and transport (although this included new loans and subsidies) and retained direct interests in strategic or military areas of the economy. The *Nōshōmushō*, which took over from the old Department of Industry (*Kōbushō*), effected the transfer of government enterprise into private hands and in doing so deliberately nurtured the state's contacts with the business elite. Mitsubishi benefited from the sale of ships, shipyards and mines as well as monopoly legislation. Mitsui bought up textile mills and the Miike coal field (see Chapter 3 p. 36, Sakamoto, Fujita and Furukawa all bought gold, iron and silver mines between 1880 and 1894 on excellent terms.

In most cases, government expenditure on establishing such enterprises and equipping them with Western technologies had been at a level twice or more that of the asking price at transfer. The subsequent investment by government in military industries added to the six factors listed above as stimulating the growth of private business activity. In addition, when new enterprises were opened up in this period, the private sector rode freely on assets established earlier in the public sector. When private iron works were established at Kōbe in early 1884 hundreds of trained workers and experts from the government's Akabane Iron Works were engaged by the managing entrepreneur (see further Chapter 4).

A major pointer to the significance of government activity and the 'selling off' policy was the frequent failure of ex-*samurai* businessman prior to 1880 and their increasing success and confidence at a later date. Many leading entrepreneurs were of aristocratic lineage with bureaucratic experience at the *han* level and privileged access to Western ideas and techniques. Eiichi Shibusawa, perhaps the greatest industrial moderniser of the era and intermittently in the service of bureaucracy and government, was born into a *samurai* family in 1840. Not only was the family engaged in sericulture and indigo production as well as rice, prior to the Restoration the young Shibusawa accepted an official bureaucratic post with the Hitotsubashi, (a branch of the Tokugawa), and then as a fief bureaucrat in 1869 established the Trading Board in Shizuoka on the lines of a public company. Later in that year he was offered an official position with the new government as head of the bureau of taxation in the Ministry of Finance, one which provided him with the practical experience for his monograph of 1870, the *Rikkai Ryakusoku*, (*Elements of Company Formation*). Amongst those who emerged in the 1880s, Sohō Tokutomi, who published his *Meiji Youth* in 1885 and formed around himself the *Min'yusha* (Friends of the Nation) group of political intellectuals, came from a familial context as close to the *gōnō* – gentlemen farmers – as to the lower *samurai*. His father attained upward status through an astute combination of intermarriage and advocation of modern technology at the *han* level, a position which led to the family's early support of the Kumamoto School for Western Studies, founded in 1871.

The juxtaposition of commercial-industrial interests, Western knowledge and bureaucratic skills carried forward well into the Meiji period. As an illustration of the industrial interests of the ex-aristocracy the railway scheme of 1875 might be briefly outlined. In June 1875 the Tokyo *Nichi Nichi Shimbun* announced the plan by a group of nobles and *samurai* to construct a line of railways between Tokyo and Aomori using their own capital. Although by that time at least six meetings of the group had taken place, a lack of accounting and financial knowledge had held back progress. Projecting a total cost for the enterprise of some 7.5 million yen the group met, symbolically enough at the rooms of the First National Bank and it was not long before the founder and manager of the bank, Eiichi Shibusawa took control. Estimating that the initial plan would require at least 10 million yen of investment, Shibusawa led the group around to the notion of purchasing, managing and further modernising the already completed government-owned Shimbashi-Yokohama branch. Under the new arrangements nineteen individuals were to pay an annual sum of 250,000 yen to accumulate to 2.5 million yen over ten years. At the fifth meeting of 6 May Shibusawa was formally elected to act for the group and he thereupon revised the prescribed annual payments to 430,000 yen, to raise 3 million yen over seven years with the government allowing a 'suitable interest' on the yearly instalments. After this period, if a clear profit of at least 8 per cent per annum was being generated by the line then it 'shall be bought from the government'. At the sixth meeting of 1 June this general plan was accepted, the members guaranteeing the money by giving their incomes as security, and this proposal was put forward in applications to the Ministries of Finance, Public Works, and the Interior. The *Nichi Nichi Shimbun* was not above suggesting to the government that it could utilise the annual contributions to finance its own construction of the originally proposed line, 'by which time some other company may be ready to take it off their hands on similar terms, and thus the Railway *System* may be satisfactorily extended throughout the country'.

Here, then, was an early conception of the promotion of technology through the transfer of government enterprises to private entrepreneurs under very favourable conditions, a process normally linked as we have seen with the Matsukata deflationary measures of the 1880s. By December of that year the plan had been accepted by the authorities. One foreign newspaper did argue that this was a matter of economy and retrenchment as much as of industrial policy, for thereby the government 'will pay much less annually to the purchasers by way of pensions, crediting them with the amount thus unpaid as so much towards the purchase of the line'. With a total purchase price of perhaps some £600,000, this was obviously a significant attempt at industrial entrepreneurship amongst the ex-aristocrats. By December of the following year the *Akebono Shimbun* was reporting that the scheme was formally under way. In fact the project appears to have failed between that time and 1879, when towards the end of that year it was rejuvenated, again under private auspices.

What were the characteristics of the initial group? The key figure was Shibusawa, (1840–1931, see p. 88) who had at one time joined the loyalist movement for the downfall of the Shogunate and the expulsion of the foreign barbarians. Indeed he, with Kisaku Shibusawa plotted the failed attempt to take Takasaki Castle and set fire to Yokohama. After the Restoration, and with a trip to the International Exhibition at Paris behind him, Shibusawa intended to continue in the financial service of Yoshinobu Tokugawa (fifteenth Shogun of that line, 1866–8) at his place of retirement in Shizuoka, but was soon caught up in the financial management of the new state. In 1873, upon resigning from the Ministry of Finance he founded the First National Bank, and thus by the date of the planned railway scheme might be defined as an ex-*samurai*-bureaucratic entrepreneur, e.g. in 1873 he established the Oji Paper Manufacturing Company. Such biography is analytically important, for Shibusawa's *pre*-Meiji background linked such other leading members of the group as Yoshikatsu Tokugawa (1825–83), Munenari Date (1818–92) and Motonori Mōri, (1839–96). Although Shibusawa was of relatively humble background the other members were from more established noble backgrounds. Common ground between members was an earlier resistance to the established Tokugawa line and a later Meiji bureaucratic role (e.g. Date was appointed Finance Minister in 1869, and Minister to China in 1871, Mōri was the Meiji governor of Yamaguchi prefecture, Tokugawa a cabinet counsellor). Such a case, one amongst several such enterprises of the 1870s, suggests a very close relationship between the innovative aristocracy, bureaucratic skills, and government stimulation of private initiatives. Clearly, too drastic a distinction between the private sector and the public sector in Meiji Japan does a disservice to the complexity of the process of industrial development.

After 1884 private enterprise developed rapidly, and men such as Shibusawa and the Ōsaka entrepreneurs began to achieve outstanding success. The number of factories with over 1,000 yen capital rose from 1,298 in 1884 to 4,133 in 1893 with a total capital of 209 million yen. Many such private firms were operating in direct competition with imports, the most impressive of which was Shibusawa's Ōsaka cotton mill, financed by a pool of entrepreneurs, in which over 10,000 spindles were powered by steam. Private railway companies using Japanese engineers now flourished, the best known being the Nippon Railway Company. Even here, however, government assured minimum profits and assisted greatly in securing trained engineers. By 1892 Japan possessed a total of 1,870 miles (3,009 km) of railway, 1,320 miles (2,124 km) of which were privately owned. Total capital invested in railways reached 45 million yen in that year. Although several companies, including the Mitsui, Mitsubishi and Sumitomo *zaibatsu*, formed their own banks, large capital was increasingly obtained through joint stock arrangements.

Private enterprise was not forever waiting in the wings. Private enterprise did not follow from failed government initiatives. Rather, the tortuous emergence of private enterprise was one measure of the success of government intervention in the economy and a sign that the initial period of the industrial drive was over. But even then, the flourishing of industry in the 1890s and 1900s cannot be interpreted other than as a supply side response to the government's involvement in military and colonial expansion and to the cost-reducing impacts of earlier and continuing public sector activity in the fields of infrastructure improvement, technological change and human capital formation.

Notes

1 Almost every significant Western intellectual may be found somehow represented in Meiji Japan. Yet to be fully analysed is the process whereby the almost infinite array of available ideas was filtered into Japan and lodged in specific groups. For an introduction see Carmen Blacker, *The Japanese Enlightenment, A Study of the Writings of Fukuzawa Yukichi*, HUP, Cambridge, Mass., 1969; R. E. Ward (ed.), *Political Development in Modern Japan*, Princeton UP, Princeton, 1968; Joseph Pittau, *Political Thought in Early Meiji Japan 1868–89*, Harvard UP, Cambridge, Mass., 1967.

2 Itagaki led the foundation of the national *Jiyūto* or Liberal Party in 1881 but was, for a while, discredited by the machinations of the regime.

3 Several categories are difficult to translate into Western terms. Most of the special schools were devoted to medicine, law and agriculture in that order of importance. Although Japanese scholars have recently re-evaluated this topic, little yet is available in English. See, however, Yoichi Yano, 'The development of technical education in Meiji Japan – an interpretation', in Ian Inkster (ed.), *The Steam Intellect Societies*, Nottingham University Press, Nottingham, 1985.

4 Given the various emergencies of the 1870s it seems surprising that inflation did not break out prior to 1878. For some discussion of this see Henry Rosovsky, 'Japan's transition to modern economic growth', in Henry Rosovsky (ed.), *Industrialisation in Two Systems*, John Wiley and Sons, New York and London, 1966, especially pp. 127–39. Prices began falling from 1881 and bottomed out in 1886.

5 Ryoshin Minami, *The Economic Development of Japan*, London, Macmillan, 1986, quote p. 155. The authorities are Lockwood's textbook p. 574 and Chalmers Johnson, *Miti and the Japanese Miracle*, Stanford University Press, 1983, p. 88. Lockwood's account is, however, far more subtle than this citation suggests, whilst Johnson uses the phrase 'a more or less orthodox version of *laissez-faire*' in passing and with no substantiation.

References

Green, R. H. (1974) 'The role of the State as an agent of economic and social development in the least developed countries', *Journal of Development Planning* 6, pp. 15–46, especially pp. 37–8.

Smith, T. C. (1955) *Political Change and Industrial Development in Japan: Government Enterprise 1868–80*, Stanford, CA: Stanford University Press, p. 30.

Moore, Barrington Jr. (1969) *Social Origins of Dictatorship and Democracy*, London: Penguin Books, p. 249.

Dower, J. W. (ed.) (1975) *Origins of the Modern Japanese State, Selected Writings of E. H. Norman*, New York: Pantheon Books, p. 447.

Bird, Isabella L. (1880) *Unbeaten Tracks in Japan* (vol. II), London: John Murray, p. 236.

Hagen, E. E. (1958) 'How economic growth begins: a general theory applied to Japan', *Public Opinion Quarterly* 22, p. 389.

Bellah, R. N. (1963) 'Reflections on the protestant ethic analogy in Asia', *Journal of Social Issues* 19, pp. 54–5.

Hirschmeier, J. (1964) *The Origins of Entrepreneurship in Meiji Japan*, Cambridge, MA: Harvard University Press, p. 43.

Further reading

Beasley, W. G. (1972) *The Meiji Restoration*, Stanford, CA: Stanford University Press.

Emi, K. (1963) *Government Fiscal Activity and Economic Growth in Japan 1868–1960*, Tokyo: Kinokuniya.

Emi, K. (1968) 'Economic development and educational investment in the Meiji era', in M. J. Bowman *et al.* (eds), *Readings in the Economics of Education*, Paris, UNESCO.

Gerschenkron, A. (1962) *Economic Backwardness in Historical Perspective*, Cambridge, MA: Harvard University Press.

Gordon, A. (1991) *Labour and Imperial Democracy in Prewar Japan*, Berkeley, CA: University of California Press.

Hall, J. W. and Jansen, M. B. (eds) (1968) *Studies in the Institutional History of Early Modern Japan*, Princeton, NJ: Princeton University Press.

Harootunian, H. D. (1970) *Towards Restoration*, Berkeley, CA: California University Press.

Hirschmeier, J. and Yui, T. (1975) *The Development of Japanese Business 1600–1973*, London: Allen and Unwin.

Inkster, I. (1981) *Science, Technology and the Late Development Effect: Japan's Industrialisation* c. *1850–1912*, Tokyo: Institute of Developing Economies.

Inkster, I. (1996) 'Into the twentieth century: patterns in the relations between science, technology and the state during the early industrialisation process', in Martine Barrere (ed.) *Sciences et Développement*, Paris: ORSTOM, 67–96.

Jones, F. C. (1931) *Extraterritoriality in Japan and the Diplomatic Negotiations Resulting in its Abolition*, New Haven, CT.

Kaldor, M. (1976) 'The military in development', *World Development*, 4: 459–82.

Kelley, A. C. and Williamson, J. G. (1974) *Lessons from Japanese Development*, Chicago.

Kublin, H. (1949) 'The modern army of early Meiji Japan', *Far Eastern Quarterly*, 9: 20–41.

Lindblom, C. E. (1959) 'The science of "Muddling through"', *Public Administration Review*, 19: pp. 79–88.

Liu, K. (1959) 'Steamship enterprise in nineteenth century China', *Journal of Asian Studies*, 18: 438–56.

Lockwood, W. W. (ed.) (1976) *The State and Economic Enterprise in Japan*, Princeton, NJ: Princeton University Press.

Minami, R. (1986) *The Economic Development of Japan*, London: Macmillan, especially pp. 7–9, 148–60, 332–68.

Ohkawa, K. and Shinohara, M. (eds) (1979) *Patterns of Japanese Economic Development: A Quantitative Appraisal*, New Haven, CT: Yale University Press, especially essays by Emi 177–202.

Ranis, G. (1959) 'The financing of Japanese economic development', *Economic History Review*, 2: 441–56.

Reed, E. J. (1880) *Japan: Its History and Tradition*, 2 vols, London.

Rosovsky, H. (1961) *Capital Formation in Japan 1868–1940*, New York: Free Press of Glencoe.

Suyematsu, Baron K. (1905) *The Risen Sun*, London.

Suzuki, N. (ed.) (1975) *Asian Industrial Development*, Tokyo: Institute of Developing Economies.

Takahashi, K. (1941) *The Rise and Development of Japan's Modern Economy*, Tokyo: Jiji Press.

Yamamura, K. (1977) 'Success illgotten? The role of Meiji militarism in Japan's technological progress', *Journal of Economic History*, 37: 113–35.

Yamazawa, I. (1975) 'Industrial growth and trade policy in prewar Japan', *The Developing Economies*, 8: 38–65.

Part II

The expansion of Japan (1912–73)

Introduction

From 1868 Japanese economic development was inherently expansive in at least the sense that it involved foreign trade and foreign investment, the construction of a merchant navy and a conscripted army, the acquisition of essential raw materials from overseas, and the deliberate penetration of other nations through treaty ports, Japanese settlement and commercial diplomacy. As in Europe and America, these were the concomitants of industrial development, although the exact pattern of colonialism varied between industrial nations for a host of reasons, including the timing of industrialisation itself, the geographical location of the nation and the nature of its physical borders and distance from non-industrial nations, the extent of its domestic market and the character of its raw material base, as well as its population dynamics. In 1893 the *Shokumin Kyōkai* or Colonisation Society put forward a demographic or Malthusian case for colonial expansion, claiming that the pressure of population growth would soon outpace the ability of Japan's resource base to feed and clothe the common people. The explicitly imperial expansion of Japan was crowded into the years from 1894 to the 'total surrender' of 1945. After the Second World War Japanese economic expansion was centred on foreign trade and, from the 1980s, foreign investment.

The global flush of imperialism from the 1880s stemmed primarily from the Atlantic industrialisers and has been variously explained as a necessary outcome of the changing imperatives of industrial capitalism. Imperialism represented a vent for surplus, a source of strategic raw materials and foodstuffs, a market for the textile manufacturers of Europe, or in some way was not contingent to but necessary to the further growth of industrial nations.

Recently the returns to colonial expansion in general have been questioned – the costs of colonies were great and certain, the returns relatively uncertain and perhaps no more than might have been gained more familiarly at home and through foreign trade and investment only. In the case of Japan, however, there would appear to have been a strong *prima facie* case for both the economic causes and the vital economic contributions of colonial expansion in the first half of the twentieth century. The colonised areas were undoubtedly sources of raw materials, foodstuffs, skills and cheap labour, and imperialism followed initial industrialisation because it, quite simply, depended on passing a threshold strength of arms, communications and organisation that could not have been obtained prior to the industrial drive of the 1870s and 1880s. Nevertheless, no convincing cost-benefit analysis of Japanese imperialism is available, and it is very feasible that the overall costs of colonialism, even prior to 1943, offset its economic returns in conventional terms. On the other hand, as we argue in Chapters 6 and 7, the *private* returns of imperial adventure were enormous, and the large earnings from colonies for some powerful elements of the Japanese elite (as against its costs for consumers and taxpayers) were essential to its sustenance, and to the hardening of a particular developmental, militarist nexus between government and big business that in turn forged the fast growth and structural changes of the 1890s and 1930s and was, therefore, responsible for the overall strong long-term performance of the economy compared to other nations. In the end, the returns to resisting imperialism in 1868 were indisputably great, but so too were the costs of imperialism as ultimately met in August 1945. Between 1952 and 1973 the Japanese economy went through its greatest period of economic growth, outpacing all other nations during an era of massive global expansion in trade, production and investment. Yet in these two decades, as shown in Chapter 8, the expansive aspects of the Japanese economy were at a minimum.

6 An outline of inter-war economic development (1912–37)

Economic performance

Japan's economic growth in the years from the end of Meiji to the outbreak of war with China (1937) exceeded that of the Meiji years and of any major industrial economy. The average annual growth rate of GNP was over 4 per cent, income per head growing at some 2.6 per cent, significantly greater than that of Germany (1.1 per cent), the US (0.8 per cent) and Britain (0.7 per cent). Yet Japan was badly mauled by the world recession of 1920–1, the traumatic Tokyo earthquake of 1923 and the financial and commercial crises of 1927–31. Given that the period is bounded by war and bisected by international depression, Japan's comparative advantage in the international growth stakes may well have related to the precise manner in which the economic system responded to externally produced shocks, both good and bad.

The good shock was the First World War, (1914–18). Between 1913 and 1920 manufacturing output grew at an average rate of 8.4 per cent per annum, led by the principal export industries of silk and cotton. Between 1913 and 1929 exports rose by 133 per cent, with the textile components increasing rather than decreasing as a proportion of the total. The severely disruptive effects of the war on international trade allowed Japan to rapidly expand exports into imperial markets in Asia, and after the war to expand her markets in the US. Japan gained from both the direct demand effects of war (through exports) and by the related indirect supply effects of the loss of Western machinery and raw material imports. Demand for Japanese manufactured exports invoked organisational and technological changes within a whole range of Japanese industries. At the same time, warfare clearly demonstrated the danger of commercial and technological dependency, particularly in the strategic heavy and engineering industries, and this induced a new surge of government intervention. Between 1914 and 1919 total Japanese industrial production increased six-fold, iron and steel production increased nine-fold with an equal increase in the usage of mining and refining equipment. During the war itself the number of blast and open hearth furnaces increased from

63 to 143 and there was a huge expansion in the number of electrical furnaces used in production. Of course, the boom in such a relatively sophisticated industry could not survive renewed competition with imports and revived technological progress in the West during the 1920s. Trade and production effects such as this probably contributed to the slighter economic growth of the 1920s.

The 1920s were dominated by the fall away in the expansion of the agricultural sector, which grew at less than 1 per cent per annum average for the first time since 1868 and ceased to be the provider of funds to industry. Land reclamation projects reached a plateau prior to 1920 and during the subsequent years agricultural labour was badly underemployed and of low productivity. The diffusion of new seed and plant varieties and techniques had already reached saturation within the existing framework of production, and in the absence of technological breakthrough conditions in the rural economy were undoubtedly worsened by cheap imports from the empire, especially Korea and Taiwan. Agriculture was in receipt of significant government subsidy in the form of aid for fertiliser and light machinery inputs, for the development of cooperatives and for price maintenance. Holdings remained very small and between 1913 and 1938 the proportion of the labour force engaged in agriculture fell from 61 per cent to 46 per cent, this representing an absolute decrease of over 1.5 million persons.

Even in the 1920s both manufacturing and construction growth was considerably greater than that of the older industrial nations, Britain, the US and Germany, and was exceptionally fast at around 9 per cent per annum average in the 1930s. This pattern suggests that Japan more or less shared in the mild or low growth pattern of the world during the 1920s but recovered more effectively from the depression of 1929–31 than did any other large industrial system. The fast growth of manufacturing in the 1930s was associated closely with a continued ease of supply of labour, imperial and military expenditures and contracts, a high level of capital formation and of technological progress through both increased internal capabilities and continued technology transfers from more advanced systems. The falling away of first agricultural growth and then transport improvement, meant that in this period the trajectory of the total economy was increasingly dependent on that of manufacturing.

The textile sector still epitomised the general characteristics of the industrial economy. Cotton textiles effectively combined very cheap young female labour, apprentices and contract workers with modern, state of the art mills, utilising Toyoda automatic looms and adapted spinning equipment to process cheap supplies of Indian short-staple cottons. Of 3 million employees, over 80 per cent were female, the routine workers amongst these being paid the equivalent of 15 (US) cents per day. Like other textile industries (wool, silk) cotton was dominated by the dual existence of small and large plants, not necessarily representing a conventional division of labour but rather the coexistent competition of small and large units producing the same or substitute goods. Around 30 per cent of cotton and rayon piece-goods, 30 per cent of wool, and perhaps 80 per cent of hosiery were produced in establishments of less than fifteen persons. In silk, 60 per cent or more of all manufactured output came from establishments of less than 5 workers. Such shops represented a combination of very variable artisanal skills or routine workers with small investments. The small-scale unit was of similar importance to the manufacturing of bicycles, wood working, chinaware and ceramics, porcelain, toys, hats, jewellery and a variety of small goods and traditional pursuits, from the *tatami* (sleeping mat) to bean curd. In the latter areas, the advantage of the small firm did arise more from the existence of niche markets within Japan. For instance, the innumerable small-scale paper manufacturers produced some 300 different kinds of paper, from writing paper to *shōji* (sliding partitions in houses) to umbrellas and raincoats.

The characteristic organisation of the small-scale firms was the putting out system of the *toiya* commission merchants, who would often obtain their own supplies of basic material from wholesale merchants e.g. as in the Kyoto silk piece goods industry.[1] The *toiya* organised production by contracting with a variety of small manufacturers to produce a general portfolio of goods for systematic sale. The *toiya* managed a great proportion of artisanal production, including its financing and its final sale, and several historians have seen the predominance of the system as a sure relic of feudal socio-commercial organisation. Whatever its lineage, the system did not prevent the diffusion of new techniques. For instance, when the General Electric patents of the Tokyo Electric Light Company expired in 1927 a mass of small companies entered into bulb production based on *toiya* advances and marketing, so that by the mid-1930s TELC's previous monopoly had been replaced by a host of small shops, all serviced by an even greater number of small shop suppliers of filaments, wiring and bases.

For the period 1921–38, the fastest growing areas of manufacturing in Japan were metals and metalworking (over 10 per cent per annum average), chemicals (over 10 per cent), machinery, ceramics and wood products, with the heavy industries growing at twice the rate of textiles and foodstuffs, yielding an overall manufacturing growth rate of some 6.5 per cent per annum, somewhat faster than the first two decades of the twentieth century. However, this result stemmed mostly from the very speedy growth of military-linked heavy industry after 1931, and the still comparatively large size of the textile sector meant overall performance in this period was a function fairly equally of growth in textiles, machinery and chemicals, which together accounted for perhaps 65 per cent of manufacturing growth.

The period 1932–7 was one of fast recovery, jammed in between the crisis and depression of 1931 and the movement towards warfare. The boom was clearly in heavy industry – pig iron production per annum doubled, as did raw steel production, and there was a great growth in the output of explosives, dyestuffs, sulphates and paints. Whereas in 1929 around 55 per cent of factory employees had been in the textile sector, by 1937 this was reduced to 36 per cent. Apart from the military inducement of supplies, the fast growth of these years has been variously explored in terms of low wages resulting from the continued depression of agriculture, a decline in the terms of trade which encouraged a speedy recovery of the export sector, a high savings rate and consequently high investment rate, itself variously explained but partially a reflection of the very pattern of industrial growth (i.e. the relative absence of consumer goods), and, finally, the reflationary or expansionary policies of the Japanese government.

The spurt of growth and structural change of the 1930s yielded a different economic structure, of sufficient extent to prompt the leading Japanese economist Miyohei Shinohara to invoke his 'law of equalisation of growth rates of industries'. By 1936, of 32 million workers in Japan in a population of 70 million, 44 per cent were engaged in agriculture, nearly 25 per cent in manufacturing, some 15 per cent in commerce, 6 per cent in government service and the rest in a variety of domestic services, fisheries, mining, transportation and communications. Of manufacturing workers, by the late 1930s, 22.5 per cent were yet employed in textiles, 7.5 per cent in food and drink processing, 7.2 per cent in wood and bamboo products, and some hefty 50 per cent in a range of heavy industries – machinery and tools, civil engineering, building, metal manufactures, shipbuilding, vehicles and chemicals in descending order of importance. Measured in terms of the value of sales, textiles remained outstanding at 29 per cent of all manufacturing, followed by chemicals at 19 per cent, and metals and metal products at 18 per cent.

Despite the increase in trade restrictions of the period – with significant tariff hikes in China, India and the British Empire – the annual average increase in the dollar value of Japanese exports for the period 1931–7 was 5.2 per cent. This compares with a world export growth of 1.4 per cent, and growth in the US of 1.4 per cent and Britain of 0.1 per cent. What is more, by 1938 nearly 60 per cent of Japanese exports were of finished goods. This export performance has prompted a view that foreign trade forged the trajectory of the economy in at least the 1930s. Arguing that the price elasticity of Japanese exports was high, Shinohara has gone on to conclude that the exchange devaluation of 1931 caused a decline in the terms of trade.

Between 1929 and 1938 (see Table 6.2, p. 109) export prices in terms of gold fell by 71 per cent, the physical quantity of exports rose by 68 per cent, much of this being in the form of cheap textiles to India and Latin America. Textiles provided nearly 50 per cent of commodity exports during the 1920s and 1930s, and of this raw silk was still of tremendous importance followed by cotton and rayon piece-goods. Foodstuffs and other consumables made up 12 per cent of exports, machinery and equipment

10 per cent, the rest composed of a medley of ores and metals (4 per cent), metal manufactures (4 per cent), chemicals and dyes (3 per cent) and a very wide variety of traditional productions in chinaware, glass, paper, toys, wood and dyestuffs. Of great importance, some 40 per cent of imports were of raw materials and fuel (including of course, raw cotton for the principal exporting industry) and 30 per cent were intermediate imports and goods for the heavy industries. Overall, the trade balance was negative for the entire period, as was that of the total balance of payments due to the sucking in of technological and raw material imports and the large exports of capital to the empire. In contrast to Shinohara's emphasis on the mobilising effects of exports, Minami summarises that 'export activities were not the engine of economic growth . . . The engine was capital formation, which created effective demand and worked with the introduction of foreign technology to increase production efficiency and thus to stimulate exports.'

Neither model is conclusive. Clearly, the import of foreign technology was financed by the exports of textiles and other goods, and the gains from exporting were not merely financial but included positive economies associated with improved foreign trade and communication facilities and the availability of a wider range of raw materials. At the same time, the low cost of Japanese exports was not solely a function of exchange devaluation but of organisational and technical innovations within industry, combined with particularly low-cost labour in the principal export sector of textiles. The increase in exports was, thus, some function of internal cost reducing factors in textiles in particular, while the increase in imports was a reflection of economic growth itself rather than of prices on international markets. This combination of forces led to an increase in the trade to GNP ratio in Japan in the face of a general fall in global trade compared to global output associated with the great depression of 1929.

It is very feasible that low export prices were mainly a result of technological and institutional progress in industry. Writing in 1940, the astute observer G. C. Allen was especially impressed with the increase in manufacturing efficiency after 1927 in terms of both costs and quality: 'The quality of her heavy products has improved and her range of output has widened. She has learned both how to manufacture good quality machinery and to use it in manufacturing enterprise with greater skill. The efficiency of her factory managers has risen. The result is that although technique and organisation have improved in other countries, the gap between Japan and the leading Western countries in industrial efficiency has appreciably narrowed.' Gross output per worker in manufacturing possibly doubled during the inter-war years. This was associated with new organisational forms and technological innovations, especially an increase in the effective mechanised power supplied to industry and the great improvement in small manufactures due to more efficient distribution of electric power and the introduction of machine tools and more specialised operations. In cotton spinning a constant output of an improved quality product was created by a significantly decreasing labour force. Transport improvements further cut the costs of export products. Improved technical capabilities still depended on a steady influx of advanced machinery from overseas. The annual average imports of machinery and equipment totalled 120 million yen in the years 1929–33, most of which came from the US. Around 50 per cent of Japanese aircraft industry at the beginning of the Second World War was supplied by foreign capital imports, equipment and training programmes. Of the relationship between the domestic machine industry and imported equipment during the 1930s, Lockwood judged that domestic output now provided a wide range of stable, standard types, and far exceeded imports in gross value. But the latter still supplied a critical technological deficit which was particularly important in the equipment industries themselves.

Dominated by electrical equipment, textile machinery and shipbuilding, the engineering industries employed 100,000 workers by the early 1930s. The great *zaibatsu* companies such as Mitsubishi Heavy Industries (shipbuilding, steel works, power stations, locomotives), Hidachi Engineering Company (electrical equipment, locomotives, steam turbines, motor cars), *Kisha Seizō* (locomotives, steel and textile machinery), Shibaura (Mitsui) Engineering Works (electrical machinery), Miike Machinery Works (mining machinery and electric motors) and Kawasaki (shipbuilders), all manufactured under licence from foreign firms including General Electric. In addition, heavy industry was characterised by joint Japanese–US operations such as Tōyō-Babcock (Mitsui and Babcock and Wilcox), Shibaura (Mitsui and GE) and the Japan Steel Works (Mitsui and Armstrong-Vickers). In several of the newest areas of industry, companies were foreign-owned: the two assembly plants of General Motors and Ford produced 80 per cent of Japanese automobiles by the late 1930s. Whereas in other nations major engineering firms tended to be highly specialised, in Japan these larger firms were extremely broad-based, a result of the history of selective government sponsorship of strategic industries and the relatively high cost of foreign technique.

The increase in manufacturing efficiency should not be unduly generalised as a function of maturing capital goods industries. Each industry was governed by its own specific techniques and inputs. The spread of best technique in spinning was a principal efficiency factor, especially in the form of 'high draft' spinning, which replaced ring spinning and saved labour whilst eliminating roving operations. In weaving, improvements arose from the adoption of automatic looms, light engineering benefited from new machine tools. Generally, Japanese industrial efficiency increased after 1927 as a result of the spread of better techniques, the introduction of some new techniques, organisational changes within firms, and increased industrial specialisation. In some cases, the introduction of imported technique did create real change. In steel-making the importation of new style open-hearth furnaces led to large reductions in fuel costs (e.g. the Rupman furnaces in Kawasaki Dockyards from 1929). Electric smelting of steel developed very rapidly, the number of electric furnaces rising from thirty in 1928, to forty in 1931, to 119 in 1934 with a daily capacity of over 400 tonnes. In rolling mills cost cutting occurred through organisational changes towards mass production, the use of conveyers cutting labour requirements by 60 per cent. Imported equipment and expertise also remained essential in key areas of the chemical industries such as ammonia sulphate manufacture (coke-gas method) and sulphuric acid production ('contact' process).

The structural shift between the 1920s and the 1930s towards the heavy industries suggests a change in the level and distribution of capital formation. The failure of private sector investment in the 1920s dampened overall capital accumulation, but in the 1930s the high rate of growth of capital formation was due equally to private and public sectors. During the 1920s gross domestic fixed capital formation grew at the rate of less than 1 per cent per annum average: during the 1930s it grew at the rate of 11 per cent per annum average, well above the rate of national economic growth. Very noticeable was the great increase in the proportion of producers' durable equipment during the 1930s and the fall away of capital formation in non-military government investment, agriculture, construction and residential buildings, a reflection of the increasing military and imperial trajectory of the economy and the associated high level of technological importing which increased expected returns on capital.

Net capital importing was minimal as Japan exported capital to the new colonies. Net savings had fallen during the 1920s but jumped in the 1930s as a result of a large increase in household and corporate savings. There is much debate over the reasons for the high personal savings rate during the 1930s and thereafter. Apart from a cultural argument centring on the inhibiting effects on consumption of traditional habits of austerity, historians have pointed to low wages, taxation and inflation as the source of high savings. Minami has posited a very convincing argument relating to the structure of employment rather than to income distribution as such. Much of Japanese output of goods and services was produced in small firms and by the self-employed. It seems feasible that at any given income level, the self-employed will have a higher propensity to save than employees of larger firms.

The outflow of labour from agriculture had slowed in the 1920s but accelerated after the depression. Around 50 per cent of the increase in industrial labour was due to inflow from agriculture and other primary sectors. Of course, this may have involved some loss of rural-based manufacturing from by-employments, but over 30 per cent of all workers were self-employed and some 40 per cent of all factory workers were female. Both these latter figures are comparatively high and together served to reduce the militancy of a labour force whose wages were suppressed through the period and who suffered enormously during the depression. Although most of the self-employed were in services and the primary sector, 20 per cent were engaged in manufactures. Unemployment was generally low, with high levels of underemployment (very low productivity work) in the rural areas and in many small services.

The evidence suggests a very elastic supply of labour for employment in the high growth industries. Shinohara and Minami have made a very strong case for the continuation of labour surplus (see Chapter 3 pp. 40–2) through this period and into the post-war years. The evidence points to a particularly high level of surplus in the 1930s. Outside of the skilled and managerial labour of manufacturing, underemployment meant a complete absence of any upward pressure on real wages and an increasing differential of wages between sectors and between firms within a sector. This trend alone was significant in producing the export surge (especially in textiles) and the high ratio of savings and investment to national income, i.e. labour's share of gross national product was small and probably declining in the 1930s.

It was within this demographic and structural context that the larger manufacturing firms adopted new organisational forms – lifetime employment, seniority wage systems and enterprise-based educational schemes. Labour productivity differences were, therefore, increasingly a function of *scale* of enterprise as against sector of employment. It was this which produced measurable wage differentials. By 1932 the wages of small-scale enterprise amounted to 25 per cent or 30 per cent of those in the large manufacturing enterprises. The depression of 1930–1 hit the smaller enterprises first, then affected larger enterprises during 1931, and the large enterprises tended to recover more speedily than the small. Not only may this pattern of recovery have been related to subcontracting and the dualistic employment structure (see p. 109), it may have exacerbated wage differentials based on scale of enterprise. As recovery occurred the larger firms bought out many of the medium size and smaller firms and instituted organisational innovations to secure trained labour in the company. This represented a dramatic episode in a longer trend. Michio Morishima captures the relationships at work succinctly:

> The wage disparity between large and small enterprises developed into a chronic illness of the Japanese economy. Able young people wanted to enter the large enterprises, and the medium and small enterprises had to take those who were left over. Therefore the large enterprises were able to recruit workers who were already outstanding when they entered the company. This contributed to a widening of productivity differentials which already existed. As wage rate differentials became even greater profit differentials also increased and large enterprises could accumulate capital more rapidly than the medium and small enterprises. The large enterprises had sufficient capital to

> take up the best technology, and the technological difference which was thus produced brought with it further increases in productivity and, therefore in wage differences. In this way a vicious circle came into being with the difference in wages between medium and small enterprises and large enterprises becoming greater and greater.

Within the large company flowed the rewards of growth. The educated and the modern skilled employees were increasingly locked into particular large companies (rather than industrial specialisms) just as the so-called 'unskilled' (in fact, generally skilled as against specialised) and under-employed competed for better conditions and wages in agriculture, services and manufacturing subcontracting. As to the latter, well over 30 per cent of manufacturing workers were in establishments of less than fifty workers, where a significantly lower labour productivity resulted from lesser skills, older equipment and a smaller amount of equipment per worker. External institutional factors were important to the configuration of this system: government policy encouraged large firm development just as small enterprises found it very difficult to obtain investment funds from the banking system.

Clearly, the emergence of industrial dualism of this sort was, in the expression of Morishima, 'inextricably linked' with the shift to heavy industries during the 1930s and thus to the government's military programme and the continued rise of the great *zaibatsu* firms. Of course, the latter two – the *zaibatsu* and imperial militarism – were themselves inextricably linked. Outstanding amongst the *zaibatsu* were Mitsui, Mitsubishi and Sumitomo, holding companies controlling operating plants over a wide range of industries in manufacturing, banking and mining. Others such as Asano and Furukawa specialised in single industries (cement, metals) and all of these and most others were descended from the 1880s or earlier (see Chapter 5). Yet others – in particular, Nissan – were deliberate creations of the state's military and imperial ambitions. The concentration of ownership was maintained and encouraged by government through cartellisation and mergers, a spectacular example being the absorption of five private companies by the Yawata Iron Works (see Chapters 3 and 4) in 1934 to form Nippon Iron and Steel.[2] Concentration of banking by merger led to the predominance of just four huge *zaibatsu* concerns. As with self-employment, historians have seen the strength of the *zaibatsu* as derived from paternalism if not feudalism in labour relations, which in turn retarded the growth of a business middle class, dampened the domestic consumer market and, therefore, created an aggressive export orientation and imperial expansion. Unequal income distribution meant a crisis of underconsumption and imperialism developed as a search for secure markets. More potently, *zaibatsu* dominance affected internal political developments by dampening medium size business and allying national economic and commercial policies to the business strategies of very large firms. On the other hand, *zaibatsu* resource concentration might have hastened overall industrial and economic growth by efficiently utilising scarce managerial and other resources, especially in the recovery from depression, and diffusing technologies and information between industries and between the financial and production systems.

The growth rate of government expenditure was consistently greater than that of national income, and measurably accelerated during times of military crisis such as the Shantung Expedition of 1927–8, the Manchurian Incident of 1931–2 and the Sino-Japanese and Pacific War after 1937. Total government expenditure as a proportion of national income rose from around 30 per cent in 1920 to 40 per cent in 1930 and 45 per cent in 1940. War brought inflationary financing through bank issues and borrowings and special accounts were established for financing imperial expenses in Kwantung, Taiwan, Manchuria and Korea, expenditures here being met by a combination of territorial taxation, transfers and bond issues. As early as 1920 total expenditure by the Japanese government in the empire equalled 238 million yen. As a result of warfare and empire expenses, special accounts rose as a proportion of the total budget to around 60 per cent. Again, the rise of government expenditure after 1931 was also part of Korekiyo Takahashi's reflationary policies. As a result of both militarism and inflation, the growth rate of government expenditure was constantly greater than that of other nations. But government utilised other means with which to influence the direction of the economy. In foreign trade, tariffs were replaced by surcharges but restrictions were removed from the import of strategically necessary capital goods and raw materials, and quality control measures were established for exports. Industrial structure was greatly influenced by legislation, particularly the Vital Industries Central Law (1931), the Munitions Industry Mobilisation Law (1937), the National General Mobilisation Law (1938) and in 1939 a series of controls over prices. As Morishima concludes, in this way 'by 1940 the government and the army had taken a complete hold over the Japanese economy'. Government was vital to the fast development of the heavy industries in the 1930s. Of these, the chemical industry, aluminium and copper processing were the least dependent, and all benefited considerably from improved supplies of hydroelectric power. Government's 'hold' over the economy was exerted through a mix of preferential tax treatments, variable levels of protectionism, direct aid, especially to strategic industries, generalised export promotion (tax rebates, export associations, subsidies) and direct contracting with firms for the increased supplies required by army, navy and transport systems. Finally, government maintained its long interest in technological importation. In the 1930s it was the government which purchased the best Swedish, Swiss and German machine tools and brought in foreign engineers and encouraged experiment in the production of Japanese machine tools. Subsequently, machine tool manufacture was strictly licensed by government, and official guarantees of orders encouraged private capital into the industry. By 1940 the machine tool industry was producing at a rate five times that of 1935 and was dominated by Mitsui, Mitsubishi and Nissan, all beneficiaries of government intervention.

Japan in context

The particular character of the Japanese economy in contrast to those of other industrial nations was illustrated best in the years of depression from 1929. Setting industrial production for each nation at 100 in 1929, the national figures for 1932 are Japan at 98, Britain at 84, France at 72, Germany and the US each at 53. The epicentres of the slump were in the US and Germany.[3] In Japan, the slump was initially transmitted through the silk trade. The value of raw silk exports fell from 781 million yen in 1929 to 417 million in 1930 and 355 million in 1931, mostly through a drastic fall in export prices rather than volumes. Although this brought great hardship to the rural community and to some textile centres, employment and production did not fall as drastically as elsewhere, as most of the adjustment to the collapse of demand took the form of wage and price falls. According to Arthur Lewis the falling export prices helped to prevent export volumes falling as much as they did in other countries; and at the same time falling internal prices enabled the farmers to maintain to some extent their consumption of manufactures.

Japan is also distinguished in terms of its speed of recovery. The reflationary policy of Korekiyo Takahashi began in 1932 – between 1931 and 1932 the national debt rose by 546 million yen and continued to increase steadily throughout the 1930s. Industrial production rose immediately, as did imports of raw materials and machinery. Yen depreciation was pursued in order to produce a reasonably balanced trade; by 1933 the yen had lost about 65 per cent of its gold value, in contrast to sterling and the dollar, both of which had fallen by around 40 per cent. The consequent rapid expansion of exports was led by textiles and was accompanied by price cutting and aggressive competition among Japanese manufacturers. Unfortunately for the status of Japanese foreign relations more generally, the nation's export performance prompted tariff retaliation in early 1933 and a British–Japanese trade conference in which the Japanese refused to restrict exports in textiles outside of the direct domain of British producers.

The early recovery of industrial Japan led to trade pressures in most world markets and over a range of products by 1933–4. In standard textiles (silks and cottons), new textiles (artificial silk and woollen goods) and a range of other manufactured goods (bicycles, electrical fittings, pottery, cement), Japanese exporters penetrated not only India (Japan's most important market after China and the US) but other parts of Asia and Europe. This early performance (to 1934) was undoubtedly a result of a variety of factors aiding the impact of yen depreciation – the considerable extension

Table 6.1 Index of industrial production, June 1932 to June 1934 (1928 = 100)

	Index numbers		
Country	*1932*	*1933*	*1934*
Japan	108.9	126.0	143.5
US	53.2	82.9	77.5
UK	89.4	91.7	104.0
Germany	60.7	69.5	68.1
France	73.2	87.4	78.0

of modernised production and new technologies, subsidised freights and falling wages. From the middle of 1932 to the end of 1933 wages fell substantially although production rose by 30 per cent, and wholesale prices for goods of domestic consumption remained steady. Table 6.1 illustrates the extent of recovery by 1932 and the continued rate of growth to 1934 compared to the four major industrial nations of the West. Note that the index is set at 1928 = 100 for each nation.

It is noteworthy that Japanese recovery was associated with armaments expenditure. Expenditure on armament, even excluding special accounts (see p. 106) rose significantly in 1931–4, to around 180 per cent of the 1929 level, whereas in the other nations of Table 6.1 armaments expenditure remained about constant, and with the exception of France failed to reach the levels of 1929 by 1934. Even other nations who were engaged in hostilities, such as Peru, Bolivia, Columbia and Paraguay, did not increase expenditure on armaments within this short period. Clearly, armaments expenditure in Japan was strongly associated with the significant structural shift away from textiles (in exports and in production) and towards engineering, metals and chemicals. In contrast to Germany or the United States, a large proportion of Japanese government expenditure was directed to armaments rather than social welfare or public works. Arthur Lewis has judged that, in Japan, 'reflation was largely war preparation'. But if Japan seems to illustrate a link between inflation, militarism and recovery, specific conditions of supply must be acknowledged. In particular, inflation was surely held down by the real wage falls of an underemployed labour force, a force acting throughout the 1930s (see pp. 103–5). At the same time, the institutional structures which encouraged a high rate of national savings and investment led to a *relative* ease of supply of capital and new (often imported) capital goods.

Interpretations

It seems possible that the earlier emphasis on the dynamic role of exports in Japanese economic growth must be qualified. This is not to say that

Table 6.2 Export indices for five nations, 1936–38 (1929 = 100)

Country	*Price in gold (A)*	*Quantum (B)*	*Total value in gold (A × B%)*
Japan	29	168	49
US	45	74	33
UK	50	78	39
Germany	64	62	39
France	51	55	28

there were not obvious gains from trade nor that Shinohara's points relating exports and the declining terms of trade to strong economic performance after 1931 are invalid. Table 6.2 (from Arthur Lewis) suggests that for Japan at least, currency depreciation and the declining terms of trade were associated with the least contraction of exchange receipts amongst industrial nations between 1929 and 1938.

But the Japanese result may as well be interpreted as a reflection of determined government reflation and promotion of exports combined with internal conditions permitting an ease of supply of labour and capital to the fastest growing and increasingly export oriented industrial sectors.

There are several pointers to the importance of industrial structures and, particularly, to the various phenomena associated with industrial dualism. Elizabeth Boody Schumpeter, writing in 1940, believed that the recovery of the 1930s could not be explained in terms of either price effects or government military expenditure, but rather the 'recovery must be explained in terms of cooperation between business, labour and government for a common purpose'. Much of such 'cooperation' in fact involved coercion and took place mainly within large firms and at the interface between them and their small suppliers. The smaller firms employed many women and temporary workers on very low wages and in insecure positions; as late as 1935 over 50 per cent of farm families had some member employed part time in industry. In contrast, the fast developing heavy industries relied increasingly upon full-time and permanent skilled male employees. In the 'first class' labour market large firms in the metal and chemical industries selected school and college graduates 'premised on a tacit undertaking of loyalty over a lifetime' (Morishima).

The domestic labour market paid growth dividends, including those stemming from paternalistic labour relations. In the large modern firms emerged the new institutionalisation of the *ie* or household notion, from the family to the workplace. The family enterprise idea readily integrated such components as age seniority, internal training (socialisation) and group incentive schemes. As Fumihiko Satofuka expresses it, 'the traditional culture was resurrected again to mollify workers'. Perhaps of just as much importance in generating quietism and limited horizons, the commitment of educated and valued workers to particular enterprises removed from the working people of Japan a potentially active and informed leadership. This divorce of the new labour aristocracy from the bulk of the unskilled was completed in the process of mobility within the large firm. By the late 1920s age seniority was increasingly linked to the movement of individual workers from manual to non-manual jobs on command at various stages of their career in the company.

On the other side of the labour equation, the great importance of subcontracting to the large firms and the elastic supply of unskilled workers together meant that the natural bargaining power of workers in small firms was minimal. Government regulation furthered control over the diverse labour force of the small firms. By the Major Export Industries Guild Act of 1925 small manufacturers were permitted to form guilds (*kōgyō kumiai*) which had rights of quality control, equipment supply and marketing.[4] Government subsidised the guilds, contracted loans for them and exempted them from business and income taxes. The number of guilds rose from 111 in 1930 to 662 by 1935. By December of 1937 the 88,000 member firms of guilds supplied around 25 per cent of Japan's total industrial production. In various ways the guilds became instruments of government control, through quality and standardisation inspections, through regulation of output, prices and sales, through the establishment of joint manufacturing facilities (pottery, rolling steel, finishing cloth) and equipment supply and through the provision of financial services, reducing somewhat the older powers of the merchant groups (see p. 99). Such guild regulation, with the emphasis on cooperation and inter-firm self-help and information dispersal, may well have served to reduce tensions between large firms and small and to ameliorate working conditions within the latter.

The speedy recovery from depression after 1931 may have owed a great deal to the domestic labour market. Unemployment effects were reduced at least partly because the larger firms protected their 'family' members by working at low capacity and offering shorter hours rather than dismissal. Costs were further cut by dismissing casual and temporary workers, cutting bonuses and supply contracts with small firms or forcing down the supply price of the small contractors. As against the micro-economic losses incurred in other nations, the modern enterprise in Japan secured the benefits of in-house training during and immediately following the depths of the recession. This may help to explain the strong rise in private investment during the earliest phases of recovery. Unemployment was minimised and felt mainly by casual and temporary workers. Small firms who could not survive the recession were in many cases bought up by their erstwhile large-firm customers who recovered the most speedily after 1932. So the recovery of Japan was firm and fast because recession was felt in the form of wage and price falls rather than through the collapse of output and resource employment. The labour cost cutting component of the fall in wages was not primarily produced through outright unemployment but through great reductions in bonuses and contract prices, reduced work hours in modern firms, the reduced wages of the self-employed, casual and part-time labour as well as the bulk of workers in small supplier firms. At the point when in many western economies workers were laid off directly, in Japan the contracts to suppliers were cut or their prices were bargained down. Conflict in labour relations was, then, at least partially shifted from the larger growing firms to the small enterprises. The large firm in Japan was in a strategically better position from which to exploit improved commercial conditions than were comparablc enterprises in Europe or America.

Synthesis

Military and imperial demands forged the trajectory of the economy. Of the success of Japanese deficit spending in the early 1930s, Arthur Lewis has judged that 'if the Japanese government had spent money on building houses and on public works instead of on armaments, there is no reason to think that reflation would have been less successful'. But this may be a little dismissive. Of the very great increases in government expenditures in 1932 and 1933, approximately 50 per cent were accounted for by increased military spending. By 1935 nearly 80 per cent of the total *rise* in government expenditure had been in military accounts. Although it may be true that large government demand in the form of public works or social overheads and services would have exerted strong multiplier effects through employment and income, it would not have had an equivalent impact on technological change, technological transfers, reorganisation of enterprises in heavy industries, and labour training processes. Again, other forms of government expenditure might have sucked in more consumer imports or discouraged the structural changes of the 1930s. As Lewis himself emphasised, in a period of just five years Japan 'had accomplished a remarkable diversification of her production and trade'. Furthermore, a high level of military expenditure is evident for the years prior to 1929 as well as for the short recovery period 1931–4, when military expenditure in other nations was far less or falling. Between 1910 and 1940 the pattern of direct military expenditure in Japan was similar to that of other industrial nations, but tended to be at a higher level. Even admitting that government bonds were often issued for several purposes, total military expenditure moved continuously upwards as a percentage of total government spending, increased during war and forced up total government expenditure *after each* war because 'military incidents permanently expanded the scope of government activity ... War seems to have been the greatest stimulus to the expansion of the economy' (Emi).

The factors behind the relative ease of supply of manufactured goods explain Japan's ability to maintain high deficit expenditures on military and imperial projects and yen depreciation in the face of increasing global prices for primary products all without instigating runaway inflation. Arthur Lewis' summary of the forces behind 1930s recovery embraces in brief most of the characteristics of the economy emphasised on pp. 97–111.

> The decline of silk production, coupled with general agricultural depression, forced hundreds of thousands of young women on to the labour market. Women's wages fell sharply, and industrial expansion occurred without any pressure on the wage level . . . only the weakness of the trade union movement made it possible. The net result was that profits increased enormously as a proportion of the national income, and large voluntary entrepreneurial savings offset the government's expenditure, and prevented inflation.

The forces behind the supply of cheap labour were by no means merely demographic but were far more clearly *institutional*. Industrial dualism allowed the absorption of large amounts of low paid labour at the same time as some skilled labour and capital were concentrated in fast growing sectors. The latter were also the sectors of the new enterprise culture, with its emphasis on labour commitment and in-house training. The burden of recession was primarily felt outside of this 'modern' sector of the economy, within the smaller, regulated enterprises, particularly in textiles, agriculture and traditional goods industries and amongst casual workers and the self-employed. The same institutional characteristics may well have generated the high savings and investment rates demonstrated throughout these years, but particularly in the 1930s. Whereas very high rates of enterprise profits in the early years created a high rate of industrial capital formation (which increased from 644 million yen in 1913 to 2,829 million yen in 1920), the capital formation of the 1930s and its associated new technologies was a function of institutionalised low wages, employment structure and taxation.

Themes

A major theme in the interpretation of the economic dynamics of this period must surely be that of industrial structure and, in particular, industrial dualism based on the size of firms rather than the industrial category of firms. The modern industrial sector of Japan in these years was overwhelmingly composed of large firms, who had grown through merger and conglomeration under government financial and other auspices. Themes for interpretation here revolve around militarism and imperial expansion (see also Chapter 7) and the characteristically complex relations between private and public sectors.

The flexibility of the Japanese economy, however, owed more to the preponderance of small firms in all industries. Understanding of the origins and workings and economic role of the small and medium size enterprises is of major concern to interpretation of the inter-war period, for this was the sector that was tempered in prosperity and bore the brunt of adjustment in recession. In 1930, 80 per cent of the industrial labour force were employed in enterprises of less than 100 employees, nearly 60 per cent in establishments of under five employees. Understanding of the *chōshō shōkōgyō* (medium and small enterprises) sector requires the acknowledgement of great variation. Those firms who provided traditional consumption items (including building materials) tended to employ artisanal workers and to be organised by merchants. The survival of these firms can best be explained in terms of traditional consumption patterns, labour surplus and, in some cases such as silk, export demand. Another category of sundry producers utilised imported and modernised technologies. Most characteristic of Japan, contractors represented a third group of Japanese smaller firms and were prominent in engineering, shipbuilding and transport and often operated in the suburban vicinity of very large producers. Less dependent on traditional skills, this last type of firm was highly dependent on orders and technological and financial assistance from the modern sector. All types of small firms were in some manner dependent on the widespread diffusion of modern technologies, from the Toyoda power loom to the utilisation of power in the form of small capacity electric motors. The common availability of small unit electrical power allowed further technical shifts, such as that from treadle looms to power looms in weaving, which raised labour productivity and allowed such firms to continue even in areas where they competed for markets with large enterprises. Minami has noted that the use of electric power in small plants followed directly on earlier transfers of foreign technology into Japanese power plants and at the same time was probably responsible for the survival of many of the small firms during the difficult years from 1927 to 1932. In particular, many workers were discharged from large firms during the 1920s and were absorbed into the small sector, a process which would not have been possible without an improvement in technology in the small enterprises.

This chapter has, thus, suggested some essential links between labour supply, industrial structure and institutional and technological change. The links were forged in a world of imperial expansion, civil contest and, ultimately, war, in which reflationary policies awaited drastic changes of regime and moderation succumbed to assassination. Once more, a key to the dynamics of the economy lies in the political system.

Notes

1 In the silk industry in particular, the *toiya* or *tonya* commission merchants provided advances to reelers and weavers and received consigned silk to sell to the large export houses in Yokohama or Kōbe or to provincial merchants for local marketing. Many merchants, including the large concerns in Kyoto, had their own mills and

factories also, and were involved in financing of retail distribution through *depāto* (department stores). In some industries *toiya* provided new power driven machinery to independent producers or paid for machine depreciation. With their highly specialised marketing and technical skills, the *toiya* were a major factor in the diffusion of information and technique amongst small firms and an important component of their survival during the difficult years of the 1920s and depression – see pp. 108–11.

2 Prior to this the state-controlled Yawata Works provided most of the iron and steel together with companies under the control of Mitsui, Mitsubishi, Sumitomo, Okura and Asano. The new company employed some 27,000 workers out of 67,000 in the industry and was capitalised to 360 million yen, over 60 per cent of which was held by the state. For Nissan see Chapter 7.

3 Between 1929 and 1932 national income in the US contracted by nearly 40 per cent and unemployment reached 15 million. It is noteworthy, in contrast to Japan, that a principal background factor was the slowdown in investment after a significant rise in the earlier 1920s. Again, in attempting to isolate Japan's relative success, the great dependence of the US economy on raw materials, the price of which fell over a period, contrasts with Japan's dependence on raw material imports. German collapse was triggered by easy credit (leading to investment increasingly financed by foreign borrowings rather than internal savings) followed by highly restrictive conditions in 1928–9.

4 Earlier, in the 1880s, government had encouraged the growth of *Dōgyō Kumiai* or trade associations for the purpose of quality control and inspection in important export areas. The *Kōgyō Kumiai* or manufacturers associations were more clearly designed to regulate and encourage small enterprises *per se.*

References

Minami, Ryōshin (1986) *The Economic Development of Japan, A Quantitative Study,* London: Macmillan.

Allen, G. C. in E.B. Schumpeter (ed.) (1940) *The Industrialisation of Japan and Manchukuo 1930–1940*, New York: Macmillan, pp. 477–786.

Lockwood, W. W. (1968) *The Economic Development of Japan*, Princeton, NJ: Princeton UP.

Morishima, Michio (1992) *Why Has Japan Succeeded? Western Technology and the Japanese Ethos*, Cambridge: Cambridge University Press, quote pp. 110–12.

Lewis, W. Arthur (1949) *Economic Survey 1919–1939*, London: Allen and Unwin, (1970 edition), quotations pp. 115–24.

Schumpeter, E. B. (ed.) (1940) *The Industrialisation of Japan and Manchukuo 1930–1940*, New York: Macmillan.

Satofuka, Fumihiko (1992) 'Some aspects to the debate on scientific tradition in Japan (III)', *Historia Scientiarum* 2(1).

Emi, Koichi (1963) *Government Fiscal Activity and Economic Growth in Japan 1868–1960*, Tokyo: Kinokuniya.

Minami, Ryōshin (1976) 'The introduction of electric power and its impact on the manufacturing industries: with special reference to smaller scale plants', in Hugh Patrick (ed.) *Japanese Industrialisation and its Social Consequences*, Berkeley, CA: University of California Press.

Further reading

Broadbridge, S. (1966) *Industrial Dualism in Japan: A Problem of Economic Growth and Structural Change,* London: Frank Cass.

Fukasaku, Y. (1992) *Technology and Industrial Development in Pre-War Japan. Mitsubishi Nagasaki Shipyard 1884–1934*, London: Routledge.

Garon, S. (1987) *The State and Labor in Modern Japan*, Berkeley, CA: University of California Press.

Goldsmith, R. W. (1983) *The Financial Development of Japan, 1868–1977*, New Haven, CT: Yale University Press.

Gordon, A. (1985) *The Evolution of Labour Relations in Japan: Heavy Industry, 1853–1955*, Cambridge, MA: Harvard University Press.

Hazama, H. (1997) *The History of Labour Management in Japan*, (translation ed. 1997, M. Sako and E. Sako) Basingstoke: Macmillan.

Klein, L. and Kazushi, O. (eds) (1968) *Economic Growth: The Japanese Experience since the Meiji Era*, Homewood, IL: Richard D. Irwin.

Large, S. (1981) *Organised Workers and Socialist Politics in Interwar Japan*, Cambridge: Cambridge University Press.

Marshall, B. (1967) *Capitalism and Nationalism in Prewar Japan*, Stanford, CA: Stanford University Press.

Mason, M. (1992) *American Multinationals in Japan*, Cambridge, MA: Harvard University Press.

Miyazawa, K. (1964) 'The dual structure of the Japanese economy and its growth pattern', *The Developing Economies*, 2: 147–70.

Morley, J. W. (ed.) (1971) *Dilemmas of Growth in Pre-War Japan*, Princeton, NJ: Princeton University Press.

Nakamura, T. (1966) 'The modern industries and the traditional industries at the early stage of the Japanese economy', *The Developing Economies*, 4: 567–93.

Nakamura, T. (1983) *Economic Growth in Prewar Japan*, New Haven, CT: Yale University Press.

Shinohara, M. (1961) *Growth and Cycles in the Japanese Economy*, Tokyo: Kinokuniya.

Yonekura, S. (1994) *The Japanese Iron and Steel Industry 1850–1990*, New York: St Martin's Press.

7 Empire, war and occupation

The 1920s

Prior to 1929 Japan emerged more fully on to the international stage, just as the nation's political system became correspondingly more democratic and open to debate and change. Japan's alliance with Western nations during 1914–18 was continued in the Siberian Expedition of 1918. The victory of the Bolsheviks in Russia after 1917 abetted Japan's emergence as an international power. The 1919 Versailles Peace Conference gave Japan a permanent seat as a member of the Big Five in the League Council of the League of Nations, and assigned to Japan former German rights over Shantung. The 1921 Washington Conference permitted Japan to maintain war shipping in the ratio of three ships to every five American or British.

Internal political developments were equally dramatic and seemingly symptomatic of an irreversible turning point in the nation's political history. The early twentieth century had witnessed the rise of political parties, popular and effective protests against government policy (including increased taxation and military spending) and demands for effective constitutional government. This last was often associated with demands for the overthrow of the old oligarchy of Meiji politicians and bureaucrats. The rice riots of 1918[1] strengthened the move towards universal suffrage that had begun in the last years of the nineteenth century. As the *Ōsaka Asahi* newspaper noted in August 1918, by this time the people of Japan were no longer automatically supportive of imperial expansion (e.g. the Siberian expedition) at the cost of what they now perceived to be their own welfare. The object of the three-party coalition of 1924 was to 'protect constitutional government' and reduce the tremendous power of the bureaucracy and the House of Peers (Upper House). Increasingly if tortuously, the party leaders realised the necessity to enlist widespread support for reform, a requisite of which was an extension of the franchise.

By the 1920s the demand for universal suffrage was backed by the labour unions and students. The number of labour unions grew from forty in 1917 to 300 by 1922, and from 1919 the *Yūaikai* (Friendly Society), the major union federation, linked extension of suffrage to the reform of legislation to free up the union movement. The manhood suffrage bill was passed in 1925 and the years from then to 1931 were ones of party government and at least a general acceptance of the notion that cabinet was responsible to the Diet and therefore to the electorate. From 1926 the period was named *Showa*, meaning 'enlightened peace', but many contemporaries also saw these years as a transition to '*Ero, Guro, Nansensu*' i.e. eroticism, grotesquerie and nonsense. Alongside the emergence of socialism (the Japanese Communist party was founded in 1922), which thrived within the newer heavy industry sector, the urban areas spawned higher incomes and Western fashions. Here thrived the Western-style youths, sharing new clothes and a disrespect for elders. The atmosphere of change and dissolution was certainly heightened with the great Tokyo earthquake of 1923, which killed 100,000 Japanese and ruined most of Yokohama and much of Tokyo.

There was something of solidity in all of this. It is true that the 'emperor system' was never convincingly tackled by the democratic forces and that the core bureaucracy never lost effective power, but, indeed, became a focus for the later transition to militarism. Within the system of competing political parties, democracy did not sit easily alongside the strong idea of *kokutai* (national polity) and notions of an organic unity between emperor, parliament and people. It was, consequently, difficult to shift the Diet uncompromisingly towards the centre of the political process. Nevertheless, the growing importance of the middle class did introduce a strong strain of bourgeois liberalism into Japan, just as the alliances of the *zaibatsu* gave power to the hands of the major parties. Businessmen were generally against the high taxes required for armaments build-up, and many were convinced that trade was a more efficient weapon of competition than were war and colonialism.

Depression outcomes

> The emotions aroused by the agony of the countryside were in a real sense revolutionary.
>
> (W. G. Beasley 1963)

It might appear that the political repercussions of economic depression would be minimal in Japan in comparison with other industrial nations. In contrast to the major powers, Japan continued to show a positive rate of economic growth throughout the period 1929–33, and was in full recovery during 1932–3. Compared to the 1929 levels, Japanese exports had recovered by 1931, industrial production by 1932. The highest level of unemployment, in 1932, was less than 7 per cent and the adjustment appears to have taken the form of falling prices and a decline in the terms of trade (see Chapter 6). Despite all of this, the depression coincided with a decisive turn towards militarism, colonialism and authoritarianism.

Even before 1929 there had developed within the army a notion of 'Showa Restoration' as state socialism administered by a military dictatorship. The widely circulated and influential, *The Reconstruction of Japan* of 1919 by Ikki Kita presented anti-capitalist formulae, advocated imperialism abroad and state socialism at home and demanded supreme power for the armed forces.[2] During the 1920s the alienation of the army was exacerbated in the corruption of Diet politics – rowdy brawls replaced debate, bribery infiltrated elections. But the years following 1932 were clearly those of the decline of democratic institutions and opinions. The break was marked by assassinations – of former finance minister Junnosuke Inoue in February 1932, of Mitsui director Takuma Dan in March and of Prime Minister Tsuyoshi Inukai in May. The latter was shot down by nine naval and army cadets, no perpetrators of murder received full punishment, and the incidents marked the end of party cabinets until 1946. Yukio Ōzaki, a progressive Diet member, long labelled the 'tribune of the people' expressed the new mixture of fatalism and violence which threatened the democratic forces of Japan in a letter to his son:

> Assassination is now much in vogue in Japan and any patriotic expression of opinion may expose me to danger . . . For a public man the best form of death is to fall victim to the cold hand of the assassin. Mr Inukai, my old friend, was killed in his official residence. I could not help envying him; it was a death befitting a statesman.

The tenets of 'national learning' had now entered the schools at the expense of the academic curriculum, and university professors had long been subject to threat. As early as 1920 an economist of Tokyo had been imprisoned for writing on Kropotkin and this had been followed by mass meetings of students. After 1931 the student movement was more visible and organised. Six thousand students of Tokyo Imperial University joined Kyoto students in protest against the dismissal of Kyoto professor Yukitoki Takigawa in 1933, which followed from his declaring that the laws of any country were conditioned by economic structure i.e. for espousing a mild form of historical materialism. Protests led to a general strike of students.

The election of 1936 symbolised the rise of militarism and the failure of the democratic process. Many militarist and extreme nationalist candidates stood for election, but most suffered disastrous defeat at the hands of the progressive parties, especially the *Minseito* and the Social Mass Party, as well as liberal independents. But this result precipitated the military uprising of 26 February 1936, the most violent *coup d'état* that Japan had witnessed since 1877. The insurgents were young army officers who, on occupying the centre of Tokyo, issued edicts against the *zaibatsu* and the political parties in the name of the Emperor. Increasingly the government acted as a branch of the military: the proportion of the budget devoted to the armed forces rose towards 50 per cent. During the general elections of 30 April 1937 (just prior to the invasion of China) the government ordered provincial chiefs of police to prohibit all statements 'charging the military with trying to provoke a war, alleging that the fighting services mean to reject the parliamentary system, arousing suspicion about obedience to orders in the services, or affecting the attitude of the people towards the conscription system'.

Yet most of foreign policy was directed by the right wing forces in the army. The invasion of Manchuria in September 1931 was undertaken by the army of its own volition, leaving the Diet with a *fait accompli*, and it was army pressure which led to the formation of the state of Manchukuo. In 1932 the advance in Mongolia compelled the Chinese to accept the political and commercial penetration of the northern provinces generally. In 1932 the Japanese left the League of Nations following that organisation's condemnation of the Manchuria incident. By 1935–6 Japan was in a position of economic and political isolation in which only the army had power. Skirmishes with the Chinese around Peking in 1936 led in effect to an invasion of China in 1937.

The collapse of liberalism and democratic institutions during the 1930s has been interpreted in several ways, some of which stress factors supposedly unique to Japan, such as the virulence of the 'emperor' philosophy. But it may instead be argued that democracy failed when economic depression was juxtaposed with late development, and that the doctrines of nationalism, expansionism, militarism and communalism which then flowed throughout the nation were measures of political breakdown rather than the *cultural causes* of political breakdown.

The failure of the US market for Japanese silk directly affected some 2 million farm families in Japan. Between 1929 and 1933 income from rice and silk dropped by 50 per cent, yet the large *zaibatsu* firms maintained the prices of manufactured inputs and fertilisers. At this time, 40 per cent of the value of agricultural produce of tenant farmers went to landlords. Small landlords attempted to secure additional rents to pay interest on bank debts by shifting the weight of their losses on to the tenantry. The impact of cheap colonial foodstuffs and the bad harvests of 1931–2 furthered the ruination of the countryside and generated a vast increase in tenancy disputes, riots, strikes and lockouts. In the Tokyo district alone during 1932 the number of persons requiring basic assistance was officially estimated at 2 million, and throughout the nation many were reduced to eating bracken, roots and rice husks. According to the journal Chūō Kōron, 614 young girls left a single village in Nagano Prefecture, 279 going to work as servants and 325 as prostitutes. In the small department of Iwate girls were sold for as little as 50 yen each. Tenancy disputes accelerated, from the 5,600 recorded for 1926–8, to 7,600 for 1929–31 and 12,000 for 1932–4, most of these being centred on evictions and involving riots and forced food distributions as well as the sacking and burning of landlord residences. Agrarian violence generally exceeded that associated with urban labour disputes. Given that the agrarian depression was seen as stemming from international factors and that the *zaibatsu* firms were seen as beneficiaries of distress and allied with major parties in the Diet, it was to some extent inevitable that much of the energy of rural protest would be generated away from the parliamentary process and towards alternative sources of power and legitimacy. Most army officers (although not necessarily those actually involved in insurrections) came from the middle and small landlord classes whose profits were severely cut by the fall in agricultural prices and the resistance of the tenants. The majority of army soldiers were from tenant or peasant proprietor families. Apart from their familial links with the peasantry, army leaders swayed the countryside through the rural school teachers, many of whom had undergone a period of military service, and the rural branches of the Society of Reservists. Extreme agrarian populists and militarists such as Kozaburo Tachibana ran doctrinal seminaries, in his case the Native-Land-Loving School which preached that the 'politicians and financiers have strayed from the spirit of patriotic brotherhood which is the fundamental characteristic of our nation'. These were the messages espoused in the urban *coups* of the young officers: 'Kill the capitalists, punish the arbitrary authorities, kill the sly landowners and the special privileged class'.

Distress spread outwards from the countryside. In 1931 there were 1.3 million unemployed. But this figure does not capture the reality of Japan's industrial structure, with its huge number of small shops, subcontracting and outworkers (see Chapter 6). In addition to the officially unemployed were the many others who were 'disguised unemployed in the many small sweat shops and as returnees to the villages where they shared the misery with their relatives without registering as unemployed'.

The correctly perceived links between government and *zaibatsu* furthered the likelihood that political solutions to the economic and social crisis would be sought outside of the democratic process. Most urban workers and small businessmen saw the Diet's political parties as unambiguously compromised by their historical links with big business, the firms who had imported depression and benefited from it. Government had long supported the *zaibatsu* (Chapters 5 and 6), and the Kato government of 1924–5 had been known as the 'Mitsubishi Gang', the premier and foreign minister both being directly linked by marriage to Mitsubishi. By the years of the depression, Mitsui was clearly associated with the *Seiyukai* party in the Diet as well as with the army, and this triad favoured aggressive foreign expansion. Mitsubishi was as closely linked to the navy and with the *Minseito* party in the Diet, a combination favouring trade and investment expansion in preference to military aggression. The depression and the initially disastrous deflationary policy of the *Minseito*-dominated government of 1931 turned the tide in favour of the Mitsui position. One Mitsui director, Ginjiro Fujiwara, in his *Spirit of Japanese Industry* summarised the new consensus as follows:

> Diplomacy without force is of no value. No matter how diligent the Japanese may be, no matter how superior their technical development or industrial administration may be, there will be no hope for Japan's trade expansion if there is no adequate force to back it. Now the greatest of forces is military preparedness founded on the Army and Navy. We can safely expand abroad and engage in various enterprises, if we are confident of protection. In this sense, any outlay for armament is a form of investment.

Mitsubishi, the largest firm in shipbuilding, was converted to a more aggressive military stance through the effect of the depression on shipping. Beginning in 1931 some three thousand million yen were allotted to the development of four naval programmes, 75 per cent of which finance went to private companies. Furthermore, the depression nurtured a new business grouping, the *Shin Zaibatsu*, the most prominent member of which was Nissan, a group which rode to prosperity on the back of very large army and imperial contracts.

As a result of the depression, in both the agricultural and industrial halves of the economy the scene was set for a swing away from the Diet. That this was so in Japan more than in other major industrial nations can probably be attributed to the relatively late development of the economy of Japan. As already suggested (in Chapter 2, pp. 24–7), it was early industrialisation which itself fostered liberal individualism and democratic institutions in Europe and, then, America. In countries of greater economic backwardness, such as Germany or Russia, industrialisation was speedily superimposed upon existing institutions and ideologies, with little time for organic adjustments. Thus, of Russia in the late nineteenth century, Trotsky wrote that 'the State strove with all its power to accelerate the country's natural economic development. New branches of handicraft, machinery, factories, big industry, capital, were, so to say, artificially grafted on to the natural economic stem. Capitalism seemed to be an offspring of the State.' State intervention and the absence of any significant indigenous bourgeoisie meant the coexistence of a growing industrial working class, centralised government intervention, autocratic privilege and very large-scale undertakings. As we have seen, Meiji Japan in fact coped with the social tensions of late development astutely, at great cost but without revolution. Nevertheless, the heritage of late development remained throughout the early twentieth century, and economic depression triggered a final political crisis that was not resolved before 1945.

More precisely, the lateness of Japan's industrialisation meant that in 1929 or 1930, in comparison to other industrial nations, the economic system was characterised by a small commercial middle class, a small professional class, a huge and important rural sector of tenants and landlords and huge business conglomerates linked to both government and the military, upon whom were dependent a vast number of small subcontracting workshops. Within this structure, however advanced and determined the progressive opinion of Japan, the institutions of democracy were yet standing on infirm ground. As Robert Scalapino has concluded from his study of the Japanese democratic movement in a comparative perspective:

> The industrial revolution was conducive to more than one political expression, depending upon the timing and intensity of its development. In the case of many late arrivals, the doctrines of economic and political liberalism were not the most logical expression of industrialism . . . the inability of Japanese capitalism to underwrite the cardinal principles of democracy was centrally connected with the timing of its development, as this related to conditions both in Japan and in the world.

Late development is a better explanation of the weakness of Japanese labourism and liberalism than is 'culture', especially given the social implications of the dual structure of the industrial sector (see Chapter 6). The layers of industrial employment did not disturb the many vertical loyalties stemming from earlier years. For instance, leaders of trade unions tended to come from non-worker backgrounds and utilised the labour movement as a stepping stone into the established political arena. The manual workers in large firms were increasingly influenced by foremen training programmes which identified the enterprise rather than the industry as a proper focus of activity and expectation, just as youth drill and military training centres within factories taught loyalty to the institution and nationalistic ethics. The state capitalism of late development transmogrified into state-led militarism because late development *also* involved a generally felt need at the political centre for defence against superior industrial powers, control over right-wing landed backlash and control over swiftly formed labour movements. All of this followed from a retardation in the emergence of a powerful middle-class presence in contrast to the relatively early development of a strong elite business grouping closely linked to older traditions (Mitsui was formed of Chōshū in much the same way as Mitsubishi was connected to the Satsuma clan) as well as new political parties. With the depression, the political parties were quite unable to withstand the dual attack from those who had suffered and from those who had gained. The very success of the military in foreign expansion during the 1930s was the final element pulling the political energies and emotions of industrial Japan away from the Diet and towards authoritarianism.

Empire and the economy

> It must be obvious to everyone acquainted with the resources of Japan and the density of her population, that she has been forced to seek territory somewhere in the world in which to gain a living for her nationals under less difficult conditions.
>
> (Kimmochi Ohkura 1932)

Until Pearl Harbor (December 1941), Japan was not fully engaged in the pursuit of war, but imperial expansion for half a century had provided a basis for a military build-up which accelerated after 1931. Japanese imperial expansion was marked by the Russian and Chinese wars to 1905 and participation in the suppression of the Boxer uprising in China, annexation of Korea in 1910, declaration of war with Germany in 1915 and the presentation of the Twenty-One demands on China, securing of Germany's spheres of influence in China as a result of the 1919 Paris Peace Conference, the Siberian expedition against Soviet Russia in 1922, the annexation of Manchuria and creation of Manchukuo in 1931–2, and the war against China from 1937. As Japanese industrialisation accelerated, the new territories of Korea, Formosa, the Kurile Islands and Manchuria were potential sinks for Japanese capital and people and a source for guaranteed, low priced strategic raw materials such as sugar, coal, iron, rice, soy-beans and sea foods. By the mid-1930s North East Asian trade (basically China, Korea and Taiwan) provided some 35 per cent of Japanese imports and received some 44 per cent of Japanese exports. In contrast, trade with non-colonial South East Asia represented about 8 per cent of Japan's total in 1936. Funds invested by Japan in the colonial areas built up an initial demand for capital equipment and a subsequent demand for a variety of consumption goods. In the late 1930s the flow of metals, machinery and other capital goods from Japan to Asia was followed by export of rayon textiles and foodstuffs, and together such items compensated for the mainly negative trade balance Japan maintained with other nations.

It has been argued that imperialism was essential to the maintenance of Japanese industrialisation either as a vital repository for Japanese capital which would not otherwise have found an equally productive outlet at home, or as a source of foodstuffs and raw materials which could not have been supplied by the ailing rural and mining sectors. In themselves these arguments are not especially strong, nor do they explain the turn from commercial expansion and diplomacy to colonialism and war. The costs of colonial aggression were more obvious and immediate than were the rewards, a point obvious to many big business interests as well as popular opinion. The surge of colonialism in the 1930s might be more usefully seen as a expression of the pattern of statist late development which began in 1868. It was success in foreign adventure which lent popular legitimacy to the armed forces during the years of depression and thereafter and, more importantly, made feasible the new understandings which developed between big business interests and the military. Whereas big business had on the whole been sceptical of military ambition within Japan, colonial excursions provided a distant but common platform upon which both business and the armed forces could find room to manoeuvre. Whatever army representatives or young insurgents might claim about the destructive character of big business at home, in Asia business interests were essential to the securing and development of new territories and, thus, to the increasing viability of the armed forces as the true representatives of the expanding industrial economy. Broached in the names of tradition, nationhood and survival, the colonial acquisitions of Japan were maintained by the forces of capitalism. It was precisely this partnership which induced the quick recovery, high rates of investment and measurable technical progress of the 1930s. Imperial militarism also provided an at least temporary resolution of the tension between traditional social and ethical attitudes on the one hand and the rapidly changing economic and political institutions of Japan on the other.

None of this is to suggest that the Japanese authorities did not make the most of their commercial operations in Asia, even from the earliest days. Japan forced low tariffs on Asia, opened ports for trade and investment and establish a great variety of manufacturing and extractive enterprises. As early as 1910 the South Manchuria Railway Company owned and managed all modern industry and railways and at least 50 per cent of North China's capital stock. Despite its name the company was directly engaged in Manchuria's mining, water and electricity supplies, warehousing, telegraphs, collection of taxes in the railway zone and management of coal mining concessions from China. After the formation of the puppet state of Manchukuo, capital poured into coal and ore mining, chemicals and electricity. By the later 1930s most Japanese investments was channelled through the SMRC, the Manchuria Industrial Development Company and its subsidiaries and the Manchuria government. SMRC was responsible for over 40 per cent of the three billion yen of Japanese investment in Manchuria between 1932 and 1939. The speed of commercial build-up is well illustrated in the complex structure of the Manchuria Industrial Development Company, formed only in 1937. Within two years major Manchurian-based subsidiaries included Showa Steel and Pensihu Colliery and Iron Works, Japanese subsidiaries including Nissan, Hidachi, Ōsaka Iron Works and the Japan Mining Company. The sum total of paid up capital for the nineteen subsidiaries in 1939 had reached 1206 million yen, matched by MID investment of 818 million yen. Of the 3 billion yen invested in Manchuria between 1932 and 1939, the greatest amount had been in the form of heavy industry investments of the SMRC, followed by bonds and subscriptions from a variety of sources. Fifty per cent of the capital of the MID was subscribed by Nissan, a company founded only in 1928, with extensive investments in the heavy industries. After 1932 the balance of trade and overall balance of payments of Manchuria became increasingly unfavourable. By 1939 Japan's export surplus with Manchukuo had reached over 900 million yen, a large amount of which was composed of the construction materials iron and steel, machinery, electrical equipment, vehicles and cement. In the same year, Japan earned some 200 million yen in the form of dividends and interest from Manchuria, and another 100 million yen as remittances and returns on private enterprise.

The variety of the mechanisms of colonial exploitation are best illustrated in the smaller-scale example of Korea, which had been annexed as Chōsen in 1910. Here all royal and public lands were alienated to Japan, as were 60 per cent of the forests. Over 50 per cent of the fish catch was Japanese owned. From 1905 a policy of forced migration of Korean craftsmen to Japan was pursued with vigour. Budget expenditure was overwhelmingly devoted to Japanese residents in the form of schooling and health facilities. The Korean language and culture pursuits were forbidden. On this basis, Maurice Zinkin has concluded that 'What distinguishes Korea from other Asian countries is the thoroughness with which the Japanese acted on the theory that the purpose of Colonial rule is to benefit the imperial power'. By 1940 Japanese investment in Korea had reached £300 million, industrial production had increased four-fold between 1922 and 1939, over 3,000 miles (4,830 km) of railway had been constructed. But, as in Manchuria, growth displaced development. As the rice crop increased so too did the volume of exports to Japan. The profits of Japanese enterprise in Korea were exceptionally high, up to three times the Japanese level in equivalent industrial enterprises at home. The riots and protests that measured low wages and appalling conditions resulted in an official figure of over 200,000 police floggings between 1910 and 1920 alone. Before 1905 Korea had been a badly governed, backward nation of low productivity. Under Japanese industrialisation and colonialism, the population of Korea rose rapidly from 14 million in 1910 to over 24 million in 1940, tenancy quickly overtook peasant ownership of the land, and real wages declined.

There is little doubt that colonies benefited Japan during the 1930s. The price of food to Japan was lower than it would otherwise have been and raw materials were more widely and securely available. High returns on Japanese private investments in empire economies were the source of further investments and colonial markets became a convenient dumping ground for inferior manufactured products at a time when many non-Asian markets remained sluggish. In effect, Japan exploited the labour surplus of colonised Asia, and this enabled the swift shifting of capital and technological resources from light industries to the heavy sector of the economy. On the other hand, perhaps the major function of later Japanese imperialism was to yield a measure of success and to weld together the relatively new nexus of internal political forces and, thereby, ensure the fast growth of the industrial economy despite the similarly growing problems faced by millions of workers in the rural sector and small-scale industrial sector.

War

> Make our country secure by military preparations – encourage and protect the people at home, and then wait for the time of the confusion of Europe which must come eventually sooner or later.
>
> (Viscount Takeki Tani 1887)

The confidence of the Japanese army reached a height during the summer of 1938, when Japanese and Soviet troops fought for possession of territory on the borders of Korea and Manchuria. Proposals for a military alliance with Germany were set back as a result of the German–Soviet Pact of Non-Aggression in August 1939. But the clear German successes in Norway, Denmark, Belgium and Holland during 1940 spurred the formation of a Japanese, German and Italian pact, a process accelerated by Japan's fear of the interests of the US in Asia. This tripartite agreement of September 1940 provided for joint action by the three powers against any neutral power (the US or the USSR) which should enter as an adversary in either the European war or the Sino-Japanese war. After June 1941, with Soviet Russia at war with Germany, only the US offered an obvious restraint on Japan's plans for a 'Greater East Asia Co-Prosperity Sphere'. Sometime in late 1941 it became very clear that the US would not allow Japan's continued aggression in China in exchange for Japan's neutrality in Europe, and on 7 December a large force of Japanese bombers launched a successful attack on the US fleet at Pearl Harbor.

Japan's first months of engagement in world war were dramatically effective, and the empire extended through the Indo-China peninsula, the Philippines, the Netherlands East Indies, British New Guinea, Guam, Wake Island, and the Admiralty, Solomon and Gilbert Islands, gains which yielded large supplies of oil, rubber, tin and bauxite. From 1942 the dogged resistance of the Chinese and the resources of the US, as well as insurgency within the empire, served to halt progress. During 1943 and 1944 it became clear that Japan's military industrial production capacity was nowhere near as great as that of the allies. Allied air power removed Japan's control over the seas. The loss of the Philippines allowed the American airforce to launch direct attacks on Japan's main islands. Tokyo was subjected to massive bombing between November 1944 and May 1945 and Nagoya, Ōsaka, Yokohama and Kōbe were burned out by incendiary attacks. In May 1945 Germany surrendered and from then Japan was totally isolated. The atom bomb was dropped on Hiroshima on 6 August and on Nagasaki three days later and was justified by President Truman and his advisers on the grounds that it thereby ended the war earlier and at less cost in human lives.[3] It was the Christians of Japan who cried out *'Shu Jesusu, awaremi tamai!'*, (Our Lord Jesus, have pity on us) as the first atom bomb landed on Japan.

Three million had died, 40 per cent of Japan's capital stock was destroyed, 6 million Japanese were returned from the lost empire. In the sixty-six cities subjected to air attack, half the dwellings had been ruined. Much productive plant had been scrapped for munitions, much else had been bombed.

Several other aspects of the war economy should be briefly noted. War meant deprivation for millions, and many thousands within Japan resisted.

From April 1941 a great series of strikes, especially in the vital heavy industries and armaments, spread over Japan, and from March 1942 labour conscription was bitterly resisted. The enormous shipping losses of the war and the dependence of fertiliser production on imported chemical supplies meant a great shortage of foodstuffs. Therefore, not only did the domestic rice harvest decrease steadily during the war, imports of rice declined rapidly from 1942. Mechanisation offered little hope in the context of Japan's rice culture and given the overriding claims of the armaments industries. Strikes, suicide, starvation and tuberculosis involving millions were the clear signs of the partiality of the war effort and of the universality of the strains it imposed.

As millions suffered, thousands gained. There can be little doubt that the *zaibatsu* won greater power over the economy during the war, especially after 1940. Administration of the colonial territories was parcelled out to various *zaibatsu* concerns. In Singapore shipping was controlled by Mitsubishi, which also gained jurisdiction over phosphate deposits in Indo-China. Mitsui controlled copper mines and other mineral resources in the Philippines as well as shipbuilding facilities in Hong Kong. Mitsui, Mitsubishi, Nissan and Sumitomo all participated in the exploitation of the natural resources, skills and labour of Manchuria. Within Japan, the war government of General Hideki Tōjō induced mergers and restricted the growth of small business. *Zaibatsu* firms bought up the many smaller enterprises who could not secure raw materials, credits and manpower. Under the Law Regulating the Application of Capital of October 1943 sellers of productive units were compelled to accept payment in the form of the issued shares of the purchaser. The subsequent Adjustment of Enterprises Law gave the authorities the right to take over all factories and redistribute their machinery and plant to war industries, usually under the control of *zaibatsu* firms, e.g. the many textile firms converted to the production of parts for aircraft under Mitsubishi control. Whereas in 1940, 216 companies valued at 3,650 million yen merged or were reorganised, by 1943 some 570 companies worth 7,500 million yen were involved. Banks were similarly affected: by late 1944 banking was dominated by Mitsui, Mitsubishi, Sumitomo, Yasuda, Sanwa, Nomura and Tokai. In contrast to the central war ministries of Europe and America, in Japan war industries were mobilised by super-trusts or Control Associations, each of which was nominally responsible to government but in effect was dominated by *zaibatsu* firms, such as Mitsubishi in iron and steel or Mitsui in coal. Until late 1942 the associations wielded massive power through their control over procurement of materials, funds and labour, a dual authority system which lasted until stockpiles diminished. But even after the military and naval defeats of 1943 government failed to remove industrial power from the *zaibatsu*, and leading *zaibatsu* magnates were attached to the Cabinet as an Adviser's Council. From November 1943 a number of *zaibatsu* representatives were brought directly into Cabinet, and in 1944 Ginjuro Fujiwara of Mitsui became Minister of Munitions.

Third, from 1937 the expansion of the metallurgical and engineering industries and all armaments was at the direct expense of the rest of industry, in particular those producing consumption goods for the home market. Consumer expenditure dropped severely during 1943–4 just as the ratio of war expenditure to GNP rose above 50 per cent. Fourth, and closely associated, the war years hastened the development of the capital goods and machine tools industries. Government led a programme of modernisation of the machine tool industry, particularly through the purchasing of prototype Swedish, Swiss, German and American tools together with the employment of foreign engineers and encouragement of the experimentation of *zaibatsu* firms in more specialised production. The Machine Tool Industry Act of 1938 provided tariff protection for machine tool producers, which itself effected an almost tripling in the output of the industry and a change within it towards the large-scale manufacture of quality special-purpose tools. Dominated by Mitsui, Mitsubishi and Nissan, production increased five-fold over the entire period 1937–45. Major wartime shortcomings, as in the case of speciality steels for machinery production, tended to be variously attributed to technological bottlenecks arising from pre-war dependency on Western suppliers, or to management inefficiencies, the latter belief boosting both a search for Western management methods and perhaps a greater acceptance of the subsequent industrial organisational reforms of the occupation forces. Finally, the Japanese war effort was clearly dependent on the viability of the empire as a source of strategic supply, particularly of coal, iron and steel, bauxite and rubber. It was the accelerated commercial development of the empire during the war which so obviously furthered the power of the *zaibatsu* firms and strengthened and complicated their links with government. Attacks on even the outskirts of empire represented blows at the heart of the Japanese industrial economy.

Occupation and institutional innovation

From the end of the war until March 1952 Japanese sovereignty was nullified and control over the nation was in the hands of SCAP, the Supreme Commander Allied Powers. Peace may be a continuation of war by political means, and many influential figures among the allies believed prior to 1945 that Japan must be contained by occupation for the good of all, including the nation's own people. The Potsdam declaration of 26 July 1945, prior to Japan's surrender and signed by Britain, the US and China, indicated in Clause 6 the elimination of the authority of all 'those who have deceived and misled the people of Japan into embarking on world conquest'. Clause 10 stated that the Japanese authorities would be made to 'remove all obstacles to the revival and strengthening of democratic tendencies among the Japanese people' and Clause 11 created a distinction between recovery industries (to be encouraged) and strategic military industries (to be eliminated).

Other opinion, represented well in the statements of the US senator J. C. Grew, former US ambassador to Tokyo, advocated 'doing business' with Japan as soon as possible, and reflected a policy of appeasement that had been adopted by the US during the 1930s in an effort to strengthen the hand of moderate groups in business and the military. Many believed that an occupation alliance with Japanese business elements would halt any resurgence of the Japanese military, an attitude opposed most clearly by the Chinese, who from an early date saw the need for a wholesale institutional reform in Japan.

The early phase of occupation took a basically Potsdam approach to Japan. The first directive to General Douglas A. MacArthur, approved by the US President on 6 September 1945, had as its ultimate objective 'to insure that Japan will not again became a menace to the United States or to the peace and security of the world'. The principal means towards attaining this goal being the strict geographical limitation of sovereignty, disarmament and demilitarisation, the encouragement of 'democratic and representative organisations' and the development of a light industrial domestic economy. Existing heavy and military production facilities were to be either scrapped, transferred abroad or converted to other uses. Of importance, the democratic ideal was to be fostered through a combination of support for labour and agrarian organisations, policies towards a more equitable 'distribution of income and of the ownership of the means of production and trade', as well as a concerted programme 'for the dissolution of the large industrial and banking combinations which have exercised control of a great part of Japan's trade and industry'.

The initial concerns of the allied powers centred on the extraction of reparations (including the wholesale dismantling and export of factory plant to China and the Far East) and the destruction of the military potential of Japan's strategic industries. Without a coherent policy of economic recovery, SCAP focused on the destruction of the material basis of Japanese imperialism and abolition of the armed forces, the introduction of a highly progressive property tax, the fostering of democratic and labour institutions, the liberalisation of the educational system and the amendment of the election laws to allow female suffrage. Of special importance were the institutional innovations invoked to carry forward basic redistribution measures, the land reform of 1947 and the anti-trust and anti-*zaibatsu* laws of 1946–8. Such measures had little immediate effect on growth – in 1946 industrial production remained at 30 per cent of the 1934–6 level and the threat of rampant inflation was curbed only through the enforced freezing of bank deposits. Within the urban areas during 1946–7 consumption was possibly only 50 per cent of the pre-war years.

In 1936 some 46 per cent of the arable land of Japan was held as tenancies. The Owner-Farmer Establishment Law of 1946 dispossessed the

Emperor and all absentee landlords and limited the amounts of land held by owner-occupiers very strictly (ranging from 1 *chō* to 12 *chō* in Hokkaido) and allowed the sale of excess lands freely to all farmers. By 1949 the percentage of land farmed by tenants had fallen to 8 per cent. Inflation greatly reduced the value of money compensations paid to the landlords as a class. Agriculture was not subject to any reparation policy nor had it been so severely damaged during the war, and manpower shortages were now readily overcome. The smallness of holdings and the return of many families to the relative security and familiarity of the land threatened labour productivity, but generally the occupation years witnessed a great diversification within the rural sector, incorporating vegetables and dairy products and stock-raising, a large input and renewed manufacturer of fertiliser to replace the soya beans of Manchuria, and the introduction of some power machinery and insecticides. The Premier of Japan, Shigeru Yoshida estimated that the reform 'greatly improved the general living standard of our agriculturists . . . such an improvement and stabilisation of our rural life made an essential contribution to the easing and stabilisation of social conditions, embroiled as they were in such a state of unrest and confusion following the end of the war'. By mid-1950 some 2 million *chō* of farm land were liberated by the reform, with some 4 million peasant households acquiring new land. The reform undoubtedly effected a radical change in the rural incentive structure. Farmers now had the security of ownership, the commitments of any investors, and a relatively low-cost structure for innovation – the land tax was based on area not productivity, the cost of purchase was eroded by inflation, and agricultural cooperatives aided in credit and the introduction of technical improvements.

Labour reforms were a second plank of the occupation authorities' initial platform in Japan. Democratic ways required a progressive and optimistic empowered, urban labour force, looking outwards towards a new Japan and away from the old. Not surprisingly, the paraphernalia of American labour administration was transferred as a model goal-set to Japan – free trade unions, collective bargaining, legislation ensuring minimum standards of health, safety, income and security. By the end of the third year of occupation some ten basic laws had been enacted. In October of 1945 there existed five labour unions with a total membership of 5,300. The SCAP directive of 4 October 1945 ordered the Japanese government to guarantee civil liberty and abolish all laws restricting labour organisations, and one week later the government was instructed to encourage the development of the labour movement. By mid-1949, 36,000 small labour unions had been formed with combined memberships of 6.7 million, about 38 per cent of the total working population outside of full-time agriculture. Once the enabling legislation had been passed, little local encouragement or organisation was required – unions sprang up throughout the localities, and from 1946 two federations (the Japanese Federation of Labour and the Congress of Industrial Unions) began to consolidate labour power.

As Miriam Farley observed at the time, the new organisation of labour was 'strong enough to make labour's voice heard, if not always heeded, in the councils of the nation'.

Industrial deconcentration, aimed especially at the *zaibatsu*, was the core of occupation policy prior to 1949. The Edwards Report of March 1946 instructed categorically that 'the larger Japanese business enterprises be systematically surveyed in order to make sure that all the *zaibatsu* have been identified and subjected to the program for ending *zaibatsu* power'. Generally, *zaibatsu* firms were taken as any which by reason of size or influence 'restricts competition or impairs the opportunity of others to engage in business independently'. In late 1947 the number of Japanese companies on the designated list for abolition was 325.

Fairly immediately, over 2,000 officers of *zaibatsu* concerns resigned from 632 firms. A separate purge of key businessmen affected persons employed in about 2,500 firms. The power of big business was further weakened by loss of assets through the new property tax. The purge may well have had profound long-term effects, but ones difficult to measure in any conventional analysis. As Morishima has stated clearly, the new managers brought in to replace the purged were mostly ex-army and naval officers who 'had spent so long in the army that they had formed a liking for the seniority and lifetime employment systems', and, thus, such practices became more widespread within Japanese enterprise culture. Factories became battalions. In addition, the younger managers were closer to the production workers, more familiar with engineering projects because of their imperial and wartime backgrounds, and set to expunge the image at home and abroad of the aggressive and selfish *zaibatsu*: 'This kind of non-capitalist, young, employed manager was far keener to improve the enterprises' national or international position than to serve its owners by striving for the greatest possible profit'.

Clearly, deconcentration policy was likely to have at least as great an effect on competitive structure as upon enterprise culture, and this was its main purpose for SCAP. In 1946 the 'Big Four' *zaibatsu* firms (Mitsui, Mitsubishi, Sumitomo and Yasuda) owned 32 per cent of total capital in heavy industry and 50 per cent of that in finance and insurance. At an early point SCAP froze the property and securities of the ten largest *zaibatsu*, assets which were disposed of amongst the public to achieve a wide distribution of ownership, e.g. MBK, a subsidiary of Mitsubishi, was dissolved into 170 separate concerns. As with the landlords (above) government bonds issued in receipt of *zaibatsu* assets were soon reduced in value by inflation. In the short run, such action was retardative of growth. As G. C. Allen summarised, the 'dissolution policy retarded Japan's economic recovery, for it disorganised the main centres of economic initiative upon which she had hitherto relied and it introduced uncertainties into the business of decision making'. A Fair Trade Commission was established to administer the workings of the Anti-Monopoly Law of 1947 and the Trade

Association Law of 1948. During the first two years of its operation the FTC investigated 236 suspected violations, prepared seventy-two industry studies and received stock disposal plans from 3,651 companies concerning approximately 70 million shares of stock.

The period 1947–8 represented a sea change in SCAP policy towards Japan on several fronts. Reforms had caused confusion and inefficiency, economic distress was not a good environment for the nourishment of democratic institutions, and the US aid bill had risen greatly, to $40 million in 1947 alone. A first indication of a move towards recovery was a report on reparations of February 1947 which recommended that the policy of enforced plant removals should be abandoned. But the real break with the early years was determined by events abroad during 1948 and 1949. The hardening of the Cold War meant that Japan was increasingly viewed in the US as a last bastion of capitalism in Asia, and this focus was sharpened with the defeats of the nationalist forces of Chiang Kai-shek in China and the division between the Republic of Korea and the Korean People's Democratic Republic. Nationalist uprisings against the colonial powers added a further sense of urgency.

Policy instruments adjusted fairly speedily – reparations were halted, additional funds for food and raw material imports were provided, the private export trade was now encouraged, the labour movement was now discouraged and the *zaibatsu* were treated with far greater leniency. In 1949 a Nine Point Stabilisation Programme was announced which incorporated the full set of conservative prescriptions of its architect, Joseph Dodge – a balanced budget, credit restrictions, expansion of trade.[4] With the outbreak of the Korean War in mid-1950 the change of policy was fully confirmed and, in the minds of many US strategists, vindicated. Spending by the US in the form of 'Special Procurements', for the supplying of materials and services during the Korean War, boosted the economy enormously. By 1951 the index of industrial production had risen above that for the pre-war years. By the Peace Treaty and the Security Treaty of 1952 full sovereignty was restored to Japan and arrangements were made for the continued presence of allied armed forces in Japan. The latter required a continuation of special procurement expenditure, which amounted to some $3,380 million during 1952–6, for any one year equivalent to above 25 per cent of export earnings.

The Dodge line invoked new restrictions, but these were now on welfare rather than on business. The reduction of subsidies and public works, the implementation of credit controls and tight wage controls, and an increase in the price of essential services all combined to threaten both real income levels and employment. According to the judgement of two American historians, 'the United States committed itself to socially retrograde policies that even sectors of Japan's paternal ruling classes thought too conservative'. It is probable that severe depression was only reversed, and therefore very serious social problems were only avoided, by the outbreak of the Korean War.

A major result of the changes of 1948–9 was the amelioration of the deconcentration policy. By mid-1948 a total of 225 firms had been removed from the original list of 325 firms designated under the SCAP legislation. Deconcentration was, if anything, replaced by a policy of industrial recovery, the chief mechanism of which was special procurement spending, which brought growth spurts to textiles, iron and steel and machinery industries. Industry was boosted by the introduction of the priority production system, whereby the importance to the nation of any industry was evaluated in terms of its influence on the entire economy by using estimates of technological linkages and input–output relationships. From 1950 technology transfer was encouraged selectively through use of the Foreign Investment Law, licences being granted for technology importing which would improve the balance of payments or provide essential public services.

Without doubt, the big tools of the occupation, the land, labour and deconcentration regulations and the subsequent Dodge line, were only ever partially applied and superficially effective. For instance, a certain democratisation of the work place did occur, but it tended to be most effective in the big enterprises, often leaving untouched the many thousands of re-emerging workshops. The trading houses of Mitsui and Mitsubishi were indeed broken up into 240 small-scale firms, but this did not necessarily mean a great change in the real production and ownership structure. Masao Takahashi has pointed out that although large firms were subject to a variety of 'democratisation' measures, in effect these were 'restricted to their accounting system, which meant nothing else but a replacement of a large, complex business with several fairly large new firms; in other words, they had the effect of making those enterprises more rationalised from the viewpoint of capitalism . . . there actually occurred no fundamental change in the dual structure of the business world'.

At this point we may note only two things. First, any meaningful impact of the occupation on the trajectory of the Japanese economy was most likely to have been exposed in later years. Institutional innovation across a wide front does take some time to show any results in terms of growth accounting. Second, although any single arena of reform may have been tackled *ad hoc* and partially, in combination the SCAP reforms both prior to and after 1947 may well have had results which were not simply those normally associated with post-war recovery processes. Certainly, the years following 1952 were surprisingly successful ones in terms of crude economic growth. During the next twenty years the economy attained a level of growth and structural change not envisaged by any major commentator at that time.

Conclusions – the political economy of Japan

The history of the Japanese economy to 1952 suggests the extreme complexity of the dynamic relations between the nominally 'political' and the supposedly 'economic'. Although we may generally claim to identify the impact of economic change on political developments (e.g. the depression on militarism), it would seem that a complex feedback process is involved, best demonstrated during periods of crisis. Economic depression in combination with late development was almost certainly central to the movement of the political system towards military authoritarianism after 1931, and this latter process was at least as clearly associated with speedy economic recovery, structural shifts to heavy industry, technological modernisation and an imperial expansion which exerted further secondary effects in both the 'political' and the 'economic' arenas.

Institutional innovation is very often the major process involved in generating linkages between the political and the economic, particularly at times of definite political momentum, e.g. during 1945–9. The economic impacts in the long term of institutional change, especially when it is overtly political tend to be unintended and are probably unpredictable to major contemporary actors. Much institutional reform is essential to statist requirements of social control, especially during and following periods of economic disaster, an example being the land reform of the late 1940s. Again, this example suggests that the retention of social control might be as essential to recovery and expansion in the private sector through its effect on incentives and risk-reduction. When institutional innovation is from one national system to another, as in the period from the 1870s to the 1890s, in the 1930s or in the years of the occupation, it is clear that the influence of the rest of the world on the national economic trajectory may be enormous, unintended and unpredictable. It may also be difficult to discover in retrospect.

If Japan benefited greatly from the transfer of technologies, information and ideas from other nations, it is just as certain that such elements neither exist in an institutional vacuum nor may be successfully transferred into an unreformed institutional complex. In Meiji Japan, technology transfer involved a massive process of institutional innovation at a tremendous social and economic cost. During the occupation something similar occurred. And in both cases there were unintended consequences, often of a long-term nature. Within Japan, one consequence was the blurring of distinctions between the private and public sectors of the economy – even those institutions of democracy and liberal individualism which offered some basis for competitive behaviour in the private sector, were initially transferred from elsewhere at the behest and means of the state, and adapted to circumstance by state bureaucracies. The economic behaviour of the *zaibatsu* perhaps epitomises private sector functions and contributions, but clearly the rising influence of the *zaibatsu* in such key periods as the 1890s, the 1930s and the war years was formed of the political activity of government and, perhaps more so, bureaucracy. Again, the transference to Japan of both advanced techniques and advanced institutions at a time when they were not in demand in the market place, meant that a trajectory emerged in which aggressive business behaviour followed the innovations of government. The significant growth of the private sector in heavy industry during the 1930s was indisputably conditioned by the environmental implications of colonial expansion, which included improved transport and communication systems, but such growth also resulted from specific government assistance in finance, technology and trade.

Some of these general points are highlighted in the case of the unintended consequences of the commercial purge and anti-*zaibatsu* legislation of the late 1940s. Here an attempt at wholesale institutional innovation from outside of Japan necessitated particular institutional reform, the dramatic decrease in the economic power of the *zaibatsu* and related firms. These were seen as harbingers and hosts of war, their removal was intended primarily as part of a general process of democratisation, a process which itself flowed from conceptions of both individualism and nationhood which were not formulated within Japan. Yet some analysts have seen in this instance of institutional innovation a key to Japan's post-war economic growth over a significant stretch of years, covering those of recovery, growth and maturity. *Zaibatsu* dissolution, even in its modified form post-1949, cleared the way for new ventures, infused new life into older enterprises and, in the words of G. C. Allen, offered opportunities for 'newcomers from outside the ranks of the favoured few, to serve the needs of the new era . . . unlike Britain, Japan entered the new era without the crippling weight of leaders who were slaves to an inappropriate experience . . . imaginative young men were given their head'. Allen goes on to make the point that, thereby, 'the US conferred a benefit on Japan that was in no sense a part of her intention'. Minami argues that 'the monopoly of the large enterprises was weakened, entry into industries became easier and competition increased', and repeats the view that such deconcentration 'helped make possible Japan's high rate of economic growth of the mid-1950s'. Furthermore, the particular form which dissolution reforms took, leaving untouched the large private banks, allowed for the development during the 1950s of the new bank-centred groups, the *keiretsu*, which have in turn been interpreted as combining the advantages of largeness of scale with real market competition. Admitting the centrality of the bank and the peculiar competitive–cooperative characteristics of the *keiretsu*, Yanaga has judged that they 'represent the particular restructuring of big business on the basis of common interests, the better to cope with common problems in such fields as production, sales and financing'. Several modern commentators have found in the occupation's break up of cartels and *zaibatsu* dissolution, the origins of contemporary Japan's competitiveness and enterprise culture. Thus Uekusa and Ide argue that the

> deconcentration measures represented probably the greatest use of government power in modern times to create a competitive industrial structure. . . . The new, competitive market structure and the decision

making autonomy of managers in the companies (in contrast to the strong ties within the prewar *zaibatsu*) led to the importation of foreign technology and the creation of a large number of new industries. Thus the deconcentration measures formed the groundwork for Japan's post-war economic development.

There are, of course, numerous contending interpretations of the reasons for Japan's industrial success, many of which we shall uncover in later chapters. Nevertheless, this example of the deconcentration policy of the later 1940s does seem to emphasise that economic dynamics may not always be either expressible or explainable in terms of narrowly 'economic factors'. In particular, non-business institutional innovations give rise to complex economic consequences yet are rarely instigated within the private sector and are seldom the result of commercial considerations in the public sector.

Notes

1 The rice riots of 1918 were the greatest of uprisings in twentieth-century Japan, and were the centrepiece of a period of unrest associated with the high price of rice. The riots spread through many urban areas, ninety civilians were killed, 7,000 or so arrested. In the same year there were 497 strikes involving 66,000 participants and there was a great increase in tenant–landlord conflicts.

2 Kita also wrote *The Theory of National Polity* (1906) and *An Unofficial History of the Chinese Revolution* (1921) and was considered the leading right-wing theorist. Kita promoted the notion of the *coup d'état* as the major vehicle of change and young, uncorrupted officers as its agents. Implicated in the February 1936 *coup*, Kita was sentenced to death.

3 The argument being that without the bomb an invasion of Japan would have been required at the cost of the lives of 500,000 United States soldiers, an estimate inflated to 1,200,000 Allied lives by Winston Churchill. Recently released materials, however, suggest the military planners were working on actual estimates of between 20,000 and 46,000 lives. Additionally, the entry of the Russians into the war may have been a decisive factor in a speedy resolution anyway. Molotov read out the Soviet declaration of war on 8 August 1945 and the Russian tanks were crossing the Manchuria border within a few hours.

4 Joseph Dodge was a conservative Detroit banker of humble background who was directly advised by President Harry S. Truman of the new importance of Japan in light of changes in China. See J. and G. Kolko, *The Limits of Power*, Harper and Row, New York, 1972.

References

Roth, Andrew (1946) *Dilemma in Japan*, London: Victor Gollancz Ltd., p. 106.

Hirschmeier, J. and Yui, Tsunehiko (1975) *The Development of Japanese Business 1600–1973,* London: Allen and Unwin, p. 149.

Knei-Paz, Baruch (1978) *The Social and Political Thought of Leon Trotsky*, Oxford: Oxford University Press, p. 179.

Fujiwara quoted in Roth (1946) p. 63.
Scalapino, Robert A. (1953) *Democracy and the Party Movement in Pre-War Japan*, Berkeley, CA: University of California Press, p. 397.
Zinkin, Maurice (1951) *Asia and the West*, London: Chatto and Windus, p. 67.
Yoshida, Shigeru (1957) *Kaiso Junen* (vol. II), Shinchōsha: Tokyo, pp. 196–7.
Farley, Miriam (1947) 'Labor policy in occupied Japan', *Pacific Affairs* 20, p. 134.
Farley, Miriam (1950) *Aspects of Japan's Labour Problems*, New York: John Day Co.
Morishima, Michio (1982) *Why Has Japan Succeeded?*, Cambridge: Cambridge University Press, p. 143.
Allen, G. C. (1965) *Japan's Economic Expansion*, Oxford: Oxford University Press, p. 181.
Takahashi, Masao (1968) *Modern Japanese Economy*, Tokyo: Kokusai Bunka Shinkokai, p. 133.
Allen, G. C. and Nishiyama, Chiaki (1974) *The Price of Prosperity Lessons from Japan*, Hobart Paper 58, London: Institute of Economic Affairs, p. 40.
Minami, Ryōshin (1986) *The Economic Development of Japan*, London: Macmillan, p. 151.
Yanaga, Chitoshi (1968) *Big Business in Japanese Politics*, New Haven, CT: Yale University Press, p. 39.
Uekusa, Masu and Ide, Hideki (1986) 'Industrial policy in Japan', in Mutoh Hiromichi *et al.* (eds), *Industrial Policies for Pacific Economic Growth*, New Haven, CT: Allen and Unwin, p. 151.

Further reading

Allen, G. C. (1940) *Japanese Industry: Its Recent Development and Present Condition*, New York: Institute of Pacific Relations.
Barnhart, M. (1982) *Japan Prepares for Total War: The Search for Economic Security 1919–41*, Ithica: Cornell University Press.
Bird, K. and Lifschultz, L. (eds) (1998) *Hiroshima's Shadow. Writings on the Denial of History and the Smithsonian Controversy*, London: Pamphleteers Press.
Bisson, T. A. (1945) *Japan's War Economy*, New York: Institute of Pacific Relations.
Cohen, J. R. (1949) *Japan's Economy in War and Reconstruction*, Minneapolis, MN: University of Minnesota Press.
Cohen, T. (1987) *Remaking Japan: The American Occupation as New Deal*, New York: Free Press.
Cusumano, M. A. (1985) *The Japanese Automobile Industry: Technology and Management in Nissan and Toyota*, Cambridge, MA: Harvard University Press.
Fletcher, W. M. (1982) *The Search for a New Order: Intellectuals and Fascism in Prewar Japan*, Chapel Hill, NC: University of North Carolina Press.
Fodor, G. (1986) 'Why did Europe need the Marshall Plan in 1947?', *Political Economy*, 2: 73–104.
Gordon, A. (1991) *Labor and Industrial Democracy in Prewar Japan*, Berkeley, CA: University of California Press.
Hadley, E. M. (1970) *Antitrust in Japan*, Princeton, NJ: Princeton University Press.
Havens, T. (1978) *Valley of Darkness*, New York: Norton.
Hein, L. E. (1990) *Fuelling Growth: the Energy Revolution and Economic Policy in Postwar Japan*, Cambridge, MA: Harvard University Press.
Johnson, C. (1982) *MITI and the Japanese Miracle*, Stanford, CA: Stanford University Press.

Levine, S. B. (1958) *Industrial Relations in Postwar Japan*, Urbana, IL: University of Illinois Press.

Milward, A. S. (1984) *The Reconstruction of Western Europe 1945–51*, London: Methuen.

Morley, J. W. (ed.) (1971) *Dilemmas of Growth in Pre-War Japan*, Princeton, NJ: Princeton University Press.

Morris, I. (ed.) (1963) *Japan 1931–1945: Militarism, Fascism, Japanism?*, Boston, MA: Heath & Co.

Morris-Suzuki, T. (1991) *A History of Japanese Economic Thought*, London and Oxford: Routledge and Nissan Institute for Japanese Studies.

Nakaoka, T. (1981) 'Production management in Japan before the period of high economic growth', *Osaka City University Economic Review*, 17: 3–17.

Okita, S. (ed.) (1992) *The Postwar Reconstruction of the Japanese Economy*, Tokyo: University of Tokyo Press.

Penrose, E. F. (1953) *Economic Planning for the Peace*, Princeton, NJ: Princeton University Press.

Sakudo, J. and Shiba, T. (eds) (1994) *World War II and the Transformation of Business Systems*, Proceedings of the 20th International Conference on Business History, Tokyo: University of Tokyo Press.

Samuels, R. J. (1994) *Rich Nation Strong Army: National Security and the Technological Transformation of Japan*, Ithica: Cornell University Press.

van der Beugel, E. H. (1966) *From Marshall Aid to Atlantic Partnership*, Amsterdam: Elsener.

Ward, R. and Sakamoto, Y. (eds) (1987) *Democratising Japan: The Allied Occupation*, Honolulu, HI: University of Hawaii Press.

Wray, W. (ed.) (1989) *Managing Industrial Enterprise: Cases from Japan's Prewar Experience*, Cambridge, MA: Council on East Asian Studies, Harvard University.

8 Recovery and growth in the golden age (1952–73)

Supergrowth: Japan in the golden age

> The increase in investment could not have taken place without the introduction of technology; new products and technology developed in the developed countries during and after the war came into Japan in great waves.
>
> (Ryōshin Minami 1986)

Japan shared in the golden age, but was not typical of it. The years from 1952 to 1973 were ones of unprecedented growth and prosperity for the advanced nations of the globe. The period witnessed the real beginnings of industrialisation and wholesale institutional change in the so-called 'newly industrialising nations' of Asia. At no period since the industrial revolution had growth of national income, national income per head, manufacturing, capital formation, labour productivity and exports been as high. Trade, most of the growth of which took place between advanced industrial nations, grew in volume at eight times the rate of 1913–50. The fast rate of global growth was accompanied by little in the way of violent fluctuations in output, employment or trade. Upon all measures, the huge economy of the US dominated the era, from the growth inducements of Marshall Aid and Korean War expenditures to the far higher level of labour productivity in America than in any other nation: as late as 1973 labour productivity in West Germany was perhaps 70 per cent of that in the US.

Japan and the US demonstrated the extreme contrasts within this general picture of prosperity. In America, growth in output and capital stock was not as marked, unemployment was relatively high and, of especial importance for the long-term health of the global economy (see Chapter 12), labour productivity *grew* far less than in the nation's major industrial competitors. This contrast between US growth and global performance at least suggests that economic growth and its variations between nations was some function of the *differential ability* of industrial and trading nations to 'catch-up' with American technological and institutional leadership during these years.

On all conventional measures, Japan was the nation which best exploited its own relative backwardness. Where in other nations the rise of consumption expenditure and business investment together created the early boom, in Japan between 1955 and 1960 the production of investment goods trebled whilst consumption rose by less than 50 per cent. As Andrew Glyn *et al.* summarised in 1988, this 'extraordinary burst of investment, probably unparalleled in the history of advanced capitalist countries defies any simple explanation; with hindsight it is clear that all the preconditions – high profits, abundant and now docile labour supply, access to new technologies, an active industrial policy and a state committed to rebuilding positions in world markets – were there, but that hardly accounts for the virulence of the upswing'. From that early investment thrust, most other indicators also pointed to an exceptional Japanese performance. National product grew at 8 per cent per annum in the 1950s, 10 per cent in the 1960s. The capital stock grew in Japan at a rate of around 9 per cent per annum, in West Germany at 6 per cent and in the US at 4 per cent. Labour productivity grew in Japan at 9.5 per cent per annum, in Western Germany at 5.6 per cent and in the US at 2.4 per cent. The volume of exports grew in Japan at over 15 per cent per annum, in West Germany at 12.4 per cent, in the US at 6.3 per cent

At the start of this phase of economic growth, income per head in Japan was lower than that of Malaysia. By its end, Japanese incomes had surpassed those of Britain. As we shall see, the state of both the economy and the society of Japan around 1952 disguised the nation's enormous expansive capacity. Domestic investment as a percentage of national income even then provided a hint: 27.2 per cent in 1952, rising to 36.3 per cent in 1971. High investment was associated with at least two notable low rates: government expenditure fluctuated around 10–15 per cent of national income compared to ratios of over 20 per cent in the US and West Germany, whilst the ratio of total foreign trade to national income stood at approximately 20–25 per cent: high compared to the US but low compared to the major industrial nations of Europe. The high rate of overall economic growth in Japan, however, means that its share of world trade trebled in these years. During the golden age of growth the proportion of labour employed in agriculture fell significantly in all industrial nations, but in Japan it fell from a much higher initial figure, from around 42 per cent of the labour force to around 20 per cent. Because total national income multiplied seven-fold in real terms during those years, Japan ended this period with a national product below that of only the US and the USSR and with a population (108 million) around twice that of the major European nations but only just over 50 per cent that of the US.

As might be expected, manufacturing led the recovery and growth process, accelerating over the period to create an annual average rate of some 15 per cent. Not only was this growth rate of the manufacturing sector above that of other nations, the acceleration was in contrast to the deceleration witnessed in such other high growth economies as Germany or Italy. In addition, the Japanese agricultural sector was rejuvenated in these years through the initiation of labour-saving technological change. Increased investment went into both chemical fertilisers and mechanisation, although the ready diffusion of better techniques may well be explained in terms of the financial incentives yielded by increased prices and the land reform of the late 1940s (see Chapter 7). Increased rural wages were a reflection of a rise in labour productivity and labour costs were offset by the decrease in the price of agricultural machinery flowing from an increasingly sophisticated machine sector.

The tremendous rate of investment throughout the economy cannot be overemphasised in any interpretation of Japan's golden age. In both the private and the public sectors, despite the absence of investment in military and defence areas, investment increased at around 15 per cent per annum. Some 75 per cent of fixed capital formation originated in the private sector, 25 per cent with government. Only a small proportion of capital formation went into housing and other social overheads, over 80 per cent was concentrated on producers' durable equipment. This incomparable experience was associated with a highly optimistic business environment, wholesale innovation in enterprise culture and organisation, the adoption of fairly aggressive market share strategies in the large-firm private sector, and high returns on capital. Over 80 per cent of after-tax profits were reinvested, and this was strongly backed by virulent bank borrowing. Business savings were boosted by generous business depreciation allowances and the high rate of government savings. Net savings (gross savings minus depreciation) reached around 25–30 per cent of national income, and the bulk of savings originated in households, followed by the government and corporate sector, which together roughly equalled the level of household savings. Again, this was a highly unusual savings pattern within the general trends of the golden age of growth. Domestic savings in Japan represented 20 per cent or more of disposable income, some three times the norm of the industrial nations at large. Also, to a greater degree than elsewhere, investment in both the corporate and government sectors owed a great deal to savings in the personal sector, especially in the 1960s, through the intermediaries of banks, postal savings and other financial institutions. The high rate of savings, as in earlier periods, has been explained in terms of the supposed retention of traditional consumption patterns, an argument which sits uncomfortably with the consumerism of the 1970s and 1980s. The rise in real incomes explains much, as do certain unambiguous institutional features of the economy. These latter, possibly of great importance, include the relative absence of social security due to inadequacies in health and insurance provision in the public sector, the bonus system in the large firms, and the remaining high incidence of self-employment in all sectors of the economy. All three institutional factors tend to work in the direction of increasing the rate of savings at any given level of income.

Japan in 1952 inherited a highly educated labour force, the size of which increased at 1.5 per cent per annum. Of more importance was the phenomenal transference of labour from agriculture, mining, forestry and fishing into manufacturing, construction, wholesale and retail trade, banking and a host of other services. Between 50 per cent and 60 per cent of the increase in the manufacturing and service labour force was due to inflow from agriculture. Demand in industry pulled labour out of agriculture just as the abolition of primogeniture (the inheritance of the land by the eldest son) arising from the 1948 reforms pushed many away from the sector. This relatively elastic supply of labour certainly had an impact in keeping wages down and the rate of savings and capital accumulation up, both in terms of its general redistribution effects and because of its effects on rates of profit as such.

Japanese foreign trade grew faster than that of the world generally because of the very high rate of national output growth. Because of the large size of the Japanese economy, the export share of GDP was modest in comparison to other advanced economies. Export shares in current prices averaged around 10–11 per cent for the whole period, and rose significantly only in the 1980s. In contrast, the export shares of the European nations of the OECD varied between 20 per cent and 25 per cent of gross domestic product, reaching over 30 per cent in the 1980s. It would seem, on simple comparative aggregate ratios, that Japan's export performance was a function of the low initial level of exporting before 1950 and the fast rate of overall economic growth. The very high level of raw material and technology importing kept the payments balance on the current account in approximate equilibrium until 1973. For the years until 1973 some 60 per cent of all commodity imports were of raw materials and fuels and some 20 per cent was comprised of heavy and chemical industrial products, reflecting the tremendous demand within Japan for advanced technologies. Luxury consumption items, light industrial products and textiles represented a very small percentage of imports, and together amounted to no more than the cost of importing foodstuffs.

Until the 1960s Japan remained an economic hermit. During that decade American and other commentators first noted the competitive impact of Japan in textiles and steel, and began to claim that the yen was undervalued and that the Japanese domestic market was protected strongly and indirectly through a variety of mechanisms, ranging from consumer preference to excessive quality control. The commodity composition of Japan's foreign trade throughout the period was distinctive in that raw materials and fuels composed such a large share of imports compared to manufactures. But from around 1968 an emerging balance of payments surplus combined with this composition to generate claims that the Japanese economy was a serious destabilising influence on the core of the golden age international economy, the payments system set up under the Bretton Woods agreement.[1] By the end of the period the situation was critical. As two leading commentators, Hugh Patrick and Henry Rosovsky wrote in 1975, 'Japanese surpluses in 1971, and even in 1972, were both a catalyst and a partial cause of the ending of the fixed exchange rate system . . . The United States had the most pronounced balance-of-payments deficit and Japan the most pronounced surplus.' The global departure from the fixed exchange rate system and the subsequent upward flotation of the yen marked (but did not in itself cause) the end of the era. (See further pp. 154–6 and Chapters 9 and 12.)

Frequently at that time, and often since, the genesis of Japan's chronic trade surplus has been located in government policy. It has been argued that government encouraged both import restrictions (for instance, through tariffs and control over foreign currency) and export promotion through special instruments such as the market research and public relations exercises of the Japan External Trade Organisation (JETRO), through the 1964 Export Contribution Award, through such financial incentives as the medium- and long-term credit facilities open to exporters by means of the Export-Import Bank, through tax incentives and through the monitoring of competitive levels amongst Japanese manufacturing exporters. The critical mood of the international economy at the time was well summarised in the Foreword to an influential publication of the Economic Research Council of 1972:

> Japan chose deliberately to promote its Exports by every possible means at the expense of its imports. As a result, year after year, it has achieved an astonishingly favourable balance which has been used by Japan to build up a vast holding of US dollars. So long as this Japanese holding of dollars remains unused for any commercial purpose it cannot help being regarded as a threat to the currency system of the Western World . . . We do not wish to imply that Japan has any evil intentions: we merely make the point that in our view governments should seek to secure that import/export trade is in equilibrium because the consequences of accumulating an excessively favourable or an excessively unfavourable balance are so disturbing to other countries.

In fact America had long been running a large deficit on her balance of payments, US exports growing at half the rate of those of West Germany throughout the 1950–3 period, and Japan had just arrived at the point of real surplus. Despite the many proclamations of the Bretton Woods system, protectionism was on the rise throughout the global economy, foreign governments targeted their own export sectors and attempted to attack Japanese imports to them through fairly particular quota, tariff and other restrictions. The balanced budget ideology of Japan, at least until the mid-1960s, removed from the Japanese authorities fiscal tools (for demand management), leaving monetary policy and industrial policy as the main planks of overall public policy. The Ministry of International Trade and

Industry (MITI) had clearly evolved a strategy of 'administrative guidance' whereby government influenced the investment and other decisions of business by informal means centring on the selective utilisation of information and persuasion in the areas of merger, competition and production control. In so far as government industrial and technological policies significantly effected *overall* economic growth (a position often denied by those who were ready enough to identify the virulence of government export policy!), the tremendous dependence of the Japanese economy on imported technique, raw materials and fuels meant that inputs were sucked into the economy at a high rate and exports were ejected out of an economic system that was fast expanding, increasing in technical efficiency and reallocating resources to the most productive sectors. In that sense at least, the end of the golden age was associated with a dynamic nexus between government policy and export performance.

To argue that the supergrowth of 1952–73 was caused by the high rates of capital and labour formation would be to claim very little indeed. Any historical interpretation of Japanese performance should acknowledge the following: (a) that the exceptional rates of change of capital and labour formation were accompanied by very speedy increases in both labour and capital productivity, and that this combination, however conceptually feasible, was unique;[2] and (b) that the Japanese economy exhibited certain other outstanding features compared to other industrial nations in these years, in particular the far greater initial rural labour base, low trade ratio, low levels of government expenditure, acceleration of the growth trajectory, especially that of manufacturing, the very high level of household savings, the persistence of industrial dualism, the concentration of capital formation in durable equipment, the similar concentration of imports on raw materials, fuels and technology, and the relatively early forging of a growth-oriented industry policy. Later sections of this chapter consider some of these elements in a little more detail. Here we are concerned only with the possible dynamic relations between them.

Much can be attempted under the umbrella of 'catching up'. Not only had Japan been badly hit during the war years (see Chapter 7), the Japanese economy was yet structurally immature despite the earlier industrial drives. In 1950 the proportion of the total labour force engaged in agriculture in Japan was 40 per cent, compared to 28 per cent in West Germany, 13 per cent in the US and 6 per cent in the UK. At that time also Japan was fairly distinctive in the youthfulness of its population, 34 per cent being under 15 years of age. By the end of the period, the proportion of Japanese employed in agriculture had fallen to around 15 per cent. Although all industrial nations benefited during the golden age from significant resource shifts into more productive employments, the greater structural backwardness of Japan in 1950 yielded a high growth result; through the 1960s the growth rate of employment in manufacturing in Japan remained around 4 per cent, that of the US 1.4 per cent, West

Germany less than 1 per cent and the UK around 0.3 per cent. The ease of labour supply was crucial to the general growth rate, but growth of employment into manufacturing as such was conditioned by demand, and this was set by the level of investment and technological change.

The catch-up thesis is an argument from both supply and demand. The large and sophisticated markets of the US and other industrial nations provided the extra increment of demand which stimulated Japanese growth. Given the level of real income growth in Japan and the relatively low trade ratio, this aspect of the argument may not be especially applicable. However, on the *supply* side, underemployed labour and relative structural backwardness enabled Japan to exploit the large technological gap between its major industries and those of the Atlantic economies, and this created a very high level of investment demand. For some years, and even at a very high level of investment, Japan was effectively exploiting a technological shelf focused in the Atlantic economy, but especially in the US. So, in *Japan in particular*, the increase in capital per worker represented an increase in superior technology per worker and may be interpreted as a direct effect of 'catching up' as it took place from a far lower initial level of capital per worker than obtained in the US or Europe.

A comprehensive 'catch-up' approach requires that the high level of investment should be at least partially explained by the availability of superior foreign technique (see further pp. 151–4). Minami is quite certain that 'capital accumulation, together with increases in labour force size and technological progress, have been the basic factors responsible for economic growth'. But more precisely, the rate of capital formation itself depended on 'external factors such as technological innovation' and the observed rapid rate of technological progress of the 1950s and 1960s 'resulted largely from the introduction of technology developed in Western countries during and after the Second World War'.

It becomes clear that foreign trade was of tremendous importance to Japan's supergrowth during the golden age, but not so much because foreign demand expanded exports and thus investment and incomes, but because the level and character of importing was essential to the process of both recovery and growth. The demand for investment funds within Japan was clearly associated with the availability of raw materials, fuels and technologies from abroad, and this relationship seems to explain much of the increased investment rate and aggregate demand of these years. If Japanese growth was not export-led, it might usefully be thought of as import-led.

Finally, growth through catch-up depended on the institutional characteristics of the Japanese economy. Improvements in production equipment resulted from the selective importation of raw materials, fuels and technologies. This in turn reduced internal costs within Japanese manufacturing and yielded a high propensity to export – Japanese goods were inexpensive not only because of an undervalued yen but because real costs of production in Japan were falling. In turn, investment demand was possibly the most active component of demand in Japan. Now, we may suggest that consumption demand was less dynamic than investment demand because increased incomes were going into savings for *primarily* institutional reasons: the bonus payments of the private sector, the high incidence of self-employment (non-agricultural self-employment still represented 25 per cent of the total in 1971), and the comparative lack of social security and insurance provisions. In conclusion, domestic demand provided the impetus to growth, rather than export demand, but a prime component of that demand was investment demand. This latter was induced by technology and raw material importing. The high rate of importing, which tended to rise particularly at the beginning of upswings and under government influence, kept the balance of payments from moving into chronic surpluses and, thus, allowed a fast growing and increasingly efficient economic system to interact with other industrial nations during the golden age through the medium of an undervalued yen.

Recovery

Table 8.1 shows production indexes for key industries in the 1950s, with the pre-war years 1934–6 as a base.

It is tempting to conclude that the era of the occupation saw full 'recovery' of the Japanese economy. Only in the production of textiles and non-durable goods was total production in 1951 not measurably above that of the pre-war years. Japan had discounted the war. But an interpretation of historical dynamics requires a little more than this. Following writers such as Jánossy and Shinohara we would suggest that recovery might more usefully be measured in terms of achievement of the output position which

Table 8.1 Major industries: production indexes, 1946–55 (1934–6 = 100)

	1946	*1951*	*1955*
Public utilities	109.1	184.7	254.7
All industry and mining	30.7	114.4	180.7
All manufacturing	28.9	115.1	189.4
Metals	15.6	144.0	218.9
Machinery	51.4	197.0	249.9
Ceramics	29.1	136.6	175.7
Lumber and wood products	60.3	157.1	186.6
Textiles	12.2	58.0	85.9
Chemicals	26.3	140.7	317.4
Rubber and leather	28.7	129.4	177.7
Foodstuffs	38.7	104.7	206.6
Durable goods	36.5	164.3	226.3
Non-durable goods	21.8	89.2	168.0

would have been obtained if the 'abnormal' war effects of 1937–45 had not occurred, i.e. the 'recovery' occurs when the level of output matches that which would have been attained in the absence of war, extrapolating the growth rates of the 1930s. The real and the hypothetical growth rates would cross around the years 1959–60. One sensible reason for taking the 1950s decade as approximately the years of true recovery is that any analysis of these years must acknowledge the time-lagged impacts of the occupation reforms (Chapter 7) and more normal 'recovery factors' such as the productive redeployment of machinery, stockpiles and military personnel. At the end of the war the Economic Stabilisation Board calculated the total value of raw material stockpiles at 25,000 million yen, somewhat larger than the national budget at that time. Around 7 million military personnel were redeployed, some 10 per cent of the total population or over 20 per cent of the potential labour force. (One estimation of total unemployment at the end of the war judged that some 13 million Japanese actively sought work.) The early years were also uniquely stimulated by the combination of US grants-in-aid and the 'special procurements' expenditures of the Korean War years. Whereas Marshall Aid designed for the reconstruction of Europe averaged about 2 per cent of the national incomes of recipient countries, US aid and war expenditure in Japan between 1946 and 1954 totalled about 5 per cent or more of Japan's national income.

During recovery, government policy was clearly growth oriented. Balanced budgets followed occupation ideology but low interest rates encouraged innovative investment behaviour amongst the large banks, perhaps 80 per cent of new enterprise investments were funded by bank loans. It was such institutional relations, set by government, which permitted the very high rate of technological transfer and adaptive innovation. The determination of the Japanese government was clearly stated in an Economic White Paper of 1956: 'The post-war period has ended; the growth as reconstruction is over. Our foremost task now is to start building a new Japan, eagerly importing the West's technical innovations.' At the onset of the so-called Jimmu Boom in 1955 investment rose 77 per cent over the previous year and orders for machinery 80 per cent. Again, much machinery investment was replacement of outdated techniques whose vintage had been extended abnormally by war and the subsequent tardiness of investment during the occupation years. Finally, the recovery phase was marked by a very significant under-investment in social infrastructure.

The highly cyclical nature of growth in the 1950s (with clear stagnation in 1953–4 and 1957–8), the huge labour absorption into manufacturing (doubling to nearly 30 per cent of the occupied population) and the great structural change caused by the differential growth of the capital-good sector (four-fold) and the consumer goods sector (2.5-fold) suggests a striking recovery period – national income grew at 9 per cent per annum average.

Indeed, many commentators predicted that special 'recovery factors' would wilt during the last years of the decade, yielding to a more mature, slower-growth economy during the 1960s. In fact, as G. C. Allen concluded, the structural changes of the 1950s moved Japan on to 'an entirely new plane of industrial achievement', wherein the future trajectory of growth would be determined by the increased weight and high performance of oil refining, ceramics, electrical energy production, electrical appliances, shipbuilding, automobiles and scientific instruments.

In 1955 the Five-Year-Plan of the new Economic Planning Board forecasted a growth rate of 5 per cent based on a simple formula centred on labour supply and labour productivity. Income growth was far higher than this primarily because of the potency of continued recovery factors – extreme technical lag combined with large reallocations of labour and capital to more productive areas. The Long Range Plan of 1958–62 predicted a higher rate of growth (6.5 per cent) and considered investment, savings, employment, production and trade targets. Monitoring of the economy would be based on a designated planned sector (where government controlled investment in essential infrastructure) and a policy sector (influenced by government through monetary measures, information dispersal and tactics of persuasion, and through control over reserves exerted by the Japan Development Bank). Once again real growth at 10 per cent per annum outstripped the forecasts. Here, improvements in the terms of trade joined with the accelerating level of investment and technical innovation. It would seem that growth in Japan during the 1950s was principally a function of the low initial level of output, occupation and subsequent American aid and expenditures, the lagged impact of occupation institutional reforms, the extreme level of relative technological backwardness and thus of technology transfer and productive manufacturing investment, the related transference of resources from low productivity sectors to those of growth and efficiency, associated economies of scale, the absence of defence expenditures, all set within the framework of an expansive world economy. Even the attention of government to growth at the expense of immediate welfare might be added to this list as a predominant 'recovery factor', for much of official growthmanship derived from a determination to retrieve status amongst the company of nations in the virtual absence of an independent military presence.

Economic growth

The phase of spectacular economic growth following the 1950s may be considered an outcome of an extension of recovery momentum associated with the lagged impact of the occupation's institutional innovations together with the operation of a technology-trade growth mechanism of a sort outlined on pp. 144–6. The relevant framework for such growth seemed to have included government growthmanship (monetary and industrial policy and the beginnings of demand management), bullish corporate behaviour linked to exceedingly high levels of gross fixed capital formation in the manufacturing, transport and communications and government sectors, a relative freedom of international trade which allowed enormous imports at stable prices of petroleum, iron ore, bauxite, timber, cotton, wool, livestock feeds and foods as well as advanced production techniques into the Japanese economy, a similar freedom of labour supply, mostly through the medium of transfers from sectors of low productivity to those of high and rising productivity, and a culture of heightening expectations amongst not only producers but consumers, workers and government.

Long before the 1960s in his *Essays in Persuasion*, J. M. Keynes had concluded that high expectations beget economic success, as 'if we are consistently on the optimistic hypothesis this hypothesis will tend to be realised; whilst by acting on the pessimistic hypothesis, we can keep ourselves forever in the pit of want'. Although a high expectations hypothesis of this type may also be applicable to the other success stories of the golden age, in Japan more than anywhere else such materialist ambition seemed most pervasive, most encouraged by the very variable interventionist instruments of government and most in contrast to the dismal condition of Japanese society in the late 1940s. Few analysts, however economistic at the outset, have finally been satisfied with conventional economic argument when leaving the relatively safe haven of the 1950s recovery for the excitement and complexity of the unexpected growth acceleration of the 1960s. More generally, Minami has appealed to 'the people's patience, industriousness and avidity for research, the absence of a rigid class system and the absence of a religion that restrained economic activity'. More specifically, the great Japanese economist Miyohei Shinohara has confessed that 'I am convinced that the unprecedented economic growth of the postwar period would not have been possible without the group-oriented psychology and social structure unique to Japan'.

We might still wish to emphasise that Japan was yet riding on a backlog. The great improvements in labour allocation and training, new applications of transferred knowledge, and high rates of investment in building and construction, together with the capturing of positive economies of scale in several key industries, were all measures of extended recovery effects. Nevertheless, to isolate such factors is not in itself to explain high growth. This requires some interpretation of the extent to which backlog opportunities were actually seized, and it is the admittance of this distinction which leads the way towards an institutional and technological analysis of Japan's economic success.

The cultural argument would emphasise such seemingly distinctive national characteristics as collectivism and consensus in explaining Japanese private enterprise efficiency and the complexity of the relations between the private and public sectors, themes returned to in detail in Chapters 9, 12 and 13. In such an analysis, 'Japan Inc.' is bounded not merely by monetary, trade and financial policy but by the intentions, understandings and institutions which facilitate the emergence of a planned rationality that overrides the activities of the market place as such. A second interpretive tactic concentrates on the role of the state during the period of high growth. Where, in Chalmers Johnson's distinction, the 'regulatory state' of common capitalism only follows in the wake of the market and the capricious repercussions of producer and consumer choice, in the 'developmental state' of modern Japan planned rationality generates a high degree of national economic competitiveness, and stems from the entrenchment of a strong bureaucratic structure which creates a flat surface of decision making and goal adjustment and information dispersals in the face of the vagaries of political change. Contrariwise, a third tactic emphasises purposive and aggressive business behaviour in the private sector. In the end nothing can gainsay the significant increases of productivity (however measured) associated with the Japanese economic miracle. Output growth per employee as well as hourly productivity growth increased at a far greater pace in Japan than in any of its economic competitors. The fact that productivity growth was sturdy in agriculture as well as in manufacturing (and far ahead of services at this period) suggests that it was a natural outcome of the utilisation of better equipment and better organisation, particularly in the manufacturing sector, which absorbed so much transferred labour from agriculture. A last approach to the growth of the 1960s and 1970s would forgo the attention given to the distinctive motivations of key agents which is common to all of the above analytical frameworks, and would shift the focus towards the inner or system logic of the catching-up process (see pp. 144–5). Given the relative abundance of labour for manufacturing expansion and a mainly open world economy showering the gifts of technique upon Japanese managers and officials alike, growth was the inevitable aftermath of recovery.

Clearly, none of these interpretive stances is satisfactory and none may be properly isolated. No extant interpretation convincingly relegates government intervention to a mere followership role, indeed most interpretations of this period highlight the unusual character of Japanese industrial policy.

Industrial policy and technology transfer

> The not-so-invisible guiding hand of MITI shaped the long-term pattern of structural change in the Japanese economy and this influence was largely exerted on the basis of judgments about the future direction of technical change and the relative importance of various technologies.
>
> (Christopher Freeman 1988)

We have already suggested that it is in the *interaction between* the public and private sectors that Japan displayed most unusual characteristics. This theme will be taken up in more detail in Chapters 9, 12 and 13.

Here we merely emphasise that such a concentration on interaction is especially validated in any analysis of the process of technology transfer into Japan during the years of the golden age. Two distinguished Tokyo-based American analysts and observers have judged that, at relatively low cost, the 'massive transfer of technology from the United States and Western Europe in fact provided the technological basis for nearly all of Japan's modern industries. Without this critical technology transfer, no amount of capital and labour could have moved Japanese companies to their present competitive positions so rapidly.' Many of the most significant transfers occurred through the medium of interfirm contracting and licensing, spectacular cases being Du Pont's nylon and ICI's terylene in synthetic fibres, Corning's glass technology in consumer electronics and, most infamous of all, Bell Laboratory's transistor technology in the semiconductors industry. Furthermore, Abegglen and Stalk rightly go on to emphasise the importance of incremental technological absorption and adaptation in explaining the success of such transfers, and see Japan's special capacity in this regard as at the very centre of the nation's economic success and as some direct function of more generalised processes of public–private sector interaction. Thus, while there was much in corporate culture and structure itself which promoted a high absorptive capacity (see Chapters 7 and 12), MITI in particular played a crucial role in both increasing the negotiating power of Japanese enterprise during the process of technology transfer and in stimulating the private sector to utilise and adapt foreign technique in a competitive, long-term fashion. Even such a strong argument for the significance of government intervention does not accord to the state the role of sole and flawless actor, but rather argues that government funding and subsidies, the deployment of R&D resources and the regulation of competition brought new technologies and products into the framework of the Japanese technological system more speedily and smoothly and, therefore, more efficiently than if left to private enterprise alone. This case also maintains that technology transfer was a crucial ingredient in both productivity growth and the stimulation of new investments in the private sector. Government did not provide much in the way of investment funds for private industry but encouraged private industry to invest in new technique, primarily by easing open the door to the West. If we follow Minami (p. 145) in his suggestion that the expansion of investment was to a large extent itself induced by technological opportunity as measured in technology lag and transfer, then the links between industrial policy, technology transfer and public–private sector institutional arrangements become quite crucial to any understanding of growth in the golden age.

Undoubtedly, technological agreements with major US companies, beginning with Hitachi's agreement with RCA in 1961, NEC with Honeywell (1962) and Toshiba with GE (1964) provided an important learning base for the growth of strategic indigenous capabilities. Yet such breakthrough transfers were set within a great wave of transfer activities. Measured in terms of royalty and license agreements, technology importing grew at a rate of some 30 per cent per annum during the 1950s and continued to grow at over 10 per cent per annum during the 1960s and 1970s. Royalty payments alone increased from $163 million in 1961 to $652 million in 1970, 50 per cent of which went to the US. At this stage most of the technology transfers into Japan were in fact standardised and generally available through trade or licensing. Of the 176,000 licence agreements signed between 1956 and 1972 most were concentrated into such areas as electrical machinery, chemicals, pharmaceuticals, synthetic fibres, transportation equipment and iron and steel. During the 1960s perhaps one third of Japanese industrial production was directly dependent upon foreign technology, a dependency at its greatest in the export industries, public works and in the industries nominated as of strategic importance by MITI.

The strength of the linkage between imported technology and internal technical capacity arose from a series of factors already discussed: the large scale of industrial operations, the very high investment rate, the continually expanding export sector, and specific institutional features. Most of the fast-growing and high technology enterprises were lead or member companies of the new business groups, or *keiretsu*. Such coordinated enterprise permitted cooperation in decision making, including the search for and selection of appropriate foreign technologies, the pooling of information, research and other resources between medium-sized production units and the sharing of risks in areas of new, high technology. With the emergence of such bank-centred *keiretsu* as Fuyo and Sanwa, the links between production, trade and financing were strengthened by means of cross-holding of stocks, interlocking directorships (especially between banks and client firms), subcontracting between 'upstream' and 'downstream' manufacturers (e.g. between large assembly plants and small component firms) and by a great variety of contractual relationships between buyers and sellers. The *keiretsu* organisational format provided two particular advantages in the process of technology transfer not found commonly elsewhere. First, the large size of the *keiretsu* company group (as against the modest size of many of its production components) assisted technology transfer by boosting the bargaining power required for contracts with foreign agencies or firms, and created an environment of certainty and cooperation in the development of technical systems shared between producing units, eliminating many transaction costs. Second, *keiretsu* banks were far better informed of technical possibilities and firm strategies than was normally the case in the financial sector of advanced industrial nations during the golden age. Banks were, therefore, that much more likely to finance venturesome technological projects, and the role of shareholders as a check on innovative activity was minimised. Together with specific processes working within the culture of private enterprise itself, such as life-time employment or in-house training, (see Chapter 9), these institutional characteristics clearly aided the process of technology transfer and ensured that imported technique encouraged rather than swamped emerging research and development capabilities within Japanese industry.

Furthermore, as Daniel Ōkimoto has emphasised, such *keiretsu* structures, combined with the existence of active business associations, provided numerous access points through which MITI could intervene directly in the workings of the industrial economy. In the words of Ōkimoto, *keiretsu* structures offer 'a variety of advantages [providing] a ready-made network for information gathering, sharing, and policy deliberations; unlike trade associations, that network cuts across industrial sectors . . . In this sense, *keiretsu* grouping organise the private sector into horizontal structures that provide the government with yet another potential point of access.'

Within this institutional context, the administrative guidance (*gyōseishidō*) or informal guidelines of government could flourish and succeed during the years of very high economic growth. It is clear that MITI's ability to gain the compliance of private enterprise in the achievement of long-term industrial and technological goals was dependent on enterprise structure, market structure (itself greatly affected by MITI's merger policies) and shared interests. Thus by the time of the Fuji–Yawata merger of 1970, arbitrated by MITI in the face of the aggressive tactics of Kawasaki steel and Sumitomo metal, production in the steel industry was dominated by about six companies, as was output in automobiles, synthetic fibres and oil refining industries. Again, petrochemicals, heavy electricals and machine tools industries exhibited similar market concentration, with the majority of production in the control of between six and nine major companies. Industrial policy was, in essence, forged from constant interactions between key government agencies and a relatively small number of aggressively competing, fast-growing enterprises. A US Department of Commerce report of 1972 recognised the power of this formula whilst dispelling myths concerning a Japanese conspiracy. What was unique was the 'extent and the scale of interaction and a qualitative difference, a style peculiar to the Japanese, derived from Japan's history and culture with its emphasis on the consensual approach'. Amongst others, Vogel has emphasised the elements of trust, closeness and repetition of contact between government and private enterprise: 'when a specific issue arises, interested parties schedule even more informal gatherings than usual. When necessary, bureaucrats from other ministries join these meetings and other knowledgeable experts and men of influence are called in.'

However idealised such formulations are, it does seem that Japan's golden age of growth was strongly associated with the forging of unusual relations between government and private sector. The emphasis on interaction serves to answer the simplistic theories of 'Japan Inc.', with their underlying vision of a national economic machine controlled by MITI and run by its private enterprise minions. Clearly, government interaction was but one feature of the golden age and its seeming success depended on enterprise culture and structure as well as a very high rate of investment and demand growth. But it is quite feasible that in the sphere of technological change and transfer in particular, government intervention through numerous formal and informal channels was of real importance. Writing at the end of the golden age, Ohkawa and Rosovsky concluded that MITI's 'postwar activities are quite new in an age when technology has assumed supreme importance . . . Miti officials continually survey the foreign technology scene, encourage and discourage certain lines of advance, set priorities – in a word they have attempted to reach and implement a national and rational policy of technological change . . . in view of Japan's performance as a technology importer it would be hard to argue that private initiative has been stifled by excessive government interference.'

Turning points

Although Japan's golden age was generally characterised by supergrowth within a global setting of speedy economic and technological change, high growth was bounded and bisected by discernible turning points. Clearly, the 1960s decade was quite different from that of the 1950s, not so much in terms of the growth rate of GNP or even of investment, as in terms of the underlying forces at work generating both high rates of investment and increased levels of efficiency. Much of the growth of the 1950s can be interpreted in terms of the fast-growing international economy, American aid and procurement, SCAP institutional reform and the exploitation of the large initial technology gap. As the economy moved towards a fuller employment of resources in the 1960s, growth was increasingly associated with large increases of efficiency generated within the private sector but under the secure auspices of long-term growth goals set by government. But, as we have emphasised, such guidance was itself the product of constant, informal interaction between the public and private sectors. The acceleration of the overall growth rate during the 1960s suggests that the Japanese achievement was not a mere reflection of global growth but some measure of the ability of the Japanese to exploit global growth most effectively. It seems that essential features of industrial structure (incorporating features *internal* to large manufacturing enterprises as well as those relating to the activity of small and medium business, self-employment and subcontracting) combined with a characteristic, competitive market structure to yield speedy diffusion of technical and commercial information and an increased ability to imbibe and adapt the best from the West, at a time when the latter was awash with new techniques and mechanisms of technology transfer. Japanese export performance was perhaps more a measure of success than a cause of high growth.

The major lesson of the years prior to 1971–3 is, in this view, that a combination of high rates of investment and increased efficiency is unlikely in the absence of both institutional *and* technological change unless an economy is riding on continued significant resource reallocations and positive returns to scale. Even these latter forces may only be best exploited by at least requisite institutional change. In the case of Japan it would appear that for this period at least, both public and private sector institutions were effectively harnessed to a fast rate of economic growth and that the interaction between institutional and technological changes may have boosted the overall growth rate to avoid deceleration during the 1960s. The high growth acceleration of Japan was unmatched elsewhere.

The end of the golden age was itself a significant turning point, often rightly analysed in terms of global forces. During the early 1970s, for a combination of reasons and at an international level, the golden age of growth came to a close, and new terms such as 'stagflation' and 'structural unemployment' entered common parlance. In Japan the advent of the first oil crisis in the last quarter of 1973 was seen as marking a 'trilemma' – price inflation, economic recession and balance of payments deficits. As in 1959–61, several experts foretold of gloom and doom. In addition to the high price of oil, the new constraints on fast growth were identified as a growing labour shortage, increased international competition, increased US pressure on Japan to liberalise foreign trade and capital movements and appreciate the yen against the dollar, and overall instability in energy supplies. In addition, government increasingly recognised that full employment and higher real wages, especially in the modern industrial sector, had created, as an unintended consequence of the growth regime, a more proactive labour movement and far greater middle-class popular concern over environmental and work conditions. Assessing such developments, an Economic Planning Agency survey of 1974–5 concluded that no stable growth could be sustained without severe deterioration of the industrial structure. The adjustment problems that were identified included excessive savings and an increasingly unstable business cycle, unbalanced government finances, strains on employment, increased rigidity in market prices, stagnation of imports, and the adverse effects of such problems 'on the neighbouring countries'.

There is little doubt that the early 1970s did witness a significant turning point and that several of the above forces did lead to greater uncertainty and instability. The surplus labour model appeared to have vanished. Between 1970 and 1977 the annual growth rate of employment in manufacturing averaged at around 0.5 per cent for Japan, as compared to 0.5 per cent in the US and negative figures for West Germany and Britain, where employment expanded more quickly in the service sectors. During 1971–3 inflationary pressures mounted for several reasons including relative labour shortage and wage hikes, increased oil prices, increased foreign reserves, and from the yen revaluations forced upon Japan by, primarily, the US. Simultaneously, increased inflation pressed down on consumption of consumer goods and hence on the rate of new investment.

On the other hand, although some of these forces appear to have been both considerable and long-term in their impact (e.g. the import cost of Japan's oil increased nearly thirty-fold between 1970 and 1980), Japan's economy was amongst the first to recover from the oil shock, and the overall approximate yearly growth of the economy between 1971 and 1980 averaged at over 5 per cent, once more well ahead of the rest of the industrialised world. Just as many of the economic problems projected for Japan did in fact operate at a global level during the 1970s, Japan itself exhibited a higher degree of flexibility and responsiveness to the lesser buoyancy of the world economy. The subsequent economic performance ushered in various explanations centring on the notion of 'flexibility', to which we shall return in Chapters 9, 10 and 12. Here it is important only to emphasise that the continued relative health of the economy after the early 1970s should not be taken as indicating the absence of a real turning point in the historical dynamics of the economy. From the early 1970s Japan did move on to a new economic trajectory as the economy and its institutions adjusted to internal social, demographic and environmental conditions, slower world growth and the collapse of older international economic institutions and arrangements.

Notes

1 At an international conference at Bretton Woods, New Hampshire, delegates from forty-four nations discussed proposals relating to international payments systems put forward by the US, UK and Canada. The system adopted depended on the working of the International Monetary Fund, which operated from March 1947 in establishing an exchange rate based on par values to the US $, an understanding which ended in December 1971. International capital movements for development by loans or by private investments was regulated from June 1946 by the International Bank for Reconstruction and Development, better known as the World Bank. The overall intention was that goods, funds and services might flow between member countries uninhibited by trade restrictions or exchange fluctuations arising from payments difficulties. In order to achieve stability and balance, the IMF utilised features of the older gold standard. For instance, each member was required to establish its par values as fixed either in gold or the US $, and the fund itself was made up from the pooling of member quotas, 25 per cent of each quota being composed of gold and dollars. Thus we might properly speak of a US-monitored golden age.

2 This is with reference to Minami as mentioned; see his textbook especially pp. 189–217.

References

Glyn, Andrew *et al.* (1988) *The Rise and Fall of the Golden Age*, WIDER Working Papers, Helsinki, World Institute for Development Economics Research of the United Nations University, WP 43, April, p. 15.

Patrick, Hugh and Rosovsky, Henry (eds) (1976) *Asia's New Giant: How the Japanese Economy Works*, Washington, DC: Brookings Institution, p. 59.

Minami, Ryōshin (1986) *The Economic Development of Japan. A Quantitative Study*, London: Macmillan, pp. 189, 180, 144, 424.

Hirschmeier, J. and Yui, T. (1975) *The Development of Japanese Business 1600–1973*, London: Allen and Unwin, pp. 242, 304.

Allen, G. C. (1965) *Japan's Economic Expansion*, London: Oxford University Press, p. 108.

Shinohara, M. (1976) 'MITI's industrial policy and Japanese industrial organisation', *The Developing Economies*, XIV, (December), p. 368.

Johnson, Chalmers (1982) *MITI and the Japanese Miracle*, Stanford, CA: Stanford University Press.

Freeman, Christopher (1988) 'Japan: a new national system of innovation?', in G. Dosi *et al.*, *Technical Change and Economic Theory*, London and New York: Pinter, pp. 330–48.

Abegglen, James C. and Stalk, George (1985) *Kaisha, The Japanese Corporation*, Tokyo: Tuttle, p. 126.

Ōkimoto, D. I. (1986) 'Regime characteristics of Japanese industrial policy', in H. Patrick and L. Meissner (eds), *Japan's High Technology Industries*, Seattle and London: University of Washington Press, University of Tokyo Press, p. 47.

Bureau of International Commerce (1972) *Japan: The Government Business Relationship*, Washington, DC: US Department of Commerce.

Vogel, E. F. (1980) *Japan as Number One*, Tokyo: Tuttle, p. 76.

Ohkawa, K. and Rosovsky, H. (1973) *Japanese Economic Growth: Trend Acceleration in the 20th Century*, Stanford, CA: Stanford University Press, p. 222.

Further reading

Aoki, M. (1988) *Information, Incentives, and Bargaining in the Japanese Economy*, Cambridge: Cambridge University Press.

Armstrong, P., Glynn, A. and Harrison, J. (1984) *Capitalism since World War II*, London: Fontana.

Barou, P. (1979) 'La croissance japonaise', *Statistiques et Etudes Financieres*, 59.

Caves, R. E. and Uekusa, M. (1976) *Industrial Organisation in Japan*, Washington, DC: Brookings Institution.

Denison, E. F. (1979) *Accounting for Slower Growth: the USA in the 1970s*, Washington, DC: Brookings Institution.

Denison, E. F. and Chung, W. K. (1976) *How Japan's Economy Grow So Fast*, Washington, DC: Brookings Institution.

Economic Planning Agency (1975) *Economic Survey of Japan 1974–75*, Tokyo: Tokyo Times.

Fruin, W. M. (1992) *The Japanese Enterprise System: Competitive Strategies and Cooperative Structures*, Oxford: Clarendon Press.

Gardner, R. (1969) *Sterling-Dollar Diplomacy* (2nd edn.), Oxford: Oxford University Press.

Goldthorpe, J. H. (ed.) (1984) *Order and Conflict in Contemporary Capitalism*, Oxford: Oxford University Press.

Gordon, A. (ed.) (1993) *Postwar Japan as History*, Berkeley, CA: University of California Press.

Horsefield, J. K. (1969) *The International Monetary Fund 1945–65*, Washington, DC: IMF.

Jánossy, F. (1972) *La fin des miracles économiques*, Paris: Senil.
Kaneko, Y. (1970) 'Employment and wages', *The Developing Economies*, 8: 453–79.
Kosai, Y. (1986) *The Era of High-Speed Growth* (trans. J. Kaminski), Tokyo: University of Tokyo Press.
Lipietz, A. (1985) *Mirages et miracles. Problèmes de l'industrialisation dans le Tiers Monde*, La Decouverte: Paris, (English translation 1987 Verso).
Matthews, R. C. O. (ed.) (1982) *Slower Growth in the Western World*, London: Heinemann.
Nakamura, T. (1981) *The Postwar Japanese Economy* (trans. J. Kaminski), Tokyo: University of Tokyo Press.
Odaka, K. (1975) *Toward Industrial Democracy: Management and Workers in Modern Japan*, Cambridge, MA: Harvard University Press.
Okochi, K. *et al.* (eds) (1974) *Workers and Employers in Japan*, Princeton, NJ: Princeton University Press.
Oshima, H. T. (1982) 'Reinterpreting Japan's postwar growth', *Economic Development and Cultural Change*, 31: 24–39.
Porter, M. E. (ed.) (1986) *Competition in Global Industries*, Boston, MA: Harvard Business School.
Price, J. (1997) *Japan Works: Power and Paradox in Postwar Industrial Relations*, Ithica: ILR Press.
Triffin, R. (1961) *Gold and the Dollar Crisis*, New Haven, CT: Yale University Press.
Uchino, T. (1978) *Japan's Postwar Economy* (trans M. A. Harbison), Tokyo: Kodansha.
van Dormel, A. (1978) *Bretton Woods: Birth of a Monetary System*, New York: Holmes and Meier.

Part III

Modern Japan

Introduction

Even at the end of Japan's 'golden age of growth' around 1973, the nation was yet a relatively small player on the global economic scene. By the end of the 1980s Japan had become the world's largest creditor and exporter of capital. By 1988 Japan's annual exports of capital were around $80 billion. At some time during this same period the economic problems of the United States became increasingly obvious and endemic and the Atlantic giant emerged as the world's largest debtor, hounded by both trade and budget deficits.

Part III considers this dramatic shift in global economic activity in a variety of ways, beginning in Chapter 9 with a substantial structural and institutional account of Japanese economic performance since the early 1970s. This is followed in Chapter 10 with a detailed account of the renewed expansion of Japan which covers trade, capital, foreign aid and technology transfers and then focuses upon Japan's changing relations with East Asia generally. In the belief that the progress of Japan will depend increasingly upon its settlement within a wider Asia–Pacific development process, Chapter 11 details the problems of, and prospects for, Japan–China economic relations, and argues that even in the absence of any final ideological resolution, the two systems may generate considerable complementarities and common industrial and commercial interests of increasing importance to the global system at large. Chapter 12 takes up the claim – voiced repeatedly in the international media of the 1980s and 1990s – that the contemporary clash between the United States and Japanese economic systems originates not merely in capitalist competition but in an underlying process which links the 'decline' of the American economy *causally* to the rise of Japan. After all, Japan was increasingly represented in United States financial markets, held a large proportion of the bonds issued to support the American budget deficit, was visibly involved in the takeover of American companies and in direct challenge to American markets overseas. In so far as such involvements affect the decision environment of enterprise within the United States, then it may be argued that Japan ultimately, if only partially, determined the structure of American commodity exports. Chapter 13 reflects on the principal characteristics of Japanese industrialisation and the major elements explaining the success of the nation since 1603.

9 An outline of recent economic change

Economic performance

A combination of factors encouraged many analysts to predict a significant secular downturn in the Japanese economy after *c.* 1971–3. Such a turning point was seen as resulting from the reduction in the amount of labour available to industry at low cost, the effects on internal and export prices of the oil price increases of the OPEC crises, and the similar effects on competitiveness of the revaluations of the yen created by the so-called 'Nixon Shock' of August 1971. In terms of the longer historical trajectory of the industrial economy itself, such gathering forces were interpreted as superimposed on an increasingly mature, high income and sophisticated industrial system, one which had now effectively absorbed the best-practice techniques and organisations of Europe and the US. The advantages of 'late development' had now been exhausted once and for all.

This combination of circumstances at the beginning of the decade was clearly neither transitory nor merely financial. Demography could not be reversed in a generation. The global pressure on the yen could not be averted by any internal official policy, even one which appeared to embrace a greater degree of 'liberalisation', i.e. reduced legal and informal institutional restrictions on foreign goods, investments, and services in Japan itself. The economic future looked very grim indeed. After all, the growth of the 'miracle' years had been commonly interpreted as some function of cheap labour, expanding export markets based on low prices, and continued technological immaturity, all of which stimulated high rates of productive investment (induced by producers' demand within Japan for advanced technology elsewhere), increased productivities of labour and capital, and foreign trade surpluses, which in turn allowed Japan to ride the crest of the global golden age. Indeed, a modified, institutional version of this sort of argument has been given in Chapters 7 and 8.

Yet, once more, the Japanese economy continued to grow, and this now in the face of a deep-rooted recession of the international economy. Japanese industrial dynamics refused to accord with the intuitions of informed observers. Table 9.1 illustrates the performance of national income compared to that of other advanced industrial nations.

Table 9.1 Growth of real GDP (annual average percentage growth rates 1971–92)

	1971–81	*1985–9*	*1988–92*
Japan	4.8	4.5	4.2
US	2.8	3.4	1.6
Germany FR	2.5	2.7	3.5
France	3.1	2.8	2.6
UK	1.4	3.5	0.8

By October of 1991, the economic expansion which had begun around late 1986 had become the longest in Japan's modern economic history. It surpassed that of any half-decade in the 1960s and was now based on an absolute size around 60 per cent of the American economy. For the fourth year in a row, Japan had invested more in absolute terms than had the US, at a rate of approximately 25 per cent of GNP. The nation's more comparable industrial competitor, Germany, was by then investing some 15 per cent of GNP. Furthermore, such enormous investments were not going principally into capacity expansion (a common enough claim at the time), but into productivity improvements and innovation (to around 60 per cent of the total) increasingly aimed at the domestic market. Of new capacity investment, perhaps 50 per cent was directed at products and services which barely existed in the late 1970s. It seemed that the boom of the late 1980s would feed the growth of the 1990s.

It is clear that throughout the twenty years from the collapse of the old Bretton Woods system of the golden age, Japanese economic growth continued to outstrip that of industrial nations elsewhere, including that of the other prime example of catch-up and late development, the then Federal Republic of Germany. From such crude comparison it is also clear that even the further revaluations of the yen in 1985 had no apparent negative effect on total export or income growth.

At the end of the period Japan was exhibiting a pattern of employment which still seemed to give some measure of late development. This is indicated briefly in Table 9.2.

Table 9.2 Structure of employment in Japan and three nations, 1981–92 (total = 1000s)

	Japan *Total ('000): Tertiary (%)*	*US* *Total ('000): Tertiary (%)*	*Germany FR* *Total ('000): Tertiary (%)*	*UK* *Total ('000): Tertiary (%)*
1981–2	56,380: 56.0	100,397: 67.6	26,774: 51.2	20,520: 63.9
1988–9	61,280: 58.7	112,440: 71.2	25,971: 54.4	22,104: 70.2
1991–2	64,360: 59.5	116,877: 72.9	29,334: 57.4	26,049: 70.3

In the two more mature industrial systems of the US and the UK, tertiary employment now easily outranked all other employments in combination, amounting to around 70 per cent of the totals. In contrast, both Germany and Japan showed a lesser move to service industries. Of all the industrial nations with the exception of Italy, Japan had the largest percentage of its workers employed in agriculture (although the trend was firmly downward from 17.4 per cent in 1970 to 6.4 per cent in 1992), and with the exception of Germany, Japan had the largest percentage of its workers employed in manufacturing industries, (with a constancy in this percentage for 1970–92 at around 35 per cent). On the other hand, as with most other industrial nations, the rate of growth of Japan's labour force was exhibiting some secular decline. It is thus possible that, in comparison to other industrial systems, income growth in Japan was coming from continued movements of labour from lower productivity to higher productivity sectors, and that this movement to an extent compensated for a demographic transition which yielded a more slowly growing and an older workforce.

Such crude aggregates point also to other possible explanations of Japan's economic performance in these years. Throughout this volume we have emphasised the complex repercussions of technology transfer into Japan from more advanced technological systems. Table 9.3 suggests that the claims of a Japanese maturity or catch-up were yet premature as measured by the technological balance of payments at this time.

Measured by the net payments made in the form of royalties and rights for international best technique, both Japan and, to a slightly lesser extent, Germany were catching up with such early leaders as the UK, but still a long way behind the much larger American economy. A great amount of new industrial development in Japan during the 1980s was still related

Table 9.3 Technological balance of payments, 1975–91 (US $ million and percentage ratios)

	1975		*1980*		*1985*		*1991*	
	$	*%*	*$*	*%*	*$*	*%*	*$*	*%*
Japan								
Receipt	233	39.3	644	66.6	982	79.9	2,751	93.9
Payment	592		966		1,229		2,930	
US								
Receipt	4,008	847.3	6,617	868.3	16,669	268.2	17,799	446.7
Payment	473		762		6,215		3,984	
Germany								
Receipt	264	38.9	430	41.9	614	50.9	5,339	66.6
Payment	679		1,025		1,206		8,022	
UK								
Receipt	589	101.9	779	115.9	848	122.5	1,933	95.6
Payment	578		672		692		2,021	

to the enormous export of technique from the US, whilst Japan was now beginning to export its own advanced applications and commercial designs and modifications of core technologies to a variety of industrial and industrialising nations. Trends in research and development (R&D) expenditure strongly suggest that a growing Japanese private industrial sector was fast investing in those techniques and research modes which would serve to optimise the use of core techniques, both Japanese and foreign. Much of US and European R&D is directly related to defence expenditure. Table 9.4 thus provides some comparative measures of non-defence R&D expenditure in the first decade of the period.

The creative utilisation and adaptation of core advanced technologies has required the increased investment in research and development. We may make a further important point by distinguishing between total gross expenditure on R&D (GERD) and the proportion of GERD financed by the public sector. Table 9.5 does this for Japan and the US in selected years.

The last column of Table 9.5 shows a clear distinction between Japan and the US. Where almost 50 per cent of American investment in research and development came from the public sector, mostly into military and strategic areas, in Japan only 25 per cent of investment was from the public sector, and because of treaty agreements and national preferences, very little of such public investment in R&D was in the defence industries directly. A spot check for the end of this first period, confirms the contrast. Table 9.6 isolates GERD, business sector expenditure on R&D (BERD), and public sector spending on R&D including higher education research (Gov. and HE).

As already suggested, comparisons between the US and Japan are especially misleading if the expenditure impact of military R&D is not explicitly acknowledged. More importantly, Table 9.6 shows that by the beginning of the 1990s, Japanese business was more actively engaged in the field of R&D than the private sectors of other leading industrial systems. We might at this stage estimate that Japan did not yet exhibit global technological leadership, was still benefiting from transfers-in of selected core technologies, but was in a technological position at least equivalent to that of its nearest industrial competitors in Europe.

Many analysts of modern Japan would argue a further case: gross comparisons of this sort are particularly misleading because they neglect the very different institutional contexts within which such R&D spending patterns were forged. We shall return to this theme later in this chapter and in Chapters 11 and 12. Here we may summarise an overall position. Japan continued to perform well industrially, even in the face of global recessions after 1971, because it optimised the growth functions of specific institutions. For instance, against the background of lifetime commitment and productivity bonuses, the large Japanese businesses developed in-house training systems characterised by recurrent management learning, the training of

Table 9.4 Non-defence R&D expenditures as a percentage of GNP, 1971–81

	Japan	*US*	*West Germany*
1971	1.84	1.68	2.03
1972	1.84	1.63	2.08
1973	1.89	1.62	1.94
1974	1.96	1.69	1.98
1975	1.95	1.68	2.08
1976	1.94	1.68	2.01
1977	1.92	1.67	2.01
1978	1.98	1.69	2.10
1979	2.08	1.75	2.27
1980	2.21	1.86	2.30
1981	2.37	1.87	2.38

Table 9.5 R&D expenditures in Japan and the US, 1975–91

		GERD GDP (%)	*GERD financed by public sector (%)*
Japan	1975	2.11	27.5
	1980	2.35	25.8
	1985	3.13	19.4
	1991	3.54	16.8
US	1980	2.57	47.1
	1985	3.02	47.7
	1991	2.50	43.3

Table 9.6 International R&D performance, total and by sector, 1991–2

	GERD (1990 US $m.)	*GERD/ GDP (%)*	*BERD/ GDP (%)*	*Gov.&HE R&D/ GNP (%)*
Japan 1991	64,834	2.87	2.16	0.58
US 1992	151,075	2.74	1.88	0.77
Germany 1992	33,817	2.58	1.76	0.81

older workers, the blurring of the very notion of 'skilled worker', the generation of social obligations within work and training projects, and an emphasis on short-term skilling or re-energising bouts of activity (such as the much-vaunted Quality Control Circles) as the most appropriate institutional system for flexible adaptation during times of technological and organisational change. Quite consistently, the concept of lifetime education (*shōgai kyōiku*) as a match to lifetime employment, filtered out from the private sector into public vocational education, union training schemes and even into a tentative revival of a modified apprenticeship system. In comparison to other large manufacturing nations, industrial education and training was probably more closely aligned to the needs of the employers of labour, more appropriate to specific industrial or commercial developments, and less dependent on the public purse or government educational policy. Such characteristics undoubtedly followed on from those institutional features of earlier years described in previous chapters, and shall be returned to later in this chapter and in Chapters 12 and 13. Here we might merely note that during the 1980s, this *institutional complex* yielded a system of high informal or non-monetary rewards for skilled employees in Japan's large-enterprise sector. Such employees worked longer hours than was common in major nations – hours per week for skilled production workers approached 43 in Japan, 39.5 in the US. Such employees were attached to strong enterprise cultures but associated within weak industrial cultures – at the end of the decade, the rate of unionisation in Japan was not much more than half that of the UK or Germany, although more than that of the US. Such employees expressed discontent through industrial action to a far lesser degree than was the case in Japan's leading commercial competitors – in the nine-year period from 1980 to 1988, labour disputes involving protest action lost on average some 429,000 man-days in Japan, 11,202,000 in the US, 7,555,000 in the UK, and 662,000 in West Germany.[1] Whether such an outcome in the manufacturing sector was principally a result of rising real wages associated with rising expectations, superior working conditions and very low levels of unemployment for permanent employees, or non-salary compensations to labour which effectively boosted wages and salaries above the nominal levels, remains a matter of dispute. It may be argued that all such factors were at work and that all arose at least in part from the precise organisation of the nation's manufacturing sector. The institutional foundations of modern Japanese industrial growth will be reconsidered later in this chapter.

Whatever the exact sources of growth into the 1980s, Table 9.7 shows quite clearly the subsequent decline of Japan's economic growth performance in both chronological and comparative terms.

Table 9.7 Average annual real growth rates of GDP (1988–96)

	1988–92 (%)	*1992–6 (%)*
Japan	4.2	1.4
US	1.6	2.6
UK	0.8	2.0
Germany	3.5	1.5
France	2.6	1.3
Italy	2.3	1.0

For the first time in over one hundred years, in the absence of global warfare, Japanese economic performance fell significantly, both in terms of its own trajectory and with respect to the performance of its mature industrial and commercial rivals.[2]

Shocks and structures: growth recurring

For reasons outlined at the end of Chapter 8 and the beginning of this chapter, it was expected that the Japanese economy would slow down as it entered the 1970s. The Miracle Economy was sooner or later bound to come up against factor constraints or exogenous limits against the backdrop of an inevitable technological catching-up process. Together such forces would dampen investment incentives. A first indication was the growing shortage of labour. The annual increase in the labour supply had averaged around 2.3 per cent for 1966–70, but shifted to 0.5 per cent for 1971–5, 0.3 per cent for 1976–80. In the early 1970s, the ratio of jobs offered to jobs wanted doubled from an average of 100 per cent per job – one job offered per applicant – in the 1960s. This was an important factor explaining the sharp wage increases of 1973 and 1974. Contemporaneously, there emerged environmental limits on investments in manufacturing, particularly water supply and industrial sites. Although this was perhaps some function of a more global environmental awareness, it was also a result of specifically Japanese limitations to growth – by the 1970s population per km^2 had reached over 300, compared to 248 for Germany, 229 for the UK, 163 for the European Community as a whole (ten nations), and 25 for the US. At the same time the land devoted to arable or other permanent pastures and meadows had shrunk to 15 per cent, compared to the 75 per cent of the UK or the approximately 50 per cent of the US or Germany. Electricity used per 1,000 km^2 of habitable land space was 268 billion kilowatt hours in Japan, only to be contrasted with the 133 billion in Germany, or the 109 billion in the UK. The infamous 'Red Tide', the abnormal proliferation of sea flora was reported to have occurred nearly 300 times in 1974, compared to around eighty times in 1970, and but four times in 1950. Not surprisingly, there was much talk of a 'turning point' in the Japanese economy, for although such forces even in combination were insufficient to halt the economic growth process, they independently coincided to increase the cost of production and generate inflationary pressures and reactions in the form of new public sector constraints on expansive expenditure or industrial targeting. But the notions of a turning point towards slower-growth maturity were strengthened by the occurrence of a series of additional, more abrupt, shocks to the Japanese economic system.

The first of these was the so-called 'Nixon Shock' of 15 August 1971, when the US authorities took the US dollar off gold convertibility and delivered the most severe of all clouts to the post-war Bretton Woods system of relatively fixed exchange rates. The bilateral background to the first shock is provided in Chapter 11. The immediate effect of floating of currencies was to expose the undervaluation of the yen (or the inflated status of the US dollar), as a host of financial interests rid themselves of dollars and bought the strong trading currencies. The 1949–71 yen price of the dollar (360) which had underpinned Japanese commodity exporting – as in Chapter 8 – had moved to 308 by December 1971, the time of the international *fait accompli* of the Smithsonian Agreement. The revaluation of the yen peaked in its first decade at 175.50 to the dollar in October 1978. Despite the increasing value of the yen, inflation within major trading partners and the quality improvement of Japanese goods and services (including, for instance, after sales services in foreign countries), combined to produce ever rising trade surpluses through the 1970s. Although a gain to GNP, this meant that pressure from other nations on Japanese trade and investment regulations and policies in fact increased, and a new policy constraint was added to the Japanese system. As Barnhart has summarised, 'it is fair to say that the central story of Japanese diplomacy since at least the mid-1970s is a story of the diplomacy of trade and currency and Japan's increasingly important role in setting the tone and pace of trade and currency negotiations'. The exchange rate of the yen to the dollar in comparison to two of its major trading competitors is provided in Table 9.8.

The inflationary impact of the secular yen appreciation was greatly increased by the second shock, that of the first OPEC oil crisis of November

Table 9.8 Exchange rates per US dollar, selected years, 1970–82

	Yen	*D. Mark*	*£ Sterling*
1970	360.00	3.6600	0.4167
1973	271.22	2.6726	0.4078
1975	296.79	2.4603	0.4501
1978	210.44	2.0086	0.5210
1980	226.74	1.8177	0.4299
1982	249.05	2.4266	0.5713
1986	168.52	2.1715	0.6817
1988	128.15	1.7562	0.5614
1990	144.79	1.6157	0.5603

Table 9.9 Japanese oil imports, 1970–80

	1970	*1973*	*1975*	*1980*
Price per barrel ($)	1.84	4.75	12.05	34.61
Import cost ($bn)	2.37	8.67	19.76	54.02
Import volume (million kl)	205.3	290.1	260.7	249.2

1973, when the Arab oil producers announced a 70 per cent increase in the price of crude oil, from $3 to $5 per barrel.[3] This was furthered in its impact on importers by an ad hoc system of physical embargoes, eased in Japan only after a nominally pro-Arab publicity tour of the Middle East by the deputy prime minister, Takeo Miki. An inflation of 15.7 per cent in 1973 doubled in 1974. The second oil crisis of 1979 simply confirmed a long-term impact, as shown in Table 9.9.

The massive twenty-three-fold increase in the oil bills had a significant effect on the prevailing trade balance. The surplus of $6.0 billion became a deficit of $3.9 billion in 1973, and again a surplus of $11.8 billion in 1978 became a deficit of $1.4 billion in 1979. After both crises, however, the deficits were reversed relatively speedily. More importantly, the adverse terms of trade effect exerted a deflationary effect on the economy at large, as exhibited particularly in the great declines in private consumer expenditures and private investment in plant and equipment during 1973–4. A generally very low level of unemployment rose from 735,000 in 1972 to 850,000 in 1974, to a peak of 1,130,000. Unemployment centred on women and older workers.

Not only was the industrial consumption of energy as a proportion of total energy consumption somewhat higher than in other industrial systems (around 50 per cent for Japan as against 28 per cent for the US), industrial consumption was particularly concentrated in iron and steel, road transport, and chemicals and petrochemicals, amongst the most important of all the industries to have generated the economic miracle of the 1960s, and sectors whose services or products were closely linked to production in other industries. For Japan this marks precisely the origins of stagflation, the coexistence of recession and inflation. Japan's energy dependency is illustrated in Table 9.10.

The third and related exogenous shock was that of 'trade liberalisation', a summary term for the series of pressures put on Japan to reduce formal restrictions on imports of goods and investment funds, to remove many subsidies or other instruments of industrial policy which were designed to

Table 9.10 Energy requirements and import dependency, 1976–81 (million tonnes oil equivalents)

	A *Total production*	*B* *Imports*	*C* *Exports*	$\frac{B - C}{A + B - C}$ *(%)*
Japan 1976	47.16	316.63	0.58	87.0
Japan 1981	59.26	314.88	3.34	84.0
Germany 1981	130.79	165.36	30.82	50.7
UK 1981	207.30	59.60	72.03	−6.4
US 1981	1,551.73	329.15	84.77	13.6

increase exports, and to simplify the enormous complexity and informal specificity of the nation's regulatory environment in an effort to deflate the incipient trade surpluses, particularly with the US and other principal trading partners. Under GATT and IMF regulations Japan had begun a limited liberalisation during the 1960s, but it was in the early 1970s that the number of protected products fell most clearly and in 1973 that Japan first agreed in principle with the OECD Convention to liberalise capital inflows. Such features of the international environment of the Japanese economy will be explored in greater detail in Chapters 10, 11 and 12.

A fourth shock, that of rapidly rising land prices, was of internal Japanese origin and very much coincided with the first oil shock of 1973–4. As astutely summarised by Tsuru, in each of these cases 'the price item which went out of balance was an almost universally used factor of production, and it could be expected that the general principle of economic efficiency would dictate either a substitution by another factor wherever possible or adoption of an alternative method with a more economic use of the factor in question'. Whereas the Japanese industrial and policy systems made a concerted effort to reduce energy consumption through both short- and long-term strategies, there would seem to have been a narrower range of options with land.

The increase in land prices impacted as an unexpected shock because the trigger was the industrial dispersement component of Kakuei Tanaka's famous 'Plan for Remodelling of the Japanese Archipelago', an almost post-modern cultural and environmental vision announced in 1972. Whereas the main goals of the previous plan projection (1970–5), had been price stability and economic growth, the new goals centred around a rich environment, a stable civil life and international cooperation The new Prime Minister intended to spread the miracle of growth both socially and spatially, and the result was the Economic Planning Agency's remodelled forecast, *Basic Economic and Social Plan: Toward A Vigorous Welfare Society 1973–77*. Intended to usher in the welfare society, an immediate effect of Tanaka's plans was widespread land speculation. In addition to its contribution to inflation, the imbalance in land prices after 1972 also served to increase tax yields from the land very significantly, encourage further land speculations and corrupt profiteering, and induce manifold smaller experiments in land alienation and amalgamation in urban areas. Of great importance to the path

Table 9.11 Increases in land and consumer prices in Japan, 1970–83 (Index 1955 = 100)[4]

	1970	*1975*	*1980*	*1983*
Nationwide City Land Price Index	1,395	2,691	3,231	3,938
Six City Land Price Index	1,832	4,148	5,844	7,160
Consumer Price Index	187	317	435	486

of economic growth, such disparities, continuing through the 1980s, exerted measurable effects on income distributions and patterns of investment, increased the status of financial institutions and services at the expense of the historic industrial culture, dampened public works programmes, and confused community life, some of which impacts will be returned to in Chapters 10 and 13.

The final major shock to the economic system of the early 1970s was the seeming collapse of 'Japan Inc.', those understandings between government, bureaucracy and private sector which had underpinned the organisation of the industrial boom. Many studies of the Japanese political system testified to the vibrancy of a bureaucracy-dominant model, best summarised by Chalmers Johnson in his central claim that 'the elite bureaucracy of Japan makes most major decisions, drafts virtually all legislation, controls the national budget, and is the source of all major policy innovations in the system'. The sites of decisions dictated their agency, the use of industrial targeting and micro-policy tools and informal administrative guidance, as well as more conventional monetary and fiscal policy instruments. Shared graduation and goals (e.g. the tremendous influence of the University of Tokyo), the practice of *amakudari* ('descent from heaven', the movement of 'retired' bureaucrats into politics or business or both), decision making by discrete channels of influence and systems of informal tacit knowledge, and other institutional elements of industrial policy and growthmanship, the agreements of Johnson's 'developmental economy', were all starkly threatened by scandals and breakdowns in the heart of the complex. Between July 1972 when Eisaku Sato gave up office, to 1994, only one of Japan's subsequent thirteen Prime Ministers lasted more than two years in office. Although the Liberal Democratic Party remained in power, a turning point had occurred in the relations between policy making, administration and profit seeking. One element in this represented a direct link with the land price shock, for the demands of the Tanaka plan necessitated a massive increase of public spending, by 25 per cent in the 1973 budget. The rise in land prices forced up public works expenditure and was a partial cause of deficit financing. The combined actions of public policy, and oil and land price increases forced up prices during 1974. In that year wholesale prices rose 37 per cent, consumer prices by 26 per cent, and the immediate result was a reversal of government short-term policy, to money circulation restriction and expenditure curtailment. In 1974, for the first time since the war, Japan suffered negative economic growth. It was from this time that deficit financing through bond issues became commonplace, beginning with the emergency revised budget of 1975, when government bonds as a percentage of the budget increased from a planned 9.4 per cent to 26.3 per cent. The subsequent level of government bond expenditure remained at around 20 per cent of the general accounts, and tended to further inflation in land and construction, increase interest rates, and direct funds away from the private manufacturing sector. (By 1996 Japanese national finance dependency on bond issues had reached 28 per cent, compared to 17 per cent in France, 14 per cent in the UK and 7 per cent in the US.)

This was set against a political context of corruption scandals, culminating in the fall-outs from the Lockheed Affair of 1972–6,[5] frequent allegations of intimate links between politicians and the *yakuza*, and a decisive movement of 'money politics' from traditional manufacturing industries towards land and construction at home and abroad. Just at the time of combined system shocks, the much-vaunted developmental state was in no position to implement innovative policies for commercial adjustment (e.g. tax reforms) or industrial innovation. Indeed, the move towards public sector reliance upon services and land-related investments may have increased the impact of the other shocks. It might be noted that the inflation of 1973 preceded the impact in Japan of the oil price shock. It is arguable, then, that inflationary pressures were raised by a failure of public policy in these years, and that this was itself at least partially conditioned by the failure of political institutions to maintain the goals and understandings of the developmental state.

In summary, five all-but independent shocks hit the Japanese industrial economy in the opening years of the 1970s, and their concerted impacts, together with the endogenous features of increased capitalist maturity (reduced sectoral movement of labour, demographic downturn, increased wages, technological catch-up, a consumer revolution in part effected by international media and communications, and so on) tended all to work in the same direction, towards moving Japan from its path of high-growth industrial development. Yet, as we have been at some pains to emphasise, the industrial and economic growth of the 1970s and 1980s, although now more prone to fluctuation, remained at a comparatively high level, as shown in Tables 9.1 and 9.7. Table 9.12 confirms that in terms of income per capita, Japan continued to outperform major industrial rivals in a period of general world recession.

Despite the well-known technical difficulties of such monetary comparisons, the figures are so stark that it may be seen that Japan performed extremely well despite its difficulties and system shocks, especially in the

Table 9.12 Per capita GNP, selected nations, 1970–88 (US $ current exchange rates)

	Japan	*US*	*UK*	*German FR*
1970	1,949	4,952	2,254	3,041
1975	4,475	7,401	4,254	6,784
1980	9,103	11,996	9,567	13,296
1985	11,098	16,760	8,134	10,355
1988	19,905	18,570	12,107	18,373

years 1975–80 (when everybody did well), and 1985–8, when income per capita went ahead of both the US and West Germany. A reasonable explanation of this performance is that the Japanese economic system responded to shocks and new conditions through a significant *structural change*, where resources were moved into: (a) new product industries; (b) the application of biochemical, electronic and communications technologies in established industries; (c) new service sectors, especially those associated with land and construction and associated financial institutions; and (d) the movement of resources overseas, encouraged by the general liberalisation theories (see pp. 169–70) and by the increasing value of the yen which lowered the Japanese price of foreign assets, especially after the large upward movement of the yen during 1985. Backed by a process of R&D investment, technology innovation and technology transfer harboured within flexible private enterprise cultures and organisations, this structural change in the total economic system served to offset diminishing returns faced in the older growth industries of the miracle years. Much of the rest of this chapter, and Chapters 10, 12 and 13 address this general position in more detail.

The extreme high-technology end of this deeper structural change has been very often noted by commentators on the modern economy – the value of computerisation within the economy increased ten-fold between 1970 and 1985, by the end of the 1980s Japan's population of industrial robots was nearly six times that of the US, ten times that of Germany. On the basis of OECD categories, by 1982, Japan outranked all its industrial competitors in the weight of high R&D intensity industries in total manufacturing output, and was second only to the US in the high-technology component of its total manufacturing exports. A serious commitment of the private sector to applied research in micro-electronics, biotechnologies, marine sciences and applications, and environmental industries or processes, especially as related to reduction of crude oil usage, illustrated in Tables 9.5 and 9.6, yielded a host of famous results. In such newer global industries, core breakthroughs continued to be dominated by the US, UK or France, as instanced in monoclonal antibodies (1975), the large programmes on fibre optic cables (1977), the construction of commercial fast breeder reactors. But commercial applications through market elaborations came increasingly from Japan – the Casio electronic typewriter with memory (1978), NEC voice data input terminals (1978), the invasion of the global computer memory market from 1981 by the Japanese 64 kilobyte computer chip, and the further improvements of Hitachi (1990) and Fujitsu (1993).

As suggested, such newsworthy developments were a result of a more underlying structural adjustment. In the twenty years following the initial Nixon Shock, employment in manufacturing as a proportion of total employment remained approximately constant at 35 per cent, but employment in the primary sector shrunk from around 18 per cent to 6 per cent, just as employment in tertiary or service industries rose from 47 per cent

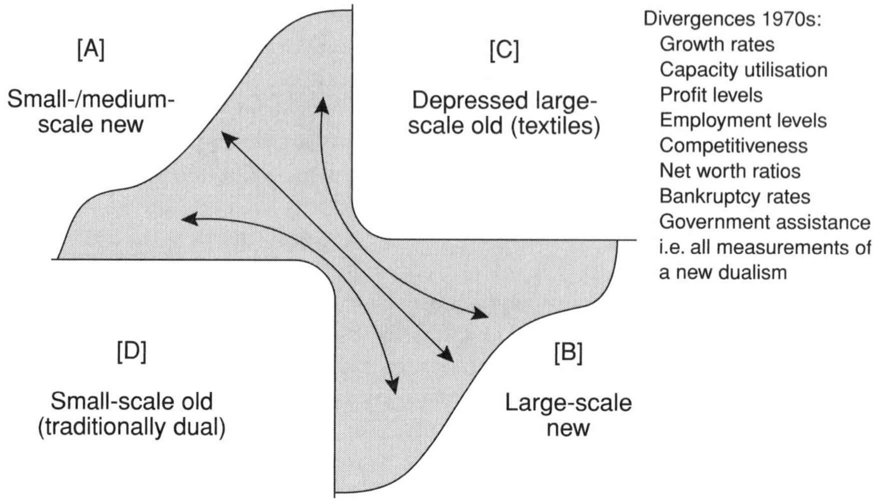

Figure 9.1 The new dualism.

to 60 per cent. Resources were moving from areas of over-capacity and technological maturity to the production of new goods and services satisfying new wants in new, more variable, markets. We may characterise the flexibilities involved in Figure 9.1, which postulates a new dualism in the manufacturing economy.

Where in the years of high boom, industrial dualism had divided small, low-wage, and low-productivity firms operating in a distinct casual labour market from large-scale, high-productivity and high wage firms operating in fast growing sectors with formally selected permanent employees, the structural changes of the 1970s and 1980s created a more complex economy. As measured by the criteria listed to the right of the figure, the old division was replaced by a manufacturing system which now placed a lesser premium on the scale of output of the individual production unit, and where the use of new electronic and communication systems (e.g. CAD-CAM) created growth in newer large-scale and small-scale producers alike. In contrast, whatever the scale of production of the individual firm, lower growth, more bankruptcies, and lesser profits were generated in industries facing diminishing returns in traditional markets and to established technologies and institutions, such as large parts of the textile, chemicals, iron and steel and electrical machinery industries. By the 1980s, enterprises located in quadrants A and B had more in common with each other (subcontracting increasingly bound them together – see pp. 182–4) than they had with the enterprises lying in quadrants C and D. In Japan, growth was recurring because of structural change. Three points shall be returned to. Structural change required institutional flexibilities. Such change allowed the total manufacturing system to dampen the effects on overall growth of decreasing returns to systems of production in older industries. An essential component of such structural change was the movement of Japanese resources into other nations.

Diminishing growth – the greying economy

During 1991 signs emerged of new problems for the Japanese economy, led by the Gulf Crisis (sparked by Iraq's invasion of Kuwait) and slowdowns in the growth of major trading partners. The first had an immediate effect on oil prices, which possibly doubled their market values in that year. The growth of the US economy was below 1 per cent prior to the Gulf Crisis, and the unification of the economies of East and West Germany reduced the growth rate for the united nation to around that of the rest of the EC. It was very likely that the long boom which followed the yen's sharp appreciation by the Plaza Accord of September 1985 would come to an end from around that time. The so-called 'bubble economy' of this period was in fact reflective of basic production growth in manufacturing associated with cost-reducing innovation, increased overseas production and industrial and geographical diversification. Such structural adjustments were perhaps overshadowed by the combined financial impacts of the *endaka* policy, which encouraged a high-value yen as a tactic towards reducing Japanese export volumes, and the true bubble economy, whereby the major banks loaned enormous sums to finance the purchase of land and shares. The higher yen value further encouraged land investments overseas as the price of such solid assets declined in Japanese terms.

Continued expansion of production seems to have come up against shortages of skilled labour from around 1990 and a consequent increase in real wages via the spring offensives: between 1989 and 1992 rates of spring wage increase in large companies averaged over 5 per cent per annum. Just as increases in labour productivity began to fall away, unit labour costs and real wages increased at a higher rate. Although something similar was found elsewhere, Table 9.13, which covers manufacturing firms of ten to thirty employees and above, suggests that the trends in Japan were more marked. Whilst wage rates almost doubled in Japan during the decade, in the US (in particular) and Germany, increases were more modest.

Table 9.13 Real incomes (wages per hour) in three nations, 1985–95

	1985	*1990*	*1993*	*1994*	*1995*
Japan (¥)	1,440	1,993	2,273	2,321	2,528
US ($)	9.54	10.83	11.74	12.06	12.37
Germany (DM)	16.20	20.07	23.79	24.58	25.46

This combination of circumstances goes far in explaining the failure of the economy to adjust easily to new short-term crises. Whereas the global financial crash of October 1987 was surmounted within Japan, the resulting escalation of the internal land boom led to a collapse of the Tokyo Stock Market in 1989, a very marked fall in land values and a rash of bankruptcies. Ironically, during 1992 and 1993, falling demand at home coincided with the first real impacts of *endaka* on the foreign demand for Japanese goods. The general election of July 1993 witnessed the fall of the LDP and the establishment of an unstable coalition of opposition parties. From then, an unsettled leadership and a fragile series of alliances found it increasingly difficult to cope with the internal economic forces described above, forces which were inexorably added to by the increased pressure brought to bear by the US over such key issues as trade and investment liberalisation, voluntary export quotas and Pacific defence.

Much has been written about the 'greying' of Japan. By 1995, the proportion of the population over 65 years of age had risen to around the 14 per cent mark. But the comparison with other high-income industrial nations illustrates nothing unusual – higher figures are available for the UK (16 per cent), Germany (16 per cent), or Sweden (17.5 per cent). What may be of more note is a seeming greying of the economy itself, a final reduction to zero of the earlier advantages of relative technological and institutional backwardness. If we are prepared to reinterpret such backwardness as youthfulness, then the 1990s may have witnessed a growing maturity in which the income yielding functions of existing industries and institutions are in decline. In a wider perspective this might be viewed as an important instance of the convergence of systems envisaged by writers such as Rostow and Tinbergen. In this perspective, Japan happens to have caught up with global institutions and social developments precisely as the growth-promoting functions of such institutions were in some abeyance.

Japan in context

Table 9.14 provides a summary picture of the performance of the Japanese economy in comparative terms.

The first five rows of the table confirm Japan's high level performance despite serious shock in the early years and a marked comparative decline in the later years. Furthermore, although the high rate of physical investment explains much of this performance, Japanese growth was also an increasing function of efficiency improvements. Over time, the tendency was for the Japanese business sector to invest more in new R&D facilities than did the private enterprises of other nations. The second group of eight rows together show that by the mid-1990s, despite its growing maturity, Japan still boasted a disproportionately high level of gross capital formation to GNP. By that time Japanese income per head exceeded that of any other nation in the table, and total national income was equivalent to the combined national incomes of

Table 9.14 Japan in context, all data *c.* 1996 unless otherwise stated

	Japan	*US*	*UK*	*Germany*	*France*	*Italy*
GDP per head $	39,687	26,580	18,849	27,604	24,973	19,021
Industrial output $bn	1,836	1,496	326	777	373	–
GDP per head growth 1980–96	55	35	47	31	27	35
GDP annual growth 1992–6 (%)	1.4	2.6	2.0	1.5	1.3	1.0
Investment per head growth 1980–96	98	98	85	14	7	5
Average labour productivity 1980–96	41	17	39	37	33	33
Average annual increase business R&D 1981–94	8.5	4.0	2.5	4.2	5.0	7.5
K/GDP 1996	28.5	17.6	15.1	21.7	18.0	17.0
GDP 1993–7 growth	1.5	2.8	2.9	1.5	1.7	1.1
Global GDP (%)	18	26	4	8	5	4
World exports (%)	9.5	13.5	6.4	9.8	6.9	4.5
World investment exports (%)	10.9	16.6	9.3	7.8	9.6	–
Manufacture value added % GDP 1987–8	32.0	19.5	20.0	33.0	21.5	23.0
Human development index	93.8	94.0	92.5	92.1	93.5	91.5
Male life expectancy 1960	65.5	66.6	68.3	66.9	67.0	67.2
Male life expectancy 1995	76.4	72.5	74.3	73.0	73.9	74.4
Density km^2	331	28	239	229	105	190
Persons over 65 (%)	14.0	12.7	15.7	16.0	15.1	–
Households VCR (%)	76	79	86	–	–	72

Germany, Britain and France. Finally, the last six rows illustrate a degree of maturity in the delivery of the high level social outcomes of economic growth. The increase in life expectancy between 1960 and 1996 was greater than found elsewhere: in the same period female life expectancy rose from 70.2 years to 82.8 years. This was despite the incredible spatial density of population distribution, which was not approached by even the UK or Germany. The relative positions on the Human Development Index[6] confirm that, in the face of problems of overcrowding and various types of pollution, as well as the historical neglect of a gamut of welfare provisions, the industrial and commercial development of modern Japan had delivered a social outcome equivalent to or better than that found in nations of far richer spatial, climatic and physical endowment. Japan had reduced its per capita air pollution (sulphur and nitrogen oxides, carbon dioxides) to a fraction of that found in the US, UK or Germany, and achieved an output of CO_2 emissions approximately 22 per cent that of the US, but failed to reduce noise levels to anything like the European norms. By this time per capita expenditure on health was approximately equivalent to that found in most European economies, but well below that of the US. Although yet to catch up in medical training, Japan provided more hospital beds per head of population than any other OECD nation and approximately four times the proportion attained in the US. Compared to major industrial rivals, Japanese were far less liable to fall victim to death through cancer and heart diseases, but more likely to succumb to pneumonia, senility, suicide and accident. Startlingly, despite maturity of industrial lifestyle in other respects, the incidence of all crime remained low in Japan, on a flat graph line far below the undulatory ascending figures for all other major industrial nations. An average Japanese was as likely as a European to possess a video-tape recorder, but far less likely to have it stolen. By the mid-1990s, Japan produced in absolute terms more movies than any nation, and in per capita terms, far more newspapers in daily circulation. Although a nation of strong cultural identity and conservatism, in these years the nationality of foreigners resident in Japan spread out from the descendents of those Koreans who had been forced to Japan under colonial rule, to embrace an increasing number of Chinese, Brazilians, and South-East Asians.

As we shall examine in Chapter 13, this was no perfect society. Despite the resolutions and achievements of the early 1990s, social security contributions lay well below those of other nations, corruption was still endemic within political and public institutions, and the social position and economic security of workers in the casual and itinerant labour markets were often no better than at the outset of the miracle growth period. But the table shows that on comparative measures, Japan had done very well indeed.

One major comparative indicator of a change in the character of the economy in Japan, was the rise of government expenditure as a proportion of GDP. As we have several times remarked, the periods of particular industrial achievement in Japan were associated with low levels of government expenditure as compared to other nations. A high level of government activity was juxtaposed with relatively low expenditures, this being particularly remarkable during Meiji industrialisation and in the more recent

Table 9.15 Government expenditure as percentage of GDP (current prices), five nations, 1913–86

	1913	*1929*	*1938*	*1950*	*1973*	*1986*
Japan	14.2	18.8	30.3	19.8	22.9	35.5
US	8.0	10.0	19.8	21.4	30.7	37.1
UK	13.3	23.8	28.8	34.2	41.5	45.9
Germany	17.7	30.6	42.4	30.4	41.2	47.8
France	8.9	12.4	23.2	27.4	38.8	53.2

Table 9.16 Trade balances, selected nations, 1993–6 in $billion

	1993	*1994*	*1995*	*1996*
Japan	141.5	144.4	131.8	83.6
US	−115.6	−104.4	−101.9	−111.0
UK	−20.1	−16.6	−18.3	−19.7
Germany	37.4	44.2	59.5	65.5
Korea	−1.6	−6.3	−10.1	−20.6
Singapore	−11.2	−5.9	−6.2	−6.3
Thailand	−9.1	−9.2	−14.3	−16.6

miracle years. As Table 9.15 (from Maddison) shows, even during the shocks of the early 1970s, Japanese government expenditures had remained remarkably low. By the beginning of the *endaka* years, Japanese government expenditure was moving towards that of its great commercial competitors.

The early 1990s witnessed a great number of claims concerning the novel failures of Japan to compete with its commercial rivals, happily juxtaposed alongside equally vehement claims as to Japan's deliberate generation of large trade surpluses through unfair cultural practices, regulatory regimes or deliberate targeting of export industries. Table 9.16 shows that Japanese trade performance remained comparatively outstanding despite yen revaluations during the years of growth downturn.

Apart from Germany, Japan was the only one of the major industrial nations to record a consistent trading surplus. Of interest from this table are the negative balances in industrialising Asia during these years. This leads to the possibility that Japan's surplus was to an extent generated by some trade switching towards East Asia in these years. By 1996, the primary destination of Japanese exports was the US, but this was followed by a grouping of six Asian economies, then Germany, followed by Malaysia. Japan's trade surplus with America was of course huge, but large trade surpluses were recorded with Korea, Taiwan, Hong Kong (the export–import ratio in the latter case being 10:1), Singapore, Thailand and Malaysia. The important exception to this trend was China, which accounted for some 5.3 per cent of Japanese commodity exports, but 11.6 per cent of imports.

A final measure of Japan in context, which shall be returned to in Chapter 10, is the increase of direct overseas investment, which we have argued to have been an outcome of both the yen revaluations and private sector restructuring of investment away from those older manufacturing industries that were facing high oil prices, increasing labour costs and skill shortages, and environmental constraints. The all-but doubling of Japanese FDI in 1985–6 reflected the yen revaluation directly. By 1900 the major recipient of FDI was North America, where the bulk of investments were in finance and insurance, trading companies and facilities, and electrical machinery. European investment was similarly well spread, although with more concentration in chemicals and transportation. Asia was the next largest recipient, and it was here that FDI most clearly took the form of oil-using, labour-absorbing and pollution-creating sectors – by the beginning of the 1990s most FDI was going into mining, iron and metal manufacture, chemicals, electrical machinery, textiles and transportation equipment. Of all Japan's FDI, the greatest bulk across the globe was directed at those financial, insurance and commercial assets which would best absorb the capital of Japan's land and construction bubble whilst taking advantage of the increased physical asset purchasing power of the *endaka* yen.

Interpretations

The several interpretations of recurring growth until *c.* 1991 may perhaps be best initially considered as falling within one or more of three large categories. The first of these relates to the claim that *Japanese growth was still an outcome of various forms of relative economic backwardness.* Such commentators would point to the lower levels (if fast growing) of labour productivity or of labour organisation when compared to more mature systems of industrial capitalism. Although fraught with well-known technical drawbacks, the Japanese statistics themselves suggest a faster growth of labour productivity in the manufacturing sector between 1978 and 1986 than could be found in any other nation, but at the period's end-point the Japanese level was clearly well below that of its competitors. Growth continued between then and 1990, at which point the level of Japanese productivity approached those of its competitors, followed by a relative decline, so that by 1995 Japan once more lay behind such major competitors as the US, UK, France and Germany.

A second type of approach would point to *specific institutional flexibilities demonstrated in the Japanese private sector which allowed it to achieve growth despite negative shocks.* Theory of this sort would point to aspects of enterprise culture and the speed with which manufacturing shifted into oil-saving or pro-environmental trajectories, or to the quickness of the move to direct investment overseas. This approach is often resorted to in attempting to explain the speed of Japan's absorption, adaptation and commercialisation of new techniques in new industries in a global environment increasingly wary of technological or informational leakage. In an astute global analysis of technical cooperation agreements between firms, François Chesnai recognises that, in the Japanese case, 'interfirm cooperation builds on enterprise structures and forms of industrial organization which are peculiar to that country'. Thus, in summary, whilst efficiency increases prior to 1971–3 might have owed most to the importation and institutional adaptation of superior techniques, continued productivity growth after the turning point has, by this argument, arisen from private sector adaptability. A strong version of this theory is provided by Masu Uekusa:

> Facing the dissolution of the Bretton Woods system and the first oil crisis, managers tried to lower costs and improve product quality as much as possible in order to survive in the domestic and international markets. There was an active effort to introduce energy-conserving and labor-saving technologies: for example, continuous casting facilities in the iron and steel industry . . . There was also increased pursuit of quality control and the learning by doing effect. For this purpose, most large companies formed quality control circles in each of their workshops . . . big businesses asked subcontractors to reduce costs and improve product quality and adopted or refined the *kanban* system. Moreover, management and administration costs were reduced through the introduction of office automation and computer-aided design systems.

The third approach tends to emphasise the *contributions of the state and public sector institutions.* Here theory points to the unusual range of industrial policies and instruments, and to the seemingly productive or growth-oriented relations with private sector banking, commercial and manufacturing enterprises. The political scientist David Williams, summarises the embrace of this approach:

> Japan has been called a 'goal-oriented society' or 'goal-achieving culture' and this fundamental orientation (determine the goal, then set about achieving it) influences all aspects of Japanese social practice. It defines the Japanese philosophy of social action, and it casts a long shadow over the activities of the individual, the family, the firm and the state. In fact, Japanese public policy, old and new, cannot be understood without reference to this philosophy . . . Japan would never have become an economic superpower in so short a time without a national commitment by policy makers, politicians, business leaders and union members to meet the challenges demanded by successful structural change.

Such themes will be returned to, particularly in Chapters 12 and 13. Here we isolate special aspects of them as an introduction to a feasible synthesis.

With direct reference to our general emphasis on the contributions of technological change, particularly in the form of transfers which generate new products or industries, the thesis of a *continued backwardness* does remain attractive into the 1980s. Pages 163–6 provided evidence of the continuation of a negative technological balance of payments, and a tendency towards drawing core technologies from the US whilst exporting Japanese refinements, adaptations and commercially viable products back to the US and to a number of smaller trading partners. This latter process meant that such technology trade went into surplus by 1994, by which time

Japanese were making almost as many patent applications overseas (139,000 approximately) as were British innovators (159,576). Such measures of high-tech payments, however, disguise the continued absorption of a huge amount of advanced technology through imports of machinery, chemicals and equipment. For the average of the three years 1994–6, imports of these three technological items amounted to 32.2 per cent of the total of all commodity imports, and fully 76.1 per cent of all manufactured goods importing. Of such technology import, over 30 per cent was coming from the US, perhaps 10 per cent from Germany, with no other nation providing more than 7 per cent of the total. In areas such as semiconductors, measuring instruments, communication instruments, power generating equipment, and aircraft equipment, the dependency was over 50 per cent. In the case of some key inputs, such as aircraft engines, some 90 per cent of imports were from the US. Equivalent Japanese technology exports were of much greater value, but tended to be more concentrated in areas such as general machinery, electrical machinery and general transport equipment; Asia took 40 per cent of all Japanese exports of machinery and equipment. It would, therefore, be difficult to postulate overall technological backwardness relative even to the US, as Japan entered the 1990s.

Arguments concerning the *unusual character of Japanese private enterprise* are perhaps the best known of all, and represent the second category. Many such approaches do tend to underestimate the total size of the small-unit components of Japanese business culture – a large number of small producers may make up most of an industry. Table 9.17 shows the far greater importance of smaller firms in total manufacturing employment and output in Japan than in other major industrial nations during the 1970s.

Interestingly, there was a slight rise in the importance of the SME sector of manufacturing between the period of very fast growth and the period of growth recurring. As late as the crisis-ridden year of 1991, firms of less than 300 workers dominated output value of leather and textile industries (over 90 per cent), food production and metalworking (over 80 per cent), and paper manufacture, publishing and printing (over 60 per cent), and produced over 40 per cent of output values in steel, rubber production, precision and general machinery, and chemicals. This is an exceptionally

Table 9.17 Small and medium size businesses in manufacturing, 1963–78

	Workers	*Labour force (%)*	*Value added (%)*
Japan 1963	(1–299)	69.0	53.3
US 1977	(1–249)	43.4	36.3
UK 1977	(1–499)	29.9	25.1
Germany 1977	(1–499)	50.0	44.0
Japan 1978	(1–299)	73.5	58.0

variable component of the Japanese economic and social system, and does not easily succumb to glib generalisations. Although returned to in detail in Chapter 12, here we merely warn that 30 per cent of the Japanese labour force is composed of self-employed workers and unpaid family workers, compared to less than 10 per cent in the US or the UK. Theories of recurrent growth based on the flexible adaptations of the large enterprise must acknowledge the limitation on generalisation which such percentages effectively impose.

Figure 9.2 stylises one approach to the flexibility model. The flow figure is based on the notion that an advanced production system of the *kanban* type may serve both as a flexible organisational device and as a link between large enterprises and the smaller employees. The *kanban* is the

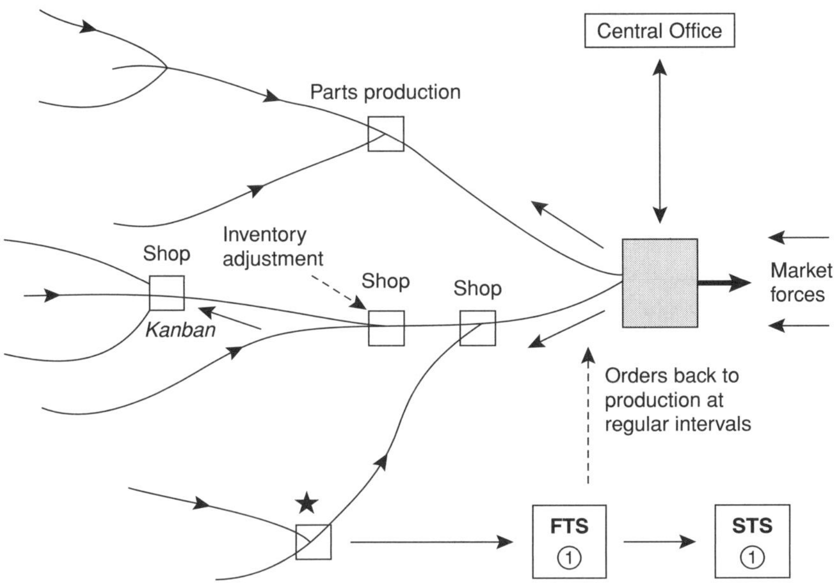

KEY

Central Controlling Office responding to market forces and centralised planning (from Central Office): **Final Assembly (FA)**.

Shops: (Including Quality Control Circles, flow controlling status etc.)

★ At this Shop information may return to Final Assembly and thus Central Office as shop innovates, learns, adjusts.

Kanban: An order placed in envelope from ▢ to each ▢ every few days, daily or hourly: ***Kanban*** and product flow to FA. Shop situated downstream dispatches its ***Kanbans*** to shops ***upstream***. ∴ Just-in-time system.

FTS/STS: First-tier subsidiaries, long-term relations with firm/second-tier subsidiaries.

Figure 9.2 Institutional flexibilities – the *kanban* system.

message passed up, down or across line in response to new instructions based on new information, and for our purposes may take the form of a computer connection.[7] Seen by many analysts as epitomising the contrast between Western-style hierarchical organisations and Japanese-style, flatter systems of information gathering and decision making, the just-in-time flexibility of the system is identified as a key to reduced inventory and production costs and a self-regulating link between main firms and subcontractors.

We might take the figure as a idealised map of the Japanese system as it may be applied (with our important reservations above) to modern production. Where flexible adjustment to external shocks might be unlikely in a production system dependent on data and orders being received and then given through a central office, the *kanban* information system involves a continual flow of information and minor adjustment to-and-fro the main shop floor and major or first-tier subcontractors (FTS), as well as the second-tier of contractors (STS). In this system up-to-date market information enters the production process through several windows, and shop floor units may adjust and reform fairly readily and without disturbing the major continuous flows of production of a great number of variations from a standard model or specification. Here are several lucrative sites for Quality Control Circles and other formulae whereby worker groupings of mixed status but common task might both receive information and prompt adaptations to changing market or technical circumstances. Most importantly, in comparison to more hierarchical structures, such a production system lends itself to quick recombination of parts (the much vaunted FMS or flexible manufacturing system) and to reception of instructions through computer networks with close suppliers, especially FTS (the OES or order entry system), rather than through a complex, time-consuming data processing by a central office,

The ramifications of this sort of institutional approach shall be further explored in Chapters 12 and 13. Here we point out only that such a perspective may provide insight into the underlying processes of recurring growth. The dampening effect of both technological catch-up and exogenous shocks (pp. 167–72) might have been offset by an acceleration of those institutional innovations within the production system which were already under way during the years of miracle growth. At the same time, subcontracting might have worked as a low-cost solution to both the earlier divergence of wages and efficiencies between large and small firms (the well-known 'industrial dualism' problem), and to the task of technological diffusion within industries or industrial complexes. Close relations between the main and subsidiary firms in a *kanban*-like system were more likely to spread technological information and tacit understandings, than were formal and distant customer-supplier distinctions. Furthermore, such relations may have acted, through repeated guaranteed orderings, as an inducement to technological up-dating in small supplier firms during the period of rising wages. Although many small firms went to the wall as they were shocked out of markets in an almost Schumpetarian manner, many more small enterprises benefited from new information networks, CAD-CAM systems, and so on. In so far as this makes sense, institutional flexibility might at least partially explain the sort of structural change suggested above on pp. 173–5 and stylised in Figure 9.1, the new dualism.

Our third category of interpretation also focuses on institutions, but switches locus to the *public sector and government economic policy*. Here the argument is that government policy aided vital structural change, both by ameliorating or diffusing the shocks emerging from the international economy and relations with the US on the one hand, and on the other by creating an appropriate internal environment for investment-led business growth, particularly following the additional strains of the Plaza Accord of 1985. Most representative of the first of these was the handling of the so-called Structural Impediments Initiative and the complex of frictions arising between the Japanese and the American economic systems. This will be addressed more fully in Chapters 10 and 12. Here we centre on some major elements of industrial policy.

Until the shocks of the early 1970s, the principal agent of government industrial policy, the Ministry of International Trade and Industry (or MITI), was concerned with orchestrating the industrial repercussions of the anti-monopoly legislation laid down by SCAP. A running battle under the various revisions of the Fair Trade Commission from 1949–53 focused on mergers and cartelisation. Thus during the recession of 1960–2 alone, the FTC ratified over 1,000 mergers, whilst 1959 had witnessed seventy major cartel restrictions on industrial output, some of which supposedly halved the market level, and all of which stemmed from 'advice' offered by MITI. By the OPEC crisis of 1973 MITI had utilised its divisions of industry into the strategic, the sick, and those of rapid growth but 'infant' international status, in order to justify a fairly comprehensive policy of reducing the 'excess competition' stemming from the unrestricted operation of earlier anti-monopoly legislation. Such a strategy had placed the Ministry, which never boasted financial clout, at centre-point within crucial sites of the industrial economy. MITI had become a crucial arm of the 'developmental state', allowing, in Arthur Stockwin's vivid phrase, 'divided politics in a growth society'. Thus, MITI was behind the 1970 merger of Fuji and Yawata Steel to form Nippon Steel, which produced 40 per cent of the country's output. This was a classic example in the catch-up growth economy – scale economies would permit technological innovation, an increase in research personnel, a spurt of patent applications (which indeed doubled during 1970–3); the development of continuous casting meant the reduction of equipment and labour costs (both fell by some 20 per cent), and so on. In addition, by the time of the shocks, MITI had emerged as a component of national planning, particularly with regard to the working of 'administrative guidance' and relocation projects, and reformulations of the pattern and siting of large-scale R&D programmes. Here the intention was to deliberately reformulate the sites of R&D endeavour in order to escape the formalities of existing Japanese innovation projects, and to merge government facilities and guidance with enterprise commercial expertise. Leading examples were the Fifth Generation Computer Program (that is, artificial intelligence using Prolog, from 1982), MITI's Sixth Generation programme which utilised neural networks and was established at an estimated costing of $26 billion, the combined enterprises project to develop the 64 megabyte D-RAM memory chip from 1991, or the establishment of the MITI laboratory for Fuzzy Engineering research in 1989.

During the 1970s the early concentration on anti-monopoly legislation was, if anything, somewhat reversed. Industries were very publicly designated for long-term growth, from which flowed a great increase of new investments and new set-ups. MITI's industrial research cartels and Agency for Industry, Science and Technology directed R&D projects in an effort to reduce duplication and encourage economies of specialisation in such fields as microelectronics, biotechnologies and new materials. MITI was similarly involved in encouraging foreign interests in new industrial locations, thereby attracting Texas Instruments to N. E. Kyūshū, and from 1983 sponsored a law which gave tax benefits to private sector projects across fifteen designated high-tech cities. By the time of the MITI-sponsored high-tech World Fair of 1985, the Ministry had located many of its new laboratories and research cartels in such new sites as Tsukuba. We might, therefore, agree with other writers that a major function of MITI after *c.* 1970 was to assist in economic restructuring through a combination of 'guidance' instruments (indicating the direction of desirable structural change), with 'sanction' methods (supplying incentives to move in such directions). The Economic Planning Agency's four- or five-year indicative plans and white papers became increasingly programmatic, that for 1981 for instance being titled 'For the Promotion of Creative Activity in the Japanese Economy', and MITI added to these its own two- and three-year 'Forward Looks', which were designed to address the 'adjustment' problem directly. In the arena of R&D, MITI identified long-term strategic projects, one of its most famous but problematic being the 1981, ten-year programme for 'The Development of Next Generation Base Technologies', which set out to distribute some half-billion US $ of funding in ten major projects whose focus was to be collaboration with private enterprise in public sector research sites. Continuing something of its earlier activity in reducing internal competition in designated 'infant industries' through 'informal investment cartels', MITI also moved to hasten or smooth structural change through a newer concern with declining industries. Designated under the alternative, more dynamic term of 'saturated industries' (meaning industries whose traditional markets were now oversupplied), areas such as textiles, shipbuilding, artificial fibres, and steel received exit compensation packages, which often included retraining schemes as well as proposals for alternative uses of fixed assets, but MITI also attempted the more traditional tactic of capacity reduction through specially formulated recession cartels. Membership in the latter involved scrapping and the shared allocation of resources, the establishment of quangos for labour compensation, subsidies and retraining, as well as the provision of interest rate subsidies for 'scrap and build' projects (e.g. in shipbuilding).

By the beginning of the 1990s, MITI had clearly regained status within the Japanese system by turning from the manipulation of legislation in order to fine-tune the competitive environment of existing industries, towards direct technical intervention in the field of restructuring through technology transfer and diffusion. The major features of this new world were global in character: the accelerated diffusion of data processing technologies, the advent of microprocessor technology and its relatively speedy transfer into manufacturing; widespread change in telecommunications; the continuous development of new materials as both substitutes for and allies of older metal products; and the rise of biotechnology. Continuous competition demanded a flow of transfers in the form of enterprise agreements, such as the technological partnership between Fujitsu and Amdahl Corporation, which provided the former IBM-compatibility.

The stronger version of the 'statist' thesis visualises such MITI activities as merely part of a growth-oriented *complex of Japanese economic institutions*, one which includes enterprise unions, or joint stock companies in which up to 70 per cent of shares might be owned by competing companies and never traded, in which bank long-term financing is of greater importance than the capital markets as a means of transferring savings to industry, and so on. In this approach there are fundamental differences between Japan and Western economic systems, differences which gave Japan an institutional edge in the economic performance stakes, but which are not necessarily the inevitable functional outcome of traditional mores and values, so much as a constructed product of a more recent process of 'conscious innovation'. In particular, this institutional complex substitutes for, but out-performs, the decision-making and information producing and processing functions performed by markets for final products, capital and information in other capitalist nations. To MITI as an information system might be added the information networks of the general trading companies and the *Keidanren* or Federation of Economic Organisations in the private sector, and such official agencies as JETRO (the Japan External Trade Organisation), which extends information search and dispersal to operations overseas (for more of which see the following chapter). Where this substitution produces problems, as with the retardation of a venture capital market for new technologies, special target-oriented institutions arise, in this case, the Japan Development Bank. To this extent, state institutions might be some measure of a remaining relative backwardness, but ones which produced a real competitive edge. This effect was sufficient to create recurring growth in the face of exogenous shocks. Although most commentators define such institutions as functional equivalents of market forces, there is an important debate on how far they generated a greater growth rate than would have occurred in their absence, i.e. in the presence of more developed market structures. Although this particular counter-factual is difficult to apply, Garry Saxonhouse has illustrated the possibilities of debate quite firmly:

> What effective elements of industrial policy exist in Japan are an effort to overcome the distortions which might result from the long-term absence of well-developed capital markets. Japanese industrial policy has been a substitute for, and not an unfair complement to, the market allocation of capital.

The political implications are, of course, important. If Japanese public policy in the industrial arena created a higher rate of export and economic growth than would have occurred under a 'western-style' policy regime, in which the market institutions of the mixed-economy would play a larger role, then American complaints of the globally insidious impacts of Japanese industrial targeting would be justified. If, on the other hand, public policy had a negligible impact on growth (in particular, if 'government successes' were merely outcomes of a high growth caused by private sector activity), then international complaints concerning Japanese industrial policy were (and remain) unfounded.

A consistent approach to the crises and downturn of the 1990s should point to a failure of one or all of these three general forces for growth. That is, if some combination of relative backwardness, private sector flexibility, and public sector over-substitution for market forces, sufficiently explains recurrent growth in the 1970s and 1980s, then a conversion of this complex of forces might explain the relative failure of high real growth in the 1990s. But to this we might add the possibility that, from the outset of the 1990s, the external context of the Japanese economy altered, especially in terms of growth rates of major trading partners and deteriorations in the commercial relations with the US.

Synthesis

It might now be possible to visualise the dynamics of the Japanese economy after *c.* 1970–3 as predominantly determined by the *diminution of relative economic backwardness towards zero.* This secular trend was confused by several factors. The first of these was the series of exogenous shocks to the economy which operated in the opening years of the period. The second was the global trend towards lower rates of industrial growth and the emergence of stagflation. The third was a growing complexity of relations between Japan and its trading partners and commercial rivals, but principally the increasing strains of the relationship with the US. *Whilst shocks could be sustained when relative backwardness remained significant, a recurrence of shocks in the later 1980s and early 1990s generated a lower rate of growth in an economy reaching institutional and technological parity with the major industrial systems of the world.* This form of synthesis of the contending interpretations does assume that the problems of the 1990s reflected changes in the cultural and historical dynamics of the economy, and were not mere cyclical phenomena.

Furthermore, such a perspective on Japan points once again to the importance of technologies and institutions as significant partial determinants of the underlying dynamics of the industrial economy. Earlier changes in supply of such conventional factors as labour or investment may well have altered rates of growth, but they never seem to have been sufficient to shift the industrial economy on to new paths, nor off the old paths of growth. At such key points in Japanese history as the early Meiji years, the inter-war years of depression, or the early 1970s, exogenous shocks stimulated structural changes which permitted long bouts of growth, within which periods fluctuations in levels of investment or labour supply undoubtedly affected short term rates of growth. Here we once more argue that such structural change could not have occurred without technologies which allowed investments to go into new product areas as well as new processes, nor without institutions which harboured and nurtured skills, provided security in eras of great change, and rewarded effort in ways that were recognisable without wholesale cultural revolution.

Themes

Chapters 10–13 examine some of the major features of the modern period with particular reference to the styles of interpretation here outlined, and in an effort to substantiate important elements of the overall synthesis. An outstanding theme of the era since 1973 has been the expansion of the Japanese economy in terms of trade, investment, aid and technology transfers, the subject of Chapter 10. The movement of assets and certain types of production to other nations may, indeed, have been an important avenue of structural change, as resources within Japan were moved into newer, high-technology, and cleaner industries requiring far less energy input to output values. Economic expansion at this rate and level cannot be a politically neutral process, nor one without important cultural implications. Chapter 10, therefore, describes the history and mechanisms of such expansion, the character of Japanese multinationalism, relations with the Pacific and with Asia, as well as the impact of the outward movement of such a very large economic system upon the economies of smaller or less-developed national systems. A major constraint of such expansion might arise from both commercial and political developments in mainland China, in Greater China and amongst the elements of the Chinese Diaspora generally. This subject is considered in great detail in Chapter 11, which argues that fundamental economic resolutions between the two systems are possible even in the absence of any final political settlements.

It has been argued that a major alteration in the wider, global context of Japanese industrial development has arisen from changing relations with the United States. This is the nation from which Japan has traditionally derived most of its advanced techniques, and the nation which in the post-war years of occupation was so decidedly influential in the reformulation of Japan's economic, and even, social, institutions. It is also a nation which has grown increasingly concerned about its internal and external deficits (and particularly Japan's share of such deficits), its trading and industrial competitiveness, its provision of profitable technologies to competing economies, and the financial burdens and logistical difficulties of its defence of the Pacific locations of what we might loosely (and generously) term liberal capitalism. The status of Japan as threat or partner remains unclear within the American policy-making world. Chapter 12 takes up the theme of the historical relations of Japan and the US, and considers the notion of whether such relations have reached a stage of global systems clash, i.e. are the two systems at some key points incompatible, and do they represent alternative models for emulation in other parts of the world?

This chapter has already noted certain *social underpinnings of the working of institutions whose character is seen as vital to the continuing health of the industrial economy*. Theses concerning secular growth slow-down or the greying of the economy at times move beyond the idea of decreasing returns to existing institutions, and towards the notion of a weakening of the *social base* upon which such existing institutions, or any other innovative institutions, might develop in the future. *How such a case of social decline is argued, depends very much on assumptions about the recent past.* We may here take the two examples of the high personal *savings rate* and the Japanese *work ethic*, both of which have been commonly visualised as fundamental social inputs into earlier high rates of growth.

It has been recognised that even when Japanese incomes lay markedly below those of other industrial systems, the Japanese ratio of household savings to income was abnormally high. For salaried worker households, the propensity to save was around 21 per cent in 1982. Between then and 1988 this propensity fell to around 13 per cent and has remained roughly constant and well above that of all other industrial nations apart from Italy. In 1994 household savings ratios in Japan were 12.8 per cent compared to 11.6 per cent in Germany, 5.7 per cent in the UK and 3.9 per cent in the US. A common argument is that earlier high rates of personal savings were a result of traditional values of frugality, that this underpinned high levels of investment (particularly in the 1980s when lower corporate profits reduced business savings), which permitted investment in new technologies transferred from other nations, a linear path to high growth. The other side of this Japan coin is the world of capitalist maturity, where higher incomes will be spent on luxuries whose purchase is increasingly determined by the power of global media and postmodern cultures. The disintegration of traditional cultural traits will, thus, lead to a downturn in

Japanese industrial and commercial competitiveness. An immediate problem concerns the assumptions about direct or sole social causation. As William R. Purcell has didactically but precisely summarised:

> An array of explanations covering cultural, economic, institutional, political and demographic factors have been advanced to explain the savings behaviour of Japanese households. Confucianism, the cost of housing, the age structure of the population, the high cost of weddings, the bonus income system, tax breaks for savings and even the prevalence of natural disasters wrought by earthquakes and typhoons are among more than 30 explanatory variables which regularly appear among the explanations of Japan's high household savings rate.

Purcell finds that, of this array of possibilities, the low ratio of aged to working population and the bonus system, together account for perhaps 90 per cent of the difference between Japanese household savings and those of other nations. There is no need to accept such precision in order to grasp the essential point. One might want to test, for instance, the effect of relatively low public financing of health and social welfare, and the impact on households of increases in such public financing during the 1990s. Any lowering of household savings in modern Japan is not an inevitable outcome of new social dissolutions, but more likely a rational outcome of population ageing, institutional changes within the labour markets, or changes in government policy towards social welfare. Our earlier arguments concerning the emergence of a new dualism might go some way towards explaining the fall away of bonus payments, which were an institutional response to the need to harbour and retain highly-educated labour whose financial reward could be linked to the efficiency achievements of a relatively backward, high growth economy.

Several very authoritative analysts have pointed to the role of a special attitude to work and its historical and cultural origins. Thus Tamotsu Sengoku describes how the Japanese employee 'looks for the reason of his being or identity in hard work and even tries to improve himself by it'. Harnessed to such claims are impressive statistics of fast-rising labour productivity. However labour productivity is a function of elements other than work input. By the late 1970s, UK motor workers may have been working at only 40 per cent of the productivity of their Japanese counterparts, but the latter were operating with more than two and a half times the value of plant and machinery, a function of the much higher rate of Japanese investment in that industry at that time. At the same time, by the 1970s total hours worked per year in manufacturing in Japan were only marginally higher than in the US or Germany, although holidays were less and thus the number of actual days worked was definitely more (e.g. at around 13 per cent more than the US figure). *Endaka* Japan witnessed decidedly falling working hours per week for production workers, so that by 1996 the Japanese hours per working week (39.6) were measurably below those of the UK (43.5), the US (42.5), France (39.8) or Germany (39.7). Is this a measure of maturity and of things to come which emanates from changing Japanese values? Our answer must depend on the factors behind hard work. In Japan from a very early period, work was rewarded in a multitude of non-wage ways, from bonuses and rewards to gifts, prizes, public acknowledgement, paternalist relations with superiors, positions of responsibility, entry to training programmes, holiday payments and arrangements, wedding gifts and so on, all this to a greater degree than in most industrial nations, although even this point should be tempered in the realisation that late development tended always to be associated with the operation of non-monetary or extra-market sanctions (e.g. in Russia or Germany from the later nineteenth century). This meant that the real reward to work in Japan departed quite considerably from its nominal monetary payment, and might have borne a very strong relationship to work input. In other words, the so-called special attitude to work would have been merely the mirror-image of a special attitude to rewards. This would have provided the illusion of a particular work effort when compared to other nations, where the monetary rewards to work were visibly higher. Any recent decline in acceptable measures such as hours worked or lengths of employment might, then, be indicators of changes in the reward systems. That is, as money rewards have risen, non-money payments may have declined, and thus contemporary complaints about the changing attitude of the Japanese towards the work-place might be misdirected. The argument becomes one about changing institutions, and this process may be quite independent of more deep-rooted cultural changes or continuities.

Chapter 13, therefore, considers several features of maturing Japan that might be broadly labelled 'social', although such distinctions between institutions should be regarded as very fuzzy at best. If fast growth did depend on some institutional variables – as described briefly on pp. 174, 180–8 and 190 – are contemporary social trends both inevitable to a maturing capitalist system, and determinants of a lesser comparative performance?

Notes

1 The union membership figures are from Ministry of Labour, *Labour Union Basic Survey*, Tokyo, 1989 and idem., *Labour Statistics Handbook*, Tokyo, 1990. The Japan and European figures probably compare quite fairly, although the UK figures include union members of branches outside the UK. The US figures comprise the ratio of union members to the number of all non-agricultural workers. Days lost averages are based on 1,000 man-days compiled in Japan from individual official national sources, Bank of Japan, *Comparative International Statistics*, Tokyo, 1990. Such latter figures are always debatable. The averages here are based on 1980–9 figures, and disguise the effect of variations. The Japanese average is

based on small variation with the exception of 1980. The performance in the German FR would have outmatched that of Japan but for the disaster of 1984, when 5,618,000 man-days were lost. The highest figures were for the US in 1980 and 1983, the UK in 1980 and 1984, and Italy in 1980 and 1982.

2 We might insert the coda that, although we have treated the 1990s as a decade of relative industrial decline associated with a greater capitalist maturity (an approach extended in Chapter 13), it is yet feasible that the period is demonstrably cyclical rather than secular. Major transitions are more easily identifiable with time, and thus the long-period historical approach of this volume has reasonably identified previous turning-points. Contemporary history is another matter. Nominal Japanese GDP growth peaked in 1990 at 7.2, troughed in 1995, but began rising quite sharply during the subsequent year or so. Growth of real GDP troughed in 1985, peaked at 6.2 during 1987–8, fell to its lowest in 1993, but climbed thereafter. In 1996 real growth was greater than in the US, the UK, Germany, France or Italy. The Tokyo Stock Price Index (TOPIX) peaked during 1989, troughed in 1992 and thereafter wavered. Urban land prices peaked in 1990 and fell thereafter.

3 Strictly, this was the Organization of Arab Petroleum Exporting Countries (OPEC), which announced the increase on 16 October 1973, during the final phases of the Yom Kippur War between Israel and the Arab nations. Within four months the Arabian light crude oil price had risen from $3 to $11.65 per barrel. These suppliers provided most of Japanese imports, in the order of importance Saudi Arabia, Iran, UAE, Kuwait, Oman and Iraq. The heightened risk associated with oil transportation increased Japanese awareness of global diplomatic imperatives and encouraged American pressure on the Japanese to extend to 1,000 nautical miles its sea-lane defences. By the mid-1990s, the eleven OPEC nations supplied 40 per cent of world oil and had faced a long secular decline of prices, with a slight peak in 1989–90 and a fall thereafter, a result of a combination of forces – low growth, low inflation, economic crises in the Far East, Eastern Europe, Russia and Brazil, discoveries of alternatives elsewhere (e.g. in the North Sea), and moves to save on oil within industries or through switching to new industries.

4 This is the base year taken by official sources because it was in 1956 that the land price caught up with general consumer prices after the war and occupation. By this time also, the real per capita income approximated that of the best prewar years. Between 1956 and our combined 'shocks', the wholesale price index was remarkably stable, rising at less than 1 per cent for each year of the period of miracle growth.

5 This began with payments by Lockheed Corporation in 1972 to secure orders from Nippon Airways for their TriStar airliner, of which enormous sums around 500 million yen went directly to Tanaka. An American Senate investigation resulted within Japan in the arrest and conviction of Tanaka, a result which did not then disturb the LDP's hold on power.

6 Initiated by the United Nations in 1990, the HDI combines GDP, adult literacy and life expectancy.

7 The term is taken from the notice board used by the leader of a household group (*gōnin-gumi*) to circulate instructions to householders as passed down from above in the Tokugawa system of local administration. Something of a measure of literacy, the system also indicated certain cultural presumptions relating to hierarchy, obedience and the recognition of a common set of goals. The most common types of many *kanban* are the withdrawal *kanbans* which are requests for parts to a workstation from a prior level, and production ordering *kanbans* which signal a workstation to produce additional lots. These now mostly take the form of formatted cards attached to the containers specifying the type of component,

quantity etc. which operate as a delivery notice as well as an order form. So, rather than conventional Western 'push' methods in inflexible production hierarchies, in kanban the quantity of stock in-process is continuously varied through the use of cards which 'pull' material periodically on the basis of more 'local' demands of assembly.

References

Tsuru, Shigeto (1993) *Japan's Capitalism. Creative Defeat and Beyond*, Cambridge: Cambridge University Press, p. 149.

Johnson, Chalmers (1982) *MITI and the Japanese Miracle: The growth of industrial policy 1925–1975*, Stanford, CA: Stanford University Press, pp. 20–1.

Rostow, W. W. (1960) *The Stages of Economic Growth. A Non-Communist Manifesto*, Cambridge: Cambridge University Press.

Kindleberger, C. P. (1962) *Foreign Trade and the National Economy*, New Haven, CT: Yale University Press.

Chesnai, François (1988) 'Technical cooperation agreements between firms' in OECD, *Science, Technology and Industry Review*, 4 (December), pp. 51–119.

Yamamura, Kozo and Yasuba, Yasukichi (eds) (1987/8) *The Political Economy of Japan*: Vol. 1 *The Domestic Transformation* and Vol. 2 *The Changing International Context*, Stanford, CA: Stanford University Press, Uekasu, p. 488 of Vol. 1.

Williams, David (1994) *Japan: Beyond the End of History*, London: Routledge, pp. 11–12.

Stockwin, J. A. A. (1982) *Japan: Divided Politics in a Growth Economy*, New York: Norton.

Saxonhouse, Garry (1983) in *World Development*, p. 81.

Purcell, William R. (1992) 'Why are Japan's savings rates so high?', *Japan Monitor* 1(3), August, p. 3.

Sengoku, T. (1985) *Willing Workers: The Work Ethics in Japan, England and the United States*, London, p. xii.

Sources for tables and statistical data

Keizai Koho Center (1983) *Japan 1983, An International Comparison*, Tokyo: Japan Institute for Social and Economic Affairs, for Tables 9.1, 9.2 and 9.3.

KKC (1991) *Japan 1991* as *ibid.*, for Tables 9.2–9.5.

KKC (1994) *Japan 1994*, Tokyo: Taiheisha Ltd., for Tables 9.3–9.5.

KKC (1998) *Japan 1998* as *ibid*, for Tables 9.8–9.13.

Jamieson, Bill (1998) *An Illustrated Guide to the British Economy*, London: Duckworth, for Tables 9.14–9.16.

Australian Department of Industry, Science and Technology (1994) *Australian Science and Technology 1994*, Canberra: AGPS, for Tables 9.4 and 9.5.

US National Science Board (1985) *Science Indicators, the 1985 Report*, Washington DC: US Government Printing Office, Appendix tables for Tables 9.3–9.5.

Monthly Bulletin of Statistics (1991) Tokyo: Prime Ministers Office, for Tables 9.4–9.6.

Science and Technology Agency (1991, 1992) *Indicators of Science and Technology*, Tokyo, STA, Tables 9.4–9.6.

Courtis, K. S. (1992) 'Beware the slumbering giant', *Japan Monitor*, 1(2), August, 3–5.

Bank of Japan (1997) *Comparative Economic and Financial Statistics*, Tokyo: BOJ.

Nagaoka, Minoru (1988) 'Financial reconstruction and economic friction: how can these dilemmas be solved?', *Review of Japanese Culture and Society*, 2(2), December.
Maddison, Angus (1989) *The World Economy in the Twentieth Century*, Paris: OECD, Table p. 71 for Table 9.15.
Suzuki, H. (1985) in *Japan Foundation Newsletter*, XI(6), p. 237, for Table 9.17.

Further reading

Brown, M. B. (1978) *Information at Work*, London: Arrow Books.
Burks, A. W. (1991) *Japan, A Postindustrial Power* (3rd edn), Boulder, CO: Westview.
Calder, K. E. (1988) *Crisis and Compensation: Public Policy and Political Stability in Japan 1949–1986*, Princeton, NJ: Princeton University Press.
Curtis, G. L. (1988) *The Japanese Way of Politics*, New York.
Dore, R. P. (1987) *Taking Japan Seriously. A Confucian Perspective on Leading Economic Issues*, London: Athlone Press.
Fransman, M. (1990) *The Market and Beyond. Cooperation and Competition in Information Technology in the Japanese System*, Cambridge: Cambridge University Press.
Hollerman, L. (1969) 'Recent difficulties in Japan's economic development', *Banca Nazionale Del Lavoro Quarterly Review*, 22.
Inkster, I. (1992) 'Japan: taking over and staying ahead', *Futures*, January–February.
Ito, T. (1992) *The Japanese Economy*, Cambridge, MA and London.
Japan Management Association (1989) *Kanban: Just-in-Time at Toyota* (trans. David Lui of revised edition), Cambridge: Productivity Press.
Johnson, C. *et al.* (eds) (1989) *Politics and Productivity: the real story of why Japan works*, Cambridge, MA: Ballinger.
Miyazaki, I. (1981) 'True causes of Japan's growth', *Japan Echo*, 8(4).
Nakamura, T. (1975) 'The tarnished phoenix', *The Japan Interpreter*, 9 (Spring).
Sato, K. (1977) 'The Japanese economy in transition', *Finance and Development*, 14(2), June.
Saxonhouse, G. (1979) 'Industrial restructuring in Japan', *Journal of Japanese Studies*, 5.
Sheridan, K. (1977) 'Understanding the Japanese economy: a review of the Japanese national economic plans 1956–1986', *The Australian Quarterly*, September.
Smith, D. B. (1995) *Japan Since 1945*, London: Macmillan.
Suzuki, Y. *et al.* (1991) 'The Japanese economy 1991', *Journal of Japanese Trade and Industry*, 10(1) (January-February).
Watanabe, T. (1970) 'National planning and economic development, a critical review of the Japanese experience', *Economics of Planning*, 10(1–2), 21–51.

10 The renewed expansion of Japan

The forces of expansion

The famous fixed exchange rate of ¥360 = $1 was set in April 1949 in the aftermath of war and in the midst of the establishment of a workable international trading and payments system. At this time the rate probably overvalued the yen, and the years 1946–55 witnessed large trade deficits, peaking at −794 $ million in 1953. The financial effects of this were to an extent offset by US aid and special procurement orders for the Korean War. This fixed exchange rate appears to have been one of the several factors taken as 'given' by Japanese public policy, which henceforth focused on reducing costs and imports. From the mid-1960s, increasing technological transfers and efficiency, and the great improvement in the trade balance, made it obvious that the 360 exchange rate was now an undervaluation: the trade balance grew significantly in 1964–5, and then enormously in 1970–1, so that in 1973 it reached $8,971 million.

Until relatively recent years Japan's foreign trade and investment were at a low level. In 1972 exports as a percentage of GDP were 10.8 for Japan, but 21.6 for each of West Germany and the UK. Although exports had grown faster than GDP during the Economic Miracle years, this was also true in volume terms for such nations as the US, Belgium, France, Sweden, West Germany, and even the UK. Similarly, for most of this period Japanese investment abroad was unremarkable, although the early comparative growth rates might be noted – between 1967 and 1974 Japan's annual growth rate of direct foreign investment averaged at 31.4 per cent, compared to 26.1 per cent for Germany, 10.4 per cent for the US, 9.9 per cent for France and 9.3 per cent for the UK. But this was from a very low Japanese base, so that even by 1980 foreign investments of US $33 billion put Japan equal to Germany but well behind the US and the UK in gross terms, well behind other OECD nations in relation to the total size of the economy. It is true that such figures do not capture the extent of loans nor the immeasurable influences overseas of Japan's giant trading companies, the *sōgō shōsha* (see pp. 209–14), nor the concentration of investments in key areas. Nor can there be much doubt that a reason for such constraint alongside massive domestic growth may be found in domestic political imperatives. The long-living party of government, the LDP, owed much of its support to small and medium-sized enterprises who were concerned with the maintenance of tight import controls. Rationalisation and the activities of MITI were considerably eased if the firms under policy treatment were not linked with foreign interests or with Japanese groups tied to foreign interests. For such reasons, Jon Halliday has concluded that 'Japan's low level of internationalisation has facilitated the maintenance of bourgeois unity within the country' in the midst of a very diverse industrial structure. T. J. Pempel argued in a similar manner that the combination of growth and isolation meant that 'Japanese government and business leaders could pursue macroeconomic policies with their eyes fixed primarily on domestic political and economic issues', a luxury hardly afforded other OECD governments at this time.

We have argued above that, until the 1970s, Japan's foreign trade was crucial to overall growth, not because of its size or balance, but because trade was a principal vehicle of technology transfer into a very fast growing, labour-surplus industrial economy reaping the benefits of the catch-up process. Purchase of foreign licences and patents increased from $20 million in 1955 to $120 million in 1961 and nearly $350 million in 1969, in spite of the growing frequency of limiting clauses which stipulated patent exchanges or restrictions on the foreign sale of goods produced with imported technologies. Imports rather than exports were the substantive trading factor in a low-wage, high investment system. With the recession of 1971 there was an increase of the current account surplus to a significant level for the first time since the war. The consequent addition to Japan's official reserves promoted, as we have seen, much talk of inflation, expansionism and a turning-point in the Japanese economy.

Such was the direct trading background to US President Richard Nixon's so-called 'New Economic Policy' of August 1971. The consequent suspension of the dollar's convertibility into gold forced the Japanese government (and others) to adopt a floating exchange, the comparative results of which have been seen in Table 9.8.[1] A real tardiness of adjustment meant that Japanese consumers did not at first benefit from the new currency regime (i.e. foreign exchange reserves in Japan were not being spent on consumer imports), nor did reserve-piling aid the trading problems of other major nations. As Tsuneo Iida observed, the 'natural result was that resentment of Japan, especially in the United States, grew daily in the period leading up to the new economic policy, and the policy itself may be regarded in many respects as the final explosion of American discontent with Japan'.

As has been shown in Chapter 9, the deflationary impact of revaluation was minimal and consolidated a public policy of demand stimulation, which indeed led to marked inflation during 1973–4. The increased trade balance marked the ineffectiveness of external pressure in reducing Japan's export surplus, and further revaluations under the chaotic global float also failed to alter the general trend of increased trade surpluses for Japan. As we have argued in Chapters 8 and 9, the underlying cause of Japan's continued competitiveness in the face of revaluations was the increased production of an increased range of industries at relatively low labour costs, a virtuous circle begun at points of technology transfer. Interestingly, much of this was underestimated in Japan itself, and the period of yen revaluation was quite commonly feared as a new invasion of Japan by American economic imperialism, rather than welcomed as an important nodal point in the renewed expansion of the Japanese economy itself. The opposition of Japanese business to yen revaluation was only bettered in that displayed by the opposition parties and *kakushin* (progressive) interest groups.

It is of great significance that the increase in Japanese direct investment overseas occurred precisely at the same time as the yen's revaluation and the large growth of the trade account. The forces at work included most of those already considered in Chapters 8 and 9 above.[2] Increases in industrial labour costs, restrictions on plant site, and environmental imperatives all curtailed investment opportunities in older industries within Japan. Natural resource problems, always present but heightened by the oil shortages of the OPEC crisis, prompted the movement of capital seeking secure supply sources abroad. Growth of industrial production in East Asian nations meant that they began to curb industrial imports just as they welcomed foreign investments into their growing industries and resource sectors. Less successful developing nations throughout the world welcomed foreign capital as integral parts of ambitious development projects. But perhaps of greatest importance were two simple supply-side factors. Yen revaluation lowered the Japanese cost of foreign assets. Second, the new Japanese technological sophistication meant that the industrial programmes of the Newly Industrialising Countries (NICs) of Asia would import technological and related inputs from Japan in exchange for raw materials and heavy industrial products (often very metal-and-oil-using) exported to Japan. The investment expansion of the economy was not merely proportional to the growth of the domestic GNP itself: between 1981 and 1988 capital outflow grew from US $4.8 billion to US $79.6 billion, the ratio of net foreign investment to GDP (the key ratio for our argument), growing from 0.6 per cent to 4.6 per cent, an increase of over seven-fold.

Thus emerged the reactions to the new Japanese presence in small or medium-sized Asian systems, from the student demonstrations in Bangkok in 1972 to the general anti-Japanese outbursts in Jakarta and elsewhere during Kakuei Tanaka's tour of Southeast Asia in early 1974. Again, the Philippine–Japanese Treaty of Amity, Commerce and Navigation was first signed in 1960 and ratified in Japan in 1961, but only ratified in the Philippines in 1973 due to thirteen years of public opposition. In many Asian places, the renewed expansion of Japan was seen as a reformulation of the pre-war Greater East Asia Co-Prosperity Sphere. Although such sentiment might be seen as an outcome of either the intensity of the Japanese presence, the behaviour of Japanese business overseas, or the history of Japanese imperialism and militarism in Asia, it is also true that Japan was the only large industrial nation to significantly renew its economic expansion just as the older IMF system collapsed and calls came for the establishment of a New International Economic Order. Whilst the destruction of the old owed much to the US, the call for a new order represented the new voice of the South in the global economy. Notions of economic justice, international cooperation, respect for the opinions of small players in the global economic system, and so on, sat most uneasily alongside the emergence of a new, individualistic and industrially efficient player on the international economic scene. The exact character of Japanese expansion was at least conditioned not only by the expected loud voice of the US, but by the somewhat unexpected voices of many less-privileged interest groups nearer at home, and including those progressive forces within Japan itself which carefully noted and vocally resisted all expansive moves. For such reasons, the Japanese expansion of the early 1970s was quick to take place but slow in its justification. Tanaka led Japan's support for the new international economic order's Charter of Economic Rights and Duties of States, but Japan abstained from voting when the issue came before the UN General Assembly. In 1977 Prime Minister Takeo Fukuda promised $1 billion in aid to the Southeast Asian nations during his tour of August 1977. Private Japanese interests sought to ameliorate the negative or enclavist impacts of direct Japanese investment in Asia by new liberal, even radical, proposals, such as the 1974 plan that at least 51 per cent of all shares in Japanese corporations abroad be transferred to local interests within twenty years of first establishment.[3]

In addition, then, to the more technical debates relating to trade liberalisation, the expansion of Japan was associated with a fairly general negative reaction in major and minor economic systems. Although Hiroyuki Hisamizu, chief economist of the Industrial Bank of Japan, could confidently define such reaction as a natural outcome of a 'pervasive flabbiness in advanced countries . . . which have fallen behind in productivity, worker initiative, and export drive', it is clear that the expansion of the economy was in the face of both international slow-down and a degree of specific antagonism directed at Japan.

As in 1971, a distinct new phase of economic expansion was ushered in by further yen revaluations following US pressure, marked especially during the meetings on the yen/dollar exchange rate in May 1984. Clearly, both the public and private sectors of the US economy still believed that Japan's trade surplus (generally, but especially with themselves!) was a function of an undervalued currency, and they had missed the message of analysts such as Michael Porter who stressed the public policy context of private sector competitive advantage. This mind-set eventually dominated the G5 meetings of 1985 which resulted in the Plaza Accord. As we have seen (Table 9.8) the result was a very significant fall in the yen/dollar ratio, from 238 in 1985 to 168 in 1986, to a low of 128 in 1988. Nominally, the competitiveness of Japanese exports compared to the nation's major trading partners fell significantly.[4] In fact, although the trade balance as a proportion of Japanese GNP did fall between 1986 and 1989, the dollar value of the yen had also increased and so the dollar value of Japan's surpluses continued to increase.

Yen appreciation affected Japanese firms and their investment strategies in various ways. The rise in domestic demand stimulated new investments in firms geared to the domestic market, and particularly those in the high technology sector. Between 1985 and 1987 there was a 22 per cent rise in R&D expenditure by the private sector, boosted further by oil price rises. Corporations dependent on imported raw materials were rewarded by drops in yen-price import costs, which boosted profits and investment levels. So, the revaluation may be seen finally as an element furthering that restructuring of the Japanese economy which is outlined in Chapter 9. It may also be seen as the principal explanation of the further expansion of the Japanese economy.

This expansion has been at times interpreted as some direct function of government policy, itself increasingly instigated by pressures from overseas to liberalise Japan's economic system. The argument is applied particularly to liberalisation of international capital transactions. Thus in December 1980 the existing Foreign Exchange and Transactions Control Law was revised to liberalise all transactions and abolish the rigid system of official approvals for every foreign securities investment. Again, in the later 1980s the Japanese government eased the constraints on the proportion of total assets (hitherto 10 per cent), which insurance companies, pension trusts, and government agencies could hold in the form of foreign securities. Nevertheless, to see the expansion of the modern economy as primarily caused by changes of government policy in response to US-led foreign pressure, would be blinkered at the least. First, there should be no underestimation of the independent and rational strategies of the private sector responding to Asian development and low foreign asset prices. As domestic rates of return and growth slowed in the 1980s (see Chapter 9) investors in Japan sought to diversify their investments abroad. Second, liberalisation progressed at a halting pace dictated very much by the Japanese government's own concerns over the balance of payments, as with the tightening of capital flows in the aftermath of the second oil price rise of 1979–80. But third, and of most importance in the argument of this chapter, the expansion of the economy was a function of overall structural change and economic maturity.

Japan invested about £4 billion overseas in 1982. By 1987 it was investing £4 billion per quarter, and by 1990 some £4 billion per month. Japan's annual foreign direct investment grew at a rate of 17 per cent during 1985–9, and by a further 22 per cent in 1990. By 1988 Japan had surpassed the UK as the world's largest net and gross creditor nation.

From about that time, the original surge in foreign securities (bonds and equities) gave way to a great increase in direct investments. Although much of this was in Asia (see pp. 211–26 and Chapter 11), much was also targeted at failing industries in older capitalist economies and illustrated new Japanese core competencies in miniaturisation, precision engineering and flexible product switching. This, to an extent, explains the reaction against Japanese investments in Britain (e.g. the minor panics over ICL or Toyota's new car plant in Derby) at a time when 132 Japanese ventures employed about 25,000 people in Britain, perhaps 2.5 per cent of the number working for American-owned companies. The European presence tended to be similarly exaggerated: during 1989 Japan invested some £1 billion in fifty-four European takeover deals, but American companies invested almost ten times as much. At that time, US overseas operations produced the equivalent of 20 per cent of domestic industry when output of Japan's overseas businesses represented only 5 per cent of the nation's domestic manufacturing output. The contrast is that the Japanese investments were both new and different in character from traditional overseas investments in and between the mature economies. Thus the much-debated Fujitsu–ICL deal of 1990 was very large at £1 billion compared to the previously largest Japanese takeover of £200 million for United Precision Industries just two months earlier. Second, this investment embraced the sort of very-high-technology which is seen as the key to future industrial productivity increases. Third, this investment represented not a new start from scratch, but the purchase of an existing, large and profitable British company. Although Britain was then in receipt of perhaps 40 per cent of all Japanese investment in Europe, such deals generated heated debate throughout Western Europe. Thus in France, where Japan had concentrated investment in machine tool manufacturing, Prime Minister Michel Rocard allayed Japanese fears of generalised anti-Japanese sentiments whilst at the same time emphasising that investments must 'create jobs, improve the trade balance and develop technical expertise'. *Le Monde* was wary: 'The lessons are clear: a sector attacked by the Japanese is a sector dead for local industrialists. This has proved to be the case in photographic equipment, radio and television, electronic components, musical instruments and perhaps – tomorrow – motor vehicles.'

The overseas securities investments of the 1980s had originated with Japanese insurance, banking and investment companies and directly fed the large current account deficits of the US economy. It was this form of overseas investment which most dramatically surged during the 1980s: in 1986 the share of securities in long-term capital outflows peaked at 77 per cent, and the great bulk of such investment was in the US and the EC. Such investment required less expert industrial knowledge than did direct investment, involved minimal risks and good yields, and was associated with highly developed and growing financial institutions. It should be noted that, despite the common enough identification of a new Japanese imperialism during the 1980s, the actual ratio of Japan's net external assets to Japanese GNP did not rise at all significantly, especially after 1985. That is, Japanese investment expansion was broadly a feature of growth and yen revaluation rather than any imperial urge or expansionist swing. Furthermore, until the 1990s most of the growth of overseas investment was not in direct investments (involving enterprise ownership) or loans, but in securities. It might be possible to hazard that expansion was less a function of a nationalist urge than of that chaos of financial sector developments which was originally centred around the land price booms and investments of the 1970s (Chapter 9, pp. 170–1). In this interpretation, the forces of expansion relate to the enormous complexities of finance capitalism and industrial maturity, and less to overt policy regimes. Indeed, the relative failure of the Japanese government to maintain its earlier more rigid 'developmental' regime (again, Chapter 9) amidst increased internal political uncertainty, might be seen as fundamental to late Japanese economic expansion. Thus a neo-Leninist analysis of changing Japanese international economic relations as an outcome of mature capitalism (or in our terminology, where relative backwardness on all fronts has approached zero after late and speedy catch-up), might be less wide of the mark than the more frequent claims concerning the potency in Japan (but seemingly nowhere else!) of official, nationalist policies of aggressive restructuring and expansion.

Again, during the 1980s real estate emerged as the largest component (21 per cent in 1989) of a fast growing flow of Japanese direct investment overseas. Although increased FDI in *manufacturing* may reflect the technological maturity, lower domestic returns, and ownership strategies of individual Japanese firms, this is possibly less true of firms investing in foreign real estate, which on the whole represents a simpler type of industry, towards which surplus domestic funds might be expected to gravitate without the need for special technical expertise or control through ownership. This notion is strengthened when we observe that much early real estate investment went to resort locations such as Hawaii, sites both familiar and highly developed as property markets where links could be fairly readily made with local banks, realtors and security houses. By the end of the 1980s the bulk of Japanese real estate investment in the US was in city offices, hotels and resorts: there was very little real estate investment for industrial purposes. Thus the land-based bubble economy and rising yen of the mid-1980s prompted a surge of activity overseas, a surge which fell away as the international price of land dropped. Roger Farrell has summarised that the 'development of the bubble economy in the 1980s had a persuasive influence on the financing and timing of Japanese real estate FDI. A range of Japanese firms, particularly realtor, leisure and construction firms, were easily able to borrow large amounts from Japanese financial institutions to fund real estate investment in Japan and overseas . . . the appreciation of land assets held by a wide range of Japanese firms, especially realtors with significant inventories, increased their purchasing power in overseas markets, reinforced by the appreciation of the yen.'

Between 1990 and 1995, the new East Asian economies accounted for over 50 per cent of the growth in world exports and over 70 per cent of the growth in world imports. In combination with the rising yen this encouraged both an increase in the export of Japanese capital goods and an increase in direct investment from Japan. Direct investment in economies whose labour prices were around 15–30 per cent of those at home encouraged a backwash of imports of Asian manufactured goods into Japan just as the technologies of the Japanese system boosted the productive capacities of such smaller Asian systems. In this period, then, structural change in the Japanese economy both reflected and was hastened by the character of its external economic relations, a claim which will be reiterated throughout this chapter. In 1990 the yen/dollar ratio had settled around 150. By 1995 the yen had reached below 100 to the dollar, falling back to 120 during 1997.

Patterns of expansion

By the mid-1990s, Japanese commodity exports were overwhelmingly in the form of machinery and equipment, this composing around 75 per cent of the total in the years 1994–6. Most other exports were of metal products and chemicals. In 1996, 40 per cent of such exports went to Asia, 30 per cent to the US, and around 16 per cent to the EC. Even in 1996, Japan's trade dependency (measured here as imports+exports as a percentage of GDP), was very low, amounting to 16.5, compared to 19.0 for the US, 46.3 for the UK, 41.5 for Germany, 36.6 for France. Japan's trade position overall could only contrast with those of the East Asian 'tigers', with dependency ratios of between 80 per cent and over 200 per cent. Even China showed a dependency ratio of 40 per cent by 1995. Clearly, Japanese trade was neither that of a well-resourced major industrial nation, nor that of a fast-developing or industrialising economy.

In terms of invisible trade (services such as transportation, finance, royalties, insurance and so on), by the mid-1990s Japan was in overall debt, particularly to the US and Europe, but also to the Asian NICs. Such debt was dominated by transport and financial services, but travel and tourism made up an increasing portion, indicating the extent to which the Japanese people were themselves increasingly facing outwards: by 1995 Japanese spent more on foreign travel than any other nation except the US (and unlike the US received little through travel to Japan), and in the previous decade over 96 million visits had been made overseas by Japanese holiday makers, the majority of whom went to the US, Korea, Hong Kong, China, Taiwan and Australia, but with a rising proportion of tourist visits to Europe (Britain and Italy being most popular) and the rest of Asia. Of special interest in terms of the notion that expansion had been associated

Table 10.1 International technology trade, selected nations, 1993–4

	Payments ($ million)	*Receipts ($ million)*	*Patents abroad (no.)*
Japan	3,627	4,521	135,250
US	5,666	22,436	628,985
UK	3,176	3,730	159,576
Germany	10,223	7,874	195,545
France	2,791	2,012	81,905

with a technological maturity which had eventually reversed the historical technology transfer relations, was the balance of invisible technology trade, as illustrated in Table 10.1.

Payments for royalties and licence fees to Japan were in surplus and thus in contrast to most other invisibles. Clearly, such receipts were insignificant beside those of the US, but the Japanese mass and balance compared favourably with nations such as the UK and France. International comparisons of patent application figures are notoriously problematic, but the column showing only the applications *abroad* originating in each of the five nations does suggest the growing momentum of the Japanese system of high technology and its global commercial applications. Such a column might be interpreted as reflecting the more sophisticated vector of recent Japanese expansion, as well as the importance of Japanese direct investment overseas in higher technology manufacturing enterprises.

As indicated on pp. 199–202, in Japan until 1990, overseas securities investments greatly exceeded new direct investments overseas. Table 10.2 shows the magnitude and regional dispersement of Japanese ODI to that time.

It is clear enough that the high rate of direct investment into the US during the late 1980s dominated the flow but also represented a long-term trend: the ratio of US to total Japanese ODI for the entire period 1951–89 was 43 per cent. Again, at the end of the 1980s, the amount of ODI

Table 10.2 Japan's direct overseas investment by region, 1951–89 ($ million)

Receptor region	*1989*	*1951–89*
North America	33,902	108,993
Europe	14,808	44,972
Asia	8,238	40,465
Oceania	4,618	13,933
Middle East	66	3,404
South America	5,238	36,855
Africa	671	5,275
Total	67,540	253,896

Table 10.3 Japan's accumulated ODI, 1981–93, by selected region and industry ($ million)

	N. America	*Asia*	*Europe*	*Total*
Iron and NF metal	5,027	3,310	734	12,040
Chemicals	5,923	4,282	2,002	14,558
Elect. machinery	12,707	5,587	5,257	24,473
Transp. equip.	6,312	2,061	3,003	14,065
Textiles	1,058	2,312	1,130	5,043
Gen. machinery	4,723	2,117	2,858	10,320
Lumber and pulp	2,508	611	124	3,711
All manufacture	**50,367**	**24,691**	**17,331**	**103,981**
Mining	2,484	7,980	1,811	18,812
Commerce	21,074	5,259	9,296	40,268
Finance and insurance	22,661	5,711	28,598	74,869
Transportation	769	1,530	365	21,652
Non-manufacture	**117,595**	**34,115**	**55,974**	**275,666**
Real estate	485	37	38	595
Miscellaneous	1,133	1,037	2,352	6,288
TOTAL	**169,580**	**59,880**	**75,697**	**386,530**

entering Asia from Japan was less than that flowing to Oceania and South America in combination. We have seen that much long-term capital export was in forms other than ODI and reflected the rise of real estate and financial sectors more than the requirements of Japan's industrial economy. The table also disguises some key concentrations of ODI into the UK (35 per cent of the European total in 1989), Netherlands (31 per cent of that total), Australia (92 per cent of the Oceania total) and Panama (39 per cent of the South American total), and the impact of smallish fractions of a large total on small or less developed Asian industrialisers such as Singapore or Thailand, (see pp. 211–26). Again, the totals represented a huge surplus over direct investment placed in Japan from overseas, which totalled US $15,654 million for 1950–89, or US $ 2,860 for 1989 alone, about equivalent to Japan's direct investment in Oceania alone.

Table 10.3 shows something of the industrial character of Japanese ODI during the period 1981–93 as estimated by the Japanese Ministry of Finance.

Of the grand accumulated total for 1981–93 of nearly US $400,000 million Japanese ODI, some 30 per cent had gone into the manufacturing sector of receiver nations generally. At 41.2 per cent, the figure for industrial investments into Asian nations was somewhat higher, and gives some credence to the idea that developing industrial systems were the receptors for Japanese industrial interests. In contrast, US and European investments focused more on commercial, financial and insurance services and

Table 10.4 Japan's accumulated direct foreign investment, 1951–95

Receptor nation	*$ million*	*%*
US	216,622	42.1
UK	37,274	7.2
Germany	8,608	1.7
Australia	26,567	5.2
Indonesia	18,577	3.6
Hong Kong	15,006	2.9
All other	191,646	37.3
Total	514,300	100.0

real estate, at around 71 per cent of their combined totals. Noteworthy were the large investments in the US electrical machinery sector, the Asian chemical industries, transportation systems in Latin America and Africa, and mining in Asia and Australasia. Globally, investments in commercial, financial and insurance services were of outstanding importance, absorbing no less than 29.7 per cent of all direct foreign investment. Recent visions of an East Asian urban corridor linking Tokyo, Osaka, Seoul, Beijing, Shanghai and Hong Kong are very much the result of recent patterns of Japanese investment into Pacific Rim cities more generally, mostly into banking, construction, shipping and tourism. By the early 1990s a great amount of all of Japan's foreign direct investment was in Hong Kong, Singapore and Los Angeles.

Table 10.4 shows aspects of the major changes in Japanese direct investment overseas by region by the mid-1990s.

Most noteworthy is the massive increase in scale during the 1990s alongside the continuation of prominent features of ODI. The US percentage of the total remained remarkably unchanged, as did the British and German. Despite some criticism of the Japanese presence at the time (see below and above), Japanese direct investment in Australia slightly declined as a proportion of the total, whilst that of five Asian nations (Indonesia, Singapore, Thailand, China and Hong Kong) moved from 9.1 per cent of the total in 1989 to 12.8 per cent, much of this arising from increased investment into mainland China, (see Chapter 11). From such very general data it would seem that increases of direct investment into specific nations in Asia and elsewhere arose from a continual general expansion of the Japanese economy rather than from drastic shifts in the global pattern of Japanese ODI. Critical reactions to such investment in receivers may, then, have related primarily to the growing absolute size of Japanese investment in smaller industrial systems (rather than targeting), or to the huge net surplus of the bilateral balances of Japanese ODI, rather than to its gross amount (the American critique). This position is bolstered by international comparisons of major investors, as in Table 10.5.

Table 10.5 Accumulated direct foreign investment of selected nations, 1970–95 ($ billion)

	Outward	*Inward*
Japan	268.3	19.2
US	707.6	564.6
UK	326.7	250.4
Germany	229.0	63.2
France	216.9	161.1
Korea	11.1	9.5
Thailand	2.1	15.1

With an accumulated inward to outward investment ratio of just 7 per cent, Japan's investment expansion appears to have been peculiarly one-way, in contrast to the investment patterns of other major nations in the modern world economy.[5] Of course, this may be seen as a potential political constraint on Japanese economic expansion as it represents a phenomenon of concern to large capitalist systems and smaller industrialising capital-borrowers alike. Whatever their other and manifold political differences, the new dimensions of Japanese investment drives home some commonality of interests amongst a very diverse section of humanity.

In particular, it has been commonly and vociferously argued that the expansion of the economy has taken place despite the maintenance of older regulations which have restricted the entry of foreign goods and capital into Japan. That is, expansion has not been effectively reciprocal, and has thereby curbed the potential growth of the global economic system and posed particular commercial problems for the US. It might be expected that the importance of the agricultural sector would serve to the continuance of protectionism there, but that the Japanese quite unfairly restrict entry into the manufactured goods trade. By the mid-1990s Japan could boast lower tariff and official non-tariff barriers than any other OECD nation. Given that the share of imports in trade in manufactured goods seemingly remained small compared to such other nations, it was then postulated that informal, institutional or cultural 'barriers' continued to dampen the foreign presence and could only yield to concerted action on the part of both the public and private sectors within Japan. In 1987 Lawrence cited the view that Japanese imports 'are also discouraged by unofficial practices, such as the strong relationships ("invisible handshakes") between local suppliers and buyers, "just-in-time" inventory practices that give nearby suppliers an edge, and an unusually complex distribution system that creates substantial entry barriers for newcomers, whether Japanese or foreign.' This was the theme repeated in US official circles, as in the claim of the Office of the US Trade Representative that 'Japan's *keiretsu* system involves close intercompany linkages which impede the importation of many US products into the Japanese market.' This remained a principal source of contention between Japan and the US during the whole period of Japan's economic expansion, and showed itself particularly during the mid-1990s disputes over the US share of the Japanese automobile market. It is claimed that the structures of *keiretsu* firms encourage collusion and aggressive pricing behaviour, whilst the character of relations between Japanese firms, dominated by pervasive networks of 'customer relationships', determines the failure of foreign products within Japan whatever the nominal price levels. In an important analysis across the range of *keiretsu* firms, Peter Drysdale has concluded that the prevailing corporate structures are not indeed inordinately (i.e. compared to the private sector in competing industrial systems) collusive or restrictive, but that there still exist important regulatory controls 'which inhibit or facilitate entry to final product markets, and they are the relevant target of policy attention'.

There can be no doubt that the large expansion of the Japanese economy is without any real precedent. During the long but much earlier period of British economic dominance, large exports of capital into railways, resource development and government infrastructures were associated with an equally large propensity to import raw materials and foodstuffs from developing commercial systems. Britain's trading dependency was higher than that of present-day Japan, its balance of trade mostly negative. During the next period, of US commercial dominance, some profound problems emerged stemming from the very rich resource base of the leading nation and its lower trade dependency. It might be argued that this, historically, led to payments problems for nations attempting to borrow long-term capital and transfer in advanced technologies in exchange for exports of raw materials and semi-manufactures. This structural problem dominated the middle of the twentieth century. The expansion of Japan has been far faster than the case of either Britain or the US, and has been associated with a very low trade dependency and an unprecedented, secular positive balance on the long-term investment accounts. At the same time, until now, Japanese expansion has not been associated with the sort of aid which could serve to counter global biases which stem from varied productivities, growth rates and industrial structures. There has been no Japanese Marshall Aid or any equivalent of Korean and Vietnamese war expenditures, nor has Japan attempted to use investment and other policies to generate political alliances to anything like the extent which occurred under American leadership during the era of the Cold War. Table 10.6 provides general evidence of Japan's emergence as an aid donor as measured by Official Development Assistance under the auspices of the Development Assistance Committee.

Japan heads the list in terms of official aid, but still spends significantly less of its income on foreign aid than those nations with imperial and commonwealth traditions whose policy institutions contain a strong bias towards providing cultural, educational and economic assistance to their former colonies. Perhaps the significant comparison is with the US.

Table 10.6 Net ODA disbursement by DAC nations, 1996

	$ billion	*To GNP (%)*	*Total (%)*
Japan	9.4	0.20	17.1
US	9.1	0.12	16.4
UK	3.2	0.27	5.8
Germany	7.5	0.32	13.6
France	7.4	0.48	13.5
Other DAC nations	18.5	–	34.6
Total	55.1	0.25	100.0

Institutions of expansion: the Japanese Transnational Corporation

A major element in the expansion of the Japanese economy was the re-emergence of the older *zaibatsu* firms such as Mitsui, Mitsubishi or Sumitomo, now transformed into coordinated enterprises, where individual units of manufacturing production were interrelated through an enormous trade-name trading company and its associated banking facility. Such a reformulation of the *keiretsu* enterprises dominated the economic miracle.[6] Coordinated enterprise encouraged cooperation in decision making, the pooling of information and the sharing of risks. With the growth of the bank-centred *keiretsu* such as Fuyo and Sanwa, the links between production, trade and financing were greatly strengthened by cross-holding of stocks, interlocking directorships – especially between banks and their client firms – increased subcontracting, and by numerous lender–borrower and buyer–seller relationships, precisely those features of industrial organisation so criticised by foreign commentators. The greatest of the *keiretsu*, such as Mitsubishi, or Mitsui or Sanwa, could each over-match the annual turnover of General Motors by the 1970s. Most important to expansionism, by 1974 the Big Six trading companies or *sōgō shōsha* held controlling stock in a total of 5,390 Japanese production companies across the entire range from huge industrial sites to small engineering units. It is often argued that this combination of weight and scale with multifarious linkages into an array of production sites has yielded the complex obligations, networks and 'flexible rigidities' of modern Japanese enterprise culture. At the high point of *sōgō shōsha* predominance in 1989, the Big Nine generated annual sales of ¥130,000 billion, of which 39 per cent were entirely within Japan, 38 per cent in export and import trade and 23 per cent in offshore trading activities.[7] What is important to note here is that over 60 per cent of the sales of the great *sōgō shōsha* were most directly linked to the outward expansion of the economy.

For many such large enterprises, foreign trade became foreign investment during the 1970s. This is not to say that Japanese TNC activity was of no importance before that. Between 1950 and 1964 there was a ten-fold increase in Japanese direct foreign investment in Southeast Asia, mostly in extractive sectors, assembly and labour-intensive manufacture. Investment in oil concerns in Kuwait and Indo-China, pulp mills in Alaska, coal mines in West Virginia and iron mines in Australia all testified to the Japanese search for secure supplies of raw materials. But this was mostly ad hoc and not on a scale comparable with US transnationalism. At this time Japanese government encouragement took the form of fiscal measures, information services, and MITI insurance schemes and exchange control measures. Foreign investment by private firms was additionally eased through foreign aid policy, which rose towards 1 per cent of GNP by the end of this period. Only 25 per cent of this was official ODA, and most was in the form of export credits, assisting trade and investment linkages with Japan itself.

But the Japanese TNC was primarily a growth of the 1970s. The forces at work in the domestic and wider economy have been already outlined above – the upward revaluation of the yen from 1971, the oil crises, increased US restrictions on trade, pollution and space diseconomies within Japan, rising labour costs and new opportunities in industrialising Asia. Together these meant that Japanese 'enterprises became increasingly interested in promoting their own resource exploration and development', leading to a fast expansion of overseas ventures in fertiliser, aluminium, copper, iron ore and agricultural products. The size and expertise of the existing *keiretsu*-trading-company structures described above meant that new Japanese producers abroad were recipients of infrastructure, services and marketing information in a great variety of host nations. These were precisely the sort of institutional features which reduced transaction costs in foreign sites and which many US or European transnational corporations would regard as necessary inputs into overseas production, inputs whose origins were external to the firm but which, especially in the absence of high quasi-rents at home, determined the viability of new production activities in new markets overseas. Whereas American and European transnationalism had historically arisen from within very large firms whose super profits and saturated markets at home had combined to encourage them to absorb large transaction costs in foreign production sites as a price of producing overseas behind the lines of tariff or quota restriction on trade, Japanese TNCs were later on the scene and more the product of the structural changes in the Japanese economy combined with the institutional and informational advantages captured abroad by Japanese trading companies who had intimate connections with a variety of productive enterprises within Japan.

This Japanese pattern of international investment and production expansion was a good historical example of the potency of a multitude of weak ties compared to the inflexibilities of monopolistic hierarchies. The timing of such new transnationalism was also influenced by those government ventures which contributed to the reduction of transaction costs overseas, especially the activities of the Export-Import Bank, development assistance agencies, and the Japan External Trade Organisation (JETRO). Long- and short-term borrowings by the *sōgō shōsha* from the Export-Import Bank for overseas activities totalled US $2,918 million at the end of March 1976. At this time the *sōgō shōsha* were transforming their foreign representative offices into locally incorporated companies, Mitsui being foremost with twenty-five affiliates. By that time, in America alone the capitalisation of affiliates of Mitsui, Sumitomo and Nichimen exceeded that of their home companies. It should be noted that such capitalisation overseas was far greater in the US, Europe and Oceania than in Asia, the Middle East and Africa.

The smaller scale and contrasting character of Japanese transnational enterprise leads to the consideration that such a non-Western model might have been more conducive to industrial development in emerging national systems than had been the case with the earlier long phase of Western dominated transnationalism.

Technology and institutions: Asian impacts

Historically, in most cases at most times, the transfer of advanced technologies into late developing industrial systems has failed, and usually after great effort and expense. Yet the outward expansion of the Japanese economy, associated more or less with a new style transnationalism, has been contemporaneous with the success of the Newly Industrialising Countries (NICs). The congery of East Asian NICs has given rise to theories that their geographical and cultural proximity to an expanding Japan has served to give them an added competitive edge within a global system in which industrial failure is still far more common than industrial success. Specifically, it has been argued that certain characteristics of Japanese TNCs meant that Japanese direct investment overseas was more likely to lead to a broader pattern of Asian industrialisation than would have emerged if only Western-style transnationalism had existed as the principal transfer mechanism in the world system. There can be little doubt, as a minimal position, that the addition to transnationalism of any very fast growing enterprises working with lower-level and more labour-intensive production techniques would have some sort of net positive effects, other things being equal.

The question arises as to whether Japanese expansion provided new types of mechanism working in such a manner that the positive impacts of foreign investment and technique were now much more likely to outweigh their historically identifiable negative impacts. From our examination of Japan's own history (see for instance Chapters 2, 4 and 13), we may postulate that a process of successful technology transfer requires that superior technique and the information or skill upon which it is based should be transferred and reduced to reasonable practice within a new operational setting. That is, foreign technique becomes part and parcel of another nation's technological system, indicated by the ability of the new technology sites to repair and adapt technique and manufacture (and perhaps even export) products based on new techniques, or manufacture products of a new sort. Again drawing from Japanese historical experience, we might suggest that the barriers to success may relate to some ill-defined 'human resistance to change' operating in receiver nations, but may just as likely be the complex product of the character of those advanced techniques, the nature of the mechanisms of technology transfer (e.g. the organisational structure and policies of the TNC), and the stage of development of the indigenous technological systems into which any advanced techniques are transferred. If technology is relocated from any TNC to its affiliate in an underdeveloped economy but never used by that affiliate, or is brought into production in such a manner as to entirely lock-out the participation of the indigenous system, then technology transfer has been severely truncated, even though there might be positive revenue or balance of payments results and the technique of production has indeed been spatially relocated. Thus the ratio of exports to total sales of Japanese manufacturing firms in Asia rose from 26 per cent in 1971 to 37 per cent in 1973 at a time of generally increased activity, but this does not itself provide a sufficient measure of long-term technology transfer.

In the face of the trade bias between rich capitalist nations, tariffs, quotas and recessions, the manufacturing exports of Hong Kong, South Korea and Taiwan in total grew from $500 million in 1959 to $20 billion in 1976. An adverse international trading environment was at that time offset by increased efficiencies generated by new technologies and low-priced labour combined with government subsidising of domestically produced and exportable manufactures. From then the larger group of NICs, including Singapore, Indonesia, Malaysia, the Philippines, Thailand, Brazil, Argentina, and more recently mainland China, have exhibited higher than world average industrial and general income growth rates, despite world recession. This achievement appears to have been associated with export-led growth and a variety of technology transfer mechanisms. Yet in most other respects, the NICs differ enormously. During the 1970s it was not possible to identify an NIC in terms of skill levels, resources, income per head, geographical location or investment levels. What identified them apart from their growth rates was the high proportion of direct foreign investment in their manufacturing sectors, export-oriented manufacturing and an increase in the extent and range of state economic interventionism. The latter included inducements to foreign investments through preferential regulations (e.g. in the labour market), and the establishment of export enclaves and free trade zones.

Most commentators noted strong adaptive capacities also, with imported machinery being used on longer, or over more, shifts and at a greater speed with shorter down times, using greater labour inputs for maintenance and repair. These features bore close resemblance to characteristics of the Japanese industrial system in earlier years. As in Japan, in many cases the setting of the new machinery was not the standard 'factory' at all, and quite sophisticated machinery was erected within proto-industrial, workshop sites. As Hernadi summarised, 'individual machines were set up in the households and by using workers and families as home workers it was possible to achieve large savings in fixed capital, while at the same time using a large mass of cheap manpower'. In cotton spinning and weaving, for instance, the number of workers per spindle or loom was decidedly higher in NICs than in, say, Japan. The Korean and Taiwanese electronics industries used far more labour than in the West or in Japan despite the prominence of transferred techniques. By the later 1970s the early group of NICs had transcended their original lowly place in the product cycle and economic activity had become more centred on telecommunications, iron and steel, shipbuilding, office equipment watches and instruments and so on. In South Korea the leading edge was with electronics, cement, oil, shipping, artificial fibres and petrochemicals. By the 1980s computers and other technology-based industries were introduced speedily.

In terms of our earlier criteria, in the NICs industrial growth almost certainly ran well ahead of growth in the capacity of their indigenous technological systems. In very many cases, TNC investments and associated transfers stipulated exclusive rights to supply materials and intermediate goods or prohibited the rights of the receiver to develop the technologies themselves. That is, they frequently forestalled key 'downstream' effects. Of a large number of Korean firms surveyed in the early 1980s, 32 per cent reported evasion of technology transfer commitments by all-nation TNCs, and a large number complained of insufficient information. To varying degrees, the costs of technology transfer included overpricing of inputs, loss of profit on capitalised know-how in the case of equity participation, and commissions paid to licensers for use of their distribution and sales services. That is, TNC enterprises were generally *internalising* the relocation of advanced techniques, a phenomenon both global and historical. In simple form this is illustrated in Figure 10.1.

During the 1970s and 1980s the flow rates measured in arrows k1 and k2 were fast and relatively unimpeded. Such technology relocation was a function of TNC communications and training systems, resource mobilisation, quality assurance, and interchangeability of components within complex systems. As Frank Bradbury commented, such features of the global production network were 'made more effective where there is majority ownership of the affiliates by the parent, leading to overall central control of operations'. But as the same writer recognised, such imperatives strengthened k1 and k2, but might dampen the operations of k3 and k4. The greater the degree of foreign ownership the more the latter processes were likely to be constrained by TNCs which viewed them as 'spillage' or 'seepage' from their own stores

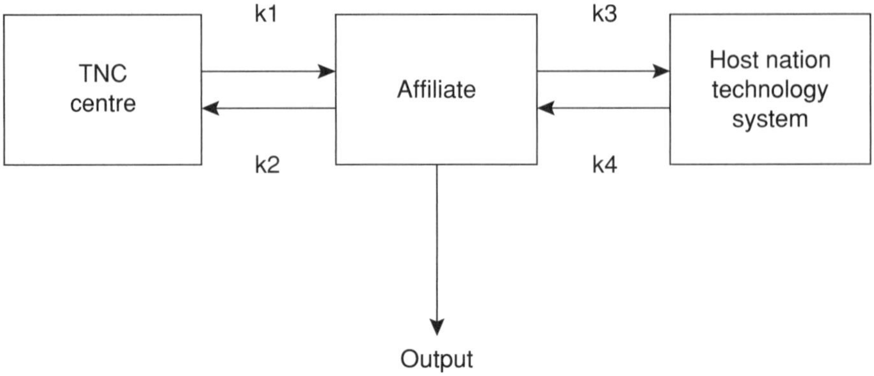

Figure 10.1 Technology transfer transactions of TNCs.

of expertise and information. At lower levels of technique this was less likely to be the case than at higher levels. A strengthening of lines k3 and k4 might come about through deliberate stimulation of sub-contracting between affiliates and host country suppliers, for instance, in the many cases where host country infrastructure might provide services to mining townships. Subcontracting in manufacturing was usually limited to maintenance and repair, transportation and communication. If linked to TNC assistance to subcontractors in the form of tools, training, quality control and even firm specific know-how, clearly such organisational systems could increase the likelihood of k3 and k4 transfers. Again, in Asia at times host country governments devised legislation which attempted to secure employment, training or consultancy agreements between TNCs and domestic firms. Thus at one point the Philippines tied the amount of foreign equity ownership permissible to the extent of forward linkages – that is, the proportion of foreign equity could rise with the increase in the extent of higher processing of materials. In Malaysia there were efforts made to place nationals in management control of major subsidiaries. There can be little doubt that the US-style TNC was well placed to resist or negotiate around such attempts at a wider process of transfer. As we have sketched above, the American TNC was generally an organisation concentrating on relatively sophisticated production lines, involving the utilisation of complex technologies in order to maximise their comparative advantage in the face of high transaction costs in new markets and cultures. Competition amongst such TNCs in new sites leads to the use of high technology as a weapon, an avoidance of joint ventures, the use of patent rights as restrictions, and the complete closure on ancillary know-how. The Japanese TNC may have differed somewhat.

The chain of events leading to Japanese production in Asia is well demonstrated in the case of petrochemicals, an area dominated at an early stage by Mitsubishi, Mitsui, Sumitomo, and Nippon Oil. The industry was

Table 10.7 Industrialising East Asia: the Japan connection

	(1) Ann. av GNP growth rate (1988–92) (%)	*(2) Export/ import ratio (1992)*	*(3) Export/ import ratio with Japan (1992)*	*(4) Japan's share of export (1992) (%)*	*(5) Total DOI from Japan (1951–92)* US $ m
Japan	4.2	1.67	–	–	
China	6.8	1.05	1.42	14.6	4,472
Four Tigers:					
South Korea	8.0	0.94	0.65	17.0	4,623
Hong Kong	4.7	0.96	0.10	5.4	11,510
Taiwan	6.7	1.13	0.45	–	3,427
Singapore	9.2	0.88	0.24	8.7	7,837
ASEAN:					
Indonesia	6.7	1.07	2.20	36.8	14,409
Malaysia	9.2	1.02	0.81	15.9	4,815
Philippines	2.8	0.63	0.66	20.2	1,943
Thailand	11.7	0.80	0.57	–	5,887

actively encouraged by MITI in Japan as part of its more general import substitution policy (see Chapter 9), and because this industry absorbed a great deal of advanced Western technology. Over-capacity then led to an export drive from Japan in the 1970s. In turn, a flood of imports from Japan stimulated Thailand, Korea, Indonesia and others to attempt a duplicate import substitution policy. In an attempt to block Japanese imports such NICs pursued restrictive trade policies which coincided with a series of problems within Japan, including a scarcity of plant sites and environmental issues. As a result, Japanese producers looked to Asia as a place for ancillary production to supply the Japanese market and as a means of protecting existing Asian markets. Thus licence agreements, first in Thailand, permitted Japanese firms to participate in the manufacture of petrochemical products in Asia as part of Asian import-substitution policy. This was followed by a spread of TNC activity into Iran, Korea, Saudi Arabia, Brazil, Singapore and Indonesia. In the next stage the production system within Japanese TNCs became increasingly standardised and export oriented, and there was an increase of competition between Japanese firms in petrochemicals. Finally, the entry of Asian indigenous producers into the petrochemical market resulted in TNC strategies of upgrading their production facilities in order to recover their earlier technological or marketing superiority. This seems to be a story of some success in terms of standard financial measures, e.g. the effect on the trade balance of certain Asian nations. In Thailand, a major recipient of Japanese TNC investments in the 1960s and 1970s, there was also a degree of increased technical capability through training processes, and a consequent Japanese

TNC enterprise strategy of upgrading and expanding. This may also have been true of the electronics industries of Taiwan, Thailand and Malaysia from the 1970s. On the basis of such rather intuitive and general evidence, the activity of Japanese TNCs may have stimulated something of a continuous, progressive and intra-product learning process, beneficial to the industrial programmes of receiver economies.

Table 10.7 illustrates the unexpected achievements of Asian industrialisers from the late 1980s and the growing importance to them of Japanese trade and investment.[8]

As can be seen from column 1, the East Asian component of the Pacific region performed in a spectacular manner into the 1990s, and much of this growth has been associated with expansive foreign trade and imports of technique. Between 1975 and 1987 the share of high technology R&D products in Japan's total exports to the four Asian NICs rose from 18 per cent to 38 per cent, a very significant trend. A prime function of such technical imports was to bring NIC capacity to a level allowing manufactured exports. In Korea and Taiwan the growth rate of exports was 30 per cent or more in 1986–7, with Hong Kong and Singapore matching such performance during 1987. As NIC growth slowed, ASEAN growth accelerated, Thailand's moving from around 5 per cent in 1985–6 to over 11 per cent in 1988 and 12 per cent in 1989. *This short period might have measured something of an East Asian turning-point* as wage rises and adverse American opinion dampened performance in the NICs just when Japanese investment turned towards lower labour costs in ASEAN. The number of Japanese-affiliated companies operating in the Asian countries at the end of 1988 was 3,770, with ASEAN accounting for 1,805. At that time the number of employees directly employed in Japanese companies in Asia was 797,000, and for ASEAN the figure had reached 345,000.[9] During the year 1988 the Japanese share in foreign investment in the NICs was in all cases above 25 per cent and as high as 54 per cent for Korea, its share of ASEAN investment being lower, in the range 14 per cent (the Philippines) to 29 per cent (Indonesia). This was associated with strong moves towards deregulation within ASEAN and generous terms to foreign investors. Clearly both Asian groups benefited from the downturn of Japanese commodity exports and increase of long-term foreign investment associated with the dual impacts of the 1985 yen increase. Of great significance, the Asian NICs began to invest substantially in ASEAN resources and cheap labour in a manner very similar to that of Japan. By 1988 NIC investment in ASEAN reached $3,901 million, exceeding that of Japan's $3,761 million.

At this time, most industrialising Asian nations boasted a better balance of trade with the rest of the world than with Japan alone, and it has been argued that this involved a significant importation of technique, a transfer process associated also with the acceleration of Japanese investment. The very large amount of DOI into Indonesia in Table 10.7 reflects large oil

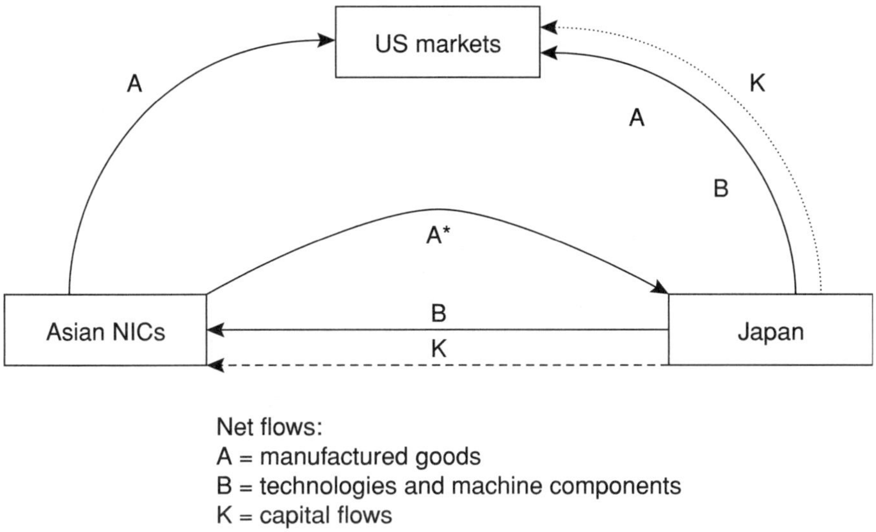

Figure 10.2 The US, Japan and the Asian NICs in the 1980s.

and petrochemical interests, this yielding an Indonesian trade surplus with Japan significantly above the average alongside a massive programme of technology transfers.

There is a clear sense in which East Asian industrialisation was sequentially dependent on both the global commitments of the US and the expansion of the Japanese economy, especially from the mid-1980s. Figure 10.2 stylises the very basic relationships.

The status and great size of the American economy permitted a fairly lengthy period during which that hegemony was challenged and the leading nation was in receipt of net flows of manufactured goods, new product technologies and large amounts of Japanese long-term capital in various forms. Such features meant that this model was bound to be transitional. The pressures on the US economy are considered in greater detail in Chapter 12. The surplus savings of the Japanese economy were increasingly linked to America's dual deficits, with an increasing Japanese ownership of US enterprises which had hitherto been considered as at the very heart of American culture and ideals. From around 1985, the further upward revaluation of the yen had the principal effect not of halting Japanese exports to the US, but of increasing the export of Japanese investment funds and technologies and of honing the competitive advantages of some Asian NICs' exports at the expense of the more labour- and energy-using products of Japan. So we might argue that although the early growth of the NICs was to a great extent a result of pull effects stemming from the US,[10] the NIC growth of the 1980s was increasingly linked to changes in the Japanese economy, which ironically enough included the increased need to replace foreign trade with overseas production through the export of private capital under pressure from American interests. The revaluation merely heightened the dynamic aspects of the emerging model: Japanese capital and enterprise surged into the earlier NICs during the mid- and late 1980s and then into the industrialising nations of South East Asia (e.g. Thailand and Indonesia) during 1988 and 1989. Until that time, Japanese activity in such ASEAN economies as Thailand had been mostly concerned with investment in labour-using textile industries, or in automobile or chemical manufacturing, which absorbed space, raw materials, lower level skills and which created pollution control expenses of a high order in Japan itself. To that extent the ASEAN nations had played a part in Japan's early restructuring processes.

The position of the NICs and ASEAN in this wider, global system was dependent on three sets of abilities, or proclivities, each of them inherently transitional:

Proclivity 1, that of the American economy to withstand very significant financial, investment and trading pressures arising from its East Asian commercial and diplomatic relations without collapse or vicious regulatory retaliation. From the late 1980s the NICs were increasingly threatened by a renewed bout of American and global protectionism and the upward adjustment of their exchange rates – between 1985 and 1988 there was significant appreciation of NIC currencies with the exception of Singapore. A more recent indication of the essentially transitional nature of these relations is provided in the so-called 'Asian crisis' of 1997–8. The Clinton administration in the US was especially critical of Japanese policy in failing adequately to stimulate domestic demand. The reasonable fear was that during the depression internally, Japanese firms would attempt to export their way out of trouble and that the US would become a principal recipient of such products: in 1998 the bilateral deficit between the two nations increased by around 40 per cent.

Proclivity 2, that of the Japanese to continue to innovate new institutions and technologies and to diffuse the pressure on US–Japan relations by foreign investment and trade dispersements. Of great importance in Figure 10.2 is the trade flow labelled A*, which served to release some of the pressures building up within this stylised global system – thus between 1985 and 1989 the ratio of Japanese manufactured imports to total imports increased from around 30 per cent to over 50 per cent, most of this increase a direct result of Japanese direct investment in NICs, which served to source NIC enterprises exporting semi-finished and manufactured goods to Japan. Between 1986 and 1988 Japan's imports from the Asian NICs grew at the rate of over 38 per cent per annum, a major feature of the *endaka* years. The trade gap between Korea and

Japan doubled between 1985 and 1986 then speedily narrowed as a result of rapid increases in exports to Japan. This represented both a continuation of Japan's restructuring strategy (as internal industry moved away from labour-and-raw-material-intensive production) and the adoption of expansionism as an alternative to a more conservative protectionist programme.

Proclivity 3, that of the NICs and the ASEAN larger industrialisers (and increasingly China) to continue to 'catch-up' through prolonged technology transfers based on foreign investment, joint ventures and so on, combined with continuation of the export drive associated with the yen revaluation. Where this led to short periods of a high Japanese presence, political strains could ensue. Inducements by the Thai authorities were an element in the rise of Japanese direct investment to 50 per cent of the foreign total in Thailand during 1986–9, at which time 80 per cent of the 200 major projects were classified as export oriented.

From this time the NICs attempted to capitalise on this conjuncture of transitional factors by adopting the more recent Japanese tactics. Many popular commentators noted the adoption of similar public sector institutions and approaches. In its mid-term plan for the 1990s the Malaysian government considered an Income Doubling Plan very similar to that of Japan in the 1960s. But more significantly, by the end of the 1980s it was becoming evident that the technological enterprise of such NICs as the Republic of Korea was at least approximating that of Japan. Following upon a focus on the internal environment for technology transfers associated with bureaucratic attempts to search and sift the gamut of global technique, more recently the centre of interest shifted away from the US and towards Japan. As NIC payment of royalties mounted and as the new middle classes found a critical voice, so too NIC state-led mechanisms of technology transfer were more directed towards indigenous users and training programmes. Early experiments with Western style liberal arts education gave way to expenditure on appropriate vocational and technical training, polytechnics and applied groupings in universities. Of greater significance, the NICs began to selectively emphasise the role of enterprise sector training processes, so famous as a characteristic of the Japanese system. International comparisons of crude aggregates do bear out the transition. Increases in business expenditure on R&D as a percentage of GDP between 1981 and 1991 averaged 9 per cent per annum for Japan and 4 per cent for the US, but 32 per cent for South Korea, 24 per cent for Singapore and 16 per cent for Taiwan. Table 10.8 provides more general evidence of institutional patterns as they developed in the early 1980s. There are important similarities between the two Asian NICs and Japan, particularly in their efforts to reduce government expenditure as a total of technological research expenditure, and to consequently raise the proportion of R&D spent in manufacturing as such.

Table 10.8 Patterns of R&D resource usage in Asia, US and Japan, *c.* 1980–3

	US	*Japan*	*India*	*Paki-stan*	*Philip-pines*	*Korea*	*Singapore*
All R&D expenditure raised by government (%)	46.9	24.0	86.0	100	76.8	27.3	37.6
All R&D funds devoted to fundamental research (%)	12.5	14.6	–	–	18.9	24.0	9.8
All R&D spent in 'productive sector' (%)	73.0	64.8	24.7	82.3	9.8	60.4	54.2
'Productive sector' R&D spent in manufacturing industry (%)	?	93.4	85.7	10.3	77.5	91.2	–
All R&D expenditure in Higher Education which is engineering, technology, agriculture (%)	28.0	26.6	87.6	–	54.7	41.1	49.6
All R&D expenditure which is aimed at goals (%)							
Industrial development	0.4	12.6	16.4	–	12.3	–	27.1
Energy	6.7	29.1	13.5	–	5.6	–	–
Defence	64.3	4.8	14.1	–	4.8	–	–
Advance of knowledge	3.9	3.6	6.8	–	2.1	–	–
Aviation/space	5.5	9.2	8.6	–	–	–	–
Agricultural development	2.6	22.7	23.9	–	46.2	–	61.2
Other goals	16.6	18.0	16.7	–	29.0	–	11.7

The Korean Advanced Institute of Science and Technology and the Industrial Technology Research Institute were good examples of new modes of high technology encouragement, attempting as they did direct linkage between global technique and local industrial needs and concerns. Again, efforts like that of Daeduk Science Town in Korea and the Hsin-chu Science-Based Industrial Park in Taiwan are clearly reflections of the Japanese emphasis on technology cities as illustrated at Tsukuba and in plans for multifunctional cities located overseas (see pp. 226–30). In contrast to the Western model, NIC universities were not necessarily seen as prime sites of the higher technology. Within enterprise culture itself, the NICs have also experimented in recent years with such institutional innovations as Japanese-style Quality Control Circles.

The Korean economy is perhaps the most apt example of a large high-growth NIC whose performance is characterised by export super-growth, Japanese investment, technology transfers and institutional innovations in the private and public sectors. The Japanese connection was early and of especial importance – on one calculation by Kwan-chi Oh, Japan supplied 56 per cent of all the technology imported into Korea during 1962–83, the US only 23 per cent. In the years 1977–83 the import of technology grew at an average annual rate of 11.5 per cent. At this end date Korea was paying out US $150 millions in royalties alone, representative of approximately 1.5 per cent of world technology trade. Government policy undoubtedly influenced the extent of technology transfers. Prior to 1978 Korea controlled such importing through the authorisation of import licences, given on condition that the import fulfilled fixed development criteria. From then trade and technology were liberalised through the effort of the Ministry of the Economic Planning Board to stimulate the heavy and chemical industries. In 1981 the Foreign Capital Inducement Act lifted most restrictions and offered positive incentives to the high technology areas of the economy. The ceiling for automatic approval of investment was raised to US $100 million in November 1989 for joint ventures where the local partner had a majority holding.

By the early 1980s some 70 per cent of total South Korean exports of electrical products were produced by foreign-owned firms. Such export orientation was induced by the two free zones, the larger of the two – the Masan – reaching its high point in the mid-1970s as a forcing ground for electronic exports. By the late 1980s the Korean electrical industry was the fifth largest in the world and was dominated by joint ventures and technology purchases. Much technology transfer was associated with the *chaebol*[11] firms, which moved from an early emphasis on joint venture towards licence agreements, technological cooperation and other joint developments.

In addition, the thriving smaller firms, utilising high (particularly micro-electronic) technologies within Japan itself, and often neglected in models of Japanese development or of the East Asian system more broadly, provided a powerful exemplar for further institutional development in the Asian NICs. CAD/CAM systems may be introduced into very small production systems. As Suzuki summarised for the mid-1980s, the small and medium size sector in Japan, was 'the source of the vitality, flexibility and general youthfulness of the Japanese economy, and the primary engine of the nation's post-war economic success'. These were the firms which were most closely involved in modern expansionism into Asia, aided as they were by the financial assistance of the *sōgō shōsha* inside Japan, by information networks established by the *sōgō shōsha* and by MITI and other organisations outside Japan, and by the widespread practice emphasised by Prasartset, of 'mutual help and collaboration within and between different industrial groups regarding their overseas operations and collective economic power'. Their importance in Japan was matched by their importance in the

NICs – some 50 per cent of manufacturing workers in Korea at the outset of that nation's industrial surge were employed in such enterprises, although this share diminished as modernisation took place. Throughout the period 1980–7, of 8,567 cases of the acquisition of the stock of foreign companies by Japanese enterprises, 3,507 were by small and medium size enterprises and represented 40 per cent of Japan's surge of direct foreign investment in these years, with some definite bias of the smaller firms towards East Asia.

Such institutional trends provide some evidence for the claim that Asian NICs have been in receipt of techniques derived initially from an array of Western nations, but adapted and filtered through the institutional and commercial operations of an expanding Japanese economy.

In a field which is open to much analytical and empirical debate, if only because of the speed and complexity of Japan's expansion into Asia, there are quite different general academic positions taken up concerning both the motives and impacts of Japan's Asian trade and investment. On one hand, Sung Jo Park has argued that Japanese affiliates handed down only the lowest levels of technical know-how. At the higher levels, Japanese TNCs employed Japanese personnel, mass production and processes appropriate to only the 'socio-cultural milieu of the Japanese management system'. This may be useful at some stage for nations such as Korea or Taiwan, which share some of the cultural or linguistic understandings of Japan, but is a mode of operation which is inherently limiting. Writing twenty years ago, Nakajo summarised this position when stressing that, although 'the case varies considerably from company to company and product to product, the usual practice is for the parent company to supply the key parts that require a high level of technology and leave production of peripheral parts and simple assembly processes to its overseas subsidiaries'. Park quoted MITI's own findings that in the 1970s some 88 per cent of Japanese TNCs in manufacturing merely relocated their own techniques to foreign production, and that 'native techniques' were being used in only 5 per cent of cases. Japanese firms brought over 70 per cent of their production facilities with them, 'which means *de facto* that the natives and investors from a third world country hardly have the chance to employ their own production facilities'. Given that Japanese TNCs were mainly operating in such mid-technology fields as textiles and electrical appliances in regions such as Hong Kong, Taiwan, South Korea and Singapore, such points become particularly salient.

In an alternative vision, Ozawa has referred to 'human centred' technology transfer, with Japanese TNCs transferring real know-how across a wide range of assembly techniques, (radio, television, trucks), treatment processes (dyes, paints) and machine operations (spinning and weaving). What remains doubtful is the potency of Ozawa's claim that such production also provided technical data, training, plant layouts, selection and instalment of machinery and equipment, quality and cost controls and inventory management *in such a manner that indigenous technological capacity was increased rather than swamped by a mixture of manifold artefacts juxtaposed with institutional lacunae.* Ownership patterns suggested that Japanese TNCs were if anything better placed than their US counterparts to provide institutional and informational back-up to hardware improvements. Kojima emphasised that the ownership of the Japanese TNC typically lay 25 per cent with the Japanese producer firm, 25 per cent with an associated trading company and 50 per cent with local investors. At the same time, indigenous producers gained something from the vast marketing facilities of the Japanese *sōgō shōsha* and the information services provided by the Japanese government. Such joint-venture arrangements should have encouraged training processes (see pp. 209–11).

While Japanese-affiliated companies operating in Asia have made real contributions to increased employment, export earnings, technology transfer and management style, there can be little doubt that they have also been responsible for regimes of insensitivity, arrogance and misunderstanding, for cultural dissonance, social conflict and labour unrest. Within Japanese enterprises in Asia Chinese partners are often favoured over natives, wage differentials between indigenous workers and Japanese workers are considerable, work discipline regimes are often both strange and strict, and in the area of work organisation, local customs and status distinctions are frequently ignored. Stories abound of Japanese TNC manipulation of their Asian partners, the *de facto* subversion of joint ventures into subsidiaries, and the financial pressures exerted on Asian partners to buy Japanese inputs at prices above those of the free market. Where native managers are officially in charge of Japanese firms they are very commonly shadowed by a truly authoritative Japanese skeletal structure operating behind the façade. Although such practices are probably more common in the less developed parts of ASEAN economies than in the more sophisticated regions of the NICs they are frequently enough talked and written of throughout the Asia-Pacific region.

Both business and the Japanese authorities have also been historically guilty of violations of seemingly settled agreements. Thus the trade treaty in force with the Philippines since 1974 (see p. 198), contained a provision that Japan would accord 'sympathetic consideration' to any attempt by the Philippines to protect the prices of its exports in the world market, yet in November of that first year Japan cut the price of lumber coming from the Philippines, Thailand and Malaysia. In August of 1975 Japan severely reduced imports of copper, and in January 1976 the same occurred with bananas. In 1976 Japan was guilty of dumping mackerel and paper products. Such moves created layoffs in Philippine industries and resentment amongst many groups. Attitudes in Asia towards Japanese expansionism has hardly been improved by official cultural policies, such as that of the early 1980s when all Japanese publishers were required by the authorities to designate the aggressions against China during 1935–7 as mere advances, the Nanjing Massacre of 1937 appearing as just a minor episode. Similarly, the Japanese extolling of their colonial history hardly sits well with the memories and perceptions of modern Koreans, especially when these are exacerbated by severely discriminatory treatment of the many Korean-Japanese now living in Japan.

It is also true that the completeness of institutional transformation is at best problematic – manuals do not constitute understanding, brief training programmes do not yield tacit knowledge, lifetime employment does not constitute the Japanese enterprise abroad. A study of Japanese enterprise in the Philippines in the mid-1980s showed that Japanese style management was to an extent transferred in the large-size subsidiaries if measured in terms of life-time seniority or some elements of skill development, but not so if measured in terms of multiple-skill creation through job rotation or quality control. Again, labour turn-over was reportedly high, though not necessarily in comparison to that of indigenous forms in the same industries.

Perhaps more significantly, it has been claimed that in the ASEAN nations the prime effect of Japanese investments has been to join a more global impact of separating the interests of local elites from those of local small investors, the middle classes and production workers, an argument which extends the 'development of underdevelopment' thesis well beyond the Western impact in South America or Africa to the Japanese impact in modern Asia. This case seems to have been applicable during the 1970s and 1980s and in instances where the large Japanese trading firms were most directly involved. Thus in the Philippines, local partners of *sōgō shōsha* affiliates were mostly drawn from very prominent Filipino families. Of an elite group of less than fifty local partners of Japanese enterprise, most had interest in more than two joint ventures, and the totality of elite partnerships accounted for over 80 per cent of all Japanese investment in the Philippines. It could thus be argued both that such investment did not contribute much to the development of grass-roots entrepreneurship or technical innovation but did tend to direct elite interests and assets away from internal industrial infrastructures and towards perhaps higher profits in international schemes, a process abetted by official activity.

There is a strong argument which emphasises that Japanese activity has often been most successful in partnership with *Hua-chi 'iau* (overseas Chinese) enterprise cultures. Thus the ASEAN nations do share the presence of important *hua-chi 'iau* minorities which are almost invariably at the centre of modernising economic activities. Perhaps 65 per cent or more of all overseas Chinese live in the ASEAN nations. The argument is not that the management practices of such significant business groups are the same as those of the Japanese, but rather that they differ from those of the West and share certain elements of a common Chinese history, and, thus, derive special advantages of interaction with Japanese business in particular, but perhaps with Western business also. In such enterprise cultures there has been strong familialism and loyalty ties, nepotism, a high degree of non-money rewards and sanctions, and an inner working which provides a platform of harmony above an underlying reality of personal hostilities and selective performance of assigned tasks. Whether such features or even a wider notion of a shared 'Confucian Renaissance' really explain the success of ASEAN or NIC nations is debatable. It is surely feasible that Japanese expansionism created closer working relationships in East Asia than could ever have been achieved by Western enterprise primarily because of clearer complementarities in trade and investment, greater proximity, and shared linguistic devices (e.g. the meanings if not the vocalisation of Chinese characters). Together these alone would have given East Asia an edge over other industrialising systems in their interaction with the modern Japanese economic expansion.

At the same time, whatever its net impact, Japanese capital has most frequently been invited into Asia, possibly because of the known strong export orientation of Japanese firms – of some 200 Japanese investment projects approved in Thailand during 1986–8, 80 per cent were classified as strongly export oriented. Complaints that Japanese TNCs did not train many Asian workers might be related to absence of a high enough basic level of education to begin the process. Again, a common argument is that at least Japanese enterprise is no worse and often better than that of its American or European counterparts, for long so dominant. And if Japanese enterprise culture does not travel, then perhaps the impact of select 'operational practices' has been nevertheless positive overall. More closely, we might here suggest that the Japanese presence in Asia, especially after 1985, might have hastened the development of a wider Asian industrialisation by increasing the scale of operations, quickening the switch towards the most recent developing systems of Asia, and acting as a virulent medium for the vital commercial, technological and investment linkages forged transitionally between the US, the NICs and the ASEAN economies.

Although it is too recent a phenomenon for historical reflection, it is feasible that the future impacts of Japanese expansion in Asia will depend principally upon a further transition towards the organisation of marketing, information search, R&D and so on in Asia itself. Hitherto, whatever their sales or basic production facilities in other nations, Japanese companies have tended to retain central control and overall strategic decision making at headquarters in Japan itself. This has been in contrast to transnationalism in Europe and America. Very recently, however, Japanese companies have developed real headquarters overseas, such as Nissan's regional centre in Rotterdam, Honda's consolidation of all American operations into one company, and Toyota's several strategic moves. This process involves a new devolution of responsibilities to local agency and a transfer of strategic R&D enterprise sites, as with Hitachi's research centres in San Francisco, Detroit and Cambridge UK, Sony's laboratories in the US, Britain, Germany and Singapore, or Mitsubishi Electric's overseas centres for handling patents and licences. This may well increase two-way flows of information and technique at the intersection of expanding Japan and the Western world. It may not do so as readily in Asia. Because of the tradition in Japan of face-to-face and highly informal information sharing within enterprise, the Japanese firm has not been notably good at devising formal means for transmitting information, technique and good guidance to others. Nor have they been notably successful at dealing with nationals, trade unions and ethnic minorities overseas. The new trend to a more mature transnationalism may therefore succeed in advanced industrial systems, where Japan has most to gain from positive interchanges, but may flounder in Asia where Japanese firms are altogether more likely to devise methods of halting information leakages from informal enterprise structures at the expense of more sophisticated processes of information dispersal and technological transfer.

Pacific partnership: the history of the Multifunction Polis

In September of 1987, MITI's Policy Planning Committee announced their vision of a Multifunction Polis, the development of a high technology city in Australia within which Japanese real estate, commercial and technological interests would play a dominant part in partnership with other Pacific nations. The documentation opened with the statement that 'the Pacific Rim is the region with the greatest growth potential in the world today' and went on to claim that Australia and Japan 'bear a substantial role and responsibilities for the development of the Pacific Rim as indispensable partners not only in economic affairs but in a wide spectrum of activity'. Entering its new expansive phase, Japan required the assistance of Australia in developing 'new projects likely to make a broad-based contribution to the Pacific Rim nations and pave the way for the Pacific Era'.

The Japanese mentioned explicitly the need felt within Japan to make a novel contribution to economic life in Pacific Rim nations, to experiment in new life styles, moving the locus of innovation beyond the established technopolis programme within Japan itself.[12] The MFP would serve as a channel of information for Japan and a mode of commercialisation of technologies and exploitation of international opportunities within Australia. Early Australian official responses, especially that of those States who were bidding for the site of the MFP, demonstrated some shared beliefs that the new high technology industries are based on human creativity and research programmes rather than on capital and oil, and that the continued progress of such industries in turn depends upon a transnational merging of different types of expertise in settings of 'mutual stimulation' and 'lively personal exchange'. Cultural and information enterprises within the MFP would provide the requisite environment which would induce technological creativity by promoting 'the germination and fusion of a wide variety of technology and know-how and spur the growth of new industries, and thereby boost the restructuring of Australian industry'. Here was an institutional gift from Japan to Australia and thereby the Pacific.

Although argued as a part of Japan's new internationalism and regionalism, the MFP encapsulated several of the ingredients associated with the nation's economic restructuring. As we have seen, it was commonly believed that a move towards environmentally friendly yet productive industries would involve the nation in a wholesale move towards creative R&D in core activities of global calibre. Perhaps a new transnationalism might capture such foreign core knowledge (see pp. 209–11), but in the future the transfer tactic was not to be relied on. At the same time, many informed Japanese commentators emphasised what they saw as crucial limitations to the internal or autonomous generation of such creativity. So, in the twentieth century, of some 440 Nobel Prizes gained in the major natural sciences, 41 per cent had gone to the US, 15 per cent to the UK, 14 per cent to Germany, but only 1 per cent to Japan. Japanese groupism and consensus modes of operation were ideal for the fusing of existing techniques, materials and sequences into modified and commercialised products, but not designed to generate paradigmatic laboratory breakthroughs. According to such arguments, hierarchical structures combine with risk-avoidance and groupism to produce a nation of innovative and cumulative imitators rather than a plethora of trail-blazing creative geniuses. Would not the industrial economy now slip down the road of diminishing returns as investment funds found fewer and fewer advanced technology outlets within Japan? Would not Japanese capital continue to escalate outwards in order to capture the technological creativity inherent in other advanced industrial systems? And would not this create more of an international backlash against Japanese economic imperialism and technological stealing on the part of powerful nations? At the outset of the 1980s, Masanori Moritani judged that 'Japan has grown to its present status through American grace', but could no more free-ride on advanced techniques elsewhere. However, Moritani departed from the opinion of many of his contemporaries by denying any *inevitable* connection between lead edge innovation, creativity and industrial efficiency. As long as the nation had some sort of access to advanced technique, then the Japanese institutional, trading and financial systems would yet ensure an effective global lead in the commercialisation of new processes and products, wherever the latter might originate. That is, lacunae in the R&D system would continue to be more than offset by global advantages in effective international commercialisation. For further discussion of this theme in the context of the transfer of technologies, see Chapter 13.

MITI in particular seems to have had both limitations and compensating tactics in mind when it planned the MFP and called for the encouragement of something along the lines of what Martin Fransman has labelled 'oriented basic research', that innovation activity within private enterprise which is commercial in its ultimate goal but wider and more searching than normal development research. During the 1970s and 1980s, MITI and other bureaucracies appear to have had some limited success through the selective utilisation of cooperative research agreements which involved very large projects such as high speed computing technologies, and through the coordination of the in-house research of a number of enterprises. The MPF was an extension of a particular vision of technological change which had already been established under various auspices in Japan itself, and symbolised in the so-called technopolis strategy.

Although commentators judged that Australia was chosen purely as a pleasant vacation location for Japanese MFP corporate members, the public justification enumerated various factors. Against the prevailing Japanese image of an Australia disadvantaged by smallness of scale, distance and labour disputes, were the countervailing notions of Australia as politically stable, skilled, relatively proximate, and in possession of natural resources and a well developed transport, communication and technical infrastructure. So, an effective MFP partnership would 'fuse' (a favourite Japanese concept of the late 1980s) Japan's marketing, production and financial capacities with Australia's 'excellent labour and technical capacity' into an innovative and dynamic pocket of Pacific endeavour in order to meet the knowledge needs of the twenty-first century. The intended concentration of the MFP was upon biotechnologies, fibre optics, advanced ceramics and new and rare metals, robotics, aerospace and computer software, all backed by the 'high touch' creativity-inducing 'industries' of convention, vacation, interaction, information, training and health. Ideally, in order to parallel the Japanese model, the MFP was to pursue such industrial activities through international cooperative projects linking governments to a great array of private enterprises. Within an Australian MFP environment of novel property rights, of individualism, and informal networking, the shared information base would then stimulate cooperation at the commercial or market end of this innovation process, leaving room for a final phase of more competitive, enterprise-based product specification. Such a planned mixture of the 'Japanese' and 'Western' modes of operation within the MFP would supposedly generate a multitude of enterprise partnerships across national borders, a tremendous learning system, a commercialisation of basic R&D activities and one very visible physical locus for new images of the coming Pacific century.

The MFP project was, thus a microcosm of Japan's restructuring and expansionism, for it was based on the idea that the necessary and sufficient condition of twenty-first century leadership was the generation, capture and commercial exploitation of scientific, technical and commercial information in new institutional sites and new industries. If the future rested on raw materials, then these were no longer coal and oil but rare earths and minerals. If research was to be the core input, then its institutional locus was neither industry nor university, but new sites which cut across such older distinctions. Leading or fast growing economies would be characterised by blurred edges between public and private sectors, and debates over privatisation, government spending or the appropriate commanding ideologies for mixed capitalist economies would fade into the past.

But the further history of the MFP also illustrates the problems of Japanese expansionism, the conflicts generated at the points of interaction between the 'Japanese system' and others, and the fundamental partiality of the Japanese technological vision in the late 1980s.

The very public character of policy issues in Australia contrasted with the mode of internal consensus building in Japan, and led to a multitude of doubts and anxieties. On the Japanese side the original MITI document was seen as a guide by which Australia would produce a less stylised and more practical proposal. Within Australia, a split between national interests and those of individual states rose to a height over the actual location of the MFP. The eventual decision in support of Adelaide, South Australia, failed entirely to incorporate all of the issues and was never accepted as a product of public consensus. A failure of Australian bureaucrats to be frank about the extent of the Japanese connection or to move beyond 'tech talk' gave space to both fearmongers and informed critics. Japanophobia arose as the MFP was characterised as a potential 'Japanese enclave of surveillance over the democratic affairs of Australia'. Those of a more liberal demeanour considered that a purely economic enclave would be quite as bad. Others were convinced that the MFP would bring in its wake Japanese and other immigrants and environmental destruction.

Other problems emerged at the point of interaction between Japanese understandings and Western concepts of intellectual property rights and commercial law. Rights, negotiation, arbitration, participation and venture capital arrangements all required legal and institutional solutions, and this at all times seemed a problem too knotty to solve. This was heightened by the obvious inequalities in bargaining power between a huge expanding industrial economy and a relatively small commercial system. Power balancing could only be achieved if Australian enterprise was aided by Australian government and financial institutions, and achieving an interface between such agencies and those of the *sōgō shōsha*, for instance, was never really attempted. Again, integration of the MFP into the Australian technological and enterprise systems required the implanting of non-protectionist incentives to private investment and expertise, carefully planned links between the MFP and existing university, enterprise and government organisations, together with some revision of organisation practices in the private sector. None of this was seriously taken on board in a manner which yielded sufficient information to both sides.

A fundamental flaw of the MFP, however, lay in its basic vision of technological change and the manner in which this may be harnessed to productive industrial activity. The project was centred on a modified linear model, in which high knowledge flows through various conduits to base applications, designs and markets. Yet in the microelectronic world within which Japan was itself so strategically placed, sites of creative endeavour need not be purely physical. In any such incubator approach a high degree of informality or flexibility must be allowed for in order that the important forces of serendipity and conflict may be encouraged to act against tendencies towards conservation, risk avoidance, gamesmanship and protectionism. Again, and conforming nicely to the regional goals announced by the Japanese, such a system works better if open to a range of influences. The failure of the MFP to properly establish Pacific partnerships (including the US West Coast) or global networking removed a source of potentially creative disturbance. The failure to incorporate NIC and ASEAN interests, in turn, greatly reduced the international compass of the project and confirmed that little attention would be given to potentially strategic innovations at the mid-technology level, which might be of interest in the agricultural, extractive or textile sectors of such economies.

The subsequent history of the MFP describes its fall from the status of Pacific high tech city to Adelaide's science city to the announcement of its official demise by the South Australian Premier in August 1997 following the termination of all federal funding. Analytical reflections concerning the MFP now refer at most to its erstwhile status as a project for urban redevelopment, rather than to its original genesis as a part of the global and regional strategies of a vastly expanding Japanese economy.

Into the 1990s: Japan and Asia-Pacific cooperation

Japan's modern regionalism began with participation in the Colombo Plan in 1954, just two years after the signing of the San Francisco Peace Treaty. In 1955 Japan first moved to effect some reparations and free economic cooperation to regions of Asia so adversely affected by earlier colonial and military damage. By 1958 reparation payments to Burma, the Philippines and Indonesia alone amounted to over US $970 million. Most of such reparations were paid in the form of construction projects and technical services to Burma, the Philippines, Indonesia, Vietnam, Korea, Laos, Thailand and Cambodia, and were followed by a limited amount of credit and technical schemes as well as training programmes for overseas students in Japan. Perhaps of equal importance, the Asian Productivity Organisation was devised in order to transfer intermediate technologies from Japan to East Asia in the textile, chemical, aluminium and travel industries and to offer advice upon such institutional innovations as the setting up of medium and small enterprises and the initiation of modernised cost and production control systems. Seventeen Overseas Technical Training Centres based throughout Asia focused on the intermediate technologies of metal processing, machine tools, bicycles, glass, electronic machines, textiles and fisheries. Such technical cooperation schemes were probably the most salient early attempts by the Japanese to forge some form of co-operative regionalism, but were characterised by smallness of both scope and official funding.

For Japan, official development aid was probably the most visible mechanism of regionalism prior to the great expansion of the economy, the mid-1990s position of which is shown in Table 10.6. Although recent statements regarding the intention of such aid do embrace the furtherance of Asian democracy and human rights, the historical tendency has been for Japanese ODA to promote both regional economic development and the construction of that infrastructure necessary to the growth of Japanese enterprise in the region. In this sense, official aid policy may be seen as an extension of restructuring policy.

By 1973 Japan was second only to the US in the amount of assistance given by the DAC (Development Assistance Committee) nations. Japanese ODA as a percentage of GNP was then 0.25, the average international level being around 0.30. Some 90 per cent of Japan's ODA was with Asia, although bilateral agreements were spread much more widely. At that time bilateral loans amounted to 54 per cent of Japan's ODA, and these specified an interest rate of 3.7 per cent per annum, long maturity periods, and, very frequently, were tied to commodity trade exchanges, i.e. a proportion of such loans were made on the understanding that money would be spent on imports from Japan. This was consistent with the international picture at that time, when most bilateral aid was designed to nurture special relations with developing systems, whether economic, political, military, historical or cultural.[13] Japan was a party to the Memorandum of Understanding on the untying of bilateral development loans in favour of procurement in the developing nations which was agreed by a number of DAC member nations in June 1974. By the late 1980s, the formally 'tied' component of Japanese aid was the lowest amongst the OECD nations, but most international economic relations are pervicacious. Robert Orr estimated that some 60 per cent of Japan's supposedly untied loans in fact resulted in purchase of Japanese goods and services.

Under Japan's initiative, in 1966 the Ministerial Conference for the Economic Development of Southeast Asia was first convened. The 1967 Bangkok Declaration, which aimed to ally Indonesia with its neighbours, minimise US military bases in the region, and initiate economic cooperation, was the basis for the formation of ASEAN and the first real evidence of a new regionalism. By the 1970s the grouping of five nations contained 68 per cent of the land area and 72 per cent of the population of Southeast Asia. Japan offered general support and was in official agreement with the principal aims of economic growth, social progress, cultural development, peace and stability, cultural and scientific cooperation, integration with international organisations, and independence not only from the US–UK axis but from China and Japan also! The regional security problems seemingly arising from the reunification of Vietnam in 1976, the Sino–US detente, the collapse of the old IMF system and the new power of OPEC, all combined to forge renewed efforts at economic integration during the late 1970s. By the early 1980s the ASEAN group boasted high rates of overall economic growth based around savings ratios ranging from 19 per cent in Thailand to 27 per cent in Malaysia. Because Japan was the single largest trading partner of each ASEAN nation it could be seen as a force for both integration and fast growth. Through the period, ASEAN experimented with a mix of integration mechanisms, from selective trade liberalisation, Industrial Complementarity Agreements and regional large-scale industrial projects sited in specific nations, including those for soda ash (Thailand), super phosphates (the Philippines) and diesel engines (Singapore). As we have seen, the appreciation of the yen and the NIC currencies and the contemporaneous increased labour costs and commercial tensions with the US amongst the NICs, opened renewed global trading possibilities for the ASEAN group at the same time as such forces also stimulated closer commercial links with Japan. This sequence meant that ASEAN growth was almost certainly but only partially an outcome of technology transfers first from Japan and then from the NIC nations. Such a sequence seemed to increase complementarities across an ever widening grouping of Asian nations, a fundamental underpinning for a more mature regionalism.

There can be little doubt that official aid continued to abet Japanese trade and investment in Southeast Asia throughout the period of economic expansion. In the early 1990s, Indonesia, Thailand and the Philippines were amongst the top five recipients of Japanese ODA, and Japan was by far the dominant force in the Asian Development Bank. The ASEAN nations have, in particular, been the focus of the *minkatsu* concept as symbolised in MITI's New Asian Industries Development Plan. The term *minkatsu* is translatable as the 'productive harnessing of private energies', and relates quite directly to a main theme of this chapter – the expansion of Japanese investment outwards as a method of exporting labour-and-resource-intensive production to other nations and deflecting US pressure on Japan's commodity export policy, as part of the long-period restructuring described in Chapter 9. The NAIDP in fact brings together the interests of private enterprise, the Export-Import Bank, the Japan International Cooperation Agency (JICA), and JETRO, public sector institutions involved in the investment expansion of private Japanese enterprise from the 1970s. More particularly, under the NAIDP, since 1987, the ASEAN–Japan Development Fund is designed to encourage joint business ventures which have been seen as in effect 'providing subsidised loans to facilitate Japanese industrial expansion into Southeast Asia'. Indeed, between 1983 and 1987 the ASEAN allocation of total Japanese ODA rose from 34 per cent to 45 per cent. As long as the major part of ODA continues to be in the form of loans, then payment must normally continue to occur in the form of exports to Japan, which in turn promotes the restructuring demands of the Japanese economy. It might be summarised that ODA served Japanese restructuring in its early years by increasing the export of Japanese products to Asia and helping in the initiation into manufacturing production of private Japanese enterprise as it swung away from the more traditional trading activities of the *sōgō shōsha*. More recently, ODA has stimulated imports from ASEAN and other nations of those products which contain a relatively high proportion of labour, raw materials and mid-level technologies in their final value-added content.

Many of the much-vaunted aspects of regionalism have been weakened by the multitude of commercial crises throughout the Asia Pacific since mid-1997, most of which have been associated with charges of corruption and bad debts, and illustrative of the claim that 'politics is fast becoming the chief obstacle to economic recovery'. Thus the Asia Pacific region is both characterised and weakened as a cooperative entity by structural bottlenecks, bureaucratic resistance to modernisation, labour issues, cronyism and bad banking practices. In Japan the LDP and the Prime Minister Keizo Obuchi visibly failed to remove the 'patronage machine' or effectively dampen the 1998 banking crisis, which was seen as an outcome of corrupt real estate development, collusion between banks and LDP political projects, and failed political leadership. The resultant failures of the Long-Term Credit Bank, of the Fuji, Sakua and Nippon banks and financial institutions spread to *keiretsu* financing and government bailouts. They also threw serious doubt on the ability of Japan to lead the Asia Pacific into continued prosperity and growth in the long-term future. From Malaysia to Korea, many similar features were witnessed through the region as it was assumed that crisis in Thailand (September 1997) would wash back through Southeast Asia, to Northeast Asia, Wall Street and Europe. The late 1990s daily witnessed the spread of what was depicted as a characteristically regional disease.

Yet Peter Drysdale has correctly and astutely summarised Japan's key role in the Asia-Pacific during the period of the economy's greatest expansion as being that of the principal promoter of a gradual liberalisation of the region's economies in the realisation that this process must be flexible enough to allow for wide differences in the production and trading strengths of a very varied group of nations. This is particularly illustrated in the Japanese role in APEC (Asia–Pacific Economic Cooperation forum) formed in 1989. Such forums as APEC are at once regional gatherings and expressive of the need for Pacific leadership in a fully global context. This dual focus has been of special concern to Japan in providing a medium for the reduction of bilateral tensions with the United States. As Drysdale expresses the point, the 'tendency of the United States to conduct aspects of its trade relations bilaterally, and to seek bilateral reciprocity in its trade negotiations, is widely recognised. It is also understandable. For a hegemonic power – which the United States still is – there is a natural temptation to use muscle to force market opening (in the name of both self-interest and the general good).' Drysdale's reflection captures the essential aims of regional cooperative activity and the role of Japan within it in recent years. As the same author is quick to realise, such balancing acts have been more or less upset by aggressive trade diplomacy, particularly that stemming from the US (see pp. 197–9 and Chapters 9 and 12). By 1992 the US President could declare in Singapore that 'we need you as free and productive as you can be, and we understand that our security presence can provide a foundation for our mutual prosperity and shared defence'. The tactic of the US was to renew pressure through GATT and other means to forge wide integration via liberal trade zones as opposed to trade blocs which 'attempt to hold the rest of the world at bay'.

Conclusions

It would seem fair to judge that the expansion of the Japanese economy on many fronts since *c.* 1970 has been closely tied to not only the rate of *growth* of the domestic economy, but to its *restructuring*. The growth of Japanese trade, investment, aid, joint ventures, technical and institutional agreements and cooperation has been at a greater rate even than that of the domestic economy. Furthermore, despite all reservations concerning the activity of particular Japanese enterprises, the hatreds engendered when very wealthy Japanese businessmen take their pleasures abroad in Asia, and the systematic blockages on processes of technological modernisation or institutional liberalisation which have certainly occurred, the net effect of Japanese expansion appears to have been positive for industrial development in both NIC and ASEAN groups of nations. The development of these latter groups took place during a time of relative stagnation in the rest of the global economy. The fast intrusion of the Japanese system made a difference, the further impacts of which will be considered in Chapters 11 and 12. It remains debatable whether the social benefits of industrialisation in Asia would have been any greater under traditional Western tutelage than under more recent Japanese expansionism.

Surely it is realistic to judge that, whatever the character of the national and international debate which took place on Japan's role in the new global system, in fact that role was structurally supportive of a climacteric shift, one which permitted continued American leadership amidst massive changes in technologies, industries and the location of productive industries. The essence of that support is, we believe, captured in Figure 10.2. Because the factors which allowed this supportive role in a changing world system were themselves in their very essence of a transitional or conjunctural nature, it would be unwise to assert either their immutability on one hand, or the likelihood of any imminent transformation in Japan's position from one of support to one of leadership. But perhaps an obvious point should be emphasised. There can be little doubt that the future of

Japan's expansionism will not depend entirely on the systematic imperatives of continued national economic growth alone. As important will be the manner in which Japanese trade, foreign investment and external political and diplomatic activities are nested into the complexities of the global economic and political system. In this respect, the key relationships will be between Japan and China and the US.

Notes

1 Presupposing a large and healthy US economy, the prevailing IMF system was a global institution in which the US dollar was linked to gold, and other currencies were linked to the dollar. A necessary ingredient was that the US would readily comply with requests from other nations for the conversion of their US dollars into gold. At the Smithsonian Conference held in Washington in December 1971, a new fixed exchange rate of ¥308 was at first adopted. In February 1973 this system collapsed as EC nations moved to floating systems amidst much selling of US dollars. Whatever the internal resistance, the yen was effectively revalued by global market forces.

2 As elsewhere in this text, the analysis of foreign investment relates primarily to the securities, bonds and direct investments of the long-term. The short-term net capital flows are of less importance in economic history and often work against the trend of the long-term flows. Thus in the later 1980s Japan's private sector was a net absorber of short-term capital from abroad, as it borrowed short in order to invest overseas over the long-term. We might argue, then, that one explanation of Japan's expansion relates to its growing status as an industrial trading economy of high savings propensity. At this level of analysis, economic growth directly fed commercial expansion.

3 For which plan see Gendai Sōgō Kenkyū Shūdan (Study Group for New Socioeconomic Institutions) 'Overseas expansion of Japanese business enterprises: a proposal', published in English version in *Alternatives*, no. 2 (1976), 151–63.

4 Using the term 'nominal' because such a change in exchange rate theoretically influences the balance of payments on both demand and supply sides. Thus, appreciation of currency such as this, lowers the price of imported goods in the yen currency of Japan, thereby raising demand, i.e. increasing imports. Appreciation also increases domestic incomes through the terms-of-trade gain, augmenting power to purchase imports. At the same time, on the demand side, consumers and producers should switch demand from domestic to foreign products, this affecting profitability and resource usage.

5 The German figures might, however be noted. In the same accumulated period, the same bias could be measured for Sweden, Switzerland and the Netherlands, but not to anything like the same extent as in Japan's case.

6 The *zaibatsu* or 'financial cliques' were formed anew during Meiji and dissolved by the Occupation authorities in 1945–46 – see Chapters 5–7. The *keiretsu* are technically enterprise groupings, linked by banking and financial networks and overall 'trade marketing', to be distinguished from the *zaikai* or financial circles.

7 A high point because by 1992 total sales of this group were ¥111,000 billion, and the proportion of overseas or foreign trade sales had fallen to 55 per cent. The Big Nine are Itochu (C. Itoh), Marubeni, Sumitomo, Mitsui, Mitsubishi, Nissho Iwai, Tomen, Nichimen, Kanematsu in descending order of sales. In the early 1970s the combined sales of the then Big Six represented about 20 per cent of Japanese GNP. They were essential to expansionism both because they were necessary to the *keiretsu* structure in linking large manufacturers with smaller

enterprises performing downstream operations as well as to the reduction of transaction costs amongst affiliated transnational producers.

8 ASEAN here is Thailand, Malaysia, Philippines, Indonesia, excluding Brunei, and in the table Singapore is entered as an Asian NIC.

9 These are Japanese figures and possibly underestimated. Counting subcontracted, related and casual workers the total might have been nearer 3 million employees throughout Asia. At the same time the Japanese investment presence ought not to be exaggerated – in these years the ratio of Japanese investment to domestic capital formation in ASEAN was probably about 1.5 per cent.

10 Apart from the impacts of Marshall Aid and Korean war expenditures, growth inducements included American liberal attitudes towards NIC protectionism during their import-substitution phases, the expanding US market for NIC manufactures and the stimulus to Asian industrialisers (especially Taiwan and South Korea) of the Vietnam war.

11 Generally the term is used for large business groups active in many, technologically unrelated industries, centrally owned by a founder family, funded in part by government banking. The four largest are Daewoo, Hyundai, Samsung and LG, and together their sales represent about 50 per cent of Korean GDP in the years since 1988.

12 In an attempt to stop flows of talent into the Tokyo–Ōsaka conurbation and to reduce environmental pressure on crowded sites, MITI had designated twenty-six areas as 'technopolis' zones in 1984. In April 1991 these were boosted with further funds and twenty were authorised to enter a new phase as developmental high tech centres. This continued a tradition of regionalism going back into the Meiji period, but also demonstrated the newer belief in the site-independency of new industries, which could draw on improved transport and communication services to produce R&D intensive products with a very high value-added to raw material ratio in new green-field locations. A further MITI precept was that more independent research centres, located well away from the influence of Tokyo bureaucracies would be more likely to yield creative results.

13 At that time, examples of such tied aid ranged from recipients in the British Commonwealth, the franc zone, nations figuring in military conflicts – such as Israel, Egypt, Vietnam – and the 'special relations recipients' of OPEC money in the Middle East and Islamic developing countries. Communist aid went primarily to Cuba, Vietnam, Afghanistan, Egypt, India, Iran, Mongolia and Turkey, although commitments to African nations rose rapidly in those years.

References

Halliday, Jon (1983) 'The specificity of Japan's re-integration into the world capitalist economy after 1945: notes on some myths and misconceptions', in Gianni Fodella (ed.) *Japan's Economy in a Comparative Perspective*, Tenterden, Kent: Paul Norbury Publications, pp. 31–47.

Pempel, T. J. (1997) 'Regime shift: Japanese politics in a changing world economy', in Pempel *et al.*, *The Politics of Economic Reform in Japan*, Australian National University, Canberra, Australia–Japan Research Centre, p. 10.

Iida, Tsuneo (1979) 'The ramifications of revaluation', *Japan Echo*, VI, Special Issue on Economy in Transition, p. 47.

Hisamizu, Hiroyuki (1982) 'Averting economic ostracism', *Japan Echo*, IX(2), p. 75.

Porter, Michael (1990) *The Competitive Advantage of Nations*, London: Macmillan.

Andreani, Jean-Louis (1990) 'Straight talking in Tokyo', *Le Monde*, 22 July, p. 23.

Farrell, Roger (1997) 'Japanese foreign direct investment in real estate 1985–1994', *Pacific Economic Papers* No. 272, October, p. 16.

Lawrence, R. (1987) 'Imports in Japan: closed markets or minds?', *Brookings Papers on Economic Activity*, 2, p. 551.

Office of the US Trade Representative (1989) *1989 National Trade Estimate Report on Foreign Trade Barriers*, Washington, DC: USGPO, p. 112.

Dore, R. P. (1986) *Flexible Rigidities. Industrial Policy and Structural Adjustment in the Japanese Economy 1970–80*, London: The Athlone Press.

American National Academy of Sciences (1967) *Applied Science and Technological Progress*, Washington, DC: US Government Printing Office, pp. 347–56.

Hernadi, Andras (1985) 'Export oriented industrialisation and its successes in the Asia-Pacific region', *East Asia*, 3, p. 4.

Bradbury, Frank (1981) 'Technological economics; innovation, project management and technology transfer', *Interdisciplinary Science Reviews*, 6, p. 151.

Suzuki, Hideo (1984) 'Industrialisation in the Republic of Korea and the small and medium enterprises in Japan', *Japan Foundation Newsletter*, 11(6) (March), p. 3.

Prasartset, N. in Yamashita, S. (ed.) (1991) (Further reading) p. 62, following also the analysis of Ozawa as below.

Oh, Kwan-Chi (1985) 'Korea as a market for technology', *East Asia*, 3, p. 67.

Nakajō, S. (1980) (full reference below), quote p. 475.

Quotes on pp. 226–30 all from MITI *Basic Concept* (Sources, below) unless otherwise indicated.

Moritani, M. (1986) *Japan's Technological Innovation and Trade Structure*, Tokyo: Simul Press, quote page 123. See also Moritani (1986) 'Japanese technology: potential and pitfalls', *Japan Echo* 13, p. 13 etc.

Conner, Rex on Japanese surveillance as quoted in the *Sydney Daily Telegraph* 8 June 1990, p. 9.

Drysdale, Peter (1998) 'Japan's approach', (full reference below), pp. 5, 16.

Asia's Failed Politics, Special Issue of *Business Week: Asian Edition*, 5 October, 1998, p. 25.

Bush, George (1992) 'US policy in the Asia Pacific Region. Meeting the challenges of the post cold-war era', *Singapore Lecture 1992*, Institute of Southeast Asian Studies, Singapore, p. 6.

Cronin, R. P. (1992) *Japan, the United States and prospects for the Asia-Pacific century*, Singapore: Institute of Southeast Asian Studies.

Orr, Robert (1987) 'The rising sun: Japan's foreign aid to ASEAN, the Pacific Basin and the Republic of Korea', *Journal of International Affairs*, Summer, 63, p. 41.

Sources for tables and statistical data

Note. All investment data, particularly between Japan and Asia, should be treated with caution, and there tend to be great differences between figures reported by investor countries, recipient countries and global organisations. Some direct investment data are not really true flows since they include projects where foreign participation is short-term and less than 50 per cent.

Higashi, C. and Lauter, C. P. (1987) *The Internationalisation of the Japanese Economy* (2nd edn), Boston, MA: Kluwer.

Das, P. (1993) *The Yen Appreciation and the International Economy*, New York: New York University Press.
Coyle, Diane (1995) 'Weak yen is Japan's route to recovery', *The Independent*, 14 September, p. 18.
IMF (1997, 1998) *International Financial Statistics.*
Survey: World Economy 'Another World', *The Economist*, 19 September 1992.
Japan Ministry of Justice (1998) *Immigration Statistics 1997*, Tokyo.
OECD (1997) *Tourism Policy and International Tourism in OECD Countries 1997*, Paris.
Japan External Trade Organization (1997, 1998) *White Paper on Foreign Direct Investment 1996*, JETRO: Tokyo.
Keizai Koho Centre (1994) *Japan 1994, An International Comparison*, Taiheisha Ltd., Tokyo especially for Table 10.7.
World Bank Policy Research Report (1993) *The East Asia Miracle, Economic Growth and Public Policy*, Washington, DC: The World Bank.
Taniguchi, Koji (1974) Measurement of economic impact of transfer of technology to developing countries: Thailand and Thai joint ventures, *Research Report* 19 July, Tokyo, Institute of Developing Economies.
Edgington, D. S. (1998) 'Japanese service sector multinationals and the hierarchy of Pacific Rim Cities', *Asia Pacific Viewpoint*, 39 (August).
Special Issue, *The Annals of the American Academy of Political and Social Science*, January 1991.
MITI (1990) *Nineteenth Survey of Trends in Japanese Enterprise Overseas Business Activities*, (in Japanese), Tokyo: Ministry of Finance Printing Bureau.
Komiya, R. and Wakasugi, R. (1990) 'Japan's foreign direct investment', Discussion Paper 90 DF-11, *Research Institute of International Trade and Industry*, Tokyo: MITI, May.
Ministry of Foreign Affairs (1975) *Japan's Economic Cooperation*, Tokyo: MFI.
Healey, Derek T. (1990) 'The use of Japanese balance of payment surpluses for Asian/Pacific economic development', *Pacific Economic Papers*, no. 181, March, Research School of Pacific Studies, Canberra: Australian National University.

Further reading

Abegglen, J. C. (1994) *Sea Change. Pacific Asia as the new world industrial centre*, New York: Free Press.
Arndt, H. W. *et al.* (1988) 'Yen appreciation: J-curve and valuation effects', *Pacific Economic Papers* No. 156, Canberra: Australia–Japan Research Centre, Australian National University.
Chaponniere, J. R. (1992) 'The newly industrialising economies of Asia. International investment and technology transfer', *Science, Technology, Industry Review*, 9 (April) Paris: OECD.
Cronin, R. (1991) 'Changing dynamics of Japan's interaction with Southeast Asia', *Southeast Asia, Affairs*, 17.
Dore, R. P. and Taira, K. (1986) *Structural Adjustment in Japan 1970–1982*, Geneva.
Drysdale, P. (1995) 'The question of access to the Japanese market', *Pacific Economic Papers*, No. 247, September.
Drysdale, P. (1998) 'Japan's approach to Asia Pacific economic cooperation', *Pacific Economic Papers*, No. 281, July, Canberra: Australia–Japan Research Centre, Australian National University.

Drysdale, P. and Vines, D. (eds) (1998) *Europe, East Asia and APEC: a shared global agenda?*, Cambridge: Cambridge University Press.

Enos, J. L. and Park, W. H. (1988) *The Adoption and Diffusion of Imported Technology. The Case of Korea*, London: Croom Helm.

GATT (1971) 'Japan's economic expansion and foreign trade 1955 to 1970', *Studies in International Trade*, No. 2, July, Geneva: GATT.

Goldsbrough, M. (1987) 'Foreign direct investment in ASEAN: its source and structure', *Asian Economics*, 61.

Hagemeister, M. (1999) 'The four largest South Korean business groups and foreign technology: acquisition of technology and foreign direct investment', *Prometheus*, 17.

Inkster, I. (1990) 'Catching up and taking over: structural change, the technopolis concept and Japanese R&D for Australia', *Journal of Contemporary Asia*.

Inkster, I. (1991) *Science and Technology in History. An Approach to Industrialisation*, London: Macmillan.

Inkster, I. (1991) *The Clever City. Japan, Australia and the Multifunction Polis*, Sydney: Sydney University Press and Oxford University Press.

Kojima, K. (1977) 'Transfer of technology to developing countries: Japanese type versus American type', *Hitotsubashi Journal of Economics*, 17, pp. 9–33.

Krugman, P. (ed.) (1991) *Trade with Japan: Has the Door Opened Wider?* Chicago: University of Chicago Press.

Lawrence, R. (1993) 'Japan's different trade regime: an analysis with particular reference to keiretsu', *Journal of Economic Perspectives*, 7(Summer) and paper by Saxonhouse in the same issue.

Ministry of International Trade and Industry (1987) *Multifunction Polis Scheme for the 21st Century: Basic Concept, MFP Planning Committee*, Unpublished typescript, Tokyo: MITI, 30 September.

Nakajō, S. (1980) 'Japanese direct investment in Asian newly industrialised countries and intra-firm division of labour', *The Developing Economies*, 17.

Nakakita, T. (1988) 'The globalization of Japanese firms and its influence on Japan's trade and developing countries', *The Developing Economies*, 31.

Nakamura, K. (1993) 'Management strategies and changes in the employment structure of small-and-medium-sized enterprises in manufacturing industry under technological innovation in Japan', *East Asia*, 6.

Nester, W. R. (1990) *Japan's Growing Power over East Asia and the World Economy*, London: Macmillan.

Ozawa, T. (1971) *Transfer of Technology from Japan to Developing Countries*, New York: UNITAR.

Ozawa, T. (1974) *Japan's Technological Challenge to the West 1950–74. Motivations and Accomplishments*, Tokyo: MIT Press.

Park, S.-J. (1983) 'Indigenization strategy between dependence and delinking, with special reference to technology policy', *East Asia*, 1, pp. 212–33.

Ping, L. P. (1979) 'The role of Japanese direct investment in Malaysia', Paper 60, Singapore: Institute of South Asian Studies.

Romana, E. R. S. (1978) 'Dependency and Philippine–Japan economic relations', *The Japan Interpreter*, 12 (Spring).

Saravanamuttu, J. (1985) 'The political economy of Japan's involvement in ASEAN: some theoretical and policy implications', *East Asia*, 3.

Saxonhouse, G. (1997) 'Regional initiatives and US trade policy in Asia', *Asian-Pacific Economic Literature*, 11(2) (November).

Schonberger, R. J. (1982) *Japanese Manufacturing Techniques*, New York.

Schwarz, A. (1994) *A Nation in Waiting, Indonesia in the 1990s*, Sydney and Singapore: Allen and Unwin.

Special Issue: Major aspects of Japanese economy in the mid-seventies, *The Developing Economies*, 14(4) (December 1976), especially essays by Yoshitomo, Shinohara and Shioda.

Stalk, G., Evans, P. E. and Shulman, L. E. (1992) 'Competing on capabilities: the new role of corporate strategy', *Harvard Business Review*, March/April.

Tsurumi, Y. (1978) *The Japanese are Coming. A Multinational Interaction of Firms and Politics*, Cambridge, MA: Harvard University Press.

Vogel, E. (1986) 'Pax Nipponica', *Foreign Affairs*, Spring.

Weinstein, F. (1976) 'Multinational corporations and the Third World: the case of Japan and South-East Asia', *International Organization*, 30.

Yamashita, S. (ed.) (1991) *Transfer of Japanese Technology and Management to the ASEAN Countries*, Tokyo: University of Tokyo Press.

Yoshino, Y. (1976) *Japan's Multinational Enterprises*, Cambridge, MA: Harvard University Press.

11 Resolutions

China and Japan

Governance and self-strengthening: Japan and China

> Inactivity and procrastination are the fundamental principles of Chinese administration.
>
> (*Hochi Shimbun* 1884)

Although the figures are heroic, acceptable guesstimates are that around the year 1800 China accounted for 33 per cent of the world's manufacturing output, Europe some 28 per cent, the US less than 1 per cent. By about 1900 the Chinese share had dropped to just over 6 per cent, Europe had risen to 62 per cent, the US to 24 per cent. By 1997, Chinese production accounted for 3.5 per cent of world GNP. Although not strictly comparable, these estimates suggest that a once strong China fell victim to the challenge of Europe and then the US and then Japan.

From his safe base back in Europe in 1880 after some troublesome Asian travels, M. de Thiersant felt able to report on the inability of China to respond to the European challenge. Not any programme of self-strengthening, whether mounted by China's provincial governors, intellectuals, Taiping revolutionaries or central government itself, could ever surmount the machinations of 'that frivolous, ignorant and vain class which takes egotism to be patriotism, and only thinks of upsetting everything, instead of using its intelligence and influence for the good of the country'. In this he sketched a vision from which a great host of commentators and experts have derived analytic inspiration. Historians who agree on nothing else all arrive at a perspective which focuses on centralised hierarchy, statism and the mandarinate. Toynbee vigorously took the 'cultural turn'. In his greatest work, he identified Confucianism as the cultural basis for the high social esteem in which the gentry were held. However energetic or innovative were the invaders and new rulers of the Chinese cultural system, over many hundreds of years all such elements had eventually 'to call in the Confucian-educated native Chinese gentry to make the wheels of public administration go on turning'.

For the writers of the earlier European Enlightenment, China became the whetstone upon which notions of progress through good governance might be sharpened. Thus, for David Hume in the 1740s, the failure of Chinese scientific and technical development lay at the door of the authority of Confucius, which 'none had the courage to resist' nor 'dispute what had been universally received by their ancestors'. The power of the mandarin class was sufficient and 'natural reason why the sciences have made so slow a progress in that mighty empire'. Similarly, for Adam Smith, the Chinese economy had settled over a long period for a stationary system because of inertia generated by prevailing 'laws and institutions'. The latter operated in a multitude of ways to hamper growth and change. The neglect of foreign commerce was some function of the control needs of the state apparatus, gained at the expense of the learning process associated with competitive trading. Investment in improvements was greatly inhibited because of the insecurity of small merchant capital, which might be 'pillaged and plundered at any time by the inferior mandarins'. The power structure created an unequal distribution of income, which allocated resources towards food or luxuries and away from industrial manufactures. In contrast to Europe, 'the great interest of the sovereign' lay in land. In a very large area this required centralism and corvée labour, in turn creating corruption and abuse and a system which favoured only the 'mandarins and other tax gatherers'. For the Enlightenment, the failures of China were political and institutional and were conditioned by size, demography and climate.

This approach has remained the dominant one. For modern geographers, settlement on rich alluvial lands meant that in China there 'was an abundance, and so long as the canals and dykes were maintained, there was less stimulus to the renewed practice of ingenuity'. The added elements of distance and isolation have led to the notion that China 'elaborated its ideals in absolute segregation from alien thought' and suffered accordingly in comparison to open, competitive Europe. Global historians like Braudel have judged that centralism and the prohibitive role of the mandarin meritocracy, who erected a systematic barrier to technical change which could not be breached, represent a sufficient institutional argument for the retardation of Chinese economic and commercial development in the modern era. In a complementary fashion, the immense studies of Joseph Needham, have appeared to conclude that China's bureaucratic feudalism might well have generated scientific enquiry in earlier years but subsequently prohibited creative breakthroughs of the sort associated with the scientific revolution in Western Europe. In the end, for Needham, 'there was something in Chinese society which continually tended to restore it to its original character after all disturbances, whether these were caused by civil wars, foreign invasions, or inventions and discoveries'. The failure of the institutions of mercantile capitalism ensured that China would not utilise the technologies of eighteenth-century Europe.

Such a brief review suggests that the major contrast between Japan and China lies in the methods and structures of governance and the manner in which good governance might be defined. In Japan a very different geography and location conditioned a multipolar system of governance as the effective system of response and adaptation during the crucial years of threat and interaction of the nineteenth century, the elements of which have been analysed in Chapters 1–5. In China, the efforts of all reforming courts, provincial self-strengtheners and rebel manifestoes eventually fell victim to the Confucian-based, authoritarian patterns of governance and control.

From this we might conclude that *governance* represents at once the principal historical contrast between these two great East Asian systems and the principal source of conflict between them now and in the near future. Whatever the immediate commercial or geopolitical issues, relations between China and Japan are bound to generate the frictions to be found in any interactions between a centralised bureaucratic communist system and multipolar democratic capitalism. Contrasting governance yields both an approach to comparative economic history and the underlying explanation of the surface tensions between modern Japan and China.

This formulation is useful but may underplay the extent of cultural commonality on one hand, whilst neglecting the more basic and mundane features of immediate imperial history, geography and location on the other, which altogether must make the real picture more multi-layered. The general perspective also neglects several specific historical points, the awareness of which might serve to modify the general view. Even in the early nineteenth century, Chinese yields per acre, low cost transport and handicrafts manufactures compared favourably with both Japan and many parts of central or eastern Europe, and even distribution of income seems to have not been as severe as the simple model would predict. The massive inter-regional trade was in per capita terms comparable to that of Europe. At one point, Eckstein concluded that the productivity of both land and labour in nineteenth-century China was *higher* than that of Japan, and this places a great burden on any cultural-institutional argument centred on governance. There is much evidence to suggest that from the proclamation of the *Tai Ping Tien Kuo* (the Heavenly State of the Great Peace, in 1851) to the broadening of the self-strengthening movement in the 1890s, there existed in China significant groupings and interests who fully recognised the need for a progressive response to the European menace of the time. Finally, although Chinese government investment was severely depleted by the military expenditures engendered by civil unrest and foreign interventions, expenditure on modernising industrial projects represented some 12 per cent of total revenue in the 1890s. In the years of industrial spurt in Meiji (1868–81, see Chapter 2), the government of Japan invested only some 5 per cent of its ordinary revenue in industrial projects, a fraction of the expenditure on education and cultural engineering (see Chapters 5 and 13). It might be sensible to argue that physical factors forged a form of governance which rendered it very difficult for China to successfully resist the nineteenth-century Western challenge whatever the proclivities of leadership or culture of control. The resulting wasting of the economic base of China meant that China could not benefit overall from the commercial interactions and technology transfers of the period. Sites of modern endeavour in Shanghai or elsewhere exerted little impact on the national income and its growth.

A crucial problem of the early and mid-twentieth century was to combine centrality and hierarchy with industrial modernisation through technology transfers in an economic system whose centre of gravity lay far away from the commercial coast lands and southern cities. Before 1937 there were fewer than two million persons employed full-time in non-rural industrial activities, a figure raised to three million in 1951. Before 1937 large-scale industrial development was confined to six regions, all relatively accessible to foreign trade and influence. From the mid-twentieth century most technological improvement focused on great advances in water control technology and its applications, Soviet-style agricultural mechanisation, which yielded to small-scale Chinese tractors for wheat, soya and vegetables, the spread of electrification, rural industrialisation based on the commune organisation, and the development, especially during the Great Leap Forward, of labour-intensive irrigation and water storage projects to address the prevailing agrarian problems of water-logging and salinisation. GLF mass mobilisation may have added some 58 million acres of irrigated land to China's total. By 1960 there were perhaps 60,000 recognised industrial units at the county level, 200,000 operated by communes, and innumerable small shops organised by brigades, covering the traditional craft industries as well as coal mining, iron production, electric power generation, agricultural tools and equipment, fertiliser and construction materials, and communications and transport. The Cultural Revolution used this institutional structure for accelerated advancement of regions and sectors – a surge in the number of hydroelectric power stations had an impact on the number of rural industries. By the mid-1970s just less than 20 per cent of industrial output came from the collective industry sector and 20 per cent of workers were employed in it. Although heavy industry was still located mainly in Manchuria, Shanghai and the North China Plain, the rural industrial programme had some positive effect on the geographical distribution of all industry in China, and many of the inputs of chemicals and machinery derived from small plants.

As we might expect from our historical review, what this planned, hierarchical system could not do was to effectively transfer modern technologies and organisations into the production processes of Chinese manufacturing, services and commerce, *a crucial problem identical with that of the USSR*. Thus between 1955 and 1978, imports of Western technology as a proportion of all Soviet equipment investment rose from 2 per cent to nearly 6 per cent but this was associated with a secular decline in manufacturing productivity. Because of ideology and economic structure, the USSR had no recourse to direct foreign investment carrying advanced techniques, but instead relied upon trade, turn-key projects, licensing and industrial co-operation agreements. By the 1980s perhaps 60 per cent or more of total Soviet imports were of machinery and equipment, petroleum and petroleum products. The proportion of technological trade to total trade in OECD–Soviet trade was 73 per cent in 1970, 57 per cent in 1982. The absence of private capital and technology markets led to a reliance on state-construed Industrial Cooperation Agreements which often involved a variety of US, British, Japanese, German and Italian firms in conjunction with such bodies as the State Committee for Science and Technology. Although these ICAs were something of a lifeline for selected Soviet firms, the impact of high technology transfer expenditures remained very limited indeed. Thus by the 1980s the USSR was clearly unable to keep pace with technology in oxygen-steel making, continuous casting, advanced coal drilling, underwater equipment for oil and gas, electronic machine tools, and computer technologies. In a world of greatly inadequate incentives at the micro-level and large and static bureaucratic structures, technological regeneration and the creation of productive linkages between domestic industry and foreign technology faced a multitude of institutional barriers. In February 1986, at the Thirteenth Party Congress there were strong indications that Gorbachev's government was attempting to increase the autonomy of enterprises as a step towards technological and organisational reformation. The experiments in that direction at the Vaz motor plant in Togliatti were well publicised, and the problem of modernised technology transfer may now be seen as an important element in the reform crises which undermined the Soviet system at the end of the decade.

Similarly, the background to the Chinese economic and institutional reforms of 1978 and onwards might be seen as including important difficulties associated with technology transfers. Throughout the 1970s there had been a considerable build-up of Chinese contracts for foreign machinery. During 1973–4 the Chinese favoured importation of complete plants and personnel, to the tune of US $2 billion. Deficits and ideological disputes hindered the process until 1979 when technology importation arose high on the reform agenda. Indeed, innovations in technology transfer devices just preceded the mainline reforms of 1978 onwards. Petroleum and iron and steel absorbed over 80 per cent of complete foreign plant purchases in the 1970s, a form of technology transfer which was costing US $7,000 million in 1978 alone. Increasingly, Japanese and German firms were entering agreements to build and equip textile and petroleum plants in exchange for indefinite control over marketing and sales. During 1978, just prior to the December decisions which brought in wholesale reforms, British, French, Japanese and Italian banking interests, as well as international agencies, engaged in lending to China for the prime purpose of technology purchase.

Hierarchies were failing to transfer advanced technologies very effectively by the 1970s, this affecting many policy issues, causing a variety of economic problems, and creating contexts for reform. China and the USSR had broadly similar problems of technological transfer and transformation. The Chinese solution to such problems eventually placed the largest East Asian system of all upon a different, very individual political and economic pathway, one of reform sequencing and regional partitioning.

Sequencing: China and the modern world economy

Historical models of late development, most famously that of Gerschenkron, describe the limits to industrial programmes under isolation and autarchy. In the transformations of the late nineteenth century which were state led, autarchy did not in itself forbid transactions in trade, investment, technology and even ideas, with the rest of the industrial world, particularly the great British trading system and the fast emerging American system of manufactures. In the rare cases of successful late development, an original surge of industrial and institutional transformation (as in Japan 1868–81, Russia in the 1890s) gave way to sustained and wider development in which competing private interests took a far greater part (Japan *c.* 1881–1912, Russia from around 1907), although even here government contracts for military industries, state controls over trade, standards, measures, rules, tariffs etc., and state training provisions, remained as essential co-requisites of sustained industrialisation. Such late development may have been multi-polar, with a variety of compelling authorities working alongside competing private interests within emerging markets for capital and information. But it was not democratic. It was not open to a global media and the artful criticisms of a more advanced industrial world, it was not yet conditioned by the growing voice of the new business classes, and its trading, foreign investment and technology transfer requirements were not dependent on the approval of its internal political and policing systems by immensely powerful interested parties elsewhere. In such systems the development of market forces and the rise of the industrial and professional middle classes (the latter class providing many of the new, sophisticated services and institutions needed by the former class) did, during the twentieth century, at least partially determine a much greater move towards democratic institutions.

Under such an historical model, which conforms to the argumentation throughout the present text (see Chapters 2 and 5), Japan, for instance, could *not have succeeded industrially under a democratic political regime* in the face of the many threats and contingencies created by the advanced Western economies, nor is it easy to imagine a democratic Germany industrialising rapidly in the late nineteenth century. From such a history of sequencing, calls for democracy and the immediate removal or root-and-branch reform of absolutist or authoritarian regimes (whether socialist or nationalist) in relatively backward economic systems may be contrary to the logistics of sustained late development. This is not by any means to argue that human agency may not transcend such discernible historical patterns, but merely that such patterns do seem to have recurred. *We argue two positions.* The example of China and perhaps the Asian NICs suggest that it is possible even at the beginning of the third millennium, to initiate substantial reforms in market structures and in non-market institutions (for instance those linked to training, education and R&D, local government regulations etc.) prior to a fuller democratisation of the central political system as such. We extend this *sequencing* argument by adding the thesis that this was only possible in a very large and isolated system such as China's because of the *partitioning* of leading points of development, much but not all of which was beyond the control of the Chinese government as such. The ready acquiescence in the continuation of a basically partitioned Hong Kong even after 1997 provides some very telling evidence that recent Chinese authorities know very well the value of allowing vigorous independent growths to flourish. Such a case cannot in itself predict the changes which might occur under a Chinese military regime, one whose priorities may place industrial and commercial development relatively low on a list headed by notions of grandeur and global face. Second, we suggest that this historically verifiable position might lead to the conclusion *that the future economic and political relations between Japan and China will be dominated by peaceful competition and a greater degree of bilateralism and regional integration. With all their differences, both are late developers in the same large segment of the globe and sharing much of the same written language.*

What might be considered the alternative contemporary Russian or Eastern European sequence, to an extent forced by external circumstances of a sort never present during the industrialisation of earlier late developers, is illustrated in the simple Figure 11.1.

This sequence does not work. Block Z has no history and would seem to have no historical precedents. Yet as the writings of Deyo, Oksenberg, Liu Binyan and their colleagues have shown, a huge amount of external pressure has been exerted by the industrial powers and by international organisations in order to try to force this sequence on Asian systems, particularly those with a growing trade surplus with the US, such as China, Thailand, Malaysia or, now increasingly, Indonesia. In the schema that we

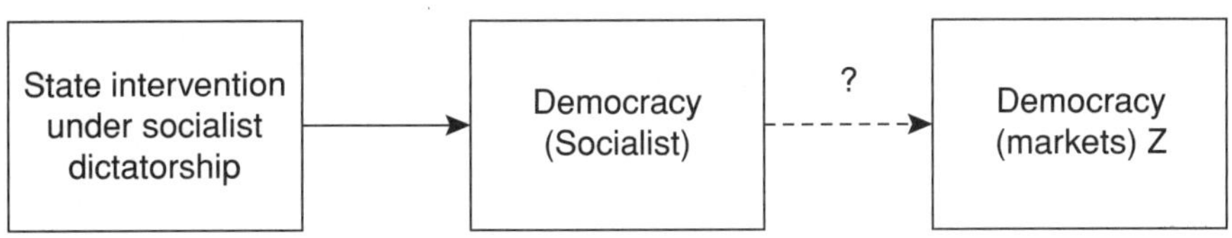

Figure 11.1 Politics, markets and industrialisation.

are presenting here, any resulting collapse of the industrialisation process, as has clearly occurred in Eastern Europe and at large in Russia, threatens to destroy the most recent political gains, holds back the fuller emergence of internal forces for change – especially the rise of a more broad-based middle class – and removes the flooring from under those institutions which have been designed to maintain a connectedness between such nations and more advanced industrial systems, particularly those relating to investment and technology transfers. *Importantly, then, the premature escalation of democratic forces may undermine precisely those current commercial and other integrations between the advanced industrial nations and the new industrial winners which in the past have acted as one key influence in the movement away from authoritarianism in both the economic and political systems of newly industrialising countries.*

The alternative sequencing is that which has taken place in China since around 1978, but becoming more certain and visible from the mid-1980s. The turning point in China's institutional reform and its relations with advanced economies was the Third Plenary Meeting of the Communist Party's Central Committee held in December 1978. This proclaimed the aim of 'openness' as a major prerequisite of economic modernisation, a position enshrined in the text of China's new Constitution of 1982. Primarily in order to attract foreign capital and technology, in 1980 the Special Economic Zones were introduced, with Shenzhen, near Hong Kong being the first of five, each of which took on the task of restructuring systems for wages, housing and prices and a series of experiments in planning, finance, foreign exchange, business and seaport management and taxation. With set-backs rather than reverses, this trajectory has been maintained, and when Zhu Rongji became prime minister in March 1998 new proposals were forwarded for reforming the state-owned enterprises and the civil service. Whilst the Third Plenum of 1994 had approved the creation of 'standard corporations' and 1996 had seen a justification for the selling of small state enterprises, the Fifteenth Congress of 1998 had broadened the definition of public ownership to embrace collectively owned elements in the mixed economy, foreshadowing a massive privatisation process. Subsequently, Shi Guangsheng, the Minister of Foreign Trade and Economic Cooperation announced that more areas of China would be opened up to foreign investors, including the oil and construction sectors along with some services. An important characteristic of Chinese sequencing has been the continued firm hold over the rural sector through quota and price controls over cereals and regulations over direct grain purchase, this strongly contrasting with the Russian case and an element in the avoidance of major strife and dislocation during the transition towards a more liberal economic regime. Given this difference in the importance of the rural sector, it might be generalised that the Chinese road has been basically that followed initially by South Korea and Taiwan.

Most economic reform issues at present (October 1999) centre on the need for new legislation for the financing of trade and investment, labour law, and the protection of intellectual property rights. A major reform policy is to attempt to privatise the troubled state-owned enterprises, through the workings of the Hong Kong stock exchange, a strategy presently inhibited by the general Asian commercial slow-down.[1] Clearly imminent problems associated with the continuation of the sequence include the daunting prospects of the 110 million people now employed in the state enterprise sector without benefit of any social security net, inflationary pressures (the high rate of around 18 per cent in 1989 is often given as a cause of the Tiananmen incident), the crisis in the banking system which is linked to state enterprise but might be exacerbated in the short-run by privatisation of such enterprise,[2] the financing of innovative private firms, the strengthening of intellectual property rights, and the reduction in the power of entrenched agencies. None of this is insurmountable in such a large system if it continues to grow, and evidence of continued institutional reform is provided in the reduction of the number of government Ministries from forty to twenty-nine during 1998. Despite general Asian economic problems, the most recent trends within China seem to have been towards further liberalism, as witnessed in the publication of the best-selling radical critique of planning, *Crossed Swords*. At the same time the authorities made real efforts to reduce inefficiency and corruption by banning the People's Liberation Army from business activity. The many thousands of businesses run by the PLA have long been a source of corruption and smuggling.

Probably the greatest ideological stumbling-block of the reforms is the recent move towards a more complete transfer of control of state enterprises to its users and managers, termed 'marketisation', as a transition towards the transfer of income and assets, or more properly 'privatisation'. The definition of Chinese 'socialist market economy' appears presently to be hovering about this distinction, an ambiguity abetted by the present fall in share prices in Hong Kong, the venue for any large-scale Chinese flotations. The debts of the state sector are the result of mismanagement and corruption, compounded by PLA interference, overstocking, and very early vintage technologies, which in combination have reduced the share of state enterprises in total industrial production from 78 per cent in 1978 to 34 per cent in 1994, with a projection of a further fall to 22 per cent in 2010. At such a rate we might expect the sector to merely wither away over the next twenty years or so. Such an irony is, however, not presently appreciated by the Chinese regime, which has spent much effort in placing the reform of the state sector in proper ideological context. Jiang Zemin has provided the contemporary lead with high-profile statements to the effect that the sector remains the base for 'revitalising the national economy as a whole', but requires an improvement of performance 'with the market and industrial policies as the leading force'. Under the conception that the 'operation of state enterprises under a share holding system do not constitute privatisation', it has been found just possible to move from a premise that 'the development of the state-owned economy is restrained by a number of objective and subjective factors', through the evolutionary theory that 'the proportion of state firms to the GNP changes along a parabolic curve' (i.e. may decline with 'maturity'), to the observation that 'international experience has also shown that state firms can be run efficiently, on the condition that they have autonomy in management and clear financial responsibilities and participate in market competition'. Although it may not be termed privatisation, the conclusion of such reasoning has been that some 'functions that are now performed by the government should be transferred to enterprises, the market and intermediary agents'.

The industrial and economic growth performance of China under the reform regime has been startling, as illustrated in Table 11.1, which is partially based on IMF calculations published in 1999.

On any comparison, these figures are impressive. The national income growth of the Chinese economy was faster than that of any major system, and the gap was especially large in 1984–8 and 1994–7. During 1998 China was the only major East Asian economy to post a positive rate of growth other than Taiwan and Singapore, where the recorded rates were 4.8 and 1.5 respectively. Whilst East Asian industrial growth rates matched those of China in some short periods such as 1983–4 or 1987–8, generally no nation matched China on this measure, and in 1998 industrial production growth fell to 2.6 for Taiwan, −0.6 for Singapore, −7.4 for South Korea. At a world level, only Singapore could match China in terms of savings and investment rates, with South Korea just falling behind

Table 11.1 Annual growth rate percentage indicators of the Chinese economy, 1983–98

	GDP	*Ind.Prod. Index*	*Manuf. Employ.*	*Savings/ GNP*	*Investment/ GNP*
1983	10.4	11.2	2.8	32.2	33.8
1984	14.6	16.3	8.0	34.5	34.4
1985	16.2	21.4	5.4	35.6	37.8
1986	8.9	11.7	8.2	35.9	37.7
1987	11.6	17.7	4.2	37.7	36.1
1988	11.3	20.8	3.5	37.3	36.8
1989	4.1	8.5	−1.2	37.6	36.1
1990	3.8	7.7	0.9	38.7	34.7
1991	9.2	14.8	2.5	39.5	34.7
1992	14.2	21.2	3.0	40.4	36.2
1993	13.5	–	2.1	41.8	43.4
1994	12.7	21.4	3.4	41.8	41.3
1995	10.5	16.1	2.0	40.2	41.5
1996	9.5	15.1	−0.4	38.9	40.2
1997	8.8	13.2	−1.5	39.6	38.9
1998	7.8	9.6	–	–	–

from around 1992. Arguments that such comparisons should acknowledge the low base from which China came[3] might be matched with arguments that China is the biggest nation on earth – a lot of productive effort at the margin must occur in order to maintain high growth rates in a system of 1.2 billion people.

An extended comment on China's modern sequence is provided by Maxim Potapov, a Secretary at the Russian Embassy in China.

> The innovations proved to be effective and were largely supported by the elite, as well as by most of the public. Examining the reasons for China's reform success, one should observe, of course, that in the early 1980s the situation in the world capital market was quite favourable, and a number of objective factors, such as the vast domestic market, cheap labour, rich Chinese communities abroad, had certainly played a positive role in developing the country's export and industrial potential, and in attracting foreign capital. But what was more important, in our view, was the fact that China had ensured political stability at home, while its market transformation effort was focused on the development of the productive forces, and improvement of production efficiency and living standards. As a result, there emerged a new society fabric and a new structure of social interests which made sure that the changes under way became irreversible . . . the robust growth rates had been achieved primarily thanks to the correct reform strategy, and not because China's backwardness was to its advantage . . . At the same time, one can hardly consider the development in this area rigidly determined and unequivocally preordained. China went the empirical way, without being unduly obsessed by abstract theorising.

Even with its Russian twist unexpurgated, Potapov's summary is astute enough. What is notable in all this is the maintenance of the economy-polity sequencing despite tremendous internal and external pressures against it over a considerable period. Throughout the reform period China has faced pressure from the collapse of sovietism, which increased cries within and without China for more democratic political institutions, just as it worried China's leaders about the over-extent of their reforms. Despite forecasts in the Western press that the death of Deng Xiaoping, the great 'architect' of the reform policy would be followed by chaos, the political crisis of 1989 did not extend into a complete rupture of the reform sequence. The so-called 'Taiwan factor', the existence of a state working successfully under a more liberal political system but adjacent and populated by ethnic Chinese with voice, advanced military capabilities and influence, caused Chinese leaders to consider the possible destabilising effects of further reform, as democrats would be quickly aided and abetted by an important component of the Greater China. The separatist risks of economic reform, particularly in the western part of the country, were heightened after the collapse of the USSR and the emergence of both the independent Central Asian states and Islamic fundamentalism. To all this we might properly add the internal dislocations which have been either instigated or exacerbated by reform itself, particularly the rise of unemployment, inflation (especially in 1979–80, 1988–9, 1993–5) rural exodus, (hastened by the widening income gap between rural and urban areas), increased urban property crime, smuggling and corruption, all set against the worrying effects of rising expectations. Fast change has brought with it water shortages, urban sewerage problems and industrial pollution in a country where domestic coal heating is responsible for vast carbon dioxide emissions.

The change in external economic relations which was engendered by the reform movement has been revolutionary. Despite the generally tougher protectionism and regionalism of the 1990s, China's external trade performed remarkably. By the later 1990s China's trade strategy was to import-substitute in power engineering, transport and communications, export-lead in textiles, light and electronic industries, whilst continuing to ease state control over foreign trade and encourage further capital importing. Opening out has been so important as to forge a vital trade–investment linkage in the Chinese system – perhaps up to 50 per cent of all the manufactured exports from China are in fact made in factories that are partly owned or managed by non-(mainland) Chinese, an increasing element as Hong Kong and Taiwanese companies relocate their export industries to the mainland. By 1997 the US trade deficit with China reached $40 billion, and China was being labelled the New Japan.[4]

During the years 1979–96, the foreign investment attracted to China under various types of contract and agreement totalled $592.9 billion, of which 48 per cent had been committed by 1997. Of the committed investments 63 per cent were by business arrangements, the rest through external loans of various types. 90 per cent of direct foreign investment has gone into the fast-growing coastal regions, into the thriving industries and services of Beijing, Tianjin, Shanghai, Shandong, Guangdong and Hainan. Although difficult to measure, foreign capital in total possibly accounted for 20 per cent of capital formation in China by 1996 and provided at least partial investment funds for up to 140,000 enterprises, who in turn employed about 17 million people, over 50 per cent in industry. The 1995 Census showed 60,000 foreign enterprises with 9 million employees, a collectivity which earned $57 billion in export revenue, or a net gain after imports of up to $10 billion. Chinese figures estimate the foreign investment contribution to total Chinese trade at around 47 per cent for 1996. Of all enterprises with foreign investment, 69 per cent were joint ventures, 11 per cent were cooperative enterprises of some kind, and over 20 per cent were owned exclusively by foreigners. The ratio of foreign to Chinese investment in such firms averaged at around 6:4, and 60 per cent of all such foreign capital came from Hong Kong, Macao and Taiwan. In contrast to the industrial and real estate bias of direct investment, most foreign loans have gone into Chinese infrastructure – especially energy projects (power stations), transport (railways, ports, airports) communications, raw materials, and machinery and electricity projects.

At US $145 billion, China's convertible currency reserves were enormous by 1998, the third largest in the world after Japan and the European Union and supplemented by a further $90 billion from Hong Kong, sufficient to help economic managers resist several international pressures to deflate the external value of the currency under the conditions of the Asian financial crisis. Following a slight fall in exports during early 1998, a switch towards Europe and the US meant that China maintained its trade surplus for that year at US $43.6 billion, or around 4 per cent of GDP.

Progress by partition – sites of Chinese endeavour

In June 1998, academic commentator Cao Jianming addressed a meeting convened by the Central Committee in order to recommend the construction of a 'firewall' between the national economy and the international economic system, then dominated by the extended 'Asian Crisis'. By this, Cao did not mean that policy should abandon the extension of the sequencing described above, but that there should exist adequate protection from external shocks. Our argument is that apart from sheer size and inertia, mainland China already is in possession of the two major weapons of control of industrial modernity and internationalism. These weapons are the established sequencing process and partition. By the latter we mean that China does not in reality react as a system at the industrial, technological and commercial levels, but as any one or several of a variety of regions, more or less exposed to foreign influence and more or less along the road towards greater economic and political liberalism. We may interpret this as a *modus vivendus* of non-revolutionary modernisation. More importantly to the argument of this chapter, we may visualise this double strategy as one which does allow a great deal of resolution of the problems of Japan–China relations, even long prior to any fundamental resolutions in terms of commanding ideologies, political institutions or global ambitions. Perhaps one reason why the USSR or Eastern European nations could not adopt the Chinese sequence with as much chance of success was the absence in those places of partition possibilities, the existence of the highly advanced areas of the mainland and Greater China and the Chinese diaspora.[5]

The sequencing of the reforms since 1978 has itself created modernisation through effective partition. Under the old regime, a basic premise of policy was to reduce the income and wealth disparities caused naturally in a massive country of huge climatic, demographic, topographic, agricultural and transport and communication diversities. In contrast, reform through markets and opening-out has meant a very rapid development of the east coast and a lag in the central and western provinces.

In terms of Chinese regions, the most industrially developed with large middle classes are the Beijing region, including the provinces of Hebei, Henan and Shandong; the Yangzi delta, including Shanghai, and the city of Wuxi and Nanjing and the provinces of Jiangsu; the Midcoast city of Fujian, Xiamen and including Taiwan; and the great gold coast of Guangdong, Hong Kong, Hainan and Shenzhen. In their different ways, these are the great points of Chinese industrial modernisation, export-led strategies and much interconnectedness. In terms of future commercial integration with the Japanese economy, there might follow such regions of lesser development as the urban areas of the mid-Yangzi, the Sichuan Plain and the northeastern industrial cities, including Harbin, areas which yet remain more state-led, and geared to import-substitution at best.

Between 1986 and 1995 the eastern region received 87 per cent of actually utilised foreign investment, the central area received 8.5 per cent, the west 4.2 per cent. Whereas the coast-to-inland ratio of investment in the late 1960s was around 2:5, by the early 1990s this had shifted to 9:7. The eastern share of Chinese industrial output grew from 60 per cent in 1985 to 66 per cent in 1995. The fastest growing provincial economy, that of Guangdong, grew at the rate of perhaps 20 per cent annually throughout the 1980s and still exerts regional leadership. By the mid-1990s the difference in per capita income production in advanced areas such as Shanghai and the most backward of the provinces was ten-fold, the per capita income disparities being around five-fold. In 1996 the World Bank estimated that some 350 million Chinese lived in poverty, a figure five times that of the official Chinese government figure. *So, the sequencing of institutional change has led to transitional disparities bordering on partition, in the sense that the fast industrialising regions may act as a cordon of modernisation, where greater freedoms and institutional advancement may for some time be considered as somewhat distant from the older, inland ideologies and realities.* We may push this conception a little further by noting a major institutional difference which exactly accords with the regional difference. Areas with large or predominant state enterprises have become the depressed regions, this being particularly true of Guizhou, Hunan, Hubei and Liaoning. So we might conclude that industrialising China is effectively partitioned from the rest of the country by a combination of geography, institutions and regulations.

The role of such multi-level partitioning is very well evidenced in the case of Guangdong. The most spectacular of the reform 'partitions', the population of some 68 million means that the province carries the weight of a large European economy, led by the high income cities of Shenzhen and Zhuhai and the capital, Guangzhou, with total populations approaching 9 million and thus considerably larger than Hong Kong, which since 1997 might be more properly seen as an integral part of a regional system which is at once highly internationalised yet segmented from the northern hinterlands of old China. Throughout the province, industry accounts for over 65 per cent of total output, and the great bulk of foreign investment has flowed into the Pearl River Delta, which harbours a development zone linking all the existing Special Economic Zones, export-processing industries, and technical innovation centres around metropolitan Guangzhou.[6] In 1992, Deng identified the province as Asia's Fifth Little Dragon. By that date Hong Kong accounted for some 80 per cent of Guangdong's investment from external sources and handled 80 per cent of the province's traded exports. The equipment, technology, raw materials and other production inputs for Hong Kong are imported from industrial systems, particularly Japan, Taiwan and South Korea. In the Chinese phrase *qiandian houchang* (front shop, back factory) is caught the functional relationship between the flows of capital, technique and know-how into Hong Kong, the subsequent marketing, design and administration of Hong Kong, backed by the labour and land of Guangdong, which provides manufacturing and assembly. This relationship encompasses a classic site of the new Asian-focused capitalism, (see pp. 262–5). Reginald Yin-Wang Kwok and his colleagues capture the essentials of the sequence-partition link when they summarise that with the post-1978 reforms 'the market system has filtered in from the metropolis. Investment from Hong Kong brings with it the free enterprise mode of production and trade . . . the new mode is quickly adopted by the provincial firms that have business deals with outside investors . . . provincial enterprise and government participate and support in developing the mixed economy'. Much in the way of entirely independent provincial action or policy has been formulated by the provincial government corporation, Guangdong Enterprises (whose shares since the early 1990s have been traded on the Hong Kong stock exchange) and the Guangdong Development Bank. By the early 1990s the province had become the most effective route through which to obtain funds, technologies, skills and foreign market access for mainland development across most industries and regions.

Penultimate resolutions – Japan and China

One of the first implementations of the opening-up policy was the Long-Term Trade Agreement signed between China and Japan in 1978, one based on a bilateralism which centred on imports of Japanese capital and technology and exports of Chinese energy and raw materials. Such strong complementarities meant that Japan was China's major trading partner as well as a close strategic ally, as measured by the signing also of the Treaty of Peace and Friendship between the two nations in the same year. In the late 1970s Japan accounted for some 25 per cent of China's total foreign trade. The trading relationship reached its height around 1985, when 22 per cent of China's exports and 36 per cent of imports were with Japan, the latter figure far greater than that of any other nation. China–Japan trade between 1978 and 1996 grew from around US $5 billion to US $60 billion. By 1994 Japan remained the greatest single source of imports into China but Chinese exports to Japan had fallen well below those of Hong Kong and were equal to those of the United States. China's trade surplus with Japan reached $17.6 billion in 1996. During that same period, Japan and the US were approximately equal contributors to foreign direct investment into China, both investing far less than the overseas Chinese through Hong Kong and Macao, and slightly less than Taiwan, but far more than any other nation. By 1996 accumulated realised Japanese FDI in China had reached over the US $10 billion mark, incorporating a peak of new investment during 1995 of $7.6 billion.

Clearly, China's increasingly sophisticated economy, and in particular the movement from resource exporting to the export of manufactured goods produced by labour-intensive techniques, has rendered the older bilateralism redundant, and the relationship of the two systems now takes place within a complexity of altering global interdependencies. *But the emergence of China has almost certainly eased the restructuring of Japan* – some 30 per cent of the production of Japanese manufacturing subsidiaries in China during the mid-1990s was exported back to Japan, the great bulk of this being the product of labour-intensive methods. Over 80 per cent of Japanese textile production in China was exported back to Japan, surely a clear reflection of Japan's restructuring strategies. But it is also the case that Japanese capital, trade and technology has been closely associated with the opening of China – by 1994 foreign trade accounted for 45 per cent of China's conventional GNP, and China was second only to the US as an importer of capital from the rest of the world. Such a record was achieved against the background of the vilification and sanctions which followed the Tiananmen Square tragedy, reactions which failed to dampen trade and investment relations between China, Japan, Greater China and the Chinese Diaspora. Thus the early 1990s saw a marked increase in the scale of Japan–Hong Kong–Guangdong economic operations, dominated by the comparatively low price of Guangdong labour and land which attracted Japanese capital as the yen inflated and the economy restructured (see further Chapters 9 and 10).

Such a secular tendency must be placed alongside the fairly frequent breakdowns in Japan–China political relations which arise from well-publicised complaints on both sides. The later 1990s have witnessed major disputes over Chinese nuclear testing (1995), military exercises off the coast of Taiwan (1996 and 1999), disputes over the Senkaku Islands in the East China Sea (1996), the 1997 US–Japan defence guidelines which placed Tokyo in support of the US on any occasion of threats to Taiwanese sovereignty, acid rain pollution of Japan from Chinese coal consumption, and Japan's repeated refusal (e.g. during Jiang Zemin's visit to Tokyo in 1998) to apologise for war atrocities committed after 1937.

Our suggestion here is that the dual sequence-partition tactic has emerged over time without trauma or political breakdown, and provides a complex conjunction of circumstances encouraging a penultimate resolution of tension between Japan and China. This conjuncture may be delineated through its six major operational characteristics:

1 *The continued and increased multiple Chinese commercial interaction with systems of advanced industrial democracy*. Thus, where in the 1980s Japan preferred to trade with rather than invest in China, during the 1990s there was a clear acceleration in Japanese investment mostly as a result of the greater certainties and commitments engendered by the continuation of reforms. Such tendencies mean that technological transfer, new institutions, ideologies and needs will permeate the Chinese system. Interaction of a more sophisticated sort demands some adjustments which have political overtones, including safety standards and inspection of exported foodstuffs, conformity to international codes of measurement, content etc. of products, together with a necessarily increased openness to international media.

2 *The continued reform of the Chinese production system, especially towards some type of 'privatisation' of state enterprises*. The major problem is still the low productivity and political weight of the state-owned enterprises which numbered some 300,000 in 1999, the total debt of which to the Chinese banking system was in the region of $200 billion. In October 1998 the State Economic and Trade Commission estimated the cost of privatisation of the sector at up to $96 billion over a three year period, a figure additional to the approximately $24 billion already spent by 1997 on reforming the small to medium state-owned enterprises. The present reform proposals include the floating of another 150 large enterprises, a forced bankruptcy of 4,000 others and new regulations requiring the increased efficiency of some 1,500 enterprises, and the merger of many small ones into more efficient units. The future proposals seem to entail something of a switch in official banking policy away from the financing of large government enterprises towards the smaller firms in order to encourage their technical updating and greater flexibility along the lines of the Japanese or Taiwanese models.

3 *The steady emergence within China of a commercial and professional middle class*. There is some evidence of increased consensus, resort to law and constitutionalism since the death of Deng. In the highly populated growth poles of the economy, foreign firms, new professionals and increasingly autonomous intellectuals may provide a basis for a new civil society, itself the stage from which middle-class demands for better education, health, information and freedoms will surely emerge. Global electronic communications render more difficult the attempts to isolate China. As Kemenade has summarised, Chinese governance may attempt to suppress the rise of the middle class 'but only at the

cost of economic growth and progress' and at the expense of the ambitions of a new generation of Western trained or influenced administrators. Greater economic pluralism supported by the louder voice of new interests might provide the space for accelerated Sino-Japanese commercial and diplomatic interactions.

4 *The resultant possibility through time of progressive internal political change through dialogue between a new civil society and an older hierarchical authority.* In this sort of model, the growth of a Chinese middle class becomes the main motor of integration through the emergence of a civil society, and what Robert Dahl has referred to as a modern dynamic pluralist society, where power and control are more dispersed towards groups and associations, possibly as has occurred recently in Taiwan. The institutions of civil society and the emergence of what Juan Linz has termed 'autonomous intermediate groups' based on new regions, interests and goals, can limit the use of autocratic power and forge greater complementarities between economic and political processes. The multipolar forces of a civil society may exercise pressures upon political regimes of even the Chinese variety. Even a sceptic such as Kemenade has judged that 'economic developments outside the old state system have drastically weakened the power of the party over society, while considerably strengthening the autonomy of the individual, the family, business and local authorities'. Such a massive growth of the new middle class of the mainland, Greater China and the Diaspora may well become the integrating device, which will allow the older ideologies to fade without losing face.

5 *Continued Chinese membership within global institutions and regional organisations* which will generate a more sustained but more informed external pressure, exerted by interest groups which have their own trade, investment, and industrial relations with China to consider before moving to condemn or sanction. China is presently a member of fifty or so international governmental organisations, as well as over 1,000 international non-governmental organisations, embracing the IMF and the World Bank, APEC and other regional bodies. As Burstein and Keijzer emphasise, such numerous and various Chinese affiliations 'weave it into a vast network of international rules, most of which it follows'. During the 1999 move of the Chinese to enter into the GATT/World Trade Organisation system, there was much pressure exerted to adopt further advances in international business practices in order to accord with the rules. Incremental or creeping acceptance of a multilateral rules-based institutional framework will through time further support China's integration into the world economy.

6 *Such forces combine to provide time for the further commercial integrations of the Diaspora and of Greater China,* this in turn offering more economic and ideological space for the continued international resolution of problems between the Chinese system and those of the industrial

systems of Europe, the US and Asia. In recent years over 80 per cent of China's inward investment has come from Chinese people resident elsewhere, a flow stalled but not stopped by the Asian economic crisis. We might hypothesise that together these elements will generate specific resolutions between China and Japan within a fundamentally altering global commercial and political system, which might not spell the 'end of history' but will be manageable without major military conflict. Characteristics 1 and 6 combine in those recent Japanese investments in South China and in Hong Kong which are designed to take advantage of the leading growth areas. By early 1999 some 2,000 Japanese firms were in operation around the southern tip of mainland China. In Hong Kong, Japan dominates foreign banking, and tourism – by the mid-1990s Japanese direct investment in HK amounted to over US $9 billion, or 20 per cent of the total of Japanese investment in Asia.

To such a list of six underlying processes we might add the pro-active role of the Japanese themselves. For some years Japanese policy makers have spent much time, energy and thought on the mechanisms whereby the nation might be further engaged with the modernising elements of the Chinese economy, a factor which often escapes the notice of analysts whose common perceptions are gained from Washington's windows. Japan's trade and investment relations with China have not resulted merely from the strength of natural complementarities, but also from deliberate policy measures. The 1997 Japanese trade deficit with China of some US $20 billion stands in great contrast with its trade surpluses with the rest of Asia, and Chinese electronics, textiles and equipment firms are now the largest receivers of Japanese capital in the region. The Export–Import Bank of Japan has provided enormous sums of money in aid of such Chinese investments, particularly those linked to large-scale infrastructural improvement. Similarly, Japan's overseas development assistance clearly supports trade links by focusing on ports, road systems, airports and railways. In addition, Japan has developed a sophisticated policy of assisting in the development and better utilisation of China's energy resources both through official loans to the Bank of China and through the exploration and development support of the Japan National Oil Corporation (see further pp. 262–3). From an astute survey of such integrating strategies, Christopher Johnstone has recently concluded that thereby 'Tokyo promotes China's development and integration into the world economy, giving Beijing a stake in stable ties with its neighbour and the outside world as a whole'.

It was a recognition of the vital importance of the economic integration of South China, Hong Kong and Taiwan which generated Tokyo's support of the simultaneous admission of the three systems into APEC during 1991. In 1997 the Japanese prime minister Ryutaro Hashimoto used the twenty-fifth anniversary of the restoration of Japan–China relations as an occasion to announce the governing principles of the relationship with China as enhancement of 'mutual understanding, dialogue stimulation, expanding cooperation, and joining forces to build a common order', pointing out that 'Japan and China should step up their dialogue, particularly on issues of security and defence, in order to ensure peace in Asia now that the Cold war is over'. Support for China's WTO bid was added to an announced 200 billion yen loan, and both sides stressed the 'inadmissibility of friction in bilateral relations between Japan and China, Japan and the US, and the US and China'. Subsequent Japanese diplomacy suggests that Chinese economic relations have come to the fore with the Hashimoto government. Although the Japanese appear to be putting much trust in such international organisations as the UN, APEC and the ASEAN Regional Forum, Japanese politicians continue to address their own business groupings to the effect that 'it is also important to expand the dialogue between Japan and China on matters directly connected with the issue of stability in our region, including the Korean Peninsula'.

Thus we suggest that the Chinese double tactic of sequence-plus-partition makes it more likely that the near future will witness a closer China–Japan relation developing, because it broadens the options, allows the economic interests full play long prior to any great or ultimate ideological resolution. Replacing highly politicised trading with joint ventures, cooperative production schemes, the activities of competing local authorities and enterprises and so on, tends to shift the origins of friction from central governments towards subnational interest groups and issues. Growing economic relations displace commanding ideologies from the centre of the global stage, and introduce from the wings the less spectacular adjustment politics of interested groups. From his examination of changing Japan–China commercial relations, Dong Dong Zhang has concluded that 'market forces and subnational interests have resulted in domestic politics taking precedence over international politics in defining bilateral economic relations . . . there has been a significant delinking of China's bilateral trade from its political relations with Japan'. Thus, through the Tiananmen incident and the traumatic realignments of the end of the Cold War, commercial relations between Japan and China continued to grow, a generalisation which remains true despite the more recent Asian economic crises. This was contemporaneous with the tightening of the economic interconnections of Greater China. By 1990 some 70 per cent of commercial investment in China flowed through Hong Kong, much of this originating in the territory, but an increasing portion coming from mainland Chinese subsidiary companies operating in Hong Kong. At that time China had perhaps $20 billion invested in Hong Kong, somewhat less than the cumulative investments in the contrary direction, which during the early 1990s were rising fast. With relaxation of Taiwanese regulations in 1987–8, a large outflow of capital poured from there into the mainland, reaching a total of $10 billion by 1992.

International condemnation of Tainanmen did nothing whatever to slow the tightening of Greater China, nor to halt the increased commercial presence of Japan. The more 'open partitions' of Hong Kong, Macao, Taiwan and Guangdong were now acting as vehicles for the resolution of political and nominal conflicts between planned and market systems. These were the thriving new sites of industrial and commercial endeavour.

From this we might conclude that very many sites of endeavour can develop between locales and agents sharing common industrial, technological and commercial interests without overt threat to the ideology and national position of China. Within this process it seems clear that Japan is already well set to gain a privileged position, and even the 'ultimate resolution' need not be dramatic at all, but merely the outcome of a gradual reduction of a political/ideological residual left over from the commonality of economic and other interests between Greater China and Japan.

For such reasons we might judge Burstein and Keijzer's 25-year forecast of the emergence of a Chinese-dominated *Confucian Social Market* as rather ill-founded, because it underplays the size and significance of Japan and overplays the role-model impact of tiny Singapore on the decision-making system of China. It is also in danger of reifying transitional features into the permanent or final characteristics of very complex social systems. In their formulation, the future will be determined by a continuation of Chinese development but along a trajectory which follows that of such a 'Confucian' state corporate system as Singapore's, in which political freedoms will remain more restricted than economic freedoms in comparison to the idealised Western model. Singapore is a small city state with clearly delimited problems and aims. Such a small city system can perhaps for a while continue to organise its commercial middle class within a politico-cultural authoritarianism. But even this is not certain for the future and surely cannot be directly applied to the massive developing middle class of China, with its greater allegiance to industry and agriculture and its lesser engagement in commerce and financial services. The Burstein–Keijzer formulation also ignores the formative role of the wider Diaspora and presumes that historical change will continue to come from the central Chinese leadership, a conservative historicism which we here reject. As we explore further, below, new technologies are creating industries which are less site-dependent than ever before, less easy to restrict and monitor. Such new industries share the same technologies as those of the international media. Thereby the diffusion of ideas has become increasingly inchoate and anarchic. Any resort to the historical point that China always reverts to some inner cohesive core based on mandarin methods and hierarchical institutions may no longer be an appropriate interpretive tactic.

Back to the future: the new sites of endeavour

The recent Asian economic crisis has provided some proximate test of the likelihood of the emergence of new sites of *cooperative endeavour* in the Asia-Pacific region which might eventually serve to further integrate the Japanese and Chinese systems both economically and politically. In 1996 and 1997 the economies of the region all showed high rates of GDP growth with the exception of Thailand in the latter year. During 1998 severe negative growth was realised in Thailand (−7 per cent), South Korea (−5 per cent), Hong Kong (−4 per cent), Malaysia (−4.8 per cent), and in the awful case of Indonesia (possibly −13 per cent). Whatever the precise causes of the crisis,[7] the speed of contagion within the region was surely conditioned by the degree of regional commercial interdependence. Table 11.2 suggests the level of trade dependency in the region by the early 1990s.

Future cooperative action may depend on analyses of the cause of the 1990s commercial crisis, and in particular the longer-term response of regional organisations such as APEC. One possibility might be to utilise the existing large foreign reserves in some systems, notably that of China (see pp. 252–3) to defend specific currencies if they again come under speculative attack from outside the region. More saliently, there is the possibility that large infrastructural projects of the Hong Kong type might in future be protected by intraregional investment and aid packages.[8] Taiwan's reaction to crisis was to offer substantial loans to overseas Chinese in the crisis-ridden areas and industries and to set up a holding company to promote investment in the region.

A type of new endeavour is already being created as a result of Japan's determination to secure future *energy supplies* through a closer Chinese alliance. The largely undeveloped Chinese oil reserves, located in desolate and distant sites, are now the focus of advanced technology projects in such remote desert regions as the Tarim Basin in the northwestern province of Xinjiang. Other energy projects include a Japan-inspired

Table 11.2 Asia-Pacific intraregional export/import share, 1991–2

Country	*Intraregional exports as % of total exports*	*Intraregional imports as % of total imports*
China	78.7	74.8
Japan	67.4	64.4
Taiwan	75.1	73.3
Hong Kong	72.9	83.9
South Korea	69.4	69.1
Singapore	71.6	73.4
Indonesia	77.7	68.8
Malaysia	77.5	78.5
Thailand	64.1	69.9
Philippines	76.1	71.8

US $10 billion, private-enterprise partnership with China, Mongolia, Russia and South Korea in order to develop the natural gas reserves of the Russian Far East, a project which alone could release some ten times Japan's current annual consumption. Overseas loans have recently funded a variety of infrastructural projects in oil and gas fields, petroleum, chemical and steel industries. Present enormous development projects such as the Three Gorges Dam and the Beijing–Shanghai Superhighway will absorb large foreign funds, and a principal global site of endeavour might well revolve around China as the single largest market for *massive infrastructural facilities*, especially those linked to energy exploitation.

Chinese privatisation (or at least 'marketisation' as above), of the *state enterprises* may serve to generate a novel site of new industries and technologies directly linked with the world economic system. Already some joint ventures in hitherto mismanaged enterprises have suggested that this is a workable mechanism to prompt changes in management and administration, alter relations with local authorities, and introduce modern technologies. Future official Chinese attempts at reducing regional income disparities might offer a further new site for foreign investment in China, particularly in the infrastructure and agricultural industry of the western and central regions. In such often inhospitable regions, whether this might bring new technologies and skills would depend on the use of preferential policies for foreign investors in joint ventures.

Potentially important sites of endeavour are the very large projects which may emerge from the *internal investment operations of Greater China*, activities which already cut across the regulations and diplomatic intents of national politics. Such new sites could become crucial nodal points for the further integration of Chinese and Japanese economic interests. This is best illustrated in the case of China and Taiwan in the 1990s. Despite restrictive policies on the part of Taiwanese authorities, that nation's business groups have for some time increased their investments on the mainland. Thus Taiwan's large plastics and petrochemicals enterprise, the Formosa Group, has since 1991 put forward billion dollar proposals for petrochemical complexes and power plants in Fujian Province to be financed by the Taiwanese corporation directly, by its overseas (mostly Chinese) subsidiaries, and by international banking partners including Japan's Mitsubishi and Sumitomo as well as several German financial houses. By such disbursement of financing, it is possible for the commercial interests of Greater China and the diaspora to circumvent national regulations and policies and to thereby create new transnational sites of production which involve both Chinese and Japanese interests on the large scale. Such projects in combination serve to forge interrelationships far beyond the boundaries set by official nationalist ideologies.

We may extend this idea to embrace the Chinese diaspora more broadly, a subject to which we return in Chapter 13. We might in the near future expect an extension of the present new triangular relations of the Chinese mainland market and labour, with Taiwanese or diaspora cultural and linguistic expertise, with capital and technology of Western and Japanese transnational corporations, combining to establish manufacturing centres and marketing networks. The most likely sitings of such triangles are in either the existing SEZs or in the strategic industries selected for special encouragement by the Chinese government, such as infrastructural development, biochemicals and advanced electronics, which may not be geographically confined to coastal or urban special zones. Presently, several MNCs are establishing 'Greater China Centres' in Hong Kong or Taiwan in order to forge multi-locational partnerships in order to invest in mainland China.

The global weight of such new sitings of endeavour may well depend upon the exact character of the geopolitical and commercial relations which develop between Japan and China and the US. Each one of these nations already expends a great deal of money and energy in monitoring and attempting to fine-tune its relations with each of the others without causing breakdown in any bilateral relationship. In Chapter 12 we conclude that the real differences between Japan and the US, although most newsworthy, are the minor problem. The major ones relate to Japan–China relations and US–China relations, with the Japan–US relation being the derived side of a crucial triangular relationship in the global economic and political systems. That is, it seems increasingly unlikely that Japan in the foreseeable future would sacrifice its expensive commitments to its giant neighbour in order to support any extreme American ideological or geopolitical positions. If it becomes no longer possible for Japan to maintain something of an isosceles triangle as the commanding configuration of its relations with the US and China, then it is most liable to opt for a shortening of the institutional and ideological distance between itself and China rather than take the risks entailed in the alternative strategy. We have suggested here that there are several sites and agencies through which such a shortening of distance might occur, without wholesale ideological confrontation or resolution. In the meantime, Japan's positive choice will surely continue to be that of aiding China in its political as well as commercial integration into the wider world economy. The resulting increased commercial competition between China and the US would emerge as a reasonable strategic result, for within such a co-existing world Japan might continue to prosper and expand.

At present there is no reason to believe that the future relations between the US and China will bear a family resemblance to the cold-war relations of the US and the USSR. Greater China and the Chinese diaspora link the mainland to capitalism in a way that the COMECON countries never could do for the old USSR, and provide innumerable sites of interaction and compromise. Despite the potency of the diaspora, China has no immediate empire to be wary of and protect. Third, there are far stronger existing trading relations between the two powers than between the earlier Cold-War superpowers. Additionally, it is surely possible that the shared cultural history of China and the largest capitalist nation in the east, Japan, provides a moderating element in the relations between China and the US. The existing degree of 'partitioned capitalism' in China is much greater than in the USSR at any time prior to the 1990s. The USSR had no Guangdong. Finally, the already 'sequenced' China has generated a completely different set of economic and political relations and more room for debate and manoeuvre. Relations between China and the US are more likely to revolve around questions of solving the conflicts between the multiply-interrelated interests of a host of diffuse groups and organisations, than to stultify in an unforgiving, cold interface between ideologies and hemispheres. All the present evidence is of rapprochement, with America standing aside from the Taiwan issue whenever possible, commending China on its responsible actions (resisting devaluation) during the so-called Asian crisis, and mostly avoiding questions of human rights and arms proliferation.

Notes

1 The fall in Hong Kong share prices during 1997–8 meant a severe drop in the value of the shares issued by Chinese corporations. An attempt during February 1999 to issue Chinese state enterprise shares was halted by lack of real investor interest.

2 The four large state-owned banks – the Agricultural Bank of China, Bank of China, China Construction Bank, Industrial and Commercial Bank of China – together with the many regional provincial government banks are presently much directed by political considerations, with lending to the state sector firms not governed by costs and profitability. Whilst creating bad debt the system can be used restrictively to control inflation, as appears to have been the case in 1993–5. In 1999 bad loans probably made up about 30 per cent of total bank assets.

3 Although difficult to compute, we might hazard from the more reliable figures that China's GDP *c.* 1992 was perhaps 7.5 per cent that of the US, 13 per cent that of Japan, 24 per cent that of Germany, 44 per cent that of the UK. In the same year, per capita GDP in China was approximately 1.6 per cent that of the US, 1.3 per cent that of Japan, 1.6 per cent that of Germany and 2.2 per cent that of the UK.

4 There are two reasons why the comparison was and is somewhat tired. Japanese exports to the US are high-tech electronics and automobiles, Chinese exports are labour-intensively produced textiles, toys and footwear. Second, just as Chinese exports to the US are often products of non-Chinese investments, so conversely Japanese investments and production both within the US and in East Asia produce goods which are sold in the US without being part of Japan's exports to the US. That is, the US trade deficit with Japan does not adequately reflect Japanese competitiveness in the US market. One calculation of 1996 was that the true US deficit with Japanese companies operating globally could be twice the official deficit of $50 billion.

5 There were of course other good reasons. Amongst them we might suggest the absence in Russia and Europe of such a large surplus labour force, the change in the global economic system between the early 1980s and the 1990s, and the greater pressure exerted on Europe by the international media.

6 General performance figures for the province underplay the very high growth in the Delta region itself, which contains Hong Kong as well as Macao and Guangzhou. A rich soil area amidst a mountainous terrain, the delta always produced such cash crops as silk, fish, fruit and vegetables, a strong basis for the entrepreneurial flourish which accompanied greater regional autonomy and the ability to seek foreign capital and retain foreign exchange earnings. In addition, regions of the delta provided the homeland of the nineteenth-century migrants to the Americas, Africa, Australasia and Southeast Asia as well as to Hong Kong, Macao and later Taiwan. Thus the region is in ready receipt of both networked information (tacit knowledge) and investment funds from throughout Greater China and the great diaspora and may also act as a centre of further dispersals. For such reasons, beyond mere physical proximity, Hong Kong became an essential vehicle of mainland development, and became 'the catalyst that drew the Guangdong provincial economy into the global economy after 1979'. In 1985 the delta was proclaimed an Open Economic Region.

7 Many newspaper and popular accounts simply blamed the old corruption, state interference, and large bank debts. Possibly heavy current account debts plus high levels of internal investment insufficiently backed by domestic savings, combined to render economies such as Thailand or South Korea especially vulnerable, and in some cases the pegging of exchange rates to the dollar would then encourage international speculative attacks. Optimistic underwriting of loans by government and central banks may at all times lead to excessive investments, as risk is reduced and the need for high real returns is less, possibly a future problem for mainland China. But the *spread* of the crisis was a function of trade, investment, and technological interdependency, rather than primarily a matter of psychic contagion.

8 Hong Kong's new airport was in receipt of large sums of money through the Japanese construction company Kumagai Gumi.

References

de Thiersant as quoted at length in, notably, *Japan Weekly Mail*, 21 August 1880 page 1075.

Toynbee, Arnold J. (1961) *A Study of History*, volume 12, quote page 179, Oxford: Oxford University Press.

Quotations for Hume and Smith taken from David Hume (1741–2) *Essays Moral, Political and Literary*, Edinburgh, as in *Works of David Hume*, Grant Richards, London, 1903, p. 123; Adam Smith (1776) *The Wealth of Nations*, quotation from Everyman's Library Edition, introduction by E. R. A. Seligman, J. M. Dent and Sons, London, 1937 volume 1 page 63–4, 85, volume 2 pages 173–4, 217–18, 319.

For the modern geography see R. H. Whitebeck and O. J. Thomas (1932) *The Geographic Factor*, New York: Jennicat Press, quotations pages 287–9, 368–9. For an extension of the approach to long-term history, Karl Wittfogel (1957) *Oriental Despotism*, New Haven, CT, Yale University Press, and his (1970) *Agriculture: A Key to the Understanding of Chinese Society*, Canberra: Australian National University.

Braudel, Fernand (1981) *Civilisation and Capitalism*, vol. 1 *The Structure of Everyday Life*, London: Collins, pages 338–77, and (1985) vol. 2, *The Wheels of Commerce*, London: Fontana, pages 117–20, 585–95.

Needham, Joseph (1986) 'Science, technology, progress and the breakthrough: China as a case study in human history', in T. Ganelius (ed.) *Progress in Science and its Social Conditions*, Oxford: Pergamon Press and Nobel Foundation, quote page 14.

Eckstein, Alexander (1975) *China's Economic Development*, Ann Arbor MI: page 130.

Dahl, Robert (1989) *Democracy and its Critics*, New Haven, CT: Yale University Press.

Linz, Juan (1990) 'Transitions to democracy', *Washington Quarterly*, 13(3), Summer, 143–64.

Licheng, Ma and Zhijun, Ling (1998) *Jiaofeng* (Crossed Swords), Beijing: Jinri Chubanshe.

Quotations concerning Jiang Zemin and reform of state enterprises are from Zhou Shulian (1998) 'Several views on deepening the current reform of state enterprises'. *Social Sciences in China*, Autumn, 5–12, quotes pages 7–9.

Quote in note 6 from G. E. Johnson (1995) 'Continuity and transformation in the Pearl River Delta: Hong Kong's impact on its hinterland', in R. Yin-Wang Kwok and Alvin Y So (eds), *The Hong Kong-Guangdong Link. Partnership in Flux*, New York: ME Sharpe, 64–86, quote page 80.

Kwok, Reginald *et al.* 'Production change in Guangdong', in *ibid.* 135–62, quote page 148.

Cao, Jianming (1998) 'Financial security and building of legal system', Renmin ribao, 18 June 1998 in Foreign Broadcast Information Service, *Daily Report China*, 24 June, 98–175.

Potapov, M. (1998) 'China's external economic strategy: significance of Chinese practice to Russia', *Far Eastern Affairs*, 2, 60–73.

Chang, David W. W. (1988) *China Under Deng Xiaoping*, London.

Oksenberg, M. *et al.* (1990) *Beijing Spring 1989*, M. E. Sharpe, Armonk.

Binyan, Liu (1990) *China's Crises: China's Hope*, Cambridge, MA: Harvard University Press

Deyo, F. (ed.) (1987) *The Political Economy of the New Asian Industrialisation*, Ithica.

Johnstone, Christopher B. (1998) 'Japan's China policy. Implications for US–Japan relations', *Asian Survey*, 38, 1067–85, quotes pages 1074, 1083.

Kemenade, W. van (1997) *China, Hong Kong, Taiwan, Inc. The Dynamics of a New Empire*, New York: Vintage Books, quote page 392.

Burnstein, D. and Keijzer, A. de (1998) *Big Dragon. The Future of China*, New York: Simon and Schuster, quote pp. 311–13.

Quotes concerning 1997 Japan–China diplomatic relations, from Anatoly Semin (1998) 'Japanese–Chinese relations in a multipolar world', *Far Eastern Affairs*, 3: 3–10.

Sources for tables and statistical data

Ginsberg, N. (1958) *The Pattern of Asia*, London.

State Statistical Bureau PRC (1984) *Statistical Yearbook of China 1984*, Hong Kong: Economic Information Agency.

The World Bank (1984) *China, Long Term Development Issues and Options*, Baltimore and London.

Asia-Pacific Economic Cooperation (1995, 1998) *1995 APEC Economic Outlook*, Singapore: APEC Secretariat, and *1998 APEC Outlook*, Singapore, for Table 11.1.

Quarterly National Economic Trends, (Taipei). May 1999, for Table 11.1 especially pages 40–49, Tables 1–20.

Mainland Affairs Council (1998) *Liang'an jingji tongji yuebao* (Monthly Report on Cross-Strait Economic Statistics), Taipei: MAC.

China Economic Information Network 'State enterprise reform costs', 27 October 1998, Internet (http:/www.cei.gov.cn).

Lee, C. (1997) 'Foreign direct investment in China: do state policies matter?', *Issues and Studies, A Journal of Chinese Studies and International Affairs*, 33(7), pp. 13–29.

Holstein, W. J. (1996) 'An economy to fear?', *US News and World Report*, 121, no. 25, 23 December, pp. 43–5.

'Backwards and Forwards in China', *The Economist*, 13 March 1999, p. 71 forward.

Pape, Wolfgang (ed.) (1996) *Shaping Factors in East Asia by the Year 2000 and Beyond. A Study for the European Commission*, Hamburg: Institute of Asian Affairs.

China's Concise Statistical Handbook 1997, Beijing.

Zhang, Dong Dong (1997) 'Transformation in the political economy of China's relations with Japan in the Reform era', *Pacific Economic Papers*, Australia–Japan Research Centre, RSPAS, Australian National University, Canberra, no. 265 March.

Luolin, Wang and Xiaojuan, Jiang (1999) 'The influence of foreign capital on China's economy and its future utilization', *Social Sciences in China*, Summer, 5–16.

IMF (1999) *International Financial Statistics*, January.

The World Bank (1996) *The Chinese Economy. Fighting Inflation, Deepening Reforms*, Washington, DC: World Bank Country Study.

Houben, Hiddo (1999) 'China's economic reforms and integration into the world trading system', *Journal of World Trade*, 33(3), 1–18.

Segal, Gerald (1999) 'Does China matter?' *Foreign Affairs*, 78(5), September–October, 24–36.

South China Post, 7 October 1998, Business Section, 3.

Further reading

Balasz, E. (1964) *Chinese Civilisation and Bureaucracy*, New Haven, CT: Yale University Press.

Baranson, J. (1987) 'Ideology versus innovation in Soviet industry', *The World Economy*, 10.

Baum, R. (ed.) (1980) *China's Four Modernisations*, Boulder.

Bernstein, R. and Munro, H. R. (1997) *The Coming Conflict with China*, New York: Alfred A. Knopf.

Bird, G. (ed.) (1992) *Economic Reform in Eastern Europe*, Aldershot: Edward Elgar.

Bornstein, M. (1985) *The Transfer of Western Technology to the USSR*, Paris: OECD.

Bryant, C. G. A. and Mokrzycki, E. (eds) (1994) *The New Great Transformation?* London: Routledge.

Central Intelligence Agency (1979) *China: Post-Mao search for Civilian Industrial Technology*, Washington, DC.

Chan, L. W. (1974) *The Tach'ing Oilfield, A Maoist Model for Economic Development*, (Contemporary China Papers) Canberra: Australian National University, no. 8.

Fairbank, J. K. (1986) *The Great Chinese Revolution 1800–1985*, New York: Perennial Library.

Financial Times, 'A Soviet experiment in autonomy', 11 July, 1986.

Funabashi, Y. *et al.* (1994) *An Emerging China in a World of Interdependence*, New York: Trilateral Commission.

Girardin, E. (1997) *Banking Sector Reform and Credit Control in China*, Paris: OECD Development Centre Studies.

Gurley, J. G. (1976) *China's Economy and the Maoist Strategy*, New York.

Hama, K. (1980) 'The Daqing oil field: a model in China's struggle for rapid industrialisation', *The Developing Economies*, 18: 167–92.

Heymann, H. (1975) 'Acquisition and diffusion of technology in China', in US Congress Joint Economic Committee, *China: A Reassessment of the Economy*, Washington, DC.

Holliday, G. (1979) *Technology Transfer to the USSR 1928–37 and 1966–75: The Role of Western Technology in Soviet Economic Development*, Boulder, CO.

Hu, C.-T. (1999) 'Challenges to economic cooperation in the Asia-Pacific region', *Issues and Studies* (Taipei), 35: 131–46.

Inkster, I. (1989) 'Appropriate technology, alternative technology and the Chinese model: terminology and analysis', *Annals of Science*, 46: 263–76.

Inkster, I. (1998) 'Lessons of the past? Technology transfer and Russian industrialisation in comparative perspective', *Science, Technology and Society*, 3: 307–33.

Inkster, I. (2000) 'Sites and agents: technological change in world history', in R. Porter (ed.) *The Cambridge History of Science, The Eighteenth Century*, Cambridge: Cambridge University Press, (forthcoming).

Krugman, P. (1998) 'Saving Asia: Its time to get radical', *Fortune*, 7 September.

Krugman, P. and Obstfeld, M. (1994) *International Economics: Theory and Policy*, New York: Harper Collins.

Lardy, N. R. (1998) *China's Unfinished Economic Revolution*, Washington, DC: Brookings.

Lehning, P. B. and Weale, A. (eds) (1997) *Citizenship, Democracy and Justice in the New Europe*, London: Routledge.

Leng, T.-K. (1997) *The Taiwan-China Connection. Democracy and Development Across the Taiwan Straits*, Taipei: SMC Publishing.

Leng, T.-K. (1998) 'Dynamics of Taiwan–Mainland China economic relations. The role of private firms', *Asian Survey*, 38: 494–509.

Lieberthal, K. (1995) *Governing China*, New York: Norton.

Metzger, T. A. and Myers, R. H. (eds) (1997) *Greater China and US Foreign Policy*, Stanford, CA: Hoover Institution Press.

Overholt, W. H. (1993) *The Rise of China*, New York: Norton.

Portiakov, V. (1998) 'Socio-political stability in the People's Republic of China', *Far Eastern Affairs*, 2: 20–34.

Qinglian, H. (1998) *Xiandaihua de xianjing* (*Pitfalls of Modernisation*), Beijing: Jinri chubanshe.

Rahmer, B. A. (1977) 'New course for China's oil policy', *Petroleum Economist*, July: 385–7.

Reynolds, P. and Young, P. (1992) *Eastern Europe: Privatization Strategy for Post-Communist Countries*, London: Adam Smith Institute.

Riskin, C. (1971) 'Local industry and the Chinese model of development', *The China Quarterly*, 46: 245–73.

Rozman, G. (ed.) (1992) *Dismantling Communism*, Baltimore: Johns Hopkins University Press.

Schlotthauer, N. (1999) 'Will the People's Republic of China trigger off the next Asian crisis?', *Intereconomics*, May/June: 124–35.

Smith, M. P. (ed.) (1989) *Pacific Rim Cities in the World Economy*, Oxford: Transaction Books.

Spence, J. D. (1990) *The Search for Modern China*, New York: Norton.

Survey of People's Republic of China Press 'Ten major contributions of Tach'ing oilfield', NCNA, English, No. 6303, 13–21 March 1977.

Sutton, A. C. (1973) *Western Technology and Soviet Economic Development 1945–1965*, Stanford, CA: Stanford University Press.

Weslowski, W. (1991) 'Transition to democracy: the role of social and political pluralism', *Sisyphus: Sociological Studies*, 7: 79–94.

Wu, Y.-S. (1994) *Comparative Economic Transformations. Mainland China, Hungary, the Soviet Union, and Taiwan*, Stanford, CA: Stanford University Press.

Yang, D. (1991) 'China adjusts to the world economy: the political economy of China's coastal development strategy', *Pacific Affairs*, 65: 42–64.

Zaleski, E. and Weinert, H. (1980) *Technology Transfer between East and West*, Paris: OECD.

12 Systems clash

Japan and the US

Sam's sequence: climacteric concerns

Ben Elton caught the notion of a modern climacteric in the reflections of Sam, the character in his novel *Gridlock* who busily pondered the fate of nations:

> Industrial dominance was a hard thing to fathom, Sam thought to himself as he took the chopper to the Global building. Why, it wasn't thirty years since the US was such an economic power it didn't seem as if it could ever end. How do these things happen? A hundred years before, the British had been the Japanese, so to speak. After them, in the middle of the century, the people of the United States were unquestionably the Japanese. These days, perhaps rather ironically, the Japanese themselves were the Japanese. Who would be the Japanese next thought Sam? Probably the Germans, but you can never tell.

Those who have mulled over Sam's sequence have at times found a ready causation. The rise of one system causes the relative plight of another in a zero-sum game. Thus many US critics of the growth and expansion of the modern Japanese economy have seen this as not only caused by unfair public sector practices but also a *cause* of the trade, investment, debt and other recent quandaries of the American economy. They would point to the character of the US trade deficit as it appeared in the early 1990s – most of the debt was with Japan, but this was notably followed by China, Taiwan, Thailand and Malaysia, a listing which bears out the relationships postulated in Chapter 10, pp. 211–26, and in the related Figure 10.2. Amongst the top half-dozen holders of the US trade debt, only the special case of Canada (at US $11 billion), lay outside the new East Asian Edge. Such critics have also spotted another irony, perhaps one not realised by Sam. This arises in a grand manner once we are prepared to identify as amongst the essential ingredients of Japan's success those which were first introduced into Japan by the Americans themselves, a position to which we shall return on pp. 274–81.

Another version of this account is to see the causation as occurring in approximately the same direction, but within a much broader scope than can be captured in bilateral relations, comparisons or accusations. It is not only Japan, Asian NICs and ASEAN who have performed well in recent years. As we have already stressed, China too grew at the 8 per cent per annum level for total GDP during the early 1990s, an estimate produced by such sceptical organisations as the World Bank and the Asian Development Bank. Spectacular growth belonged not merely to particular industries, regions within nations or even industrial sectors. A huge system such as that of China witnessed growth diffusing away from favoured coastal free-trade areas to deeply interior zones (Chapter 11). The possibility arises that the end of the Cold War was associated with a broad transition towards markets and outward expansion amongst a goodly range of nations whose bureaucracies were targeting reform in commercial life whilst withholding wholesale change in the political structures which had initially supported those older economic institutions. In this thesis, particularly derived from the Chinese experience which we have documented in Chapter 11, a gradual sequence of institutional reforms allows a number of nations to benefit from relative economic backwardness through a rebirth into the global flow of commodities, capital, skills and techniques. Countries in the former Soviet Union, Eastern Europe, the Balkans and elsewhere[1] which chose the shock therapy of greatly speeding up the reform sequence or even reversing it – by yielding real power to democratic political and cultural interests ahead of a programme of planned liberalisation of economic institutions over time – appear to have fallen into recession, confusion and violence, leading to the new outbreaks of tension and warfare in a post-Cold-War world.

The theory of global transition spins a causal thread which links the Japanese and the US economies more indirectly than through bilateral trade and investment flows. Thus in postulating the global transition thesis in research programmes of the United Nations University, Vladimir Popov has judged that it is 'natural to assume that China and Vietnam are developing a type of market economy that is broadly consistent with the existing regional patterns: ASEAN countries and South Korea may show China and Vietnam what their immediate future looks like while Japan provides visions of the more distant future'. In Chapters 10 and 11 we have suggested that Japanese economic expansion has been influential in the industrial and commercial development of Asian systems and, in particular, has acted as an essential ingredient in the process whereby Asian development was interlinked with the US economy, especially during the key years of the 1980s, e.g. as in Figure 10.2. In this chapter we would modify the existing approaches to transition on at least three levels. First, the measures of transition are very confused and do not sufficiently account for important areas of *renovation* within older industrial and service economies, including that of the US. For instance, the period of extraordinary Japanese expansion coincided with the move of many resources within the US economy from the East to the West (see p. 295), a move which took time to yield net economic rewards. Second, the downturn in the rate of overall economic growth in the established capitalist systems might be interpreted as the *setting-in of diminishing returns to older institutions of both private and public enterprise.* In other words, the climacteric represents a clash of systems in which earlier developers grow more slowly in political economies increasingly oriented towards making decisions which maximise many social goals other than those directly obtainable from an increase in the economic growth rate. Early starters exhibit lower growth rates when juxtaposed with very late developers. Third, transition becomes *climacteric* when we acknowledge that *integral to differential performances is the creation and application of an array of new technologies* whose major characteristics are in great contrast to those of the West or of Japan in the years up to and including the golden age of the 1950s and 1960s (Chapter 8). That is, it is highly unlikely that any institutional reform in struggling East Asia or China would yield competitive industrial growth if only the metal- and energy-based tools and heavy chemicals of the old Western-dominated machinofacture were available for exploitation. Very late catch-up seems to have been predicated on both some institutional reforms which served to open up hitherto very closed economies in combination with the availability of new techniques of communication, transportation and industrial production. Although it is yet adventurous to say so, it is quite possible that the paradigmatic shifts in communication, service, environmental and production technologies have already converted what might have been transitional and non-sustainable spurts of growth in new locations into permanent features of a vital change in the global balance of economic power and wealth. *It is to this vital change we refer when adopting the notion of a modern climacteric.* Sam's sequence is legitimate, but the switch of much productive activity to Japan, China and East Asia more generally is not a mere move in a Western game of follow-my-leader. It may represent a climacteric in which the location of core activity shifts eventually not only from the West to the East, but from the nation state towards regional groupings or even cross-national projects whose integrity is based not on heavy investments in physical sites protected by national public sector regulations and policies, as much as upon the systems-logic of advanced techniques in new industries and services. Harbingers of such sites may be the developments we tentatively put forth in Chapter 11, pp. 262–5.

So, the developments of the years since *c.* 1970 described in our last chapters may serve to sharpen the perspective offered by Noam Chomsky in 1973. Writing of Indo-China and the Vietnam war, Chomsky noted that Japan was the first of the capitalist powers to exploit Saigon's new policies of investment and trade linkages. Both aid and investment could rightly be explained as attempts by the Japanese to secure reliable inputs of such materials as silica as well as to produce agricultural machinery, diesel engines, and electronics through Japanese–Vietnamese joint ventures. For instance, the newly formed Vietnam National Company was a joint product of Vietnamese interests and Matsushita to manufacture radios, televisions and other electronic products. On such evidence, Chomsky then predicted that the post-Vietnam era would be one within which would be constructed a 'Japanese–American co-prosperity sphere' at a time when Japanese wages were only 25 per cent of those in the US and when the US had tremendous commercial commitments in South East Asia generally. In this view, the US policy makers were encouraging Japan to take up the burden of the Cold War in Asia through foreign aid, investment and an accompanying political suasion. Such a perspective adds a fascinating colouration to any picture of the modern climacteric, for its ultimate position would surely be that, however antagonistic the relations between the two capitalist superpowers *appeared* to be, and whatever the *cultural* significance of the locus change from West to East, the modern period has seen sufficient adjustment to allow the continuation and increased strengthening of capitalism just as the Cold War collapsed and communist regimes crumbled in most of their traditional places. In such a global perspective, the expansion of the Japanese economy and even the frictions engendered with the existing capitalist hegemony of the US, were essential mechanisms of the process whereby the challenging technologies and institutions of the modern climacteric were effectively captured by an older capitalism.

Historical interludes and ironies

From the beginning, the Americans believed in the Japanese. After the signing of the Treaty of Kanagawa, Townsend Harris was appointed as the first US Consul General. He arrived in Shimoda in 1856 and immediately considered that the Japanese 'are superior to any people east of the Cape of Good Hope'. The murder of the US official interpreter in January 1861 and a chain of anti-foreign activities and responses led to the British bombardment of Kagoshima and a withdrawal of foreign residents to the fortified residential base of Yokohama. After the burning of the US legation building in 1863 and the closure to foreigners of the Straits of Shimonoseki, the US retaliated and was soon joined by an allied battle flotilla of seventeen ships which bombed the harbour. In November 1865 the Emperor sanctioned previously signed concessions, and the uneasy relations between the West and Japan had really begun.

In the subsequent years of treaty negotiation, the US authorities took an altogether more liberal position than the other great powers and, more generally, America was seen as a model for emulation. Just when in 1884 the *Jiji Shimpo* was claiming that American influence in Japan was giving way to that of Germany, a graduate of the University of Tokyo was entering the senior class of the University of Pennsylvania's Wharton School of Finance and Economy. Just as that same newspaper reported on a lynching of a Japanese in Ogden, US after supposedly shooting a woman in a restaurant, so too the *New York Herald* reported on the healthy and growing Japanese communities of New York, Boston, Chicago and San Francisco, so noted for their 'intelligence, industry, sobriety and a strict observance of the social duties'. Such US communities of Japanese were made up of merchants and artisans in tea, silk, porcelain and toy trades, and by the mid-1880s they boasted their own American bank and their own New York club, and numerous Japanese were utilising their fluent English in lively discussions of American politics and culture. But even the Japanese sailors in American ports were reportedly well-behaved. The good influence of Japanese communities in America was even lauded by the British press, the *Manchester Guardian* claiming that such overseas communities 'in constant communication with the home country, should have some influence on the progress of an enterprising people is natural enough'.

Although Mexico was the first outside nation to fully recognise Japanese autonomy, in November 1894 America was the first of the nations to sign a treaty which demanded no special concessions. In turn, the Japanese had seen the Americans as a special case. In his great compendium of foreign information and culture, the *Seiyō-jijō* (*Conditions in the West*), Yukichi Fukuzawa singled out America amongst the nations as 'republican in the best sense of the word. This is the country in which real representatives of the people meet and discuss national politics without any private interests. Although nearly a century has passed since it was established, the laws of the country have never been thrown into confusion.'

By the end of the Meiji period, the *yōkō-gaeri* ('returners from abroad') were encouraging further Japanese migrations to America and arrests were mounting within Japan of those miscreants who were forging or swapping passports and other travel documentation. In 1913 the *Yokohama Bōeki Shimpo* was claiming that half the inhabitants of Mihomura, in Shizuoka Prefecture had reached America 'securing their permits by clandestine means', and wage remittances from the US received at the Ejiri post-office amounted to almost 100,000 yen. Nor were American authorities in any way opposed to the forging of close relations. The US exchange lecturer Dr H. Wright Mabie successfully toured the Imperial, Waseda, and Keiō Universities in Tokyo as well as several other venues, including Kyoto Imperial University and Dōshisha College, in order to bring to the Japanese the way of life, constitution and institutions of the Americans. And there was much generous reciprocity. When Dr Henderson of the University of Chicago arrived in Tokyo, a dinner was given in his honour by the Tokyo Sociological Association in the house of none other than Count Shigenobu Ōkuma, statesman and founder of Waseda University. Table 12.1 indicates the pattern of Japanese business settlement overseas at the end of the Meiji period. Listing only the business offices, factories or agricultural and fisheries enterprises whose annual incomes were over 10,000 yen, the official data shows the clear bias towards America.

Table 12.1 Japanese business communities overseas, 1909–11

Overseas location	*1909*	*1910*	*1911*
China	592	621	618
US	1,260	1,450	1,841
Canada	78	73	98
South America	12	7	18
Australasia	138	130	149
Europe	25	21	29

In doing business, the Japanese had turned primarily to America. An official breakdown of the figures for the Japanese business community in America for 1911 shows that of the 1,841 known cases, 46 per cent were engaged in farming and brokerage, 21 per cent in general merchandising, 16 per cent in restaurant and hotel keeping, and the rest in a sundry group of occupations including washermen, gardeners, tailors and labour contractors. Of Japanese overseas whose annual transactions were in the range 100–200,000 yen, sixty-nine businesses were in China, fifty-six in the US, and twenty-nine were elsewhere. In the next range, annual incomes of 200–300,000 yen, twenty-four were located in China, twenty-two in the US and thirteen were elsewhere. Although Japanese business communities were clearly comparatively numerous and prosperous, their very success and visibility engendered sporadic outbursts of anti-Japanese feeling within America.

The seeming victory of democracy in the First World War confirmed the opinion of many Japanese about the superiority of the Anglo-American way, and paved the road towards '*Taishō* democracy', (see Chapter 7, pp. 116–17). However, the 1920s also witnessed both popular agitation and discriminatory legislation against the Japanese communities settled on the Pacific coastal states of America, culminating in the Immigration Act of 1924 with its infamous exclusion clause.

At a time when Japan's export economy had little real impact on the West, one of the most astute of commentators identified structural problems which would echo distortedly throughout the rest of the century. Stressing that trade between Japan and America was not especially significant and probably complementary, in 1936 William Lockwood went on to argue that instability within economic policy regimes might lead to a future volatility in political relationships.

> Is a country like Japan to be allowed to procure raw materials and foodstuffs abroad through the processes of peaceful selling in world markets (and for Japan this means especially the Pacific area), or, in the face of rising barriers against her goods in the United States, and in the British, Dutch and French empires, must she seek the extension of political controls abroad by armed conquest and other means in order to assure

> herself of access to necessary supplies? To call attention to this alternative is not to imply a justification of Japanese imperialism as practised today; but there is little doubt that the unreceptiveness of the outside world to Japanese goods provokes a feeling of insecurity and offers an incentive and a rationale for attempts at empire-building.

As we have seen, the depression years set the political face of Japan against both democracy and the West, although the immediate targets of the nation's aggression continued to be the powerful northern neighbours, China and the USSR. The investments of the 1930s meant that by the eve of Pearl Harbor Japan had an army of one million and a reserve force of some two million, besides a high technology capability in the form of the Zero fighter aircraft, itself a product of technology transfers from Britain and America. The navy may well have looked towards Oceania, America and even Britain as potential military targets, but as late as 1941 the army and most opinion saw threats from Russia in Asia as being most real, and this was the background to the invasion of northern China. By the end of 1937 there were more than 700,000 Japanese troops in China. Ironically, this tactic itself depended on large imports of materials and goods from the US and Europe. In 1939 the US began to impose economic sanctions by abrogating the United States–Japan Commercial Treaty and soon after placed direct embargoes on strategic materials to Japan. When the Japanese invaded the southern region of French Indo-China in July 1941, the US, the UK and the Netherlands embargoed oil supplies.

As the goal of materials security took over, a southern movement began to seem a logical extension of aggression. This was the reasoning behind both the Tripartite Pact of September 1941 with Germany and Italy, and the neutrality treaty with the USSR, which together were designed to offer time in which to move south, a decision which changed the course of the whole war as Stalin was enabled to switch energies westwards, against the Germans. For the first time since the 1860s Japan engaged in military conflict with the US. In the six months following Pearl Harbor (7 December 1941) the Japanese forces ran rampant in the Pacific and Southeast Asia, overwhelming the European colonial empires, encircling China from the south, and threatening India, Australia and Hawaii.

The 'benevolent despotism' of the Japanese Occupation was to be the starting point for an American crusade against Communism in the East. It has been argued (see also Chapter 7, pp. 128–33) that the SCAP reforms of the US occupying forces in post-war Japan instilled the ideologies or goals of both equality and competition. Within the educational system was laid the foundation of egalitarianism in the elementary schools whilst college education was characterised by *batsu* (cliques) which were the effective institutional genesis of networks of influence, mobility and loyalty in the wider world of business and politics. Again, problems surrounding the labour reforms of 1950–5 led to a formula of nursing skilled labour by large firms and the emergence of new foreman systems, company training programmes and the seniority (*nenkō*) system. An aim of SCAP was to affirm enterprise loyalties by encouraging Japanese workers to compete within accepted structures of enterprise, including some form of enterprise unionism. It has been suggested that this in turn led naturally enough to the system of subcontracted workers who are easily shed in times of recession, who provide inventory space for the major company, and who are least likely to institutionalise their grievances. Such institutional impacts lead to a belief that the American Occupation created the basis for the 'economic miracle' of the 1960s.

A belief in the strategic contribution of the US to Japanese industrial success may be furthered in consideration of post-SCAP activities also. The Korean war procurements and the Western alliance of the early Cold War artificially boosted demand for Japanese goods and supplies. The encouragement of an ideology of balanced budgets during the SCAP years served to effectively remove demand management from the potential range of public policies and thereby encouraged moves to more direct intervention through industrial policy, much of which was organised by MITI, an agency whose conversion from original military to market tasks was encouraged by US authorities. Subsequent MITI activities under the rubric of the occupation's anti-monopoly legislation promoted mergers, competition and hence increased productivity. The behavioural theories of the American business guru, W. Edwards Deming (neglected in the US at the time),[2] became the ideology of Japanese private enterprise, a consequence of which was the emergence of an unusual but efficient Japanese enterprise culture (see pp. 285–9 and 309–10), just as the US overlordship of the Pacific allowed Japan to save on defence and concentrate on new technologies in the private sector under the encouragement of public sector institutions which could devote their energies to winning the hot business war rather than the military cold war, (pp. 289–95). Furthermore, the global creation by the US of key international agencies aided the entry of Japan into the golden age. The UN, the World Bank and the IMF, the principal enabling institutions of Japanese foreign diplomacy, trade and investment, have been interpreted as complex outcomes of the Roosevelt–Churchill Atlantic Charter of September 1941. The US overtly aided Japan's membership of GATT and the OECD, with US governmental support overriding the opposition of US protectionist interests. Again, as we have seen, the revaluations of the yen which were implemented directly under pressure from the US in 1971 and 1985 combined to speed the outward expansion of the Japanese economy rather than to curtail its export of commodities. *The list of American contributions towards Japanese growth and expansionism is seemingly relentless.*

An ultimate effect of such a range of US post-war activities lay in the governance of technology transfer, a phenomenon at the heart of Japanese industrial modernisation. During the 1940s and 1950s the Marshall Plan dominated the financial relations between the world and the US and provided access to new markets for American entrepreneurs, who were also given additional incentives to invest abroad. Although US dollars and US technology flowed into Europe, Asia, Latin America and elsewhere for quite deliberate political reasons, it was the devastated but previously efficient industrial nations, such as Germany and Japan, which optimised the 'catch-up' opportunities presented within the new global system. As we have seen in Chapters 7 and 8, in Japan a combination of severe technological lag, high rates of investment, and ready supplies of semi-skilled labour led to efficient technology transfers as a basis for industrial transformation and export expansion. According to the productivity estimates of Nishimizu and Jorgenson, the technology gap between the US and Japan closed quite dramatically between 1952 and 1974, indeed to the extent that Japan could be seen as equal to or superior to America if measured by aggregate productivities. Whereas at the beginning of the period this catch-up was primarily due to Japanese labour surplus, by the latter years the difference was most attributable to high levels of Japanese industrial investment. This accords neatly with the interpretive structures of Chapters 7 and 8 and isolates the key conventional economic variables explaining the peculiar ability of Japan to benefit from its special institutional relations with the US. As we have stressed throughout this volume, the actual technological and institutional environment within which such variables worked demands proper acknowledgement and specification.

American global political strategies and transnational activities were fundamental in the optimal positioning of Japan within the post-war golden age. Of the nearly 200,000 licence agreements signed by Japanese companies, nearly all were with American enterprise, and were concentrated in electrical machinery, chemicals, pharmaceuticals, synthetic fibres, transportation equipment and iron and steel. The greatest foreign technology dependency ratios were in precisely those Japanese industries nominated as of prime strategic importance by the Ministry of International Trade and Industry, a bureaucracy which developed its *ikusei* philosophy of monitoring new industries under the auspices of legislation first laid down by SCAP. In testimony before the Subcommittee on International Trade of the US Senate Committee in May 1971, George Meany listed eighty-four major items licensed by General Electric to Japanese firms, these including radar, machine guns and boilers for nuclear reactors. The US taxpayer was paying for Japanese industrial growth through the financing of General Electric contracts with the US Defence Department. The US was losing its competitive edge due to the inexorable linkages between technological progress, defence spending and technology transfer.

Much transfer during the golden age occurred through international patenting and licensing. Of 343,000 patents issued to corporations in the US between 1939 and 1955 just less than 33 per cent went to the 176 largest corporations, less than 65 per cent to other corporations, and some

Table 12.2 US corporate and individual patenting, 1956–80 (1000s)

	1956–60	*1961–5*	*1966–70*	*1971–5*	*1976–80*
All patents issued	237.5	260.0	325.1	375.5	312.3
Individual issues	76.6	69.9	73.4	87.0	65.0
Corporate issues:					
US	133.9	152.5	190.6	192.9	150.4
Foreign	21.0	31.0	52.8	86.0	90.4
US Government	5.9	6.5	8.5	9.6	6.5

Table 12.3 The top Japanese firms in numbers of US patents granted, 1969–81

Rank among Japanese firms	*Name of company*	*Number of US patents*	*Rank among world firms*
1	Hitachi	3,754	17
2	Matsushita Electric	2,299	37
3	Fuji Film	2,063	45
4	Toshiba	1,685	56
5	Nissan Motors	1,576	60
6	Canon	1,537	63
7	Sony	1,511	65
8	Toyota Motors	1,438	69
9	Sumitomo Chemical	1,270	77
10	Ricoh	1,093	85
11	Nippon Electric	1,091	86
12	Minolta	815	117
13	Olympus	796	120
14	Mitsubishi Electric	705	130
15	Nippon Gakki	703	131
16	Asahi Kasei Kōgyō	626	153
17	Takeda Chemical	605	160
18	Aisin Seiki	592	163
19	Nippondensō	592	163
20	Nippon Kōgaku	549	171

7 per cent to foreign corporations or partnerships. By 1955, nearly 60 per cent of all patents lodged in the US derived from corporate research, 40 per cent stemming from individuals, 2 per cent from government. At that time the biggest patentees were the research-based firms such as General Electric, ATT, Westinghouse and du Pont. Table 12.2 provides an outline of the pattern of US patent issuing since that time and shows the increasing importance of foreign patentees.

The working ties between this system and the emergence of a high technological capability in Japanese enterprise is shown in Table 12.3, which captures the impacts at the end of the golden age period.

Between 1969 and 1981 the largest number of US patents were those of the great American corporations, such as GE, IBM or Westinghouse.

The first non-US firm was Bayer (Germany) with a ranking of 8 and a total number of US patents in that period of 5,134. The first Japanese firm was Hitachi, ranked 17, and clearly the Japanese invasion of the US system was dominated by large *sōgō shōsha* affiliated firms. In the period 1963–83, amongst foreign nations Germany generally secured most patents in the American system, but by the late 1970s Japanese applicants were in fact numerically greater. By 1990, the top ten patent winners in the US were in correct sequence Hitachi, Toshiba, Canon, Mitsubishi, General Electric, Fuji Film, Eastman Kodak, Philips, IBM and Siemens.

The global platform: trade and investment

Between 1985 and 1987, the years of the great yen revaluation, the US current account deficit rose from $120 billion to $160 billion, most of which was held by Japan. The negative trade deficit on automobiles alone approached $60 billion. In contrast, in 1988 Japan's global trade surplus reached US $100 billion, nearly 50 per cent of which was with the US. At that time American economic activity yielded a 1 per cent growth rate, an even lower growth in productivity, high welfare and military expenditures, a low savings rate, difficult labour relationships and highly questionable management practices and enterprise structures, alongside a measurable loss of leadership in such global high technology markets as semiconductors and computers. Vintage problems seemed to be delaying the industry-wide application of such important new technologies as the basic oxygen process in steel making.

At the same time, as we have suggested above, many US interests identified Japan as a source of such problems, not only as an expansive economy but as an unfair trader and dealer. The Japanese response was to deny any deliberate tardiness of liberalisation or to defend specific protectionist policies as designed to support Japanese agriculture or small businesses, the prosperity of which were traditionally essential to social solidarity and economic confidence at large. At the same time they claimed that other nations have been more guilty than they of abrogating GATT's trade regime requirements of non-discrimination, predictability, transparency and openness, and its preferred mechanism of negotiated tariff levels.

Nor on the face of it had Japan been particularly reticent at the international level. Japan had proposed the Tokyo Round of GATT negotiations in 1971 in order to negotiate tariff reduction. This did not begin real work until after 1975 due to US Congressional delays concerning enabling legislation for the US President to begin the negotiations. This was a successful round, with international tariffs on a wide range of manufactured goods reduced by a third. More obviously perhaps, Japan repeatedly agreed to yen revaluations throughout the decade of the 1970s and instituted some genuine investment liberalisation. It is true that this was also the decade for the formulation of a security perspective which did not involve much increase in actual military expenditure. It is additionally true that Japan was caught in a dilemma with US calls for an oil embargo during the price hikes of 1978–9. After all, unlike Europe or the US, Japan possessed nothing in the way of alternatives, and a disappearance of oil would have created a fall in the economic growth rate which would have curtailed internal demand and abrogated promises made earlier to the US concerning the taking in of increased US imports! At times, Japan could do no right. There were moments when American car workers threatened to commit a form of global luddism as they prepared to smash Japanese-made automobiles during Japan's prolonged quandary over Iran. Eventually the Japanese Prime Minister, Masayoshi Ōhira, rejected Iranian price demands, which meant that Iran cut off oil shipments to Japan in April 1980.[3]

The principal reason for increased tension in the first half of the 1980s lay simply with a change in the dimensions of the international platform – the US current account deficit grew greatly, the Japanese surplus mightily. The Japanese current account surplus moved from less than US $5 billion at 0.4 per cent of GNP in 1981, to US $86 billion at 4.3 per cent of GNP in 1986. The US current account moved from a surplus of US $6 billion at 0.2 per cent of GNP in 1981 to a deficit of a staggering US $141 billion at over 3 per cent of GNP in 1986. During 1987 the US deficit grew further to US $161 billion. There is nothing boring about statistics when their pattern of alteration is of this character. Politically, the concurrence of this opposite movement meant that the Japanese surplus became a symbol within America of that nation's own severe economic problems. In fact, there is little reason to believe that the one caused the other in any direct fashion. An estimate by the Institute of International Affairs in Washington concluded that a removal of all Japanese non-tariff barriers might increase imports from the US by about US $5–8 billion, a calculation which omitted what might happen in the opposite direction if at the same time the US was forced to yield up all of its own non-tariff restrictions. Contrasting fortunes of the two superpowers were due to more underlying differences of growth and efficiency combined with the medium-term phenomenon of particularly high private sector savings in Japan and very high government expenditure in the US. The calibre of any causal link between the medium-term policy contributions on one hand and the more underlying or historical factors on the other remains debatable but is explored thematically on pp. 285–97. *What is notable is that it was precisely pressure from America to further liberalise the Japanese economy that provided an institutional mechanism allowing Japan to so quickly emerge as the greatest of capital exporters.* As Drysdale then summarised, Japanese 'capital market liberalisation provided the avenue for Japan to finance the growth of American debt'.

The 1990s opened with a reduction in the level of official antagonism, despite the failure of Japan to send Self-Defence Forces personnel to the

Persian Gulf. American public opinion, however, remained critical, and it has been argued that the collapse of the communist enemy in Europe left Japan as a very different but now more exposed target. The *Wall Street Journal* reported how a North Carolina group called 'Help Save America for Our Kid's Future', were engaged in a mailing campaign which argued that Japanism had replaced communism as the major threat to the nation. At the populist level the Japanese were depicted as a serious threat, as different and immoral, and as long-term and cunning in their ultimate aims. At the death of the Japanese Emperor in 1989, journalists such as James Fallows seemed to use the coverage as an opportunity to report only on negative features of Japanese social life, and this became a leading feature of American attitudes to the Japanese during the 1990s.[4] In an important article in the respectable *Atlantic Monthly*, Fallows accepted the need for partnership between the powers on such matters as defence, financing the US debts, and global and bilateral business partnerships, but then went on to accuse Japan of generating an economic expansion through unfair trade and investment practices directly detrimental to the US economy.

> The expansion is one-sided because Japanese business does to other countries what Japan will not permit to be done to itself. It is destructive because it will lead to exactly the international ostracism that Japan most fears, because it will wreck the post war system of free trade that has made Japan and many other nations prosperous, and because it will ultimately make the US–Japanese partnership impossible to sustain . . . Unfortunately, the major external threat to America's ability to pay the costs of leadership is Japan's uncontrolled, unbalanced economic growth . . . If Japan cannot restrain the excesses of its own economy, then the United States, to save the partnership with Japan, should impose limits from outside.

The essence of this particular American position seems to illustrate the Chomsky claim. That is, Japan as junior partner in a shared leadership of international capitalism throughout the global economy was an acceptable choice, but one fatally marred by imputed practices unacceptable to American opinion. Not only did such a voice neglect Japan's efforts to liberalise and America's own considerable protectionist devices, as well as the squeeze that would have occurred in US global debts if Japan had not utilised surpluses to expand trade and investment. It also showed little understanding of causation. As the more technical analyses illustrated, removal of any restrictive practices in Japan would have failed to restore equilibrium to the relations between the nations, as they were based on public expenditure policies, private savings propensities and underlying historical factors all of which were little touched by such global rhetorics. In the Fallows model it was fine for America to be protectionist because of that nation's $10 billion monthly trade debt. Japan's trade balance must have arisen from artificial restrictions. Failure to expend on social services in Japan allowed cash surpluses for unfair government stimulation of overseas trade and investment. Japan dumped products into the US market. The insidious money politics of Tanaka and the LDP meant that the Japanese system hinged on politicians supporting budget expenditures for their favoured agencies or industries. Although Fallows repeated his assurance that he believed in the potential partnership between the two systems, all he listed was *system clash caused by warped institutions and foul intentions.*

In contrast, one of the more astute of US experts, the historian and economist Gary Saxonhouse, was quite firm in his alternative ascription of causation. Underlying performance factors determined our 'platform' of trading outcomes, an analysis confirming the approach of the present chapter (and book) and one readily obtained from economic historical perspectives. In particular, even by 1986 it was 'difficult to argue that American producers of industrial goods are protected by fewer overt barriers than are their Japanese counterparts'. In terms of identifiable non-tariff barriers, Japan made very little use of these to protect her industries, but 'she does make considerable use of such barriers to protect her agricultural producers'. In contrast, non-tariff barriers in the US provided only some protection for agriculture, for 'most overt protection is concentrated on the manufacturing sector', the latter especially being in textiles and clothing, steel and shipbuilding, radio and television products, and motor vehicles. In conclusion, if any balance could be struck then the overt trade policies 'of both countries help Japanese agriculture at the expense of American agriculture and help American manufacturing at the expense of Japanese manufacturing'. This was hardly a conclusion supporting Fallows-type arguments, which centred on unfair Japanese practices in manufacturing industry trade. Saxonhouse went much further. By using a model developed at Michigan he estimated the reciprocal effects of any equivalent reduction of Japanese and US tariff or informal barriers, i.e. an estimate that captured the decline in imports from the US (or the increase of Japanese exports) that would occur if Japan removed protective barriers. In light of the continuing debate, the conclusion of such a technical exercise is worth preserving here:

> The removal of Japanese tariffs and non-tariff barriers would result in the United States in a significant expansion of agriculture, forestry and fisheries and a contraction of virtually all manufacturing industries. By contrast, in Japan the removal of both Japanese and American tariffs and non-tariff barriers would lead to a sharp contraction of agriculture, forestry and fisheries and the petroleum product industries and an expansion of virtually all other manufacturing industries.

Saxonhouse also addressed trade barriers which went beyond the conventional notion of overt non-tariff barriers into the murky world of certification, standardisation, quality and environmental assessments and so on and to those inter-enterprise 'understandings' which were arguably potent elements in the exclusion of US goods to Japanese markets. Such elements were discussed in Chapter 10, pp. 207–8. Saxonhouse suggested that such intangibles are both difficult to measure and almost certainly exaggerated by the deliberate selection of adverse effects from a normal range, the sort of range that we might expect from any other foreign-language culture. Furthermore, Saxonhouse went on to demonstrate that bias in the manufacturing trade balance of Japan was far more likely to have occurred because of those characteristic patterns of resource endowment, investment and human capital formation which generally distinguished Japan from other nations. This accords well with our present analysis, although we might perhaps place more stress on the growth- and expansion-inducing features of technology transfer and institutional innovation.

Contrasts 1: enterprise cultures

In strategic terms it is perhaps understandable that Japanese commentators eschewed the trade platform in explaining the trade imbalance and frictions with the US. Long before Fallows went to Yokohama, Japanese analysis centred on the failure of the American system of manufacturing. Thus Kawai Mikio in his book (in Japanese) *The Decline of America as a Technological Superpower*, had identified short-term contracts amongst American managers as generating a distaste for long-term technological development and a failure to place those trained in engineering into strategic decision-making positions. In other words, from the outset of Japanese expansionism the Japanese themselves have tended to identify aspects of enterprise culture as of the essence in explanations of differing trading outcomes.

American enterprise was condemned by its own analysts, particularly during the 1980s decade of overt Japanese–American antagonism. A multitude of official and academic publications indicted American industry on the grounds of expense and shoddiness, inefficiency, a failure of technological awareness and competitiveness, the employment of ill-trained workers, and protection by ill-advised governments. A central question concerned whether such lacunae originated deep within American enterprise culture or in other institutions such as education and the family or, rather, were the ultimate consequences of a faulty public policy. Thus it could be cogently postulated that the focus of American enterprise on short-term profit-making – which held back major technological or organisational innovations and contrasted so strongly with Japanese long-term strategies – was a function of the high cost of capital which demanded high returns over short periods but was itself a partial result of government deficit financing.[5] On the other hand, the high price of capital was not merely a function of demand but perhaps also of the supply of savings for investment. Again, in simple contrast to Japan, where household and other savings were relatively high, the lower savings of higher-income groups in America could be seen as reflective of a stark contrast in underlying social or cultural factors, *a difference in the way that the social elites were configured within their respective societies.*

So, it seems difficult to usefully isolate apparently ingrained features of US enterprise culture from both the historical and contemporary pressures working on business from the external economic and social systems. Analysis of the American failure to compete with Japan could begin with the maldistribution of public funds towards defence (see pp. 289–90), continue with the failure of national nerve in areas such as education, and be completed in condemnation of those enterprise strategies which repeatedly underutilised what MIT referred to as such 'essential downstream engineering functions as verification and testing of design, manufacturing and product and process improvements'.

One of the most powerful of analyses at the time was *Made in America*, a product of an expert team of academics from the Massachusetts Institute of Technology in 1989. Although involving a subtle and embracive approach, *Made in America* blamed enterprise culture fairly and squarely. In contrast with Japanese firms, private industry in the US overwhelmingly concentrated on costs and profits rather than production, product array and markets. American exceptions, such as the chemical industry, resulted when enterprise exhibited a 'rich technological tradition and commitment to innovation', but leadership in core applied science was not a necessary requisite of success. From transistors to numerically controlled machine tools, America's original research lead had not sufficed to sustain any competitive edge at the level of global markets. Within such a general perspective, MIT pointed the contrasts. Thus, Japanese multi-functional design teams aimed for simplicity, elegance and quality of production, building the last two into overall production at an early stage rather than applying quality control retroactively. In contrast to America, advantages flowed to Japan through the key roles played by project managers, the early rather than late solution of goal conflicts, and the simultaneous pursuit of multiple development activities. Such organisational features yielded greater speed and flexibility and lower costs at the engineering base of the firm, characteristics especially well illustrated in the automobile industries of the 1980s. Again, in common with many approaches, the MIT analysis emphasised differences in education and training for and within industry. In contrast to America where an overworked public education system bore the brunt of training responsibilities in the absence of much in the way of industrial influence or authority, in Japan rotation of employment within the firm, special training courses in firm- and industry-specific centres, employer-sponsored correspondence courses, quality control circles and so on, together delivered precise training at points of utility without taxation. Directing industrial training at Japanese 'saturated' firms (those operating at well below full capacity in such industries as textiles) as well as innovating firms served in turn to reduce the social costs of the 'laying-off' phenomena so common in America and Europe.

It is possible to stylise the contrast in enterprise cultures between America and Japan as an exercise within the wider task of analysing the 'cultural factors' which may have been at work in Japanese economic development. This is a theme raised already with reference to modern Japanese enterprise, (see Chapter 9, pp. 180–8) and returned to in Chapter 13. Figure 12.1 presents in short form the possible relationships between the four factors of: (1) *time*; (2) the *internal culture* of the firm; (3) the *external economic environment* of the firm (in the reasonable belief that public economic policy helped determine enterprise rationality); and (4) the *external socio-cultural environment* of the firm or industry (in the reasonable belief that enterprise behaviour is not a mere outcome of enterprise structure but also partially a result of attitudes, visions and biases brought into the firm from the outside world). Any 'cultural' argument would need to effectively isolate and integrate either factor 2 or factor 4 in explaining the contrasting behaviours of industrial enterprise in Japan and the US. All else is time and institutions.

As has been emphasised throughout this volume, timing or sequencing may explain a great deal. Thus the MIT team were quick to admit that several features of enterprise culture may have been primarily outcomes of the natural history of the modernising process. The fairly unproblematic but tremendous growth of American manufacturing after the war was based on market size, technological superiority, accumulated skills, and high income per head. A high level of effective demand meant that new products developed in the US well ahead of Europe or Japan, and this had led to a high rate of investment together with the formation of a new meritocracy closely linked to industry and commerce. But the obvious success of such massive historical advantages served to entrench the organisational and attitudinal structures which were initially so complementary to the high rate of physical investment. In the meantime, Japanese firms entered the low-cost niches of existing markets which had been hitherto dominated by US firms. In this process they utilised technology transfers from the US in order to exploit the potential advantages of relative economic backwardness.

	1. Time	
Institutional layers	Historical rigidities	Contemporary processes
2. Internal culture of enterprise	1A	1B
3. External economic environment	2A	2B
4. External socio-cultural environs	3A	3B

Figure 12.1 A stylised model of enterprise 'culture' and its determinants.

Returns in such markets were relatively unattractive, this enabling low-cost Japanese enterprise to increase its share of total output and ride a global learning curve which took Japan to the point of a frontal challenge to the central processes and products of such industries. This sequencing, then, served as the effective context for Japan's harnessing of its advantages – late vintage techniques and institutions, lower labour costs and superior skilling systems, government industrial policy and the adherence to longer time frames in public and private sectors. Again, sequencing might explain the securing of such advantages. That is, sequential catching-up was associated with a real conjuncture of circumstances. Thus, MIT recognised that 'every manager does need to understand how technology relates to the strategic positioning of the firm, how to evaluate alternative technologies and investment choices, and how to shepherd scientific and technical concepts through innovation and production processes to the market place'. Yet perhaps only 7–10 per cent of US managers had a background in engineering, and the so-called US New Mandarins flowed out of MBA rather than M.Sc. programmes. In Japan, perhaps 40 per cent of enterprise executives were trained in engineering, a New *Samurai* phenomenon which Morikawa explained principally in historical terms. As the newly united Germany had shown in the late nineteenth century, concentration of limited resources into engineering training instead of general or commercial education was an imperative of late developing systems rather than a cultural predilection.

One of the aspects of science, technology and the defence imperative (pp. 289–95) is the suggestion that American economic and industrial policy is conditioned and constrained by the nation's global military commitments. There may be little doubt that factor 3 in Figure 12.1, the external economic environment of enterprise, has not been favourable to American enterprise competitiveness during precisely the years of Japan's economic expansion. The culture and choices of American industrial capitalism have developed firm commitments to high levels of public expenditures on social welfare, defence and space programmes, all of which could be justified in terms of a Cold War environment which demanded that the US economy outmatch socialist systems across an array of most visible measures. At intersection 2B of Figure 12.1 this produces a fairly inflexible pattern of public expenditure, leading to large government deficits. Whereas in 1996, national defence and social security together composed around 25 per cent of government expenditure in Japan, the comparable expenditure in the US totalled 73 per cent. Contrariwise, in the US, expenditures on education, culture and local public infrastructures, all representing positive external inputs into private enterprise (e.g. improved urban, transport and communications infrastructures), totalled some 6 per cent of government expenditure at most, in Japan the equivalent expenditures totalled 26.5 per cent. It is possible that levels of public expenditure on social welfare relate directly to the sequencing of development. The proportion of social welfare expenditure in total government expenditure rises as income per head increases, and this is a feature of time passing within all industrialised capitalist systems.

It might thereby be reasonable to conclude that the so-called 'culture' of American enterprise, its short-termism, rigidity of labour markets and work practices and so on, is explicable within the parameters of Figure 12.1 and that, thereby, the economic problems of the US are understandable without recourse to the effects of Japanese economic expansion and competition. In such a perspective, the non-competitive behaviour of much of American private enterprise until recent years was an outcome of forces operating at intersection 2B (government policy, itself conditioned by international financial and military 'responsibilities') and 3A (a version of the 'disadvantages of the early start' thesis). In contrast, Japan's more robust enterprise and technological systems have been reliant on a buoyant 'culture of enterprise' (1B) forged out of forces operating at 2A and 2B. The role of forces at 3A – the much-vaunted 'cultural argument' for the success of Japan's economic and technological system – may thereby be rendered redundant.

Contrasts 2: science, technology and the defence imperative

In 1985 the US expended 6.6 per cent of its GDP on defence, Germany spent a similar 3.2 per cent, Japan a lowly 1 per cent. Although Japanese defence expenditure had risen at an average per annum of around 6 per cent during the 1980s, the Japanese had not lifted the level of expenditure above the level of 1 per cent of GNP. Prior to and since that date, much of the antagonism between the two nations has surrounded regional and global defence roles. Thus the 1979–80 international crisis over Russia's invasion of Afghanistan showed Japan hesitating between calling for UN discussion and imposing sanctions at a time when the US was calling for the latter and a boycott of the Moscow-scheduled 1980 Olympic Games. As the old Cold War tensions mounted and the US moved forces into the Indian Ocean, the more hawkish Japanese thinkers led by Yasuhiro Nakasone (who seemed to have genuinely feared both the USSR and the scorn of the Japanese public over American gibes about a pygmy polity clothed by a giant economy) began to offer promise of overturning the established 'Yoshida Doctrine' which advocated economic expansion within a retreatist military framework. But more deeply representative of Japanese opinion were books such as Jun Eto's *The American–Japanese War is not Over* or Shintaro Ishihara's *The Japan that can say No*, which on the whole focused on the idea of a victory over the US as being entirely a technological and commercial affair involving little in the way of any military presence. That Japan could not win the battle over defence expenditure in the eyes of American opinion was well illustrated in the FSX affair.

Table 12.4 Defence and ODA expenditures of Japan and the US, 1985 and 1995 (totals in $US billion)

	Japan	*US*
Defence expenditure 1985	29.4	352.6
Defence expenditure 1995	50.2	277.8
Defence expenditure as a percentage of GDP 1995	1.1	3.8
ODA 1995	14.5	7.4
ODA to GNP 1995 (%)	0.28	0.1

The FSX or experimental fighter was an aircraft designed to refurbish the Japanese military. By 1988 America had persuaded Japan to modify the original plan and purchase a jointly produced FSX as a means of reducing its trade surplus with the US. A host of US interest groups and Congress itself then claimed that this would be a mechanism of both technological stealing and covert Japanese rearmament. The original plan for direct production by the Japanese would have caused far less friction than the attempt at joint military production.

From 1990 high level diplomacy has converted hitherto vague declarations of an emerging 'Japanese doctrine' into a clearer conception of global partnership. The Bush–Miyazawa meeting of January 1992 in Tokyo confirmed that such a partnership should involve Japan's assumption of more international political and security responsibilities. Table 12.4 indicates the comparative financial burdens of defence systems in 1985 and 1995 set against 1995 expenditures on Overseas Development Assistance.

It becomes clear that to 1995 the US defence burden was in a league quite other than that for Japan, although Japan's commitment had considerably risen in the previous decade. Again, although Japan had also greatly increased its contribution to Pacific and global diplomacy and commercial harmony as measured by the ODA figures to beyond that of the US, the cost of this to the Japanese economic system was insignificant in comparison to the cost of defence to the US economy. The maintenance by Japan of a total of 236,000 regular forces simply did not compare with the maintenance by America of 1,484,000 regular forces in the same year of 1996.

This contrast has led to the claim that a portion of Japanese prosperity has been free-riding upon US defence expenditures in the Pacific and throughout the globe. It is admitted that a great proportion of American expenditure is through NATO and into Europe, to perhaps 30 per cent of the total. Although Japan has shown compliance and at times financial support for actions taken by the US in international crises and conflicts both prior to and since the end of the Cold War, it is argued by many interests within the US that such support should become more of a military partnership, at least in the Pacific and in cooperation with other

Table 12.5 R&D military expenditure, *c.* 1979–83

	R&D in defence (%)	*Military expenditure as percentage of GNP*	*Armed forces as percentage of population*
US	64.3	5.2	0.93
UK	48.8	4.8	0.59
France	36.5	3.9	1.07
Thailand	24.6	3.5	0.49
India	14.1	3.0	0.17
Australia	10.2	2.3	0.23
Germany (FR)	8.5	3.3	0.81
Canada	6.6	1.9	0.34
Japan	5.8	0.9	0.21
Argentina	1.1	2.5	0.57

Table 12.6 R&D expenditure by socio-economic aims, *c.* 1982 (%)

	US (1982)	*Japan (1983)*	*UK (1981)*	*Germany (1984)*	*France (1980)*
Industrial development	0.4	12.6	6.3	10.2	9.3
Energy	6.7	29.1	6.4	14.9	7.5
Transport	2.3	2.9	–	2.1	2.7
Health	11.5	5.2	3.7	3.9	4.4
Advance of knowledge	3.9	3.6	15.2	44.5	22.2
Defence	64.3	5.8	48.8	8.5	36.5
Space	5.5	9.2	1.9	3.9	6.2
Other	5.4	31.6	13.7	12.0	11.2

nations or regional organisations. We may pursue this further by examining the possible effects of different defence expenditures on the industrial R&D capacities of the two systems. Table 12.5 ranks ten nations in terms of the percentage of their R&D expenditure which is committed to defence.

On all measures the US ranks number one. Through the years of noisy system clash, America's innovation system was swamped by Cold-War expenditures of a sort that reduced the mission-oriented R&D expenditure within industry and service sectors. Table 12.6 shows the comparative expenditures on R&D in terms of the socio-economic aims identified by UNESCO.

It is very clear that fast industrial growth in both Japan and Germany was associated with a low commitment to defence which was reflected very directly in their ability to put scarce institutional, skill, training and knowledge resources into immediate industrial R&D activities. The table gives one argument as to how restructuring in Japan was directed at energy saving and high technology industrial pursuits. Hardly surprisingly, the US

Table 12.7 Expenditure and personnel in R&D: Japan and the US, 1983–4

		US	*Japan*
1	All R&D as percentage of GNP	2.7	2.6
2	Total expenditure R&D which is *from* 'productive enterprise' (%)	49.6	75.9
3	Current expenditure *by* 'productive enterprise' as a percentage of all expenditure	73.0	64.8
4	*Manufacturing* R&D expenditure as a percentage of all 'productive sector' expenditure	–	93.4
5	R&D as percentage of GNP deflated for expenditure on *space* and *defence*	0.82	2.21
6	Scientists and engineers per million of population	3,111	4,436
7	Technicians in R&D per million of population	–	810
8	Total number of scientists and engineers in R&D	728,600	531,612
9	Scientists and engineers in 'productive sector' as a percentage of all S and E in R&D	73.5	56.57
10	Scientists and engineers in 'productive sector'	535,600	300,730
11	All scientists and engineers in *higher education*	100,000	187,350
12	Percentage of row 11 who are engaged in engineering and technology studies	20.5	16.4
13	Percentage of row 11 who are engaged in the *natural sciences*	46.0	6.8

Commissioner on Industrial Competitiveness reported in 1984 that science and technology 'need a higher level of attention, greater predictability of support, more coherent policies, and better long range planning to enhance the competitive status of our nation'. Table 12.7 documents in some detail the contrasts in the R&D systems of the two nations at the time in which the Commissioner spoke.

In Japan, over 75 per cent of all expenditure on R&D was raised in 'productive enterprise', but only 65 per cent was expended in that sector. If there was any redistribution effect it was from the private to the public sector. In contrast, in the US only half of all R&D expenditure was formed in the private sector, but that sector spent 73 per cent of all financing. Although Japan boasted considerably more scientists and engineers in higher education than did the US, a lesser percentage was engaged in engineering and technology. Not shown is the fact that Japan had a higher percentage of university personnel engaged in non-technical research, with many nominated scientists being researchers in social and medical fields. At this time in Japan, the universities were not the strategic sector for basic research in science and technology. We might postulate that the long commitment in the US both to close relationships between universities and industry and a military-oriented R&D regime, has meant that a great amount of US

Table 12.8 US government R&D by departments and agencies, 1975 and 1980 (%)

Department/agency	*1975*	*1980*
Departments:		
Agriculture	2.20	2.17
Commerce	1.12	1.08
Defence	47.33	44.13
Energy	10.75	15.01
Health and human services	12.58	11.93
Interior	1.59	1.29
Transportation	1.63	1.14
Agencies:		
Environmental Protection Agency	1.35	1.08
National Aeronautics and Space Administration	16.09	16.04
National Science Foundation	3.12	2.78
Other agencies	2.18	3.32

government-financed research is actually located in the private sector itself, whether institutionally or by military contracting, but has also served to direct much high level applied university research into military and related space systems. Apportioning a very large amount of its budget to atomic, space and defence objectives, the US government provided huge resources through specialised agencies – the most famous being the National Science Foundation, established five years after the end of the Second World War – and into selected industries by means of formal contracts with individual enterprises. In Japan or Germany, where defence R&D is of little importance, such a mechanism is less developed. The agency orientation of the US system of R&D is illustrated in Table 12.8.

During the 1970s and 1980s the dozen or so agencies received general policy directives from the executive office of the President, but once applications had been received by the agencies further distribution within them was remarkably autonomous. The budget office generally took advice on priorities from the Office of Science and Technology Policy, established in 1976. Such a regulated pluralism may not have been productive of that sustained synergy between public policy and private industrial enterprise which we have seen as one hallmark of the Japanese system of that time. In the US, only from 1979 was there any convincing public questioning of the agency-contract system for 'stimulation of innovation in industry to sustain economic growth and improved productivity', but even this did not survive the early years of the Reagan administration and its emphasis on both defence spending and overall budget conservatism. During the early 1980s the great challenge of Japan and a growing belief that existing institutions were failing to provide for even fundamental research led to new attempts at reform. A 1985 report by the Presidential Commission on Industrial Competitiveness recommended that agencies should be rationalised in order to create a Department of Science and Technology to administer all non-defence-related R&D. However, comparison with neither Japan nor Europe provided robust evidence of the economic efficacy of institutional centralism. We would more precisely claim that the barriers to closer relations between R&D fund providers and the applications in the industrial economy were (and still are) found in the enormous expenditures on military R&D together with the workings of the agency-contract system in the neo-civil sector.

This history and institutional complex may only be contrasted with that of Japan. Between 1980 and 1985 expenditure for R&D in Japan rose at an annual average of over 11 per cent amounting to over 3 per cent of GDP in 1985, a surge of spending which came predominantly from the private sector. Over 90 per cent of private enterprise investment in R&D came from manufacturing as such, 30 per cent of this from the electronics industries alone. Enterprise R&D in 1985 took the form principally of product development (64 per cent), followed by general applied research (24 per cent) and basic research (13 per cent). In that year spending on genetic engineering rose by 46 per cent. The dispersement of public funds by the three major Japanese agencies in the years 1985 and 1986 took the pattern indicated in Table 12.9. Of the total science budget, the Science and Technology Agency (STA) received 64 per cent, the Ministry of International Trade and Industry (MITI) 29.5 per cent, and the Ministry of Education, Culture and Science (MECS) 6.5 per cent.

Such agencies did contract with individual corporations in a similar manner to that of the US. Thus Mitsubishi heavy industries were the main contractors for the STA space station project. The difference lies with the strategic position and freedoms of MITI, the industrial impact of which has been outlined in Chapters 8 and 9. MITI spread its influence well beyond direct financing and contracting to provision of incentive allowances, instigation and implementation of the technopolis strategy, telecommunications provisions, the encouragement of venture capital and selective import

Table 12.9 Major activities of agencies in Japanese R&D, 1985 and 1986

STA	*MITI*	*MECS*
Expo '85	Basic technologies for future industries	Maintenance of research systems
Special promotion funds	Agency of Ind. Sci. & Tech.	Energy research:
Space	Sunshine Project (energy)	Nuclear fusion
Nuclear energy	Moonlight Project (energy)	Accelerator programme
Cancer campaign	Fifth generation computer project	Space research
Ocean research	Large-scale industry projects	Marine science
Disaster prevention		Polar researches
ERATO (group research)		Cancer research
		International academic exchange

promotion, little of which was captured in formal R&D aggregates. Thus MITI, STA and others combined to sponsor joint leading-edge applied research which was actually performed in corporate laboratories. Nine of MITI's sixteen national laboratories of the 1980s were located in Tsukuba Science City, northeast of Tokyo. In some cases MITI would fund up to 50 per cent of the research costs of a major project through special conditions loans (*hojokin*), repayable when the recipient could generate profits. In a multitude of ways, the Ministry's R&D activity became privatised as it increasingly acted as an organiser and coordinator of innovative industrial activity. In unison with MITI's continued use of tax credits, patenting legislation and special depreciation allowances, such arrangements helped to induce the very high levels of private industrial R&D.

Conclusions: climacteric causation

An absolutely crucial feature of the US economy in the 1970s was its move westwards. Some 4 million Americans shifted to the Pacific Coast in that decade as the smokestack industries of the frostbelt lost ground to the high-tech industries of the sunbelt. Even the political centre of gravity notably shifted westward – California moved from its quota of twenty-five Congressional Representatives in 1946 to forty-five Representatives by the 1980s. For Ronald Nairn, writing in the *Wall Street Journal* on 15 December 1981, the prospects for the US economic system as a whole were beginning to 'stagger the imagination . . . when we measure the near-optimized market of Europe and its 250 million persons against the near-unoptimized 1.5 billion to 2 billion people of the Pacific basin alone, Europe seems a puny affair'. A year or so later, Sir Oliver Wright, the British Ambassador to Washington, in a speech at Tufts University lamented how the Atlantic had 'grown wider'. Of course, Europe too has grown wider and bigger in the interim, and the Americans were altogether too sanguine concerning the underdeveloped character of Pacific markets. Nevertheless, it is clear that the move of resources westwards took time to furnish any net results for the American system at large. Although the US economy may have been better positioned for global competition by the end of the Cold War, in the meantime there may be little doubt that such a restructuring and relocating occurred alongside a particular expansion of the Japanese economic system, exacerbating the differences in performance and promoting views of inevitable US decline caused by 'unfair' Eastern trade and investment competition.

On pp. 285–95 we argued that the competitive performance of Japan in contrast to the US, especially in the 1970s and 1980s, was not a result of unfair trading, but of underlying determinants of performance centred on the actual behaviour of the private and public sectors. Here we might more formally theorise that our modern climacteric of catch-up and take-over, is explicable in terms of *late development effects*, and that the case for cultural causation has yet to be made. Even the high defence expenditures of the US and the so-called 'free ride' of the Japanese are inexplicable in cultural terms but perfectly accountable in general historical terms. The earlier industrial and technological sophistication of the US helps explain the course of events in the war of 1942–5 (or 1937–45), the character of the American occupation and the global position of the US in the Cold War. The resultant high expenditures on defence and space programmes in turn served as a major constraint on American economic performance and hence on the behaviour of American private enterprise. More generally, as postulated in Figure 12.1, earlier development makes it the more likely that any large system will be both highly sophisticated and inflexible, productive of world-class core developments on a given trajectory, less able to adapt to changing circumstance, to new markets or industries. Other things being equal, that is, *discounting cultural difference entirely*, then the private enterprise sector and its external economic and socio-cultural environment, are likely to exhibit less flexibility than the equivalent institutions as forged and reinvented in late developers. This contrast is more likely to be reflected in differential economic performance in a period of paradigmatic change in technologies. *That is, enterprise culture does not directly reflect a nation's culture in a broad sense, but is simply a congery of behaviours within enterprise which emerges from a conjuncture of historical, technological and institutional forces.*

Modifying von Clausewitz's adage we might reflect that in everything but war it is easier to take ground than to hold it: catching-up is ever with us. The catch-up which has dominated the global system since the initial post-war recovery of Europe has been that centred on the expansion of the Japanese economy and its East Asian ramifications. This has not disturbed the central logic of a global capitalism that has been centred somewhere in the Atlantic since the eighteenth century and that can boast the recent seemingly final victory over state socialist systems. But it has involved a climacteric shift of capitalism from metal-based industries to knowledge-based industries, from industry to services, and from the Atlantic towards the Pacific. It has disturbed old understandings and what were fondly but often mistakenly thought to be 'gentlemen's agreements' about what was good in the world and how that world should be run in order to promote such a good. It is this which has been for more than a generation at the centre of the US–Japanese antagonism. But as Chomsky spotted back in the early 1970s it is precisely what we have here referred to as the central logic of a global capitalism which defines the limits of such antagonism as demonstrated on the global platform (pp. 281–5), between transnational corporations (pp. 285–9) or in disputes over global defence strategies (pp. 289–95). Chomsky's more vivid new 'co-prosperity sphere' of the 1970s has transmogrified into the contemporary notion of collective leadership in global development, which may have at its bifocal centre both the US and Japan, but can no longer be envisaged in the absence of China and Europe as much more than voices off stage. As Peter Drysdale summarised in 1988, an increasing 'leadership role for Japan must be found within a pluralist structure of world economic power, encompassing the effective representation of broader Pacific and global interests, as well as those of the United States and Europe'. Since then, the continued economic success of mainland China and the collapse of the political and economic systems in Russia and Eastern Europe add much further real evidence of multi-polar power relations and the essential commonality of interests between the two capitalist superpowers. Tensions between capitalist superpowers do not a revolution make.

Notes

1 The theory of transition through institutional change towards liberalisation of markets cannot draw clearly from Latin American experience, which is thus neglected in our general account. The nations of this region differ radically in institutional ethos from both Europe and developing East Asia. Particularly they may be characterised as demonstrating poor compliance with laws and regulations; vicious social tension arising from very great maldistributions of wealth in nations of strong elites many of whose economic allegiances lie outside the indigenous economy; large unreformed latifundia in agriculture and inefficient industries bolstered by government subsidies; politically weak governments with a low level of tax base which thereby preside over failures in the provision of public goods and social transfers; large foreign debt, low savings and investment, frequent inflation and capital flight. A short reflection will show how such features work as a negative feedback system based on regressive institutions.

2 It was SCAP who invited Deming, originally a statistician, to Japan in 1947, and in 1950 the Union of Japanese Scientists and Engineers invited him back to deliver lectures on quality control, the first of an almost annual series as well as a multitude of contacts and influences lasting to Deming's death in 1993. The notion of using statistical analysis to maintain control over quality of production was adopted in Japan rather than in the US, and an annual Deming Award remains much-coveted in Japan today. For, therefore, perhaps the greatest irony of all, see the works by Deming, Aguayo and Tsutsui listed in the bibliography.

3 When Ohira became PM in December 1978 he had already formulated his version of *Sōgō anzen hoshō senryaku*, or a 'comprehensive security strategy', which was stipulated on the belief that Japan could be made secure without military expansion.

4 This was not peculiar to the US. Whilst working in Sydney, the present author was woken up at 6 a.m. on more than one occasion by establishment and right-wing radio and television interviewers determined to unearth a negative tone about both the state of Japanese society and the likely conservative backlash within Japan upon news of the Emperor's death. The latter was seen as a potential threat to Australian security interests by at least one such, well-known journalist.

5 A large government deficit increases the public sector borrowing requirement and thus puts pressure on the capital market and the rate of interest. Interest rates were certainly some function of such 'crowding out', as the US government failed to either reduce expenditure or raise tax revenue.

References

Elton, Ben (1991) *Gridlock*, London, quote page 166.

Popov, Vladimir (1997) 'A fresh look at the transition debate', *Wider Angle*, Helsinki: World Institute for Development Economics Research, UNU, no. 2/96, January, quote page 3.

Chomsky, Noam (1973) *For Reasons of State*, London: Collins and Fontana, quote page 71. The term was drawn from the use by John G. Roberts (1971) 'The American Zaibatsu', *Far Eastern Economic Review*, 24 July.

'American Influence in Japan' (in Japanese), *Jiji Shimpo*, 28 June 1884.

Kennedy, Paul (1989) *The Rise and Fall of the Great Powers*, New York: Vintage Books, quote page 347.

Lockwood, W. W. (1936) *Trade and Trade Rivalry Between the United States and Japan*, American Council, New York, Institute of Pacific Relations, quote page 62.

Hood, N. and Young, S. (1979) *The Economics of Multinational Enterprise*, London, quote page 18.

Abramovitz, Moses (1986) 'Catching up, forging ahead, and falling behind', *Journal of Economic History*, 46, see especially page 385.

Nishimizu, M. and Jorgenson, D. W. (1978) 'US and Japanese economic growth, 1952–1974: an international comparison', *Economic Journal*, 88, see especially pages 721–6.

Fallows, James (1989) 'Containing Japan', *The Atlantic Monthly*, 263(5) May, quote pages 41 and 42.

Saxonhouse, Gary R. (1986) 'Japan's intractable trade surpluses in a new era', *The World Economy*, 9(3) (September) quote page 240.

Drysdale, Peter (1988) 'Japan as a Pacific and world economic power', *Pacific Economic Papers*, Research School of Pacific Studies, ANU, Canberra, No. 166, December, quote pages 8 and 25.

Dertouzos, Michael L. *et al.* and the MIT Commission on Industrial Productivity (1989) *Made in America: Regaining the Productive Edge*, Cambridge, MA: MIT Press, quotes from pages 66, 67, 79, 162.

Morikawa, H. (1975) *Gijutsusha-Nihon Kindaika no ninaite*, Nihon keizai Shimbunsha, Tokyo.

Sources for tables and statistical data

World Military and Social Expenditure 1983, Leesburg US, 1983 (Table 12.4).

US Arms Control and Disarmament Agency (from 1984) *World Military Expenditures and Arms Transfers*, Annual, Washington, DC.

Japan Weekly Mail, 8 February 1913 (Table 12.1 etc).

Statistical Abstract of the United States 1982–83, Bureau of the Census, Washington, 1983, page 548 Table 925 for data in Table 12.2. etc.

Bergsten, C. Fred and Cline, W. R. (1988) *The US–Japan Economic Problem*, Washington, Institute of International Economics.

Azumi, K. (1985) 'Nippon Kigyo wa Dokusosei Yutaka', *Nihon keizai Shimbun*, 30 November, and (1987) 'Creativity of Japanese companies', *Japan Foundation Newsletter*, 14, for Table 12.3.

UNESCO (1986) *Statistical Yearbook*, Paris (Tables 12.5–8).

Business International Corporation (1984) *Worldwide Economic Indicators, Annual Comparative Statistics for 131 Countries with World and Regional Reports*, New York.

The World Bank (1981) *World Development Report 1981*, Oxford: Oxford University Press.

UNESCO (1984) *Manual for Statistics on Scientific and Technological Activities*, doc. UNESCO ST84/WS/12.

US National Science Foundation, *Federal R&D Funding by Budget Function*, Washington DC, annual, which uses sixteen categories comparable with UNESCO definitions of socio-economic aims.

Further reading

Aguayo, R. (1990) *Dr Deming: The American who taught the Japanese about Quality*, New York: Lyle Stuart.

Battistini, L. H. (1960) *The Rise of American Influence in Asia and the Pacific*, Michigan State University Press.

Bellon, B. and Niosi, J. (1988) *The Decline of the American Economy*, Montreal: Black Rose Books.

The Business Roundtable (1987) *American Excellence in a World Economy*, New York: The Business Roundtable.

Cohen, S. S. and Zysman, J. (1987) *Manufacturing Matters: The Myth of the Post-Industrial Society*, New York: Basic Books.

Deming, W. E. (1982) *Out of the Crisis*, Cambridge: Cambridge University Press.

Destler, I. M. *et al.* (1979) *The Textile Wrangle: Conflict in Japan–American relations 1969–71*, Ithica: Cornell University Press.

Dunn, L. (1983) *In the Kingdom of the Blind: A Report on Protectionism and the Asia-Pacific Region*, London: Trade Policy Research Centre, Special Report No. 3.

Hayes, R. H. and Abernathy, W. J. (1980) 'Managing our way to economic decline', *Harvard Business Review*, 58: 67–77.

Heiduk, G. and Yamamura, K. (eds) (1990) *Technological Competition and Interdependence. The Search for Policy in the United States, West Germany and Japan*, Tokyo: University of Tokyo Press.

Inkster, I. (1991) 'Made in America but lost to Japan: science, technology and economic performance in the two capitalist superpowers', *Social Studies of Science*, 21.

Inkster, I. (1993) 'Education, human capital and technical change in Japan – a skeptical evaluation', *East Asia*, 6.

Inkster, I. (1996) 'Into the twentieth century: patterns in the relations between science, technology and the state during the early industrialisation process', in Martine Barrere (ed.) *Sciences et Développement*, Paris: ORSTOM Editions.

Iriye, A. (ed.) (1975) *Mutual Images*, Cambridge, MA: Harvard University Press.

Johnson, C. (1995) *Japan, Who Governs? The Rise of the Developmental State*, New York: W. W. Norton.

Kamei, S. (1976) 'Japanese see America: a century of firsthand impressions', *The Japan Interpreter*, 11(1) (Spring).

Krugman, P. (1990) *The Age of Diminished Expectations. US Economic Policy in the 1990s*, Cambridge, MA: MIT Press.

Lincoln, E. J. (1990) *Japan's Unequal Trade*, Washington, DC: The Brooking's Institution.

Maswood, S. J. (1997–8) 'Revisionism Work? US trade strategy and the 1995 US–Japan auto dispute', *Pacific Affairs*, 70.
The President's Commission on Industrial Competitiveness (1985) *Global Competition: The New Reality*, Washington, DC: US Government Printing Office.
Prestowitz, C. V. (1988) *Trading Places: How America Allowed Japan to take the Lead*, Tokyo: Tuttle.
Schwarz, J. E. and Volgy, T. J. (1985) 'The myth of America's economic decline', *Harvard Business Review*, 63(5).
Shimada, H. (1992) 'Japanese capitalism: the irony of success', *Economic Eye*, Autumn.
Stewart, T. A. (1991) 'The new American century: where we stand', *Fortune Magazine*, Spring–Summer.
Tsutsui, W. M. (1998) *Manufacturing Ideology. Scientific Management in Twentieth-Century Japan*, Princeton, NJ: Princeton University Press.
Tsutsui, W. M. (1998) 'W. Edwards Deming and the origins of quality control in Japan', *Journal of Japanese Studies*, 22(2) (Summer).
van Wolferen, K. G. (1987/7) 'The Japan problem', *Foreign Affairs*, 65(2) (Winter).
Vogel, E. (1970) 'Pax Nipponica', *Foreign Affairs*, 8(4).
Yashiro, N. (1994) 'The Hiraiwa report: goals of economic recovery', *Economic Eye*, Spring.

13 Reflections on Japan

Social causation and capitalist maturity

During the 1970s and 1980s, the continued success of the economy encouraged the view that specific, perhaps unique, cultural and social forces were at work in Japan, encouraging thrift, hard work, loyalty to business enterprises, and responsiveness to the guidelines laid down by a growth-centred political system. With the slowing down of Japanese growth in the 1990s this sort of perspective faded, to be replaced by assertions concerning the failure of Japanese society to support a more mature, complex capitalist system. On one hand it was argued that the social characteristics of Japan are not of the sort that will sustain further expansions in the economy and in social welfare in the coming century. On the other hand, it was also suggested that economic growth has occurred too fast, at the cost of retardation in social and psychic welfare, that capitalist success has kept Japanese democracy at bay, and that Japan is a powerful example of the problems of aggressive capitalism – socially divisive and environmentally disastrous.

The inadequacy of such perspectives may be easily summarised – Japanese society is in many respects similar to that found in other industrial economies, it is not homogeneous and so cannot be dismissed in generalisation, and many Japanese institutions are of recent vintage rather than of ancient lineage.[1] In addition, late-development and the activities of the occupation forces (Chapter 7) together explain much that seems at first sight unique. Clearly, the exigencies of relative backwardness from the late nineteenth century stimulated the direct industrial interventions of the state in an environment in which normal trade protection was forbidden, just as the importance of elite networks, such as those surrounding the tremendous influence of the University of Tokyo, is explicable in terms of the deliberate creation of an industrial meritocracy at a time of Western technological superiority. The high rate of personal savings may be attributable to a lag in social welfare systems accompanying fast industrialisation from a low base. Again, the disproportionate importance of agrarian interests in modern Japan may be thought of as a reflection of a time-lag in the adoption of Western ways due to the strength of rural traditions, but it might be better seen as a direct outcome of the occupation land reforms, which removed much tenancy, transferred land to small-owner households and thereby encouraged a trend towards dual occupations that has led to a society in which stake-holder agrarianism is common.

If we must beware of too-ready generalisation we might nevertheless address the possibility that Japanese industrial society has benefited especially from the character of the social institutions in which it is embedded, and that the present downturn in economic growth has resulted from either some key change in such characteristics or from the failure of such older social formations to carry growth through industrial catch-up into capitalist maturity. One of the more convincing of approaches is that which focuses on loyalties and duties, on the historical relations between individual obligations and group identities, a theme that we first broached in Chapter 2, pp. 15–20. The emphasis on elements of groupism (hierarchy, loyalty, seniority, all bonded by complex obligations) is frequently set within arguments concerning Japanese-style Confucianism, as in Morishima's approach to the long history of Japan's economic development. Here, the individualism of the 'Western model' is set against the needs of late-development, where the prime requirement was to harness the innovations of the advanced economies to the attributes of Japan without undue or costly social disturbance. According to Koschmann, inherent to the social system which emerged during and after Meiji, 'are the preservation of harmony through repression of conflict and the failure of a universal concept of individual rights to fully replace power as the central principle of hierarchical relationships', perhaps best represented in Nitobe's summary of *Bushidō* (the *samurai* 'way of the warrior') as that which forged Japanese society as 'an encampment'. The question arises as to whether such cultural elements were naturally and comprehensively formative of industrial development or whether they were deliberately mobilised by a modernising elite bent on survival and success at all costs, as seems to be suggested in Koschmann's formulation. The first possibility inscribes an ancient cultural story, the second a tale of power and intent under conditions of relative economic backwardness operating primarily (but by no means solely) in the nineteenth century.

The cultural story was given credence generally through the cultural anthropology of 1946 and beyond. American observers like Ruth Benedict isolated specific cultural features, such as the reciprocal obligational system, which Japan owed 'to no Chinese Confucianism and to no Oriental Buddhism', thus effectively isolating Japanese culture, and thereby the Japanese industrial trajectory, from other East Asian experience. In turn, Japanese analysts have transposed general theories of culture to specific institutions in the private sector. Obligational relations determine specific characteristics of household and family, and these translate into private enterprise characteristics such as the lifetime-employment system and the whole framework of 'vertical stratification by institution or group of institutions', which leads to the networking and consensus-formation associated with Kaisha business and production organisation, (see Chapter 9, pp. 180–9).

Such conceptions are nominally neat and serve to isolate Japan as unique within Asia and thus appear to address the specific cultural causes of Japanese success. But the simple cultural argument suffers from obvious drawbacks. The approaches tend to slide over such terms as 'lead to' or 'follow from', i.e. what precisely is the historical relation between Japanese culture on the one hand and particular institutions in the private enterprise sector on the other? Second, post-war cultural anthropology and its successors tended to exaggerate social homogeneity and depended on problematic psychological assumptions concerning 'national' motivation and response. Third, as we have suggested, institutional innovations may be direct outcomes of late-development and post-war reforms introduced by the Western occupying forces.

It might be expected that the confusions and reverses of '*Endaka* Society' may offer short-term evidence for or against the cultural argument. That is, if Japanese social institutions are now undergoing severe alteration, is this because they no longer serve the interests of economic growth, or has the failure of industrial growth during the 1990s itself undermined the veracity of key institutions? Is cultural change a function of increased influence from abroad, accelerated by globalisation and international media technologies, or is it an outcome of catch-up and a greater capitalist maturity? Have some key cultural variables withstood the test of economic downturn and survived as strategic institutions or behaviour patterns into the twenty-first century? Certainly, the notion of lifetime employment has become less attractive to young graduates, saving for house purchase has given way to spending on luxuries, travel overseas has shifted cultural perceptions and material expectations. The land boom of earlier years (see Chapter 9) has provided opportunities outside industry as well as for closer alliances between the black markets of the youth culture, older gangsterism and right-wing political parties. More trenchantly, the suburban localities of the contract and casual workers, the small firms and the self-employed that were a necessary component of fast late-development in the modern enterprise system, have become in many cases wasteland communities, eroded by under-investment in necessary infrastructures through time, and infested increasingly by an *endaka* underbelly of youth gangs and *furōsha* (street tramps).

Whether any or all of this measures a reason for Japan's poor industrial performance in the 1990s, or is predictive of future economic decline, is another matter entirely. Japanese industrialisation always carried its negative impacts along with it. As we have seen for the earlier twentieth century, such failures of distribution or investment in welfare were merely more visible during economic downturns. More importantly, it remains feasible that many of the key institutional characteristics of Japanese industry were always features of late-development and thus temporary phenomena, tractable with catch-up. In this view an erosion of the Three Treasures does not spell an erosion of some 'underlying' Japanese culture.

More likely is the case that social change in Japan may not be dramatic *enough*. The institutions of late-development may not be those required in a climacteric world economy of services and 'dot com', in the ever shifting but growing non-industrial sectors of tourism, leisure, sport, entertainment and the 'life-needs' of the growing number of older, retired people inhabiting not only Japan but all the prosperous nations of the world. This vision is behind the present movement within Japan for wholesale reform of major national institutional structures, from the political system to the working of education and public health. A most recent manifestation of this view is the report entitled 'The Frontier Within: Individual Empowerment and Better Governance in the New Millennium' that was commissioned by former Prime Minister Keizo Obuchi but handed down to his successor in mid-January 2000. This is a report that advocates the reform of education, the use of English and Asian languages in the school curriculum and in public places, a greater ease of entry for foreign residents, and the creation of a 'global literacy' that welcomes the new, embraces creativity and fights all precedents. More importantly, the Commission overtly attacks the institutions of late-development as those which have 'ossified society and the economy and leached Japan's vitality' and calls for the construction of a new relationship between the individual citizen and the public domain. With reference to the latter, the new view is that the old hierarchical governance has ignored the potential rewards of 'creative tension between those who entrust authority and those entrusted with authority', a suggestion that strikes at the heart of groupism and hierarchy.

This report is one significant link in a chain of reform proposals stemming back to the 1970s. However, for reasons already sketched, there seems to be little evidence that the effective limits of Japanese industry lie more with Japanese culture than with Japan's immediate relations with the wider world, as postulated in Chapters 10–12. In the rest of this chapter we argue that many so-called 'cultural' attributes are in fact behavioural outcomes of the working of Japanese institutions, many of which have no ancient lineage. So, high personal savings have related to low public investment in insurance and health, a strong work ethos may have reflected a high level of indirect reward to work, the long-term investment and technological horizons of private enterprise were outcomes of long-term bank financing and relative technological backwardness. These counter-arguments have been advanced throughout this text and serve to both reduce the saliency of cultural explanation *per se*, and lead to a reasonable expectation that catch-up would inevitably weaken the institutional basis for such behavioural outcomes. This does not necessarily implicate culture as more broadly conceived. Second, we posit that 'cultural engineering', the selection and mobilisation of cultural attributes was of greater importance historically than the mere existence of such attributes. Third, we argue that a key to Japanese success lies in the process whereby this cultural engineering shifted from its original location in a crude, growth-oriented public sector into a private sector which devised specific institutional innovations in order to capitalise on such deliberate cultural manipulations. Whatever the inadequacies and costs of the interventions of the Japanese state in industrial transformation, a sure benefit to the private sector was the relative ease with which enterprise could subsequently devise institutional innovations, such as the Three Treasures, which were overtly geared towards the fast expansion of the industrial and commercial sectors in the absence of effective dissent from workers, intellectuals or ideologues.

Fundamentals: late development and technology transfer

If Japanese industrialisation depended on the transfer of technologies from other nations, it is equally true that the success of this developmental strategy depended on much more than elite intent and investment resources. As previous chapters have demonstrated, transferred techniques were justified by ideas and harboured within institutions. Such generic requirements of major programmes of technology transfer, indeed, explain why they have so frequently failed, why the great liberal project for 'third world' development in the twentieth century came normally to nothing. Transfers over time from areas of advancement to areas of relative backwardness involved both a linear movement of technologies between systems as well as a horizontal movement of information transfer from the level of reliable knowledge and research towards its applications, improved design and commercialisation. For Japan from the beginnings of Meiji or even earlier, both types of transfer were crucial to late industrialisation. In the absence of something of a learning process, costly transfers would have faced diminishing returns as internal capabilities failed to keep up with the increased sophistications of advanced techniques. Clearly, in this case learning was captured alongside technology, for Japan was one of the few nations of the world in which strong programmes of technology transfer were paralleled in sustained developments in indigenous technological capacity associated with the search, selection and modification process described in Chapters 4 and 6. It was this combination that measured the deeper success of Japanese industrialisation.

Particularly prior to 1890, much was accomplished in the face of a manifest lack of investment funds, yet without resort to foreign capital but utilising the mechanisms of foreign trading firms. From then a major mechanism was the acquirement by foreign producing firms of minority interest in Japanese firms in exchange for patent rights or equipment, and this involved such famous global technological agents as Siemens, Otto Wolff and General Electric and such fundamental techniques as the Haber-Bosch and Fischer-Tropsch.[2] During the 1930s licensing predominated, especially in engineering and shipbuilding, and was increasingly dominated by the *zaibatsu* firms. Indeed, the increased costs of transfer and of patent rights exacerbated existing market concentration, particularly during the 1927–31 years of speedy catch-up in the technologies of the heavy industries. The relatively low dependency on foreign capital and the very fast growth of the Japanese engineering industry suggest that these years saw the emergence of technological sovereignty, aided by the subsidies of government and its spreading military contracts, which together induced the rapid growth of Mitsui, Nissan and Mitsubishi. Government further assisted autonomy with research institutes and scientific missions directed at specific industries, metallurgy and nitrogen fixation. After the occupation, licensing and technology importing remained crucial to industrialisation, but were joined by a much more formidable array of public sector interventions. The Japan Development Bank's policies of cheap loans to innovating firms was followed by MITI's policy of monitoring new industries through information gathering and dispersal, provision of loans and licences, and tax assistance and cartelisation. Such interventions were also important in the control of declining industries during the 1970s and 1980s and took the form of retraining schemes and equipment conversion.

All of this suggests certain crucial features. Local screening of the most appropriate techniques was important and lay primarily in private hands, whilst bureaucracy deterred transfers into non-strategic industries. The major agency harbouring foreign technique was the large firm, whether originally a trader, a *zaibatsu* or a *keiretsu* enterprise. Large network structures permitted cooperation in decision-making, the pooling of information, search and research facilities, and the sharing of risks, and were enabled to institute chains of incremental innovation, necessary for the adaptive absorption of advanced techniques designed for other systems. Network firms in the private sector and their several connections with the public sector and with long-term bank financing, generated a complex that encouraged research cooperation between otherwise competing firms and through transfer agreements with foreign firms such as Honeywell (with NEC) or General Electric (with Toshiba).

Although much has been claimed concerning government encouragement of high technology industries in the 1980s and 1990s, many of the more advanced areas owed more to private sector financing and skills, as in the early move towards the private sector funding of the applied life sciences, core developments in microelectronics, the huge increase of Japanese patenting in the US, or the high-tech diversifications of firms such as Kōbe Steel (into biotechnology) and NKK (into electronics). Similarly, much has been written about catch-up and the necessity for the Japanese system to lurch into core creativity. The case remains unproven, for the Japanese enterprise may still retain its lead in the capture and commercialisation of core breakthroughs, wherever they may occur. Here the government might play a vital role through cooperative schemes for private–government research and development and through international participation in such large projects as the Human Frontiers Project.

We may generalise that Japanese history illustrates the fundamental importance to technology transfer of institutional adaptation, which utilises indigenous assets and foreign resources of ideology and institutional practice. Japan was aided by its size and the density of its population settlement and markets. Distance acts as friction within the mechanisms of information and technology transfer or diffusion, and in Japan effective distance had been further reduced by the communications and transport improvements of the Tokugawa period. So, mundane factors are important. Dense settlement on navigable rivers, high levels of urbanism and good roads, as emphasised in Chapter 2, may be of far greater importance to effective technology transfers than any number or category of cultural traits. Again, the character of transfer mechanisms is vital. Japan utilised trade and patents, joint agreements and American aid. It is at times forgotten that the total flow of private and official US capital into Japan, much of which embodied very advanced techniques, reached a peak at the end of the 1950s, the time of Japan's move into 'miracle' economic growth.

Dynamics: cultural engineering

We have suggested that on several grounds any argument from culture requires modification. To enrol an extremely long-term factor (culture) in order to explain a relatively short-term result (industrialisation) might be to take a hammer to a gnat. More promising is the notion that at crucial points of industrial transformation, particular cultural traits were mobilised in order to secure a result at relatively low cost to the public sector. Furthermore, we might postulate that this process of cultural engineering passed from the institutions of the public sector to those of the private sector sometime in the years between 1912 and 1937, but that this shift was quickened by the institutional innovations introduced during the years of post-war occupation.

It is not enough to claim that Japan has always borrowed cultural and material artefacts from other places and then engineered them into indigenous cultural forms. Although it is certain that traditional Japan revamped Shintoism, sanctified a borrowed emperor system, and generally took over Chinese conceptions of centralised administration as well as literary forms, the same talent for absorption may be found in the histories of China or of Korea. But it was Japan that industrialised. Although we would adhere to the theory that the contrast stems from a group of mundane factors – as described – we would add to this the particular factor that only in Japan in the more modern period were so many public resources brought to bear on the more recent great adsorptions, those involving advanced machinery from the West. Interpretation becomes a matter of degree, but much seems to centre on the ability of a sovereign state system to choose and sustain a reform project that utilised existing mores and belief systems and depended on freedom from colonial intrusions.

The Tokugawa instruments of cultural suasion that we described in Chapter 2, *sankin kōtai*, isolationism, revivals of Confucianism and so on, may be interpreted as part of the institutionalised response to the outside world. During the crises of late Tokugawa, *bushidō* was enlisted as a means of control and Harootunian has written of how *samurai* values were 'transmuted and creatively adapted, became the emblem of an entire society and in the process the class was robbed of whatever special identity it once possessed.' The equivalent in Meiji was the commutation of stipends, the award of property rights in land, and compulsory primary education, all surrounding the Imperial proclamation of 1868 demanding the rejection of the totality of 'absurd customs of former times'. But the media of cultural suasion were even more insidious. Thus the 'Civilisation Ball Song' invited the children of Japan to recite the ten objects of Western culture while bouncing a ball to an emphatic beat of repeated listings: gas lamps, horse carriages, steam engines, cameras, lightning conductors, telegrams, newspapers, schools, letter post, steam boats. During Meiji, Shintoism was once more revamped and the Imperial rescript of 1890 emphasised an official version of native customs, ancestor worship and filial piety. In this, cultural engineering rode on the back of very large expenditures on human capital formation, to a level far greater than any direct public investment in the industrial programme itself. Expenditure on mass education during Meiji reached perhaps 1,000 million yen, about 30 per cent of all local government expenditure. Reformulated mass education was a main vehicle of cultural engineering, with basic texts offering the 'most important means of instilling values among the people'. Of real significance, in the important years of 1873–7 when there was a heightened drive towards industrialisation (see Chapter 3) some 43 per cent of all government expenditure took the form of human capital formation, from basic education through to income transfers as compensation for loss of feudal incomes.

If we define culture as the values and norms of an historical social system, then it seems likely that the intrusion of vastly different foreign technologies and ideologies will necessarily stimulate a degree of cultural crisis. In this sense, culture becomes a limiting factor in industrialisation, in a manner analogous to the supply of investment funds. Just as in the latter case, success came to those systems that both mobilised such investments and transformed them into new technical processes and products, so too in late-developers the mobilisation and transformation (through selection and reification of particulate traits or traditions) of cultural assets was a key to success.[3] But this process depended for its sustenance as much on mundane factors, those of public financing and institutions (e.g. schools) and upon spatial and communications givens, as it ever did upon the original character of the cultural stock. This may be our best explanation of the contrasting industrial histories of Japan, China and Korea in the nineteenth century and beyond.

The culture of enterprise

There have been many approaches to Japanese enterprise that have directly linked its outstanding characteristics as reflexes of the national culture in which such enterprise is embedded. Perhaps the best known is Ōuchi's 'Theory Z', which draws a fairly exact parallel between the slow and traditional emergence of Japanese clans and the more modern version of 'industrial clans', and therefore concludes that features of coherence and stability within enterprise are functions of cultural history.[4] Following this argument, Giddens has summarised that in Japanese firms 'there is far more effort to secure consultation at all levels, and to encourage a developed sense of corporate loyalty'. In opposition to such a style of argument, in Chapter 12, pp. 285–9 we suggested that enterprise 'culture' could be considered the product of an amalgam of internal and external processes, whereby the institutional forms and behaviour of private enterprise in an early industrialiser might be expected to differ from those of any late developer. Given some agreement with this second perspective, it becomes difficult to move directly from a judgement about a 'national' culture to any necessary argument about industrial 'enterprise culture', for there cannot be any direct identities between the two, mediated as they are by the relative stage of development, public policy framework, commanding technologies and institutional imperatives – in the latter case these incorporate relations with other private, non-industrial institutions such as banks, schools or universities. Then the cultural question concerns the historical development of particular institutional formulations within private enterprise. If such features of Japanese business as groupism and familialism, *kanban* or just-in-time may be traced to exogenous cultural forces, may these themselves be traced to a concomitant or earlier process of cultural engineering in the public sector? Historically, has cultural engineering in the public sector acted as a positive external economy in the growth of Japanese private enterprise, with the existing 'cultural stock' acting as a permissive factor only?[5]

It seems certain that the 1950s was the time when the public sector most deliberately attempted to transfer cultural engineering out of the public sector and into the structure of private enterprise itself. Acting under a certain weight of American influence, the Japanese Labour Ministry and MITI proposed the establishment of a Japan Productivity Centre in 1951 that adopted a mix of Western management styles but in doing so overtly harnessed them to notions of groupism and familialism. Prior to and since that time it is possible to identify many instances of deliberate fostering by corporations themselves of corporate familialism based on 'imitation of the family' strategies. Is it possible to devise any test of the strength of such cultural engineering? The social changes of *endaka* Japan and the so-called 'Asian crisis' of the late 1990s (see Chapters 9 and 10) and the sudden weakening of modern corporate forms does suggest that the latter were not deeply entrenched within an underlying Japanese culture. In particular, the enterprise labour system characterised by lifetime employment, enterprise unions and seniority wages was under threat as soon as industry suffered lower real growth. This suggests that enterprise forms in Japan are more malleable than might be expected in the 'strong' cultural model. Second, we do not perceive the same 'cultural' modes of behaviour and social relations in other parts of the industrial economy. For every salaryman working under model conditions there are several casual and contract workers operating under unsafe, insecure and sweated conditions, in which work relations are not even a pale reflection of those posited by the analysts of the modern enterprise. Why did the culture of consensus and respect not permeate all corners? The answer may simply be that it was an engineered culture, created for specific purposes in appropriate sites.

Japan in the new climacteric

Few global pundits would have predicted in the 1980s that by late 1999 Japan's annual rate of economic growth would have fallen below 1 per cent, nor that this would have contrasted with over 4 per cent in the US and some 2 per cent in Britain. Although the industrial production growth rate in Japan remained at around 3 per cent and equivalent to that of the US, the overall performance for the entire 1990s seemed to mark a real turning-phase in industrial history, one that demonstrated the weaknesses of Japan's peculiar institutional relations, public policy and market development. Rather than joining in the global chorus proclaiming the fall of Japan, an argument that follows from this book, particularly Chapters 9–12, is that such variance amongst industrial and commercial leaders is a principal feature of the years since the collapse of the golden age *c.* 1971. The subsequent years have witnessed a profound global shift from the Atlantic towards the Pacific. In particular, for the first time on such a scale, East Asian development arose from a series of institutional and political reforms that acted as necessary conditions for the full and sovereign capture of Western capital and technologies. Following the earlier Japanese lead, the new industrialising economies reformed their public institutions and policies, gave greater attention to guidance than to autocratic planning, and prepared the way for greater Western commercial involvement. By the beginning of the 1990s the US was already now in massive trade deficit to Asia – annual trade deficits approximated at $60 billion with Japan (population at 122 million or 50 per cent that of the US), 25 billion with China (1,072 million or 435 per cent), 11 billion with Taiwan (20 million or 8 per cent), 7 billion with Thailand (54 million or 20 per cent) and 7 billion with Malaysia (17 million or 7 per cent).

As has been suggested, several commentators have taken the poor growth performance of the Japanese economy in the 1990s to represent a real turning-point in the global balance of economic power. But, in a more stark reality, the new millennium opened with Japan as the major ally of the industrial West. Whatever the view (and the astonishing neglect) offered by the US media, Japan remains a major partner of American commercial, political and military ambitions, not only in the Pacific but at the global level. Japan's economy is seven times the size of China's and accounts for 65 per cent of East Asia's total economic output. American military bases in Japan continue to be vital to Washington's global military strategies. The 1990–1 Gulf War, together with continued tensions across the Taiwan Strait from 1996, have encouraged some increase of Japan's military capabilities and pressure for revision of Article 9 in the Constitution, which commits Japan to 'forever renounce war as a sovereign right'. This outward move has been consistently supported by the US, eager to discount expenditures in the Pacific through Japanese financial and hardware support of American forces, but has recently been reinforced by advisers seeking a more independent military role in the face of North Korea's launching of ballistic missiles into Japanese airspace and incursions of military shipping into Japanese territorial waters. Modernisation in China has been associated with an increase in military expenditure of around 10 per cent per annum between 1988 and 1997 and is an important aspect of Japan's global vision which is often neglected by Western commentators.[6] The recent Asian economic crisis has led to some deflation of national military programmes alongside affirmation of the importance of the ASEAN Regional Forum and a variety of bilateral security dialogues involving Japan, the US, China and Russia. Within this complex post-Cold-War framework, the Japan–US bilateral security arrangements are, in the words of Masahiro Akiyama, probably the 'world's most important bilateral relationship in all political, economic and security aspects', and were strongly reaffirmed in the Joint Declaration of April 1996.

More importantly, diplomacy and short-term fluctuations should not be confused with major global turning points. Clinton's America surfs the wave of success at a time of Asian financial panic. But the American economy still depends for its long-term growth on private sector institutions, public sector welfare, defence, and global commitments, and social and urban infrastructures which remain little touched by 3 per cent growth, West-coast fashions, and Presidential visits to China. The underlying features of the modern global climacteric include major shifts in technology, the relocation of new industries and services, the altered character of economic and political interactions between nation states, and the rising importance of super-national regions and non-national sites of activity. Although we have highlighted major tendencies in Chapters 10–12, it is far too early to define the exact contours of that global shift, and there is no theory that excludes America and Europe from competitive resurgence. But there is just as little evidence to show that the achievements of the Asia-Pacific over the last thirty years were illusory, partial or subject to reversion. The well-known economist Joseph Stiglitz was right when in February 1998 he reiterated the reality of the East Asian 'miracle', which had created 'higher standards of living for hundreds of millions of Asians', and which 'will be far more permanent than the present turmoil'.

In the case of Japan *per se*, we would argue that a longer, historical perspective does serve to identify a conjunction of a growing social, economic and industrial maturity with the global switch to a new climacteric. Both these forces have been working since the early 1970s, but they did not combat the high rate of Japanese industrial growth because of huge opportunities of economic expansion, many of which were exploited (Chapters 10–12), and because surplus labour and technological-lag combined to increase the efficiencies of the production system well into the 1980s. No other large industrial system faced such a combined effect over this same period. An historical perspective might also emphasise that the location of Japan within a fast-changing East Asian system meant that a growth pattern that depended on trade and investment expansion was bound to be affected by the growing sophistication of neighbourhood traders, and in particular by the startling industrial development of mainland China. How the Japanese industrial and trading system survives the immediate future may well depend upon management of the switch between external and internal paths of development. Much of this depends on decisions in the private sector, and in particular on exploitation of technology as a factor in keeping prices down in the face of yen appreciation. But it is possible that public policy may serve to ameliorate both the difficulties of growth and the relations of the Japanese commercial economy with the major economies of the Asia Pacific and the world more generally. To be successful, public policy must switch to structural and sectoral concerns and away from budgetary and monetary interventions, so much the subject of political discussion at the turn of the twentieth century.

Given the continuation of trade surpluses and high levels of foreign investment, a useful tactic might be for the Japanese to lead the developed nations in the transferral of trade-surpluses to poorer nations. In the bubble days of the late 1980s, this was precisely the prescription offered by the World Institute for Development Economics Research of the United Nations University, and could yet be revived under Japanese leadership.[7] As a strategy for the rejuvenation of Japan's own economy through increased trade and investment opportunities with Asian and other nations, the mobilisation scheme might be as apposite as continued restructuring and deregulation. More importantly, such a scheme would be eminently visible and a convincing proof of Japan's intention to take a more active role in the manipulation of the global system in the continued absence of a national militarisation programme. In its widest, global perspective, such a tactic might be seen as representing something of a Japanese move to occupy the position taken earlier by Britain and later by the US. This seems an unlikely historical outcome in a world which is moving into multipolar leadership and non-national sites of endeavour.

A second public policy tactic would be to encourage the development of those new sites of endeavour which we first identified in Chapter 11, pp. 262–5. We might elaborate on this as a special case of positive exploitation by Japan of the opportunities offered by the new climacteric. Here we cite the many plans which stem from Japanese cities and regions on the Japan Sea coast and centre on new sea lanes and air routes, (the Yamagata–Harbin sea route of 1992, or the Vladivostok–Toyama sea route 1993), and the surge of new economic missions, as well as the development of special access zones. There has been a massive increase of cross-border trade between China and Russia since the early 1990s, one which seems to be very complementary and incorporates basic foodstuffs and raw materials such as sugar and steel, with textiles, chemicals and machinery. This is the immediate historical background for the great investment surge into northeast China by Japan, South Korea, Taiwan and Hong Kong, aided by large-scale infrastructural improvements by the Chinese provincial authorities, e.g. Liaoning's large investments in roads, harbours, railways, power plants and water supplies, or Heilongjiang's port and airport constructions. Recent moves towards the establishment of a single international zone jointly between China, North Korea and Russia, have been strongly supported by China since its conception at a conference on economic and technological development held in Changchun City, Jilin, in July 1990.

The notion that Japan may effectively exploit regionalism (defined here as optimisation of interactions between nations) is not so far-fetched, and would probably emerge as a more sturdy tactic than so-called globalisation (defined here as those interactions amongst institutions which are no longer nested within the sovereign decisions of nation states) for the next generation or so. Japan might be the capitalist nation which first fully exploits the coming Neo-Orwellianism of the three super-regions of North America, Europe and East Asia.

Do the developmental assumptions of an old world of 'modernity' still operate in a 'post-modern' global system? The rise of new industries and locations is not merely a technological phenomenon but represents a climacteric change which might reverse the historical sequencing of site and agency, as perhaps seen now in China. Historically, in Western modernity, the attributes of physical sites, as described by leading economic historians such as Sidney Pollard, did condition the character of industrial agency. As we have described in this volume, then there was a need for large physical capitals and power sources, a mass of raw materials, large congregations of labour and skills contingent to new institutional freedoms from the older restrictions on the workings of markets (from royal monopolies to the proscriptions of religion to apprenticeship or guilds). Perhaps all of this really determined the nature of the factory, of entrepreneurship and its institutions, whether in eighteenth-century Britain, or nineteenth-century Europe, or twentieth-century Japan. Even late-developers, however different from early-developers (see other chapters of this volume), were reacting to the physical requirements of the metal-based machinofacture of modernity and its technological paradigm. But the present climacteric seems only most loosely associated with special sites of capital, physical resources, labour or land, and more strongly associated with clusters of disembodied initiative, the exploitation of timely and quick-vanishing 'windows of opportunity', information networks and communication systems. Thus, in most new industries or service sectors, the proportion of basic labour costs plus raw material and energy costs to the market value of the final outputs is much lower than in the year 1900 or the year 1950 or even the year 1980, and possibly falling still. So, agency and its associated networks is less constrained by the earlier sites of machinofacture resources, and more or less free to determine new sites of production, a general proposition only modified by institutional factors determined in the public sectors of the great nation states e.g. tax regimes, trade regulations, or environmental restrictions on private sector activity. *Japan, then, may have been the last major nation to industrialise within the older 'modern' technological paradigm of machinofacture. It may thus be in the best position to respond to newer paradigms and agencies of the climacteric, this explaining its faster absorption and commercialisation of the post-1970 technologies despite its relative weakness at the creative core of the system.* If future economic change is, in our limited sense, post-modern and presently unpredictable, will the capitalist nation which was *both* the last industrialiser and the furthest from the cultural core of historical capitalism, be the nation which best adapts – is best placed to adapt – to new circumstances, and thus snatches the lead into the new millennium?

Much will depend on the evolving character of the East Asian system and the cultural and commercial relations between China and Japan. If culture matters, it will matter more now. For Japan, perhaps the cultural site which needs most consideration does not belong to a national setting, but to the elusive Chinese Diaspora and its potential role as an integrating force. By the late 1990s, 51 million Overseas Chinese[8] controlled US $700 billion of annual sales, similar to the gross national product of China itself. Wealth held in the diaspora is equivalent to the combined gross national products of France and Germany. McKeown writes of the ability of the historical diaspora to utilise symbols to mobilise loyalty and trust within complex networks and associations, and of the possibilities of a 'diasporic nationalism'. Although the political crises after 1949 served to curtail the mainland–diaspora links, these have since been reinvigorated and are following centuries-old routes and networks, where the family is still the basis for status and decision-making. For Ong and Noningi, China is 'one among many sites within and across which Chinese transnational practices are played out . . . an Asian cultural space of capitalism'. For these writers such cultural spaces are complementary to the new climacteric phenomenon of 'a polycentric global capitalism with multiple nodes of geopolitical and economic power'. It might, therefore, be feasible to see Chinese transnationalism as an 'outcome' of the transformations of late modernity, or what we call the climacteric. Could not such transnationalism be part and parcel of such transformation? David Shambaugh has summarised that in the contemporary industrial and cultural developments of Greater China, 'the relevance of nation-states and political entities is minimised. People, ideas, investments and goods are transcending political and territorial boundaries largely irrespective of the governments under which they live'.[9] It is true that informal networking across formal ideological and legalistic boundaries may come more naturally in Pacific than in Atlantic sites of industrial transformation, if only because the diaspora of the Chinese business class is more accustomed to *guanxi*-based ties than formal regulatory environs monitored by state legislation.[10]

Our claim is that in such cultural complexity and movement there is a great potential for continued Japanese expansion and commercial interaction. This at least points to a possible pattern of regional expansion which is not dependent on any resolution of the ideologies of the Japanese and Chinese systems, or on any 'end of history' scenario of the Fukuyama type. We might even note that the totality of the diaspora is very similar to Japan itself in terms of entrepreneurial innovativeness and an historical escape from the prohibitions of traditional Chinese institutions and ideologies. As the cultural and commercial associations of the diaspora with Guangdong are of fundamental importance, so too the strong commercial presence of Japan in that region of the mainland means that, in combination, Guangdong and South Chinese interests could become the principal site for the greater and sustained integration of Japan and Greater China. This could be one of the major processes in the world economy in the next few decades.

Given what has been said about social change and environmental constraints in modern Japan, a third public policy tactic for renewed growth might lie in devolving resources away from real estate and back into industrial research and development. This would be a continuation of 1980s pursuits, but with far greater attention to the development of environmental high-tech industries geared to energy saving, raw-material-substitution processes and products, for which Japan is particularly well-placed – Japanese customers would provide a large internal market from which to derive learning and scale advantages in preparation for a new surge of exports of environmental services and techniques. The nation which joined the industrialisers despite a lack of obvious raw materials and under strict spatial and topographical constraints, might be the nation to first move more wholeheartedly into environmentally aware re-industrialisation.

We would suggest that these three policy elements of trade-surplus dispersals, enhanced regionalism based on cultural proximities, and increased focus on R&D and environmental industries, are highly complementary and allow the pursuit of industrial growth as a major objective whilst accommodating several of the new international constraints on the Japanese political and economic system.

Notes

1 The more convincing argument might be that a combination of overloaning by banks within Japan (or under-investing in industrial companies by independent shareholders) plus the global financial crisis *c.* 1987, led without much regulation to a great exit of Japanese finance to projects that soon became bad debts,

particularly those in Asia. More generically, long-term easy funding by banks has been interpreted as an endemic East Asian problem, yet might be restated as a function of rapid development under conditions of relative economic backwardness.

2 In 1909 Karl Bosch improved on the original Fritz Haber process for extracting nitrogen from the air in the form of ammonia used in fertiliser and explosives manufacture, replacing the costly use of potassium nitrate. The Fischer-Tropsch method synthesised gases with the aid of a catalyst, and was bought by Mitsui Mining (coal).

3 This is by no means to deny the importance of cultural engineering to such earlier industrialisers as Britain. It is to say that this factor was much more of an effective limiting factor in late-developers facing speedier industrialisation based on advanced techniques and institutions, inevitably involving cognitive dissonance and ideological intrusion. In cases of this sort, where cultural engineering was ineffective or not associated with expensive projects of human capital formation, then the social and political cost of late-development caused political turmoil and regime breakdown.

4 However, it is important to note that Ōuchi does not fall into a *nihonjinron* camp in that he goes on to argue that such uniqueness does not spell an exclusive and necessary cultural trajectory, and that clan features may be adopted within Western systems, leading to the secondary-level institutions of lifetime employment or consensus decision making.

5 We have not the space here to challenge the normal characterisations of Japanese enterprise, to posit the realistic approach that power is more important than trust in the relations between managers and workers, that labour market conditions rather than internal mechanisms of consensus have generated both a sense of company solidarity and quietist trade unions, nor that even a modified Japanese model does not represent the many tens of thousands of casual or contract workers. However, such points have been made throughout the historical analysis, and follow quite naturally from the approach in Figure 12.1 above. See also papers by Sullivan, Hofstede and Inkster (1993) in the bibliography to this chapter. It might be worth pointing out that the general image of Japanese enterprise culture promoted and (at some levels) held in Japan, has itself been a product of a cultural engineering process.

6 It should be noted that between 1965 and 1981, the growth rate of Japanese defence expenditure was well over the 10 per cent mark, peaking in 1975 at 25 per cent and in 1978 at 20 per cent, the year of China's initial economic reforms. Because of very healthy growth in the overall economy, the defence to GDP ratio remained almost constant around 1 per cent, the ratio to general government expenditure also constant at around 6 per cent. As Japan entered the 1990s it was already spending through the Self-Defence Forces (created from the Safety Force in 1954) around $40 billion as defined by NATO, making Japan the third largest military power in the world. This capacity of course excludes the positive effects of burden-sharing with the US, which incorporated about $40 billion US spending in Asia. By the 1990s capacity included most of the best of US technology – the F-15 interceptor, the Patriot surface-to-air missile, the P-3C ASW aircraft, the E-2C early warning aircraft, and the Aegis-equipped destroyer which was made in Japan under co-production agreements.

7 At that time – 1987 – Japanese trade surpluses stood at around $90 billion, Germany's at $35 billion, as transfers from major developing nations stood at around $30 billion annually. So, transfer of the one to the other was seen as preferable to endless attempts at reduction of current account surpluses in nations such as Japan or Germany with their increasing productivity, high rates of savings and heady export expansion. This was seen as a Japanese Marshall Plan. It may be argued that adoption of such a move might have alleviated pressure on the yen, opened up new opportunities for US political and commercial alliances in

the new post-Cold-War environs, and accelerated economic development and hence liberalisation and deregulation in industrialising East Asia. A result might have been the absence of any Asian crisis in the late 1990s.

8 There seems to be no one acceptable terminology. Probably most acceptable is 'diaspora' and 'ethnic Chinese', avoiding 'Chinese overseas' and 'overseas Chinese' altogether. The Chinese government still regard the people of the diaspora as *Huaqiao* or 'Chinese nationals who reside overseas', from the Imperial Chinese claim on its Chinese citizens abroad. More accurately they are *Huaren* or ethnic Chinese, or *Huayi*, meaning 'of Chinese descent'. But for Chinese specifically of Greater China, i.e. Hong Kong, Taiwan and Macao, they are *Zhongguo ren* (those from the central kingdom). Most of the SE Asian Chinese who have recently invested in mainland China are in fact first generation migrants who speak Chinese and follow Chinese cultural and associational patterns. They are precisely the ones in the best position to assess the conditions for trade and investment on the mainland.

9 One measure of this might be the escalation of Overseas Chinese investment into the mainland after the Tiananmen Square incident in 1989. The move was composed of excess funds, the need to exploit cheap Chinese labour, especially amongst Hong Kong investors, the improved atmosphere for capital under the Chinese economic reforms, and the special attractions of Guangdong province, Shenzhen and the other SEZs, combined with the 'open spigot' character of Chinese capital.

10 In the mid-1990s, Hong Kong was the world's eighth largest trading economy and increasingly functionally interdependent with industrialising Guangdong, symbolised by the proximate airport competition between Hong Kong, Macao, Shenzhen and Zhuhai. During the previous decade and more, direct investment from Hong Kong to other nations had been massively in favour of Mainland China, followed far behind by Indonesia, Thailand, Taiwan, Japan and South Korea.

References

Morishima, Michio (1982) *Why Has Japan Succeeded?* Cambridge: Cambridge University Press.

Koschmann, J. V. (ed.) (1978) *Authority and the Individual in Japan*, Tokyo: Tokyo University Press, quote page 14.

Nitobe, I. (n.d.) *Bushido: The Soul of Japan* (10th rev. edn.) New York, quote page 169.

Benedict, Ruth (1974 [1946]) *The Chrysanthemum and the Sword*, New York: Meridian.

Prime Minister's Commission on Japan's Goals in the 21st Century (2000) *The Frontier Within: Individual Empowerment and Better Governance in the New Millennium*, Tokyo: National Science Foundation, 3 February 2000. http://www.twics.com/~nsftokyo/rm00–04.html

Harootunian, Harry D. (1966) 'Introduction' in B. S. Silberman and Harootunian (eds), *Modern Japanese Leadership*, Tucson, AZ, pp. 16–20.

Ouchi, William (1981) *Theory Z*, Reading, MA: Addison Wesley.

Giddens, Anthony (1989) *Sociology*, London: Polity Press, quote page 284.

Akiyama, M. (1999) 'Japan's security policy towards the 21st century', *Royal United Services Institute Journal*, 143(2): 5–11.

Stiglitz, Joseph (1998) in the *Asian Wall Street Journal*, 2 February, quote page 56.

Pollard, Sidney (1981) *Peaceful Conquest*, Oxford: Oxford University Press.

McKeown, Adam (1999) 'Conceptualising Chinese diasporas 1842 to 1949', *Journal of Asian Studies*, 58: 306–37.

Ong, Aihwa and Noningi, Donald M. (eds) (1997) *Ungrounded Empires. The Cultural Politics of Modern Chinese Transnationalism*, New York: Routledge, quotes pages 12, 14.

Shambaugh, D. (1995) *Greater China. The New Superpower?*, Oxford: Oxford University Press, quote p.2
Fukuyama, Francis (1989) 'The end of history', *The National Interest*, Summer: 3–18.

Further reading

Aoki, M. (1990) 'Toward an economic model of the Japanese firm', *Journal of Economic Literature*, 28(1–27), with an excellent bibliography.
Benedict, R. (1934) *Patterns of Culture*, New York: Houghton Mifflin.
Economic Planning Agency (1994) 'White Paper on the Life of the Nation', Ms Typescript Tokyo: Foreign Press Centre, February.
Edquist, C. (ed.) (1997) *Systems of Innovation; Technologies, Institutions and Organisations*, London: Pinter.
Funabashi, Y. (2000) *Alliance Adrift*, New York: Council on Foreign Relations Press.
Hamabata, M. M. (1990) *Crested Kumono*, Ithica: Cornell University Press.
Hofstede, G. (1984) 'Motivation, Leadership and Organization: Do American theories apply abroad?', in D. Kolb, *et al.* (eds) *Organizational Psychology: Readings in Human Behaviour in Organizations*, (4th edn), New Jersey: Prentice-Hall, pp.309–29.
Hopp, W. J. and Spearman, M. L. (1996) *Factory Physics*, Chicago: Irwin.
Inkster, I. (1993) 'Antithesis on peculiarity – or, a dialogue on labour organisation and the Japanese economy, *circa* 1960–1980', *East Asia*, 6, 111–19.
Inkster, I. (1998) *Technology and Industrialisation. Historical Case Studies and International Perspectives*, Aldershot: Ashgate.
Inkster, I. and Satofuka, F. (eds) (2000) *Culture and Technology in Modern Japan*, London: I. B. Tauris.
Iwata, K. (1999) 'The Japanese big bang and the financial crisis', *Japan Review of International Affairs*, Spring: 55–73.
Kinzley, W. D. (1991) *Industrial Harmony in Modern Japan: The Invention of a Tradition*, London: Routledge.
Morris-Suzuki, T. (1988) *Beyond Computopia. Information, Automation and Democracy in Japan*, London: Kegan Paul International.
Nakane, C. (1974) *Japanese Society*, London: Penguin Books.
Nathan, J. (1999) *Sony: The Private Life*, London: HarperCollins.
Nelson, R. (ed.) (1993) *National Innovation Systems, A Comparative Analysis*, New York: Oxford University Press.
Ong, A. (1997) 'On the edge of empires: flexible citizenship among Chinese in the Diaspora', *Positions*, 1(3): 745–78.
Rozman, G. (1999) 'Backdoor Japan: the search for a way out via regionalism and decentralization', *Journal of Japanese Studies*, 25: 3–31.
Selvarajah, C. T. and Cutbush-Sabine, K. (eds) (1991) *International Business*, London: Longman.
Sullivan, J. Z. (1983) 'A critique of Theory Z', *Academy of Management Review*, 8(1): 132–42.
Taylor, R. (1996) *Greater China and Japan. Prospects for an Economic Partnership in East Asia*, London: Routledge.
Trends in Japan 'Facing the Fallout', 6 January 2000, http://www.jinjapan.org/trends/honbun/tj000104.html
Vlastos, S. (ed.) (1998) *Mirror of Modernity: Invented Traditions of Modern Japan*, Berkeley, CA: University of California Press.

Index